For Etta & Clay!
Best Regards
Bob

THE SEEN AND THE UNSEEN: SHAMANISM, MEDIUMSHIP AND POSSESSION IN BORNEO

Edited by
Robert L. Winzeler

BORNEO RESEARCH COUNCIL MONOGRAPH SERIES

VOLUME TWO

BORNEO RESEARCH COUNCIL MONOGRAPH SERIES

Published by

THE BORNEO RESEARCH COUNCIL, INC.

Department of Anthropology
The College of William and Mary in Virginia
Williamsburg, VA 23185 USA

Series Editor: Vinson H. Sutlive, Jr.

©*Borneo Research Council, Inc.*
1993

The chapter on Melanau Shamanism by H. S. Morris originally appeared in a slightly different version in *Social Organization: Essays Presented to Raymond Firth*, edited by Maurice Freedman, pp. 189-216, c 1967 by Frank Cass & Co., Ltd. London, whose permission to republish is acknowledged with gratitude.

Library of Congress Catalog Card No. 93-072413
ISBN 0-9629568-1-3
ISSN 1055-7792

Printed in the United States by
Ashley Printing Services, Inc.
Shanghai, VA

DEDICATION

For the shamans, priests, priestesses, and spirit mediums of Borneo--keepers of tradition and bearers of innovation.

THE SEEN AND THE UNSEEN:
SHAMANISM, MEDIUMSHIP AND POSSESSION IN BORNEO

BORNEO RESEARCH COUNCIL MONOGRAPH SERIES
VOLUME 2

Robert L. Winzeler, Editor

Preface vii
    Vinson H. Sutlive, Jr.

Introduction xi
    Shaman, Priest, and Spirit Medium: Religious
    Specialists, Tradition and Innovation in Borneo
    Robert L. Winzeler

PART ONE

To Converse With the Gods: Rungus Spirit Mediums 3
    George N. Appell and Laura W. R. Appell

To Do Battle With the Spirits: Bulusu' Spirit Mediums 55
    Laura W. R. Appell and George N. Appell

Shamanism Among the Oya Melanau 101
    H. S. Morris

From Shamans to Priests: Towards the Professionalization
    of Religious Specialists Among the Kayan 131
    Jérôme Rousseau

Canoes for the Spirits: Two Types of Spirit Mediumship in
    Central Kalimantan 151
    Sian E. Jay

PART TWO

The Shaman's Destiny: Symptoms, Affliction, and the
    Re--interpretation of Illness Among the Taman 171
    Jay Bernstein

Spirit Possession as Exculpation:
    The Chinese of Sarawak 207
    Richard C. Fidler

PART THREE

Performance, Effectiveness and the Iban Manang 235
    Robert J. Barrett

Shaman and Fool: Representation of the Shaman in Iban
    Comic Fables 281
    Clifford Sather

Notes on Contributors 323

PREFACE

VINSON H. SUTLIVE, JR.
The College of William and Mary

The thesis of Claude Levi-Strauss's tour de force *The Savage Mind* is that all people everywhere think in the same ways. Written as corrective to Lucien Levy-Bruhl's *The Primitive Mind*, with its hypothetical co-existence of two modes of thought, the "primitive" and the "civilized," and with accompanying "laws," *The Savage Mind* refuted the earlier speculations, established the similarity of processes of thought among all people, and has become part of the "canon" of anthropology.

So widely has Levi-Strauss's thesis been accepted that the possibility of *radically different modes* of thoughts has become unthinkable to many anthropologists. Without reviving the deservedly-interred "laws" identified by Levy-Bruhl, it is important to reaffirm another of the axioms of anthropology, viz. that people perceive the world in widely differing ways, that they behave on the basis of these perceptions, and that such perceptions may represent insuperable barriers to understanding.

The papers in this volume illustrate widely different contents of thought and an apparently unbridgeable gap between Euro-American systems of thought and the epistemologies of societies whose members include shamans and spirit mediums. Even if we think in the same or in similar ways, one wonders whether it is possible for practitioners of western cultures to comprehend the subtleties of those societies which feature shamanism. This is not for a moment to suggest that the subjects of these papers are in any way incapacitated, an issue joined frequently in analyses of shamans and mediums. As Jane Murphy has written (1976), the societies whose members become shamans or mediums are able to distinguish normal and abnormal behaviors, and these specialists are well within the parameters of normality.

Western intellectual history has been dominated by two philosophical traditions, monism and dualism. The former, conceptualized by Pythagoras, reinterpreted by Comte, Durkheim, and Sartre, contends that only the observable, the measurable, the demonstrable are admissible to human knowledge. The concept of dualism, explicated by Plato and Aristotle, and reinterpreted by Boas and Levi-Strauss, among many others, insists that unobservable, immeasurable, and non-demonstrable "social facts" are critically significant to human knowledge.

Western scholars have accepted as intellectual imperative Soren Kierkegaard's "either/or" proposition. The polarity of monism and dualism, however, fails to capture the world of the shaman and medium. The "either/or" proposition is meaningless to believers of societies in which discontinuity is lost to continuity, death in life, self in society, and society in all.

Convinced that there are forces beyond the capacities of the senses to apprehend, true believers in shamanism and mediumship are equally convinced that such forces interact with and influence human lives. They participate in a continuous universe, what George Appell insightfully has called "a seamless world," in which traffic between humans and non-humans is part of the regularly established order of things. This seamless world includes but extends far beyond what may be explicit in visual and non-visual experiences.

This is not to suggest that there is not considerable variation among and between societies whose members select some for the roles of shaman and mediums. For example, Robert Barrett's sample of Iban described in this volume is quite different from Iban shamans I knew, who in temperament and behavior seem much more like the Taman described by Jay Bernstein.

Nor is there consensus on differences between "shaman" and "medium." A minimalist definition of the former is "one who works with spirit beings," and of the latter, "one through whom spirit beings work." Concern for neatly-packaged categories is part of our scientific approach, but is irrelevant in societies whose multi-functional specialists may at one time "work with spirit beings," at other times be the medium "through which spirit beings work." Both shaman and medium function as "a lightning rod" for other members of society, affirming in chant and other ritual form the existence of what Georg Simmel identified as a continuing, metaphysical realm in which a majority of the world's societies attempt to establish themselves as part of an ongoing and living stream.

Nor do ancient beliefs in the efficacy of shaman and medium appear to be waning. It is important to recall once again the important distinctions between "manifest" and "latent" cultures. The trappings may change, but the core-values and belief persist. The persistent integrity of such cultures through time is remarkable, even in situations of rapid sociocultural changes.

One must question whether popular courses in the United States in "cross-cultural shamanism," with weekend experiences in "spirit journeying" and "getting in touch with your familiar," can transport participants beyond the predominantly non-spiritual characteristics of the western world into the subtleties of the shamanic world. This question is intended not to disparage efforts to educate persons new to an appreciation of shamanism, but rather to emphasize that just as in most of our studies, we rarely approach, let alone glimpse the heart, soul, and genius of ways of thinking that are untranslatably different from our own.

These ways of thinking can be understood only with intensive study of the languages of the shamans and mediums. Such languages are not merely add-ons, nor are they composed of loan words. They represent distinct lexicons whose meanings are known only to their singers. If, as the author of one proverb observes, "one's thoughts can go no further than one's vocabulary," perhaps the greatest contribution of this volume is to identify the limitations of vernacular language and a recognition that research must be extended beyond research on rituals to shamanic texts to discover the mysteries of languages and of ways of thinking that are in fact and in faith *radically* different from our own.

REFERENCES

Murphy, Jane. Psychiatric Labeling in Cross-Cultural Perspective. Science, Vol. 191:1019-1028, March 12, 1976

SHAMAN, PRIEST AND SPIRIT MEDIUM: RELIGIOUS SPECIALISTS, TRADITION AND INNOVATION IN BORNEO

ROBERT L. WINZELER
University of Nevada, Reno

The essays in this book describe and analyze Bornean ritual practitioners, individuals who all deal in one way or another with supernatural power. Interest in such persons has a long history in Bornean studies. The attention that early colonial and missionary scholars and travelers gave to religious lore was overshadowed only by that devoted to headhunting, another ritual activity. Particularly in Sarawak this fascination eventually waned and has only been renewed in the second half of this century.

In a similar fashion, after a period of decline during the early part of the present century, Bornean ethnology was revived following the Second World War in the form of social anthropology, and initially focused on practical issues of development. This revival began with Sir Edmund Leach's (1950) post-war socio-economic survey of Sarawak that made recommendations for various specific studies, none of which concerned matters of religious life. The first reports based on Leach's proposals also neglected religion except as it related to other concerns. Even so, the authors of most of these reports--Stephen Morris on the Melanau, William Geddes on the Bidayuh (Land Dayak), and Derek Freeman on the Iban--went on to write important papers about ritual and belief, especially shamanism. By and large, however, it was left to later scholars to deal more systematically and fully with the study of religion.

Recent scholarship on Bornean religion has tended to focus on specific topics. Peter Metcalf, (1982, 1989) for example, conducted detailed studies of Berawan mortuary belief and practice and of ritual language, and Penelope

Graham (1987) published a monographic interpretation of Iban shamanism. With the partial exception of Erik Jensen's *The Iban and Their Religion* and Rodney Needham's translation of Hans Schärer's study of Ngaju cosmology, no new comprehensive overview of the religion of any Bornean people has been published in the last several decades. The only available material on Bornean religious specialists and their activities is uneven and available in scattered monographs, articles, chapters, and reports.

The present volume attempts to assemble and lend insight into current scholarship, and to provide a more thorough consideration of shamanism, spirit mediums, and possession in Borneo. The effort originated in response to a suggestion at the Borneo Research Council's symposium during the Annual Meeting of the American Anthropological Association in 1989, that the topic merited closer study. Approximately half of the papers included here are drawn from ones given at the organized session the following year. The remaining entries have been added to consider a broader range of societies. As in the previous volume in this series, Sarawak tends to be more fully represented than other areas of the island, reflecting the greater number of researchers in Sarawak in recent decades. Several of the following essays address societies which lie outside of Sarawak (the Rungus of Sabah, the Bulusu' of East Kalimantan, the Taman of West Kalimantan and the Ngaju of Central Kalimantan), as well as ones found both in Sarawak and elsewhere. The latter category includes the Iban, the Kayan, and the Chinese, who dwell both in Sarawak and in other political divisions, especially, of course, Kalimantan.

TRADITIONAL BORNEAN SOCIETY AND RELIGION

Here the reader who is unfamiliar with Bornean ethnology may appreciate a thumbnail sketch of the societies represented in this book and of the nature of indigenous religious traditions. In addition to Chinese communities which are both large and long established, Bornean ethnic populations include various "coastal" groups. In some areas these groups speak only a dialect of Malay and are identified as *Melayu*, but in others they speak different languages and are identified accordingly. Among the latter are peoples such as the Melanau of central Sarawak, who include Muslims and Christians in addition to those who remain adherents of traditional belief and practice. The remainder of the population consists of various indigenous groups spread over the vast expanse of the island, many of which are lumped together as "dayaks." With the exception of remnant nomadic hunter-gatherers, the different groups live (or lived) in longhouses along rivers, practice swidden agriculture, in the past engaged in warfare involving headhunting, and have bilateral forms of family and kinship. Some communities have a ranked or stratified social order, and others an egalitarian one. While the indigenous Bornean populations of the coastal zone, when converting to an exogenous religion, have often acceded to Malay influence and entered Islam, the interior peoples have generally embraced Christianity, though with varying degrees of thoroughness and enthusiasm.

Traditional Bornean religions include beliefs, practices and organization relating to the symbolic or the unseen reality and its counterpart, the normal reality experienced through the senses. Knit together by common symbols, general cosmological principles, mythological lore and the like, the indigenous religions comprise a series of complexes of belief, ritual and organization often referred to as "cults"--a term which has taken on new meanings and may therefore no longer be appropriate in this present context. With respect to any one society (let alone indigenous Borneo generally), it would be a mistake to suggest that a particular complex constitutes the heart or essence of religion. It would also be misleading to suppose that it is possible to distinguish between "practical" and "transcendental" dimensions of belief and practice. The various Bornean ritual complexes are all practical in that they relate immediately to the material fortunes of daily life; at the same time, however, they are all based upon cosmological notions and principles. Notwithstanding considerable variation from one group of people to another, it is possible to identify five focal points of ritual activity that are (or were) of widespread significance. These include fertility (especially of rice), the taking and use of heads, birds and the reading of omens, the treatment of the dead, and the healing of the sick and troubled.

Rice

Swidden agriculturalists in Borneo typically emphasize the cultivation of hill rice over other crops, both materially and spiritually. Throughout the island, as elsewhere in Southeast Asia, rice is thought to have a spirit or a soul, and its cultivation is regarded as a ritual endeavor as well as a practical one. Freeman notes that in Iban societies, the

> whole system of agriculture is based on an elaborate fertility cult...Every *bilek* family possesses a strain of sacred rice called *padi pun*. Although all kinds of *padi* are animated by spirits, most important of all are spirits which dwell in the *padi pun*, for these are 'the lords of all' (*raja antu magang*). Year by year each *bilek*-family plants in the middle of its farm, a small plot of *padi pun*,

and this spot becomes a center for the performance of manifold rites (Freeman 1970:153-154).

The annual cycle of locating fields, clearing, burning, planting and harvesting is based upon augury, sacrifices and ritual celebrations, and usually culminates in grand harvest festivals.

Heads

Bornean beliefs and practices about headhunting and the value of collecting and retaining the skulls of enemies are intimately connected with concerns for fertility.[1] They also reflect a widespread and ancient understanding of the head as the focus of spiritual energy (cf. La Barre 1983). The conscious beliefs, unconscious motivations, social functions and ecological implications of headhunting in Bornean societies in general and among particular groups such as the Iban have been the source of much controversy (Freeman 1967; McKinley 1976; Needham 1976; Vayda 1976; cf. also Davison and Sutlive 1991; and Mashman 1991). Headhunting practices differed from one group to another, as did the ritual treatment of skulls, the latter having implications for male virility and fertility. Heads have been used as sacrificial gifts to the gods and ancestors; whether newly acquired or old, skulls have been the focus of elaborate ceremonial attention. Skulls are associated universally with spirits, as reflected, for example, in the Iban term *antu pala'* (ghost head), and in the great care taken to welcome and treat properly heads that have been brought to the village.

Augury and Birds

Ritualized rice cultivation and headhunting in turn relate closely to a third ritual complex, that of divination. Both of the former matters are associated with a good deal of uncertainty and risk that invite concern about the disposition of spirits and unseen forces affecting human life. It is the business of shamans, priests or spirit mediums to communicate directly with spirits. The spirits also may initiate contact with humans through dreams, to which much attention is devoted. In addition, divination involving external signs in the natural environment is generally very important. Focusing on the movements and the calls of various living creatures, above all certain birds, augury and the association of birds with the spirit world have developed into highly refined techniques. Birds are one of the main forms in which divinities may appear to humans. Though common everywhere, the identification of birds as spiritual messengers appears to be particularly important among many Bornean peoples.

Again, however, specific omen-birds vary from one Bornean group to another, as do methods for interpreting their messages (cf. Freeman 1960 and Metcalf 1976).

Death and Ancestors

While birth, maturation, and marriage merit relatively little ceremonial attention, death and the transition of the soul from the human world to its final destination are events given great ritual emphasis. The immediate concern is to remove the soul of the dead person from the living as quickly as possible, and hold it at bay. The soul is believed to become a spirit which, at least initially, will remain in the vicinity of the body. As such it is a potentially harmful force, particularly in the case of individuals who have died "bad" deaths (see e.g. Metcalf 1982:254-256; Sather 1978). Travel from the land of the living to the realm of the dead is frequently made by river, accounting for widespread boat symbolism in ceremonies involving death and other interaction with the spirit world. The spirit world is thought to bear many similarities to that of the living. Spirits are said to plant rice, go hunting, live in longhouses, and hold ceremonies of their own.

The successful transition of the souls of the dead to the spirit world favorably disposes them to humans, to whose calls for assistance they may respond (though apparently more as a category than as particular deceased relatives). The spirits are invited to return to the village for festivals and are contacted by religious specialists, earning such beliefs and practices the sometimes inappropriate appelation of "ancestor worship." Some groups conduct two- or three-stage funerary rituals which involve an initial and then a later, more elaborate ritual handling of the remains of the dead. Their systems of sacrifice and prayer seem to show greater concern for ancestors than other groups who, although mindful of the souls of the deceased, do not practice secondary interment.

Healing

The matter of healing requires little initial comment, for it is treated extensively in the remainder of this introduction and in the papers that follow. Of the various focal points of Bornean symbolic belief and ritual practice, those involving healing may be the least distinctive in comparative terms. The fundamental notion of a person has several components: a person consists of both a body and a soul (or souls); the latter has a life of its own. Illness is apt to be caused by the wandering of the soul or by its capture by a spirit; and death involves the final departure of the soul. Healing thus focuses upon the retrieval or rescue of souls, and the driving away or even slaying of malevolent spirits. Although this conception is widespread throughout Southeast Asia and much of the rest of the world, it varies considerably from one Bornean group to another.

RELIGIOUS SPECIALISTS IN BORNEO

The present papers fall into three categories and are organized accordingly. The largest number deal in a straightforward way with the positions and roles of various religious specialists. To begin, George and Laura Appell provide particularly important and interesting information on the Rungus *bobolizan*, which they identify as spirit mediums. *Bobolizan* dominate ritual life and, since they are women, provide an important foundation for the gender-equality characteristic of traditional Rungus society in general. The extensive involvement of women as religious specialists in important domains of "central-morality" ritual activity has been noted of other Bornean peoples, including the Bidayuh (Geddes 1954:31, 41) and various Ngaju groups (Schärer 1963 and Jay, this volume). In these latter instances, however, the ritual involvement of men appears to also be extensive and to overshadow that of women.

Laura and George Appell also provide a valuable account of spirit mediumship among the Bulusu' of East Kalimantan. Beyond a wealth of descriptive information on trance states and healing rituals, they note important contrasts between the two cases. They also argue strongly that the notions of "shamanism" and "possession" have frequently been misapplied and should therefore be abandoned. Their point that we need to be succinct is certainly well taken. Other contributors, however, have retained these terms, suggesting that we may not want to throw the conceptual baby out with the bath water of ambiguity. Also, the notion of spirit medium, which they favor in place of both priest/priestess and shaman, is not without its own range of meanings and ambiguities, as can be seen in the very different character of the Rungus and Balusus' patterns.

The Melanau as described by Stephen Morris also have several types of ritual specialists in addition to the *a-bayuh* or shaman. These include *dukun* (in this instance a herbalist healer), and a carver of sickness images, both of whom, like the shaman, cure illness. Morris' main concern is with the practicing shaman. In addition to curing, the *a-bayuh* also performs funerary rituals in which his soul travels to the land of the dead to carry gifts and to escort the souls of the relatives of the deceased person back to earth. The term *a-bayuh* also applies to other spirit mediums who possess spirit familiars but who are not practicing shamans. Finally, there are guardians of the ritual object (*beligieng*) which houses the spirits used in the annual cleansing of the village ceremony, who may or may not be shamans.

The existence of these and other ritual offices indicates that the role of shaman is not sharply differentiated from that of a **priest**. At the same time, the ambivalence of the Melanau people towards shamans who are potential threats to the hierarchical social order could more clearly distinguish their roles from those of priestly functionaries. Melanau aristocrats and elders tend to look disapprovingly on the power of male shamans who present a challenge to authority. A male shaman from an aristocratic lineage would thus be intolerable, as would one from the strata of former slaves. As a result, women assume the role of shaman more often than do men, accounting to some degree for the male aversion to unseemly behavior displayed during possession.

Jérôme Rousseau's analysis of ritual specialization among the Kayan, one of the Central Bornean groups of Sarawak and Kalimantan, reveals a pattern that is different from, but quite consistent with, the one noted by Morris. In what is probably the most detailed and lucid treatment of the religious roles of any of the *Orang Ulu* ("up-river people," as they are known in Sarawak) ever produced, Rousseau shows that there are presently two main types of specialists. One of these is the *dayong*, which he renders as a **priest**, the other is a *dayong na'ah*, which he terms a **shaman**. This dichotomy might be expected in Kayan society: differentiation and hereditary inequality are driving forces, and political and religious power are closely linked. The *dayong*, trained with study, is charged with administering the sacrifices and other central rituals of the society. He or she enhances status by assuming the priestly role. The *dayong na'ah*, on the other hand, recruited through spirit possession, is primarily a curer of lower status. As might be suspected, gender is a differentiating factor: although other issues complicate development, men are more likely to be *dayong*, while women tend to become *dayong na'ah*. Despite this, however, both priestesses and male shamans are by no means rare; and, priests and priestesses as well as shamans may have possession experiences. Rousseau argues that the distinction between *dayong* and *dayong na'ah* is probably a recent phenomenon in that it is not common in Central Borneo. He suggests it derives from an effort by Kayan nobles to preserve their power in a period of change, stemming particularly from the ritual and religious transformation of the Bungan reform movement.

The final paper in this section, Sian Jay's account of the Ngaju, supports Rousseau's inference that the differentiation of Kayan religious specialists is relatively recent. In it she suggests a development that may be widespread in

Borneo. Among the most ethnologically famous of Dayak peoples, the Ngaju have been to studies of Bornean religion what the Iban have been to those of ecology and social organization. Though studied by various colonial scholars, the Ngaju gained most exposure from the scholarship of the missionary-ethnologist Hans Schärer (1963). In an interpretation of Ngaju cosmology that subsequent observers (Miles 1976:76; Weinstock 1987:78) suggested exceeded what even the Ngaju themselves knew and understood, Schärer described what are among the more lurid beliefs and practices (transvestite priests, prostitute priestesses, human sacrifice) to be found in any religion. All life, he postulated, was closely tied to a grand symbolic design of Upper World and Lower World, to pervasive distinctions between Male and Female and to the central mythical figures of Hornbill and Water Serpent. While generally supporting and clarifying Schärer's interpretation of Ngaju cosmology and symbolism Jay notes the transformation of the older system of officiating *basir* ("priests") and *balian* ("priestesses") into a contemporary one led by male *basir* and female *tukang sangyiang* (or "shamans").

The papers in Part II offer more distinctly psychological interpretations of Bornean religious specialists and their activities. In the first of these, Richard Fidler discusses functional aspects of possession among the Chinese of Sarawak. He places special emphasis on "involuntary" possession as providing exculpation, the lifting of blame and guilt for transgression or failure, by attributing causation to supernatural forces. Fidler describes two instances (the first in graphic detail) in which a spirit medium determines that possession led to error, and in which the ensuing exorcism of the offending spirit serves to restore harmony and honor. The value of what occured moreover, may account for the willingness of some Chinese, who tend to be skeptical of folk religion, to suspend their disbelief.

Aside from presenting a valuable insight, Fidler's account raises an issue that might be pursued in future research: To what extent might Chinese folk religious beliefs, ritual practices, symbols and paraphernalia have affected those of surrounding indigenous Bornean communities? Other scholars have noted such Malay influence. While in general having much more in common with Chinese elsewhere in Southeast Asia than with the other ethnic sectors of Borneo, the Bornean Chinese, nonetheless, have a long history during which, in some regions they have intermarried with local inhabitants and assumed a local rural life style. Such marriages, and the ties between Chinese and indigenous populations that they create, encourage a mutual exchange of ritual belief and practice. While visiting a Bidayuh family several years ago in rural Lundu, I happened to witness a healing seance conducted by a Chinese-Selako shaman. The ceremony was divided into two parts. The first was a Chinese exorcism performance similar to that described by Fidler; the second involved a Selako ceremony. The competitive and innovative character of shamanism and spirit mediumship in Borneo would appear to make them particularly prone to alteration by dialectical forces.

The second paper in Part II is Jay Bernstein's detailed account of the shamanic career among the Taman, a Maloh people of the Upper Kapuas in West Kalimantan. Taman *balien* are a classic example of a shamanic career path in which the afflicted individual becomes a reluctant initiate only as an alternative to a life of chronic illness. Bernstein notes that the sorts of illnesses from which prospective *balien* suffer are ones which in western psychiatric discourse are referred to as **hysteria**. Since Taman shamans are in nearly all instances women, for whom the cause of the affliction is often diagnosed as being the erotic interest of a male spirit, Bernstein concludes that shamanic hysteria in such cases is rooted in sexual tension and conflict. He concludes further, however, that the symptoms of mental disturbance displayed by potential shamans may be "pathomimetic" rather than "pathogenic" in nature. This is to say that in order to become a shaman--for whatever inner motive--it is culturally expected that a person will display overt symptoms of distress and disorientation.

The two papers in Part III have several things in common. First, they both concern shamanism among the Iban, a topic about which, despite a wealth of scholarship (as both papers clearly show), there remains much of interest to be said. However, a more fundamental connection between the essays lies in the concern of each with cultural, phenomenological, and experiential interpretations that complement the sociological and psychological orientation of previous ones. I stress this because it often seems that such differing approaches constitute competing, alternative lines of analysis (cf. Geertz 1973 and Lewis 1986). Here again the significance of the Iban material demonstrates the important contributions that can be drawn from cultural, psychological, and sociological perspectives.

In the first of these papers, Robert Barrett, an anthropologist and a psychiatrist studying cultural constructions of physical and mental illness among Saribas Iban, is concerned with shamanism as cultural performance. Following an approach established most notably by Bruce Kapferer (1983) in his study of Sinhalese exorcism, Barrett's study of performance draws upon Victor Turner's (1982) formulation of drama as symbolic process, and includes a critique of these earlier approaches. He argues for an extended and reflexive concept of ritual performance and effectiveness, one which considers fully the impact of ritual on individual members of society and the cultural practitioners' metacommentary on the nature of ritual. Barrett's ethnography stresses the importance of the discussion that ensues on the periphery of ritual action, focusing on the critical role of deception in the *manang*'s work. Analyzing this discourse from a phenomenological stance, he proposes that *manang* effect transformations in the fundamental dimensions of Iban experience.

In the last contribution, Clifford Sather approaches Bornean concepts of religious roles from yet another perspective. He assesses the Iban *manang* as he appears in the Iban oral tradition of comic narrative or morality fable. The stories in question concern *Apai Aloi'* ("Father-of-Aloi") who in fact is not a real shaman but a Fool or trickster. On several occasions, *Apai Aloi'* pretends to be a *manang*, but in so doing proves to be a very clever man indeed. By drawing upon theories of play and ritual, Sather nicely reveals Iban attitudes about shamans and about themselves. As marginal figures outside their ritual domains, Iban shamans are the focus of skepticism as well as fascination and admiration. Often believed to be master deceivers, their appeal stems in part from the fact that success in dealing with the spirits is thought to involve trickery. If people may be fooled, so also may the inhabitants of the unseen world in which the shaman operates.

SHAMAN, MEDIUM, AND PRIEST

Taken together the accounts which comprise this rich collection raise a number of questions. To begin with, an immediate consideration must be made of the terms **priest**, **shaman** and **spirit medium** themselves. Although the original title of the symposium which led to the present volume was "Spirit Mediums in Borneo," it was readily apparent that initially this phrase would have to be broadly defined, and subsequently looked at more closely. In the past several decades, the terms used for religious specialists in anthropological discourse have sparked a good deal of controversy (Turner 1982:81-93). The discussion revolves around a distinction between "priest" and "shaman," although some scholars have preferred to use the term **spirit medium** in lieu of either of these.

According to I. M. Lewis (1986:78-80), the use of such terms is a matter of national academic tradition. American anthropologists have generally employed the term **shaman** to identify any specialist using possession for purposes of curing and dealing with non-routine crises. This usage derives, Lewis suggests, from traditional American ethnological familiarity with Eskimo and Amerindian versions of shamanism, which display affinity with the paleo-Siberian pattern. Continental scholars (most notably Eliade [1951, 1964]), interested in Euro-Asiatic religions have also been comfortable with the term for the same reason. This denotation of shaman, then, is used to distinguish the shamanic role from that of the priest. British social anthropologists, in contrast, understand shamanism from the African perspective, in which their research interests have been most deeply rooted. In Africa, classic shamanism has either been thought to be unimportant or has been overlooked, accounting for the British preference for **spirit medium**. The term describes a role not intended to oppose that of **priest**, but one which in many ways has subsumed it.

The semantic issues posed by anthropological studies of ritual specialists increasingly are becoming matters of the past. Many, though not all, anthropologists have begun to adopt the interpretation of American and Continental scholars (see also Firth 1959:129-148; 1967), as evidenced by the generally uniform application of the term in the following essays contributed by affiliates of both American and British traditions. However, within the broader context of Bornean studies, the use of these different terms has not been entirely consistent. What one scholar calls a shaman another, writing of a similar specialist in different society, has sometimes referred to as a priest or spirit medium. Occasionally, a single account will use the several terms interchangeably to refer to the same practitioner.

Our special concern is with the meaning of these terms in the present essays. However, it may be noted that not every major religious activity which requires special knowledge or skill is performed by an individual who is recognized by a title. A number of ritual functions may be fulfilled by untitled, yet nonetheless knowledgeable, adults. Among the Berawan, as recently described by Metcalf (1989), sacrifices and the ritual recitation of prayer are central to religious practice. These and many other more specialized activities are conducted by senior adults: they possess detailed, esoteric knowledge, skill and status but are not referred to by any particular Berawan term that might be translated "priest," "medium" or even "ritual leader."

In most Bornean societies, including all of those considered in the present collection, certain ritual positions are clearly recognized with titles. Many contributors to this volume thus write about shamans, often contrasting them with priests. Rousseau notes that modern Kayan clearly distinguish the two types. Priests are agents of established authority who conduct communal as well as private household ceremonies. Both priests and shamans have been selected by spirits, but priests complete a formal apprenticeship and learn a fixed body of ritual and prayer. Each practitioner also may practice beyond his or her local community, acquiring prestige in doing so. However, unlike priests, shamans may move beyond ethnic boundaries, by virtue of the individualistic and innovative character of their activities.

As already noted, Laura and George Appell employ the term "spirit medium" in their accounts of both the Rungus and the Bulusu'. There seems, however, to be a distinction between the practitioners they describe: the Rungus female *bobolizan* is (as they note) more a priestess than a shaman, while the Bulusu' *ulun gantu* shares more characteristics of what other contributors call a shaman. Sian Jay similarly refers to both sorts of modern Ngaju practitioners as **mediums**, but it is again evident that the male *basir* may also be described by the term priest, while the female *tukang sangyiang* fits neatly into the category of shaman. Finally, in his account of the Chinese folk ritual practitioners, Richard Fidler also uses the term "medium." His usage, in this case, is conventional though as he notes, the Chinese medium is more of a shaman than a priest.

Whether ritual practitioners specializing in personal crises and possession should be referred to as spirit mediums or shamans may be difficult to resolve to complete satisfaction. If, following Firth, one defines a shaman as a "controller of spirits," then most ritual specialists discussed in this volume who deal in possession are shamans. If, however, one follows Eliade and others who characterize the shaman as a **psychopomp**, a specialist who goes on celestial journeys to deal with spirits and to guide and retrieve souls, then a somewhat narrower range of religious practitioners qualify. Finally, if following Lewis (1986:78-93) and others, "shaman" describes a person afflicted or coerced by spirits who then masters them, the term is again applied differently. In Borneo, however, there is often considerable overlap in these several characteristics; as a result, some ritual specialists are shamans according to all three criteria.

If one accepts the classic shaman as being a controller of spirits, **and** a psychopomp with a career involving initial affliction and subsequent transformation, there remains the question of how to address the other practitioners: as **spirit mediums** or as **priests** and **priestesses**. In this regard, it seems important to keep the possible implications of the use of the term **medium** or **spirit medium** in mind. Such use should not imply that the practitioner (unlike a shaman or priest) serves only as a mere channel for communication between humans and spirits. This is certainly not the case for any of the various specialists described as "mediums" in this collection. The Chinese medium (*dang ki*) is an exorcist, a controller of spirits, an herbalist, a preparer of charms, and a diviner. He is known as a Master. Similarly the Rungus *bobolizan*, the Bulusu' *ulun gantu* or the Ngaju *basir* or *tukang sangyiang* are much more than vessels through which humans and spirits engage in discourse and conduct transactions.

PRIESTS, SHAMANS, AND DEVIANCE

A second concern is the personality and social role of Bornean ritual specialists. In what manner and to what extent does Vinson Sutlive's (1976) well-known phrase regarding the Iban shaman as using "an alternate route to normality" apply to shamans throughout Borneo? Some scholars may prefer the more neutral term spirit medium to that of shaman because the latter implies dysfunctional or pathogenic behavior, which may or may not be present. Particularly for Bornean and other practitioners, "shaman" carries connotations of androgyny. The issue of mental instability either as a temporary episode or an inherent characteristic of the shamanic personality has long intrigued scholars. Are shamans, in contrast to priestly practitioners, and to other individuals in the society, apt to be mentally unstable? Is the service they render the product of a perfected technique in their own recovery from mental instability? Or, alternatively, are shamans entirely "normal," "average" members of society?

The disinclination of observers to make psychological (as opposed to "ethnographic") assessments of the personalities of shamans, makes such questions difficult to answer. While many authors of the following papers make observations about the mental health of shamans, they do not attempt detailed analyses. (Jay Bernstein, who deals with Taman shamanism at some length, is an exception.) Another difficulty observers face involves the time period within which research activities are bracketed. Field data always reflect specific situations in particular periods of time, while the crucial phase in the development of the shaman's career, the events which led him or her to accept the call, may have taken place long before the arrival of the ethnographer.

The data provided by various accounts suggest that Bornean shamanism is characterized by significant variation. At one extreme, the Rungus spirit mediums are socially and psychologically normal, as George and Laura Appell emphasize. In this and other respects, Rungus mediums seem more priestly than shamanic.

By contrast, Iban shamans, about whom considerably more has been written than other Bornean peoples, represent a more complex case. The *manang bali'*, the "transformed" or transvestite shaman, is said to represent the highest, most spiritually potent sort of practitioner. While the focus of much scholarly interest (including an entire chapter in Graham's [1987] monograph on Iban shamanism), the transvestite Iban shaman appears to be a phenomenon based upon earlier--usually nineteenth-century--accounts. No *manang bali'* has been described or identified in the recent period, as far as I am aware. The transformed shaman may be important to the Iban and to researchers as a cultural possibility or symbolic prototype, rather than as an ethnographic reality. Further, as a cultural prototype, the Iban *manang bali'* is an example of a widespread symbolic category. Blind, crippled, or androgynous, the *manang bali'* is distinct from other humans and thus a capable intermediary between the human and the spirit realms.

Symbolic categories aside, most Iban shamans described in modern ethnographic accounts are apparently sexually, mentally and physically normal. Manang Bugang, the Baleh River Iban shaman, described in vivid detail by Derek Freeman (1967), embodies characteristics of the ideal Iban warrior: he embodies bravery, self-confidence, exuberance, sociability, and vigor. Similarly, Barrett (a psychiatrist and anthropologist) reports on 14 shamans from the Rimbas and adjacent regions of the Saribas area, all of whom are "mentally robust, neither psychotic nor pre-psychotic, neither effeminate nor hyper-masculine." His conclusion is based on a clinical assessment of the shamans' mental state during performance and on extensive biographical data, focusing on their mental health when they received their vocation in dreams. These reports indicate that while Iban shamanism may have been an alternate route to normality during periods when the main road to achievement was the warpath, it has now become one among many avenues to power and influence, as Sather notes at some length.

The contrasting personalities of shaman, priest and spirit medium are addressed in a number of other contributions as well. Rousseau tells us that while Kayan priests would not be recruited from persons with physical or psychological handicaps (though he notes an exception), this is not the case with shamans. On the contrary, peculiar behavior, as testimony to a Kayan shaman's effectiveness, increases the demand for his services. This would suggest the association of material reward with the cultivation of eccentricity or an image of instability. Again, however, Rousseau reports that the lives and personalities of most Kayan shamans (like the Iban ones noted by Barrett) are indistinguishable from their fellow villagers, except for their shamanic career and services. He also notes that while transvestites among the Kayan were not uncommon, they were unlikely to become shamans.

The shamanic vocation among the Melanau, the Taman and the Ngaju more closely approximates a culturally defined alternative route to normality. Reporting on the Melanau, Stephen Morris notes that **all** successful shamans are men and women of intelligence and imagination, who have histories of emotional disturbance and physical illness that often begin as early as adolescence. Moreover, echoing 19th century Iban accounts, he notes that the Melanau shaman "is in many respects androgynous." Male shamans have been known to live as transvestites, just as female shamans may affect a masculine persona.

In the case of the Taman, Bernstein reports that **all** shamans are said to be initially troubled, and that becoming a shaman is thus culturally defined as a matter of coercion. Specifically, physical illness or mental disturbance often may be attributed to the sexual interest of a spirit. If the condition persists, the only remedy may be shamanic initiation. However, unlike the Melanau, the Taman do not appear to associate shamanism with male transvestism. The fact that virtually all Taman candidates for shamanism are women does not, as might be assumed, "emasculate" a man who assumes the role. Finally, like the Melanau and Taman, the Ngaju *tukang sangyiang* are culturally expected to have suffered difficulties which are explained in explicit cosmological detail.

RELIGIOUS SPECIALISTS AND THE SOCIAL ORDER

A third issue that is raised by these papers concerns the relationship between religious roles and the social order. As we have seen, many indigenous Bornean peoples have egalitarian social structures, while others are marked by notable hereditary distinctions between nobles, commoners, and (formerly) slaves. Additionally, while there is significant variation, the overall tendency is for priests and priestesses to be "normal" (or exemplary) and for shamans (at least by reputation) to be "abnormal," or troubled at one time or another. The question thus arises whether differences in the social order produce varying attitudes towards shamans and priests. There is reason to suppose that where both shamans and priests or priestesses are recognized, the traditionally egalitarian societies would be less likely to differentiate socially between the various roles. Conversely, hierarchical societies would be more likely to denigrate shamans as opposed to priests. Gender differentiation also may alter the social status of practitioners. That is, egalitarian societies tend to have priestesses as well as (or even, as among the Rungus, instead of) priests, in contrast to hierarchically organized ones.

The cultural logic on which such expectations are based is not hard to follow. Priests are recruited according to fixed rules as purveyors of routine ritual services and mediators between humans and spirits. They are thus agents of established authority and social order. Conversely, shamans are typically selected on the capricious whims of spirits and use their skills to handle crises and cure illness. Because shamans tend to be less controllable and reliable, their social value in hierarchical societies is diminished. Similarly, in hierarchical societies women are less likely to hold positions of established religious authority; they will be more likely to channel their spiritual energies into shamanism.

Egalitarian societies, in contrast, are less suspicious of shamans, a role which often is assumed by men.

Overall both the present reports as well as other accounts of Bornean societies tend to bear out such expectations. The Taman case initially appears to be problematic, but Bernstein asserts that Taman shamanism is not linked to traditional stratification. This implies that shamans may come from any class, though Bernstein notes that the position is avoided if possible. The study, however, was made at a time when the Taman already had undergone a great deal of social and cultural change. As a result, little may be left of traditional patterns of stratification and rank. Further, almost all of the Taman he studied had become Christians, dissolving the need for former priests to preside over important domains of ritual.

The relationship between social order and types of ritual specialists is clearest for the Kayan, the Melanau and the Ngaju, all of whom conceptually recognize both practicing shamans and priests. As we have noted earlier, Rousseau suggests that the shaman-priest distinction does not appear to be a general feature of Central Bornean societies. From this (and from the absence of mention in earlier accounts), he infers that it **may** be a recent Kayan phenomenon,[2] indicating "professionalization" within Kayan religion that has taken place in the recent past. However this may be, it is clear that priests are part of both the religious and political establishment of Kayan society, whereas shamans are not. For the Ngaju, whose situation also has been complicated by change, and for the Melanau, similar patterns can be observed. In the latter case, Morris notes that a shaman will not normally come from the aristocratic sector of Melanau society. There is an aura of ill repute surrounding shamans, stemming from a belief that they are controlled by their familiar spirits, who may direct them to witchcraft.

The social implications of gender also are fairly clear. Among the more egalitarian but highly competitive Iban, shamans are primarily men (for example, 13 of the 19 *manang* Freeman [1967: 315] found in a 1951 Baleh River survey, and 13 of 14 Saribas shamans that Barrett describes in this volume). In Rungus society, also with an egalitarian structure, priestly spirit mediums are women. Conversely, in present day, hierarchally-ordered communities, priests are more likely (for example, among the Kayan) or almost exclusively (among the Ngaju) to be men, and shamans to be women (among the Melanau and Taman). Further, a particularly interesting example not included here is provided by the egalitarian Bidayuh who have both what Geddes (1961:xii-xiv) terms **priests** and **priestesses**, and male "spirit mediums." The latter category appears to denote shamans, as the Iban namesake (*manang*) would suggest. It has been suggested that such

xxvi

shamanic mediums are a recent phenomenon, borrowed in this case from the Malays, according to Geddes. Nonetheless, it is significant that they are men rather than women. The situation among the Bulusu' is less certain but George and Laura Appell report that male spirit mediums appear to be displacing female practitioners.

SHAMANS, PRIESTS, AND CULTURE CHANGE

The final matter raised by these papers thus involves the fate of Bornean ritual specialists with respect to processes of social and cultural change. The issue has emerged as an important theme in several of the articles, and clearly warrants attention as an important topic for future discussion and research.

As we already have noted, conversion to Christianity in the interior areas and to Islam in the coastal zone has been a powerful form of religious change for Bornean peoples. For some groups including the Melanau of Sarawak and the Ngaju peoples of the far south, such conversion has been a matter of more localized choice. In any case, while these developments are by no means unprecedented, even in the interior, they have accelerated in recent decades, especially in relation to broader processes of modernization. In Kalimantan, national Indonesian principles, such as the Pancasila, which encourages all inhabitants to follow a monotheistic religion, have been important factors in promoting, if not coercing, conversion. The extent to which formal conversion to Christianity and Islam has pervaded Borneo remains to be known, though clearly many inroads have been made (see Avé and King 1986:104-107).

While by far the most common options, conversion to religions other than Christianity and Islam has also occured. In southern Borneo, the Ngaju and other peoples of Central Kalimantan Province have succeeded in modifying their traditional religion (known since the late 1930s as Kaharingan) into an officially recognized form of acceptably monotheistic "Hinduism" (Weinstock 1987:71-79; Jay, this volume; Schiller 1989). Other areas have seen syncretic or revitalization movements (King 1978). The Bungan movement of Central Borneo is one of several that have been noted with some frequency in the literature, but doubtless others have been overlooked. In some areas religious leaders and ritual specialists thus include not only traditional priests, priestesses, shamans, or spirit mediums and the like, but also **prophets** or innovators who mediate between, or synthesize, competing religious traditions (see Metcalf 1989:216-217; and Tsing 1987 for recent examples).

For the most part, anthropological students of Bornean ethnology, while acknowledging universal rights to religious self-determination, have lamented the passing of traditional religious practices, and have devoted their energies to recording and analyzing those that remain. The religious traditions that have emerged or may yet appear will likely include not simply Christianity or Islam, but folk religions as well. While Hindu Kaharingan in Central Kalimantan has attracted substantial interest, Christian and Islamic folk religions in Borneo have received little ethnological attention (with the exception of Miles 1966 and 1976).

The question of central concern here is the effect of conversion and other patterns of change on traditional ritual specialists and their activities. The fact that shamanistic practitioners are often viewed as being disreputable when compared to priestly types might suggest that shamans are most vulnerable to forces of culture change. In actuality, although reports are not conclusive, this does not appear to be the case. In Taman society, for example, conversion to Christianity has apparently been relatively complete. The new religion, however, has effectively proscribed or displaced the domain of activity which formerly was associated with priestly functionaries. This may account for the absence of priests in accounts of many groups in which shamanism appears to thrive.

The endurance of shamanism in the face of such developments may be attributed to several possible factors. First, a shaman's capacity as curer is neither competitive with nor mutually exclusive of "religion," despite some Christians branding the role as "deviltry" in societies like the Taman. Second, the various needs and stresses which shamanism serves to heal and express may have increased in recent years. Although modern western or other non-traditional curing may provide an alternative to shamanic curing, neither modern medicine nor the ritual activities associated with Christianity appear able to remedy the social and psychological difficulties produced by change.

Finally, the implications of conversion in terms of gender has contributed to the endurance of shamanism in a changing world. As we have seen, many egalitarian Bornean societies are notable for the participation of women in religious life as priestly functionaries. Of the religious roles of women in Christianized groups little, if anything, has been written. The adoption of Christian or Muslim beliefs appears to have a likey consequence: the religious involvement and status of women as central ritual specialists will be diminished. It is possible that the previously existing ritual positions held by women might survive in some form, however improbable this may be. The more likely alternative is that women will turn instead to the more durable traditions of shamanism. In fact, as much as "tradition," this may explain why shamans among such Christianized groups as the Taman are exclusively female.

ACKNOWLEDGEMENTS

I wish to thank Jérôme Rousseau, George Appell, Anne Schiller, Jay Bernstein, Clifford Sather, Sian Jay, Vinson Sutlive and Robert Barrett for helpful comments and corrections on an earlier draft of this essay.

NOTES

1. George Appell (personal communication) points out that headhunting among the Rungus does not appear to have been related to notions of fertility.

2. Rousseau also notes (personal communication) that the priest/shaman distinction may have been present in earlier periods and was simply overlooked by Hose and Niewenhuis in their studies of the Kayan.

REFERENCES

Avé, Jan B. and Victor T. King
    1986   People of the Weeping Forest: Tradition and Change in Borneo. Leiden: The National Museum of Ethnology.

Davison, Julian and Vinson Sutlive
    1991   The Children of *Nising*: Images of Headhunting and Male Sexuality in Iban Ritual and Oral Literature. *In* Female and Male in Borneo: Contributions and Challenges to Gender Studies, edited by Vinson H. Sutlive, Jr. 153-230. Monograph Series of the Borneo Research Council, Volume 1. The College of William and Mary, Williamsburg, Virginia.

Eliade, Mircea
    1964   Shamanism. Translated by Willard R. Trask. New York: Pantheon Books.

Firth, Raymond
    1959   Problem and Assumption in the Anthropological Study of Religion. Journal of the Royal Anthropological Institute 89(2):129-148.

Firth, Raymond
    1967   Tikopia Ritual and Belief. Boston: Beacon Press.

Freeman, Derek
    1960   Iban Augury. *In* The Birds of Borneo, by Bertram E. Smythies, 74-97. Edinburgh: Tweeddale Court.

    1967   Shaman and Incubus. Psychoanalytic Study of Society 4:315-343.

    1970   Report on the Iban. London: The Athlone Press.

Geddes, W. R.
    1954   The Land Dayaks of Sarawak: A Report on a Social Economic Survey of the Land Dayaks of Sarawak Presented to the Colonial Research Council. London: Her Majesty's Stationery Office.

    1961   Nine Dayak Nights. Melbourne: Oxford University Press.

Geertz, Clifford
    1973   Religion as a Cultural System. *In* The Interpretation of Cultures: Selected Essays, by Clifford Geertz, 87-125. New York: Basic Books.

Graham, Penelope
    1987   Iban Shamanism: An Analysis of the Ethnographic Literature. An Occasional Paper of the Department of Anthropology, Australian National University, Canberra.

Kapferer, Bruce
    1983   A Celebration of Demons: Exorcism and the Aesthetics of Healing in Sri Lanka. Bloomington: Indiana University Press.

King, Victor
    1978   'Revitalization Movements' in Kalimantan (Indonesian Borneo). Indonesian Circle 17:14-27.

La Barre, Weston
    1983   Muelos: A Stone Age Superstition About Sexuality. New York: Columbia University Press.

Leach, Edmund
    1950   Social Science Research in Sarawak. Colonial Research Studies 1. London: Her Majesty's Stationary Office.

Lewis, I. M.
    1986   Religion in Context: Cults and Charisma. Cambridge: Cambridge University Press.

McKinley, Robert
    1976   Human and Proud of It: A Structural Treatment of Headhunting Rites and the Social Definition of the Enemies. *In* Studies in Borneo Societies: Social Process and Anthropological Explanation, edited by G. N. Appell, 92-126. Center for Southeast Asian Studies, Special Report no. 12. Northern Illinois University, Dekalb.

Mashman, Valerie
    1991   Warriors and Weavers: A Study of Gender Relations Among the Iban of Sarawak. *In* Female and Male in Borneo: Contributions and Challenges to Gender Studies, edited by Vinson H. Sutlive, Jr. 231-70. Monograph Series of the Borneo Research Council, No. 1. The College of William and Mary, Williamsburg, Virginia.

Metcalf, Peter
    1976   Birds and Deities in Borneo. Bijdragen tot de taal-, Land- en Volkenkunde 132:96-123.

    1982   A Borneo Journey into Death: Berawan Eschatology from its Rituals. Philadelphia: University of Pennsylvania Press.

    1989   Where Are You, Spirits: Style and Theme in Berawan Prayer. Washington: Smithsonian Institution Press.

Miles, Douglas
- 1966 Shamanism and the Conversion of Ngadju Dayaks. Oceania 37(1):1-12.

- 1976 Cutlass and Crescent Moon: A Case Study in Social and Cultural Change in Outer Indonesia. Center for Asian Studies, University of Sydney, Sydney, Australia.

Morris, H. S.
- 1953 Report on a Melanau Sago Producing Community in Sarawak. London: Her Majesty's Stationery Office.

Needham, Rodney
- 1976 Skulls and Causality. Man 11:77-88.

Sather, Clifford
- 1978 The Malevolent Koklir. Bijdragen tot de taal-, Land- en Volkenkunde 134:310-355.

Schärer, H.
- 1963 Ngaju Religion. Translated from the Dutch by R. Needham. The Hague: Martinus Nijhoff.

Schiller, Anne L.
- 1989 Shamans and Seminarians: Ngaju Dayak Ritual Specialists and Religious Change in Central Kalimantan. Contributions to Southeast Asian Ethnography 8:5-24.

Sutlive, Vinson H., Jr.
- 1976 The Iban manang: An Alternate Route to Normality. *In* Studies in Borneo Societies: Social Process and Anthropological Explanation, edited by G. N. Appell, 64-71. Center for Southeast Asian Studies, Special Report no. 12. Northern Illinois University, Dekalb.

Tsing, Anna L.
- 1987 A Rhetoric of Centers in a Religion of Periphery. *In* Indonesian Religions in Transition, edited by Rita Smith Kipp and Susan Rodgers, 187-210. Tucson: The University of Arizona Press.

Turner, Victor
    1982   Introduction. *In* Celebration: Studies in Festivity and Ritual, edited by Victor Turner, 11-30. Washington: Smithsonian Institution Press.

Vayda, Andrew
    1976   War in Ecological Perspective. New York: Plenum Press.

Weinstock, Joseph A.
    1987   Kaharingan: Life and Death in Southern Borneo. *In* Indonesian Religions in Transition, edited by Rita Smith Kipp and Susan Rodgers, 71-97. Tucson: The University of Arizona Press.

PART ONE

TO CONVERSE WITH THE GODS:
THE RUNGUS *BOBOLIZAN* -- SPIRIT MEDIUM AND PRIESTESS

GEORGE N. APPELL
Brandeis University
and
LAURA W. R. APPELL

From the perspective of Borneo, we frequently find ourselves uncomfortable with the generalizations that arise from comparative studies. The comparativist takes a sample of societies from Africa, Asia, the Americas, but seldom Insular Southeast Asia much less Borneo, and by this limited comparison he reaches conclusions on universal or near universal features of sociocultural behavior. However, such conclusions are frequently either inapplicable to Borneo societies or are invalidated by the Borneo ethnographic data.

Why Borneo studies are so ignored eludes us. But the result is that the major contributions that Borneo studies have to make to anthropological theory remain unexamined.[1] The problem of Borneo studies being the spoiler of comparative studies and anthropological theory is clearly exhibited in studies of spirit mediumship.

In Lewis' (1989) admirable study of the sociology of spirit possession, his approach to explaining the "seizure of man by divinity" is explicitly sociological. And he reaches important conclusions. He distinguishes what he has termed "peripheral possession cults" from central morality religions, or central possession religions. The former are in ritual rebellion against oppression. The shamanistic performances in the latter represent the central morality of the society. Yet the characteristics that he attributes to each of these types hardly matches the function of spirit mediumship among the Rungus of Borneo. The activities of the Rungus spirit medium reinforce the central morality of Rungus society, as will become apparent in our discussion. Yet spirit mediumship is in the hands of females, which Lewis claims is characteristic of peripheral possession cults. Thus, Rungus spirit mediumship shares characteristics of both his types of possession cults.

Lewis (1986, 1989) also claims that assuming the role of shaman is first preceded by a major event of illness, deprivation, or affliction that is interpreted as possession and which eventually leads to the afflicted individual gaining control over the afflicting spirits. While this occurs among the Bulusu' of Borneo (see this volume), becoming a spirit medium among the Rungus with the capacity to go into trance and communicate with spirits and control them is not precipitated by an event of affliction.[2]

However, Lewis' work is critically important for he outlines many of the dimensions of trance behavior and its sociological correlates that need to be investigated in each ethnographic case. And he points out (1986:78-93) that in cross-cultural studies of spirit possession, such as that done by Bourguignon, many of the categories used can be simplistic and do harm to the complexity of the cultural phenomena. Yet the work of Bourguignon on trance behavior also has produced a number of empirical questions that must be raised in any ethnographic study attempting to describe faithfully the nature of spirit possession.

But Lewis' point on the inadequacy of the categories currently employed in cross-cultural analysis is a crucial one. This inadequacy is also found in those concepts that are used for ethnographic inquiry, which confounds studies of ecstatic behavior involving both divine and demonic forces. The problem is nowhere more salient than in the concept of possession.

"Possession" is a term used by anthropologists to cover a multitude of phenomena. It is an invasion of the individual by a spirit, according to Lewis (1989:40). He includes in this both the state of altered consciousness in which the religious practitioner goes into a trance and has a relationship with divine or demon and the nontrance states in which possession indicates a change in health or behavior without an altered state of consciousness. But the use of the concept of spirit possession to refer to behavior in two radically different behavioral environments only muddies the water and leaves out crucial ethnographic detail that might provide greater specificity to each case.

As many different culturally specific explanations for behavior have been conflated under the rubric "possession," it becomes an inadequate analytical or explanatory category. In any specific behavioral environment, what does possession refer to? To possession of the body? The consciousness? Or the soul? Does possession involve intrusion into the body by a spirit? Riding on the body? Or only control from an external position? Does it involve loss of a part of the personhood, as when the shaman's soul goes wandering in the classic Siberian case, which is also referred to as possession in some of the literature?[3] When possessing a spirit medium, does the divine spirit exercise minimal control or full domination?

This confusion in concepts and terminology could have been avoided both in such comparative studies and in ethnographic inquiry if the behavioral environment of altered states of consciousness had been adequately defined rather than ignoring the indigenous perspective. Early on in her work Bourguignon (1965) drew attention to the importance of viewing possession in terms of its behavioral environment in order to understand it, following Hallowell's (1954) theoretical perspective. But Bourguignon in her later work, like Lewis, does not fully analyze each case of spirit possession in terms of the behavioral environment of the spirit medium or shaman and his or her spirits.

The indigenous explanations for trance behavior and its purposes are a first step in describing it, as Bourguignon has argued. But any such description must include not only the social geography of the soul and spirit world but also the temporal processes of the relationships between the divine or demonic and the spirit medium. Lewis (1986) nicely delineates this temporal procession in his discussion of the shaman's career, but as defined it has limited applicability; his conclusions do not apply to the Rungus case.

Firth warned of this lacuna as early as 1959:

Despite the erudite and massive analyses of the personality, powers, and role of shaman or spirit medium, we still have very little data on exactly who these spirit presentations purport to be in terms of the social order (1964:248; orig. 1959).

But this requires extensive fieldwork, as we have discovered in our investigations of Rungus spirit mediumship. The dimensions and content of the spirit world are frequently the most difficult aspects of culture to ascertain.

Among the Rungus, the spirit medium (*bobolizan*) is a female. She communicates with the spirit world in trance. But in this form of dissociative behavior no part of her social identity, either body, soul, or consciousness becomes usurped, displaced, or appropriated by any member of the spirit world.

There is no intrusion into body or mind of a spirit. Her soul is not absent. In trance she enters a different state of consciousness, a dissociative state. This occurs usually on her own volition, or when her spirit familiar appears in a dream and wishes to communicate with her so that she awakes already in trance. Whatever the source of the trance, it enables her to converse with her spirit familiars and permits her to serve as a channel for the discussions that go on between her spirit familiars and other spirits, which are heard by the audience. This state does not represent control in any form of body or soul by spirits. It is her own state of changed consciousness just as is dreaming. For this reason we shall avoid using the term "possession" as well as the term "shaman," since the role of *bobolizan* is not similar to that of a shaman.

Thus, the Rungus form of spirit mediumship has not yet been adequately discussed in the theoretical literature. For example, Bourguignon (1968, 1973, 1976) in her now classic studies of the altered states of consciousness does not put enough emphasis, in our opinion, on that type of practitioner that Firth (1964:247-8, orig. 1959) has referred to as a spirit medium. She makes the critically important distinction (1968) between possession trance, in which spirit voices speak through the shaman in trance, and nonpossession trance in which the shaman's soul goes on a voyage to the land of the spirits and is heard to converse with spirits. But she does not identify or discuss the type of spirit mediumship found among the Rungus. Nor has Winkelman (1990) included this type of spirit mediumship in his extensive classification of religious specialists that use trance as part of their healing performances.

Thus, Bourguignon's (1968) classification of types of explanation for trance behavior needs revision. The subcategory of nonpossession belief that she breaks down into the three types, (1) witchcraft victim, (2) soul absence, and (3) mystic state, should be expanded to include a fourth class. This would be a form of nonpossession trance such as occurs among the Rungus, which, as we will explain in our analysis, might be identified as lucid trance.

But before we discuss the *bobolizan* and her activities in detail, it is critical to outline the nature of Rungus social and cultural organization and the context in which the Rungus spirit medium works for a full understanding of the behavioral environment of her trance behavior.

ETHNOGRAPHIC PROFILE OF THE RUNGUS OF NORTHERN BORNEO[4]

The Rungus are a people of northern Borneo inhabiting the Kudat Division of Sabah, Malaysia (G. N. Appell 1965, 1966, 1967, 1976, 1978, 1988, 1991; Laura W. R. Appell 1988, 1991; Doolittle 1991). They speak a Dusunic isoglot (G. N. Appell 1968) and identify themselves, their *adat*, and their isoglot by the autonym "Rungus."[5] In addition to the Rungus, there are a number of other self-conscious, named Dusunic-speaking, ethnic groups in the Kudat Division.

The Rungus are the most visible and most numerous of these Dusunic groups. In the early 1960s the size of the Rungus population was approximately 10,000 out of a total population of 29,456 speakers of Dusunic or related languages in the Kudat Division (G. N. Appell 1965). The Rungus are found on the two major peninsulas of the Kudat Division: the Kudat Peninsula and the Melabong Peninsula. This description of the role of the *bobolizan*, however, is based on our research among the Rungus living on the Kudat Peninsula, with whom we resided. It may, nevertheless, be extrapolated with caution to the Rungus of the Melabong Peninsula on the east side of Marudu Bay.

Major Features of Rungus Social Organization

The Rungus are primarily swidden agriculturalists. They have a bilateral kinship system with no corporate descent groups. Cousin kinship terminology is essentially of the Eskimo type, although in certain situations the Hawaiian type may also be used to indicate social solidarity. The terminology for parents' siblings is lineal. A kindred type of social isolate is not present (G. N. Appell 1967). The major social units are the domestic family, the longhouse, and the village.

The Domestic Family. The domestic family is the only producing, consuming, and asset-accumulating social unit of Rungus society. It is thus the most important corporate entity in the economic, jural, and ritual realms. It is ideally and most frequently a conjugal family consisting of a man and his wife--the two founders--and their children. This conjugal family lives in its separately owned longhouse apartment. Marriage is normally monogamous, but rarely a man may have two wives. Post-nuptial residence is uxorilocal. First cousin marriage is considered incestuous and ritually dangerous, but it may occur if the proper ritual payments are made.

The domestic family's economy is based on (1) the swidden cultivation of rice, maize, cassava, and a variety of vegetables;[6] (2) the raising of pigs, chickens, and frequently water buffalo; (3) the planting and cultivation of a large variety of fruit trees; (4) the trading or sale of domestic manufactures, the most important of which are the woven clothing of various types that is made exclusively by women from cotton they have grown, spun into thread, and dyed; and (5) the work of the *bobolizan*, who receive payments for performing sacrifices and for teaching girls and women the long, complicated ritual hymns known as *rinait* that accompany such ceremonies.

Agricultural surpluses of the domestic family are invested in a variety of brassware, gongs, and ceramic ware. And these are held corporately by the domestic family as a jural entity. When a son wishes to marry, a substantial bride-price is provided for him from these accumulated assets. The bride-price items received are held corporately by the bride's domestic family and are used to provide bride-prices for sons. This type of bride-price G. N. Appell has termed "corporate," and it contrasts with what G. N. Appell has termed "redistributive" (G. N. Appell 1985a). In redistributive systems, as among the Lun Dayeh (Crain 1970, 1982) and Bulusu' (G. N. Appell 1985b), various items of bride-price are redistributed among a network of kinsman who have provided help in the wedding ceremony, who have provided help to the family in the past, and who it is hoped will provide help in the future.

The bride-price, as well as the other institutions which lead up to marriage and the eventual foundation of a new domestic family, is justified by the major value premise in Rungus society that all sexual relations are potentially deleterious for the participants, the rest of the society, the domestic animals, the crops, and the countryside itself unless they are properly entered into through marriage.

The corporateness of the domestic family is symbolized in the Rungus religious system. A number of sacrifices are made to cure illness in the family or to create an enhanced ritual state between the family and members of the spirit world who are responsible for protecting the family from illness and harm and for promoting fertility in the swiddens and fecundity of the family's domestic animals.

The Longhouse. The Rungus longhouse comes into existence through the lateral accretion of individual domestic family apartments. There is no section of the longhouse that is jointly made and collectively owned by the constituent members. It is in essence a condominium. The members of a longhouse are also not involved in any corporate action or even collective action in the economic realm. However, they do take collective, but not corporate, action to protect themselves against pathogenic spirits (*rogon*). For example, when there are wandering spirits abroad bringing epidemics, all the member longhouse families together will take a ritual offering to the head of the path leading to the longhouse to keep the wandering spirits from entering. This is collective action as the longhouse is thus not symbolized as a corporate entity. The longhouse is not considered to be a structural isolate, i.e. a ritual entity, in most activities of the ritual realm, with but one minor exception. Nor is it considered a jural isolate in seeking restitution after a ritual delict has been committed against its members (see G. N. Appell 1976, 1983, 1984).

The Village. The village is the fundamental political unit of Rungus society. It is not a kin grouping. Membership in it is open to individual domestic families whether or not they have kin resident there. And it may consist of several hamlets in which one or more longhouses may be situated.

Like the domestic family, the village is considered to be both jurally and ritually corporate. But unlike the family, the village is not an operating social entity since it does not have the capacity to enter into economic relations and accumulate assets, with the exception of the goodwill of the gods. However, through jointly organized sacrifices of its members the village can increase the state of ritual goodwill between it, as a corporate entity, and the gods to improve the fertility of its territory, its plants, animals, and inhabitants.

This ritual status of the village as a corporate entity is illustrated in the ceremony held by the village every decade or so in which a pig is sacrificed to renew the fecundity of the village land and the community. During this ceremony the village territory is closed off to nonvillagers. A person violating the boundaries is sued by the headman for a pig to repeat the ceremony and re-establish goodwill between the village and the spirit world.

The number of inhabitants of a village can vary from approximately 40 to 400 people.

Land Tenure System. The village holds residual rights over its territory, the boundaries of which are actively defended (see G. N. Appell 1976, 1988). Domestic families resident in the village may cultivate their swiddens there, but no family from another village may do so without prior permission of the headman. Each year a resident domestic family selects a section of forest in the village reserve to be cut for the family swidden. After all the crops of that year have been removed, it reverts back into forest and is available for anyone else in the village to use for a swidden. No permanent use rights over secondary forest are created by the cutting of primary forest. G. N. Appell has termed this type of land tenure system as "circulating usufruct." This system contrasts with those found in Borneo in which permanent use rights are created by the cutting of primary forest. G. N. Appell has termed this latter form "devolvable usufruct" rights (see G. N. Appell 1986).

Role Symmetry Between the Sexes and Its Justification in Myth

Among the Rungus there is sexual role symmetry. The sex roles are not identical, but are they balanced and of equal value (see Laura W. R. Appell 1988, 1991). The division of labor is critically interdependent, and on it rests the prosperity of the domestic family. Thus, the work done by males and females makes up an interdependent whole with their contributions being viewed as equivalent.

The interdependence of husband and wife is exemplified in Rungus myths and legends. In the creation story the Creator God, *Minamangon*, sets off to create the world. The stem *mamangon* means literally "to make the fate (of the world and all living things in it)." With the **-in-** infix, indicating narrative past, the name for the creator god may be translated "he made the world," "he created the fate of the world." But before he could do this he had to be prepared for the task by his wife. She had to weave for him a ceremonial jacket and a headcloth. The woven designs in the jacket included a man, a crocodile and other animals, while the designs of the headcloth included lightning, thunder, floods, wind, etc. Until he put on the jacket and headcloth he could not create the world and all living things, which he then did with a flick of his headcloth.

RUNGUS COSMOLOGY: THE RUNGUS SELF AND ITS BEHAVIORAL ENVIRONMENT

The *Osunduw*: Gods

The Rungus distinguish humans (*riniba*) from supernatural beings (*osunduw*). The term *osunduw* is used in two contexts. First, it is a cover term for all "supernaturals." It includes not only celestial gods but also the terrestrial "spirits" or "demigods" (*rogon*), and the rice spirits as well. At a lower level, it contrasts both with these *rogon*, who are the embodiment of the social and physical environment and who can be harmful to humans, and with the rice spirits (*odu-odu*).

However, in everyday discourse the term *osunduw* is primarily used to contrast with *rogon*. In this context *osunduw* refers just to the celestial gods that inhabit the various layers of the upperworld and are helpful, not harmful to humans, while the *rogon* are referred to as inhabitants of the earth, *putana'on*, "to be of the earth." The earth (*tana*) is separated from this upperworld (*avan*) by a river that can only be crossed by *osunduw*.

The *Rogon*: Demigods and Spirits

The *rogon* are spirits both of the natural and social world. They inhabit the same world as human beings do in both space and time. It is a seamless world in which the *rogon* are found in aspects of the landscape that have distinctive features: a landslide, a large group of boulders, a grove of trees with a spring or wet place, banyan trees, etc. Those *rogon* inhabiting wet places were originally human beings. In crossing a log bridge, some of these human beings slipped off and from then on became *rogon*. Thus, in this context these *rogon* might be translated as "demigod." But, as we shall see, the terms "spirits" and "demigods" only roughly approximate the semantic value of *rogon*.

The *rogon* are the most salient *osunduw* in everyday discourse for they are the most potentially dangerous to human beings. They are capricious, irascible and cause afflictions if they are not properly treated or if their living space is intruded upon. *Rogon*, like human beings, have families and engage in the same activities as human beings. Thus, in addition to *rogon* who are essentially Rungus, there are *rogon* who are Muslim, as for example, those who inhabit certain species of trees in the forest and the particularly malicious *rogon* found at sea.

These Muslim *rogon* will accept only a sacrifice of chickens, not a pig. This mirrors the social environment of the Rungus, for historically there have been villages of Islamic peoples at various locations along the coast who trade fish for agricultural produce with the Rungus and also trade certain types of woven cloth to the Rungus (see Illustration 1).

Invading the living space of a *rogon*, such as cutting a grove of trees in which a spirit dwells, can anger the spirit, and he will in turn cause illness in the family of the perpetrator of this ritual delict. Other *rogon* can also cause misfortune and infertility. These afflictions can only be removed by a sacrifice of pigs and chickens to re-establish the state of goodwill. In the past a human sacrifice to remove the afflictions of a whole village might occur. There are also the wandering *rogon* who bring epidemic diseases.

In addition to the wandering *rogon* and the *rogon* who personify the natural world, there are *rogon* called *rusod* who mirror the organization of the social world of the household. On the birth of a child, his *rusod* comes into being. Thus, each household has a family of rusod mirroring their family, and these dwell in the longhouse apartment along with the domestic family. When a young person marries and moves in to live with the family of his spouse, his *rusod* follows and becomes a member of that *rusod* family.

The *rusod* are the guardians of the proper cultural order in the household and protectors of the household members. They do not die when their human counterparts die, but continue to protect the rest of the family. However, when a family moves to a new longhouse apartment, the *rusod* of dead family members are left behind. The household members can offend the *rusod* by violating the cultural order of the family. If a member breaks any prohibitions, such as frying food in the apartment, bringing in certain prohibited citrus fruits, etc., which are only permitted during the major renewal ceremony especially for the *rusod*, the *rusod* thus will not only cease to protect members of the family, allowing other *rogon* to make a household member ill, but also they themselves will actually cause a member to become ill, until propitiated by ceremonies and sacrifices.

However, most men and even many women are not fully aware of their *rusod* counterpart, even though they know about the *rusod* that dwell in the longhouse apartment and their irascibility if the cultural order is violated which results in illness in the family. The full explanation of the nature of the *rusod* counterpart can only be obtained from *bobolizan* in whose hands lie the placation of the *rusod* and its care and feeding. For it is in the trance performances of the *bobolizan* and the ritual texts she sings over sacrifices that the *rusod* is defined and described.

While *rogon* are generally feared, because when offended they produce sickness, there are other *rogon*, in addition to the *rusod*, that an individual can appeal to for help. There are *rogon* located at the edges of village territories, which if sacrificed to, will prevent the wandering *rogon* bringing epidemics from entering the village. And there are *rogon* of place that can be become guardian spirits for the individual if appealed to and sacrificed to with a chicken or pig. Thus, females can acquire *rogon* as spirit familiars. *Rogon* that inhabit boulders, when acquired are referred to as *sondihon* (literally, "one that can be leaned upon"). *Rogon* spirit familiars who dwell in the earth of sacred groves with springs or seeps, are called *luhuban* (see below).

In the past, particularly during the period of intergroup warfare and head-taking, men would call upon similar *rogon* of place for help.[7] Such *rogon* that become protectors of men are called *ansamung*. But while these *ansamung* are guardian spirits and will appear in transmogrified form when called upon *in extremis*, men did not go into trance to get into communication with them but simply called to them for help. Unlike spirit familiars of *bobolizan*, *ansamung* do not respond verbally when called upon.

The *Odu-Odu*: Rice Spirits

The third major class of spirits are the rice spirits. These rice spirits, like the *rogon* of the household (the *rusod*), mirror the social order of the family and reflect its social and jural substantiation (see G. N. Appell 1976 for a discussion of the implications of this ritual symbolization). Thus, as a new child is born into the family, a new rice spirit comes into being, who is then called to come to the swiddens during the agricultural season along with the rice spirits of the other family members in order to ensure a good harvest. At the end of the agricultural year they are sent home again across the sea.

In addition to these rice spirits there are specific swidden *rogon*, such as the spirits of mice, and other agricultural pests. Ceremonies for all these various agricultural spirits involve prayers and exhortations, and every few years the sacrifice of chickens. Communication with the spirits in the swidden that affect agricultural yields is predominantly handled by males. There are also a few women who are equally as skilled as men at performing the agricultural rituals that involve the sacrifice of chickens. But at no time do these ceremonies and sacrifices involve going into trance to communicate with the gods and spirits.

Divato and *Lugu'*: Celestial Counterparts of Human Beings

Dwelling in the lower level of the upperworld with other celestial *osunduw* are the celestial counterparts of individuals. These are called *divato* for a woman and *lugu'* for a man.[8] A celestial counterpart is born with each individual, along with his multiple souls, his rice spirit, and his *rusod* counterpart. When an individual is in danger, the celestial counterpart looks out for him and protects him. Thus, a *lugu'* or *divato* is called upon for help when frightened. For example when alone and lost in the jungle a person will call out to his celestial counterpart, saying he can't see him but needs his help. There is no response on the part of the celestial counterpart, but because he is an *osunduw*, he comes to help and will hover above the individual until safety is reached.

Luma'ag: Spirit Familiars

The celestial counterparts of living or deceased individuals can become spirit familiars of practicing bobolizan particularly if they are or were efficacious *bobolizan* or individuals of renown. The term *luma'ag* is used to refer to any spirit familiar, god, *rogon*, or celestial counterpart, that communicates with a spirit medium. And thus the cover term *luma'ag* is frequently used also to refer to the celestial counterpart of a living individual, male or female. However, only *bobolizan* obtain replies from their celestial counterpart when called upon in trance.

It is through the help of these *luma'ag* that a *bobolizan* while in trance diagnoses illnesses and obtains information on the proper sacrifice to achieve cures, which then involve the performance of hymns to the gods and spirits over sacrifices of pigs and chickens. The primary *luma'ag* of a *bobolizan* is usually her own celestial counterpart, although sometimes it can be that of her mother or teacher.

The *luma'ag*, except for *rogon* spirit familiars who inhabit the earth, live in *libabow*, the lower layer of the upperworld.

The Rungus Self In Its Behavioral Environment

The Rungus self is composed of body (*inan*), multiple souls (*hatod*), the *rusod* counterpart, an individual's rice spirit (*odu-odu*), and the celestial counterpart (*divato* or *lugu'*). These all appear on the birth of the individual, but it is only the celestial counterpart that dwells in the first layer of the upperworld. On the death of the body the main soul goes to the afterworld, *Nabalu* (Mount Kinabalu). Other souls reside in the individual's joints, and these go wandering during dreams and become exposed to malicious or angered spirits (*rogon*), who capture and torture these souls, causing illness. When the spirit medium retrieves these souls at the end of a ceremony, she returns them to the body through the whorl of the hair.

Beyond this, Rungus exegesis on the nature of the behavioral self is contradictory and unsystematized. Thus, there is considerable variation in explanations given for number of souls or their loci. Men will state their understanding of the subject but then defer to *bobolizan* for the proper and fuller explanation. And even *bobolizan* themselves are not consistent on the subject. Thus, the number of souls given varies from two to seven or more depending on the informant. But all agree that the joints have a soul or souls. Thus, there are souls that reside in the joints of the knees, elbows, and shoulders. Some say that there are six, one for each joint, while some say there are three, one for each pair of joints, and some say that there is just one for all the joints. In those instances when the number given are less than six, it is stated that the soul or souls move around between the joints.

Furthermore, a few individuals who are not *bobolizan* respond that the celestial counterpart is the main soul of the individual, confusing it with the soul of the body. Also a few men say that the *lugu'* resides in or near the body. As the term *lugu'* also refers to the heartwood of a tree, this suggests the source of this interpretation.

Our most knowledgeable *bobolizan* informant divided an individual's souls into "bad" souls, the souls of the joints that wander and actually seek out agents that cause illness, and the "good" soul, the "soul of the body." It is generally stated that this good soul does not go wandering--although one informant stated that it did--and it does not leave the body till death. However, it does not reside within the body but follows the individual about, watching out for his well being. It can even go up to the first layer of the upperworld to consult with the celestial counterpart when concerned over the health of the individual. It is this soul that goes to the afterworld on death, although one informant stated that it was the soul of the knees that went to *Nabalu*. Some say that if the *rogon* have "eaten" all an individual's souls, he no longer will become ill but will have a long life.

Most say that the souls of the joints on death turn into *bubuha*, "ghosts," which frighten people and cause illness. These ghosts are also said to hover around a woman giving birth as they like to drink blood. However, an authoritative *bobolizan* disagreed, insisting that these ghosts are derived from the *rogon* of the grave, which are created from improper burial procedures. She said that at death the souls of the joints become *rogon* called *namatai* (derived from the lexeme *matai*, "to die"). Others have also said that not all souls of the joints become "ghosts," but some become *namatai*. These live near *Nabalu*, and visit the world of the living most frequently during ceremonies where rice wine is being drunk. They appear in the form of a dead relative and try to entice souls of the living to *Nabalu*.

The Issue of Invisibility as a Defining Characteristic of the Category *Osunduw*

The *osunduw* are normally invisible to humans beings in their ordinary mode of consciousness, but they can be seen in a change in mode of consciousness. In dreams the soul goes wandering and may meet up with *rogon* and other *osunduw*, as well as the *hatod* of other people. In ordeals to solicit a guardian *rogon* to provide protection in fighting, a man may see the *rogon* indistinctly or in transmogrified form. However, in trance state the *bobolizan* does not always see the inhabitants of the spirit world, although she becomes the channel though which information is passed on from these to the human world. Occasionally a particularly skilled *bobolizan* will say that she has seen her *luma'ag* standing on a leaf of a variety of banana plant (*kudau*), although no one else can see her, nor are there any indications of her presence such as the movement of the leaf itself. Itulina, the *bobolizan* who worked closely with Laura W. R. Appell, felt that when in trance she actually became partially a member of the spirit world; she saw *rogon* walking in front of her eyes, and at times they handed her something. When she came out of trance, there was nothing in her hand, and her interpretation of this was that the *rogon* had returned the soul of the sick person directly to her rather than via her spirit familiar, the more usual mode.

Various *rogon* also occasionally reveal themselves to humans when they are traveling in the forest. This happened more often in the past when there was more primary forest, as *rogon* are believed to frequent the primary forest. But the presence of the *rogon* are more usually indicated by certain occurrences or changes in the natural environment. For example, the appearance of slime in wet places is an indication that a *rogon* is dwelling nearby. This slime is called *ta'i rogon*, "*rogon* feces."

The upperworld *osunduw*, however, have never revealed themselves in normal states of consciousness to Rungus, according to our informants. But they appear in myths and other religious texts. Since many of these are the result of dreams, the *osunduw* must also appear in dreams from time to time.

The spirits, demigods, and gods all appear like human beings and have most of the same emotions and motives, except that they have superhuman powers. They are able to become visible or remain invisible. They have superhuman powers of movement, such as riding on the wind. And they have the capacity to transform themselves into other forms and shapes. Thus, they can transform their bodies into those of animals, human beings, or monsters.

Sather and Barrett (in this volume) argue that the fundamental distinction in the Iban cosmos is not between the natural and supernatural but between the visible and the invisible. However, this distinction does not seem to hold for Rungus conceptions of the cosmos. While it is recognized that the gods and spirits are generally invisible, invisibility is not the sole characteristic of the gods and spirts nor a characteristic of them alone. The souls (*hatod*) of human beings are also invisible, with the exception that they can be "seen" along with gods and spirits in dreams. Furthermore, gods and spirits sometimes, though rarely, actually appear before human beings. The term *sumindatu*, "to appear," to become manifest," refers to this act taken by gods to become visible to human beings. Thus, invisibility is not the sole defining characteristic of the *osunduw*. Their capacity to materialize in the sight of Rungus and their appearance in dreams suggest that the Rungus live in a seamless world that cannot be described by such oppositions as "invisible:visible" and "natural:supernatural," which are commonly found in western culture.

EXPLANATIONS FOR HUMAN AFFLICTIONS

Illness and the Soul

Illness is explained as the result of harm done to the soul when it is absenting itself from the body or when it has been captured by a *rogon*. And bodily impairment is a consequence of soul involvement. For example, a *rogon* may capture one of the souls of an individual and subject it to tortures. This is then reflected in his physical body through various symptoms. The torment of a soul being subjected to the heat from a fire will produce an illness with a high fever.

An offended *rogon* may not necessarily make ill that member of the domestic family that has caused him to be offended. Thus, if a man in cutting his swidden inadvertently damages the dwelling of a *rogon* family, the *rogon* will seek revenge by causing any member of that man's family to become ill.

Upon occasion a *hatod* (especially that of a child) is itself capricious and will wander away from its body and cause illness by repeatedly jumping out of a tree or falling while in a running contest with other *hatod*. This is experienced in a dream, and such activity will cause sore bones and joints. But the *rogon* have no part in this. At other times the *hatod* will play tag with *rogon* or hide and seek, and if caught by the *rogon*, will become ill. Sometimes a *hatod* will simply get too close to the house of a *rogon* and will be chased by a *rogon*'s dog. By the time the *hatod* returns to his body, it is exhausted and sore from tripping and stumbling as it tries to run away from the dog. A special ceremony in which a chicken is offered is held to bring back such wandering *hatod* to the body.

In charting the social geography of the Rungus cosmos and the relationship of the *bobolizan* to gods and spirits, it is important to note that when the soul goes wandering or is captured, its geographical scope encompasses only the earth (*tana*). It does not go beyond the boundaries of the earth into the upperworld, the realm of friendly *osunduw*.

Accidents may also be caused by a *rogon*. This could be any *rogon* of place that has been angered, or a special *rogon* whose particular field of endeavor is causing accidents. There are sacrifices specifically for those *rogon* who cause accidents.

The identity of the *rogon* that is causing illness is revealed to the spirit medium through the help of her *luma'ag*, whom she has communicated with in trance. At the same time she is told what sacrifice of pigs and/or chickens must be offered to the *rogon* to return the soul.

While the primary explanation for illness given by the *bobolizan* is harm done to the soul by *rogon*, in every day discourse an individual will refer to illness as the result of being eaten by a *rogon*. For example, a bruise is an example of a *rogon* who has tried to eat you. Thus, clear-cut distinctions of which parts of the self, body or soul, that are involved are frequently not made. When it is said that the body is attacked, it is in fact the *hatod* that has been captured, as all know. But the use of the body as reference in this discourse is in effect a shorthand way of dealing with an elaborate etiology.

Explanations for Infertility, Bad Harvests, and Misfortune

Swidden failures can result from the rice spirits being scared away or offended by ignoring the customary rules of swiddening. Ceremonies to right these misfortunes are generally in the hands of men, but not exclusively. Trance behavior to locate the source of the misfortune is not part of these ceremonies. Only the reciting of sacred texts and the sacrifice of chickens, or occasionally a pig, are required.

However, there are times of misfortune for everyone in a village. Children die. Domestic animals do not reproduce and die. Women are unable to conceive. Harvests of fruit trees are bad. There are major crop failures. And many people are sick. This type of total misfortune is caused by incest or illicit intercourse.

There is a basic value premise that no sexual act may take place outside of marriage. If incest, fornication, or adultery occur, it is perceived that the whole world becomes hot, with this malicious heat spreading out from the couple who have violated the rules on sexual conduct, but not involving them, to those closest to them and eventually the whole village. And this will anger a class of *rogon* who retaliate with these massive afflictions.

When this happens, the situation cannot be reversed without a ceremony to appease the *rogon* and "cool" the country. A fine must be paid by the offending couple of pigs and chickens, which are sacrificed. And all members of the village must be ritually cooled by having blood of the sacrifice put on their ankles.

There are larger ceremonies to make the village fertile, and in the past this included a human sacrifice. This ceremony has not been held within the memory of even the oldest members of the village or their parents, although the ritual texts are still remembered by some of the *bobolizan*.

Another ceremony for the village only requires a pig. This pig is either bought jointly by all the domestic families who join in the ceremony, or is raised jointly by them. Blood from the pig is put on the ankles of all village members, and shavings dipped in the blood are buried in a ritual plot in the garden and placed with rice seeds. This ceremony rids the longhouses and gardens in the village of all pests and dangerous *rogon* that cause infertility and crop failure as well as the failure to accumulate brassware and gongs. These ceremonies to return the fertility to the village as well as the ceremonies for illness are performed by the *bobolizan*.

THE *BOBOLIZAN* AND HER SPIRIT FAMILIAR: CURING ILLNESS AND INFERTILITY

The *bobolizan* serves as an intermediary between human beings and supernatural beings, both upperworld *osunduw* and the terrestrial *rogon*, to alleviate afflictions of disease, misfortune, infertility, and crop failure. *Bobolizan* are universally females (with the exceptions described below). They go into trance to communicate with the spirit world in order to diagnose and cure illness and misfortune, and they then sing the long sacred texts that accompany the necessary sacrificial offerings to the spirit world. Thus, the term *bobolizan* may be glossed both as spirit medium and as priestess. The fact that both glosses are applicable and may shift in applicability with the work of the *bobolizan* indicates that the concepts and terminology currently available for describing and analyzing religions, and in particular spirit medium performances, are inadequate to map this cultural domain. They are still ethnocentric.

Consequently, we shall use the term *bobolizan* when we are referring to the total role, both that of priestess and that of spirit medium. When we refer to the dissociative aspects of this role, we shall use the term "spirit medium." And when we refer to that aspect of the role that involves reciting and singing the long sacred texts that accompany a sacrifice, we will use the term "priestess."

The origin of the word *bobolizan* is far from clear but it may be from the stem *momoli*, "to transact," as their main function is the transaction of sacrifices with the spirit world for the return of the souls of ill people.[9]

As a result of their ability to go into trance and communicate with the spirit world, women are considered the authorities on the nature of the cosmos and are the interpreters of most forms of misfortune except those relating to farming activities, where there are male experts as well. Responses by men to queries as to the nature of gods and spirits, their locations, their powers and activities are frequently concluded with a statement that they really don't know about *osunduw*; women are the ones that know the ultimate answers to such questions.

The Relationship Between the *Bobolizan* and Her *Luma'ag*

While each person has one personal celestial counterpart and a terrestrial counterpart (*rusod*) created at his birth who look out for him and try to prevent the *rogon* from capturing his soul and causing illness, the *rogon* often prevail against these despite their efforts. Then, a *bobolizan* is called in to help.

Her natal *divato* usually becomes a *bobolizan*'s first spirit familiar. But as she becomes more skilled in trance performance she will establish communication with other *luma'ag*. By the time a *bobolizan* attains such proficiency she has been married for some time and has had children.

Various *luma'ag* that communicate with a *bobolizan* may be those of family ancestors, both male and female. If her mother, aunt and/or sister still are living and are *bobolizan*, their *luma'ag* will also assist her when needed, as will that of her husband and occasionally even a friend. The *luma'ag* of her children will not communicate with her if the child is living, nor will the *luma'ag* of a child who died at a young age. However, if a child has died as a mature adult, that *luma'ag* may communicate and help the mother. A *bobolizan* will also call upon the *ansamung*, the guardian *rogon*, of her grandfathers to come near when in need, though these do not communicate.

Occasionally, her *luma'ag* perceive a *bobolizan* to be filthy (*asakau*) because she has not performed the special ceremony to cleanse herself. *Luma'ag* do not like filth, and when a *bobolizan* is unclean they will become angry and refuse to communicate with her, though they will relent if it is a case of an emergency and a life or death situation for a patient. However, when they are finished with the immediate situation, they will chastise the *bobolizan* and ask her to perform a cleansing ceremony. If she is too lax in this regard, her *luma'ag* will not take care of her, will not readily respond when invoked, and will actually allow her and her family to become ill.

A *bobolizan* can become unclean by going under the longhouse where she may come into contact with human or animal feces. Even mud is considered filthy by spirit familiars. For example, a spirit familiar of Laura W. R. Appell's informant suddenly ceased talking with her while she was attempting to cure a sick grandchild. The next day when she was able to contact her familiar again and asked why she stopped talking so suddenly, she learned that her familiar was angry with her because she had touched cat vomitus and was filthy (*asakau*). The spirit familiar told her what she must do to purify herself. It is stated that generations ago one particular class of *luma'ag* was said to find pregnancy particularly repugnant, and preferred *bobolizan* either not to marry at all or, if they did marry, to bear only one child. However, this was no longer the case when we did our field work in the 1960s.

The purification ceremony for a *luma'ag* in which a chicken is sacrificed is called *mangaraha luma'ag*, "to blood *luma'ag*." A diligent *bobolizan* will perform this once a month at the time of the full moon, but most do not do it that frequently. The other term for this ceremony is *momugas*, which means "to cleanse," "to polish." This refers to the cleansing of the *bobolizan* who might have been contaminated by filth. The *momugas* may also be held for people who are frequently ill, whether or not they are a *bobolizan*, as anybody's *luma'ag* may fail to protect them if offended in any way.

There is a more elaborate ceremony for *luma'ag*, called *monimbang*, which is less frequently held. This is also a ceremony to cleanse a person who is ill, so that his *luma'ag* will be more "considerate." The help of the *luma'ag* of a particularly efficacious *bobolizan* is sought to do this. At the *monimbang* a platform is built outside the longhouse with a bridge to it from the apartment of the person for whom the ceremony is being held. Offerings of pigs as well as chickens are made to his *luma'ag*, and the best brassware is brought out, polished, and used for the presentation of special oil and other offerings to please his *luma'ag*.

The Trance: *Rundukan*

Rungus classify trance behavior into two types on the basis of the manner by which it is entered. Spirit mediums can actively induce trance to ask help from their spirit familiars, or they may spontaneously go into trance during a dream or on returning from visiting a *rogon* in the forest to ask for his help.

The term for trance is *rundukan*. And the term for induced trance is *rundukan mangambo*. The lexeme *mangambo* is used also to refer to the act of calling upon young men and women for help during a ceremony, and so in this context it can be understood to mean to call upon the spirit familiars for help. The *mangambo* here refers to the ritualized invocations that are memorized and used to call up the spirit familiars.

Rundukan mangambo is also auditorially induced by the use of a hand clapper (*gonding*) with the chanting of invocations. The *gonding* has a wooden handle and bits of broken brassware and gongs attached to it so that when it is shaken it produces a sound like a bag of coins being bounced (see Illustrations 2 and 3).

Trance is induced when a *bobolizan* is asked to communicate with her spirit familiars to determine the causes of illness, and it also occurs as part of the curing ceremonies.

In curing ceremonies the *rundukan mangambo* that occur at certain stages are ritualized trances in that they differ little in content each time. In these the *bobolizan* calls upon her various *luma'ag* to assist her in communicating with the *rogon* to make sure that the sacrifice has been sufficient to placate them and thereby insure the safe return of the wandering souls of the ill person. In essence they describe the journey of the *luma'ag* as they travel to the villages of the *rogon*, bargain with them for the return of the souls in exchange for the sacrifice, gather up the souls, and return them to the *bobolizan*. At this point the *luma'ag* tell the *rogon* to remove their agents of pain and to refrain from any more soul capture or torture.

In the case where trance is not part of a ceremony but is induced to determine the cause of illness, onlookers will gather around to listen to whatever news the *luma'ag* has to impart, and after a *bobolizan* has finished communicating with her various *luma'ag*, other people can ask questions of the *luma'ag* and tell them their worries about ill family members. The *luma'ag* will answer them through the *bobolizan*. These usually occur at night, and, as *luma'ag* do not like bright lights, they are held in semi-darkness with the *bobolizan* covering her head with a cloth.

Spontaneous trances, *rundukan tomod*, occur often as a result of a dream about a *bobolizan's luma'ag*. The lexeme *tomod* indicates in everyday language an action taken intentionally by an individual because he wanted to. In this instance it is the action of a *luma'ag* who wants to communicate with his or her medium. When this occurs, she wakes up already in trance. It is said that the *luma'ag* misses his or her spirit medium and wants to talk with her. At other times this happens if a *bobolizan* has tried to call upon her *luma'ag* when he was busy and couldn't communicate with her. He now is contacting her to see what it was she wanted.

Upon occasion a *luma'ag* will bring news of an ill child or other relative in another village before the news has reached the person who has had the dream, although the informant of Laura W. R. Appell said she was very dubious that this could happen. She believed a person who heard of disaster via her *luma'ag* was embellishing on a story she had already heard.

Acquisition of Spirit Familiars

After a woman has a reasonable command of the ritual texts she must learn to go into trance to get in communication with one or more spirit familiars before she can perform a ceremony for illness.

A novice *bobolizan* can have her first contact with a *luma'ag* when she is performing a ceremony. As stated above, the *rundukan* during a ceremony does not vary. During the *moginum* ceremony (described below) a *bobolizan* who has been teaching a young woman the ritual texts will help her *rundukan*. The *bobolizan* sits behind the young woman during the *mangambo* invocations guiding her hand as she shakes the *gonding*. They *mangambo* together, and when the *bobolizan's luma'ag* arrives she will let go of the woman's hand. If the young woman continues in trance it means the *bobolizan's luma'ag* has been transferred to her. This *luma'ag* will become a spirit familiar of the young woman and will continue to help her throughout her life.

If a woman has difficulty in getting a *luma'ag* to communicate with her she will hold a *momugas*, a cleansing ceremony, and ask the help of a *bobolizan* to persuade her *luma'ag* to begin to talk. At that time a mother can also bestow her *luma'ag* on her daughter and ask her to help her daughter during trance. Often during such a ceremony a woman will be visited by her spirit familiar for the first time.

The learning of the invocations, *mangambo*, for trance or holding the *momugas* ceremony do not, however, guarantee that a *bobolizan* who controls the ritual will be able to enter the trance state and be acknowledged by spirit familiars. This depends upon how receptive she is to the idea of going into trance. A woman with a rigid personality is not likely to be able to *rundukan*, as her *luma'ag* feels she is not trusted.

A woman can also acquire, as a spirit familiar, a member of the class of *rogon* that dwell in sacred groves. Like any other *rogon* these will cause illness. However, these *rogon* of sacred groves, if properly appealed to, will become spirit familiars of *bobolizan*. There is a ceremony called *sumombol do rogon*, "to visit the *rogon*," in which a single individual or a group of people both male and female will take offerings and ask for help. When such offerings are made, a woman may call upon the *rogon* to ask him to become a spirit familiar. If her request is granted, shortly after returning home she will spontaneously go into trance, and the *rogon* will communicate with her and offer protection as a spirit familiar.

There are occasionally women who can call on their *luma'ag*, as well as other spirit familiars, and enter trance, but who do not control the *rinait*, the ritual texts that are sung over a sacrifice or offering. As a result, they cannot perform ceremonies. These women are particularly sought after to communicate with their spirit familiars to diagnose the causes of illness or other troubles and determine how to correct misfortune. This can include locating a relative lost in the jungle. Such women are looked up to because it is thought that their *luma'ag* are particularly o+ohis, "straight," but they are not referred to as *bobolizan*.

Diagnosing the Cause of Illness and Misfortune

In addition to calling upon her guardian spirits to determine the *rogon* source of illness, a *bobolizan* will also analyze dreams of the person who is ill. It is during dreams that the soul goes wandering and becomes vulnerable to attack by *rogon*. After a person describes his dream in detail to the *bobolizan*, she can call upon her spirit familiar to find out just what class of *rogon* has been angered, and what must be done to appease them. The *bobolizan* herself at times is also able to ascertain what *rogon* are guilty after she has heard a description of what happened to the soul of the person who had the dream.

Although no form of divination is used to find out why a person is sick, a *bobolizan* will examine the intestines and other organs of the sacrificed animals at the end of the ceremony. The appearance of these organs is an indication of whether or not a cure has been effective.

The Behavioral Environment and Physiology of Trance

When a *bobolizan* wants to enter the trance state she must first go through the invocations (*mangambo*) to call her *luma'ag* and alert them to the fact that she needs their assistance. A woman about to invoke her spirit familiars sits upright on the floor with her legs straight in front of her. The following is based on a description by Laura W. R. Appell's informant, Itulina, of what happens to her when in trance.

Before beginning the path to dissociation the *bobolizan* first makes a fresh "chew" of betel and *sirih*. She chews this and at the same time starts shaking her ritual clapper (*gonding*). She then starts singing the ritual invocations, the first step of which is to wake up the spirit (*divato*) of the basket that contains her ritual paraphernalia (see below). As she progresses, the rhythmical shaking of the *gonding* becomes faster and faster. Next she takes a small piece of the root of the *komburungo* plant (Sweet Flag, *Acorus calamus*; see also Evans 1953:60), which is believed to have a soul of its own. Prayers are uttered over the *komburungo*, and its soul precedes the words of the *bobolizan* in summoning the *luma'ag*.

When the *luma'ag* arrive, they do not enter the body of the *bobolizan* but hover above her in the lower layer of the upperworld and look down on her. There is a symbolic "bridge" between the dwelling place of the *luma'ag* and the *bobolizan*. Across this bridge the words of *luma'ag* arrive at the whorl of the hair of the *bobolizan* and cause her to speak. However, the terrestrial spirit familiars, the *sondihon* and *luhuban*, do not speak from the bridge but sit beside the *bobolizan* when she is in trance.

With the arrival of her spirit familiar the *bobolizan* feels her body "enlarge" (*gumazo*). She feels goose pimples and begins to shiver, her legs begin to twitch and shake and her trunk sways from side to side. As her *luma'ag* travels back and forth mediating between her and members of the spirit world her movements become more frenzied, her body sways faster and her head moves rapidly from side to side. Depending upon which spirit is speaking through her mouth, the voice will become louder or quieter.

The spirit familiars talk through the mouth of the spirit medium, as do the *rogon*. However, the *bobolizan* herself rarely converses directly with the *rogon*; the spirit familiar is always the intermediary. All discussions that the spirit familiar has with other spirits are voiced through the mouth of the *bobolizan*. It is said that she does not say the words herself; the spirit familiar makes her mouth move, and the words come from them. Each type of spirit speaks with a different voice, and onlookers who are knowledgeable will know which of the spirit familiars is talking.

The arrival of each of the various spirits, *osunduw* and *rogon*, is signaled by yawning and belching on the part of the *bobolizan*. The success of a trance is usually indicated by the *rogon* saying that they have removed the cause of illness because the people have pleased them and fed them. At the very end the spirit familiars say, "We're going home now."

It must be emphasized here that at no time does the soul of the *bobolizan* leave her body to go in search of the souls of people, as is said to happen among the Iban of Sarawak where "the *manang*'s soul (*semengat*) leaves his body to seek out and return with the missing soul of the patient he is treating" (J. D. Freeman, personal communication).

Luma'ag and other *osunduw* have their own vocabularies, which the *bobolizan* understand but onlookers often don't. *Rogon*, however, usually use the everyday lexicon when communicating with the *luma'ag* and other *osunduw*.

Upon occasion the *rundukan* will take on a humorous aspect as a capricious *luma'ag* speaks in metaphors which are not understood, and says the opposite of what he or she means. At other times the spirits called *sondihon* (see above) occasionally carry on a long diatribe in "Malay," and, though rare, in "Chinese" or "English." Though the sound of the language is skillfully mimicked, it is not the actual language. One *bobolizan*, when a spirit familiar, who was Chinese, started to talk, told the *sondihon* to "stop talking like that, I cannot understand you." The spirit abruptly ceased talking.

One form of *latah* behavior can occur in trance. The Rungus form of *latah*, exhibited by women, primarily involves repetition of words, speaking the wrong word, or voicing an obscenity, when an individual is startled (see Doolittle 1991). It is called *kasała*, "to make a mistake." Itulina, who was an extreme case of *kasała* behavior, often exhibited *kasała* when she was in trance, as long as she was the one who was talking. However, when *luma'ag* or the *rogon* were using her mouth to talk through, she never exhibited *kasaḵa*.

The trance state will be broken if the *bobolizan* is interrupted by such things as a dog fight, being intentionally touched by an onlooker, or if someone does something that angers her *luma'ag*. A *bobolizan* does have recall of the conversations that took place during her trance state, but does not know anything of what went on around her while she was in trance, although she can recall the questions that were put to her by onlookers asking for help as well as the answers received via her *luma'ag*.

Most of the time a *bobolizan* does not have any adverse physiological reactions when entering trance, during trance or leaving trance. Though her breath is somewhat short and she perspires from the physical exertion, she does not have an elevated pulse at the end of a trance. She does not faint or pass out during trance, nor does she fall into a cataleptic state after leaving the trance state, as in some societies.

Thus, a skilled *bobolizan* whose *luma'ag* are straight and truthful will not feel any different at the end of a *rundukan* than she did before starting. It is not unusual, however, for a novice *bobolizan* to fall over in a semi-faint for a brief time the first time she is visited by a *luma'ag*. This is merely attributed to her inexperience at such an emotionally charged happening. She does not lose consciousness, and is only momentarily incapacitated. This is called *otimporon*. *Otimporon* has been known to occur during the *rundukan* of an experienced *bobolizan* if a *rogon* becomes angry with her or has come too close to her and makes breathing difficult. A young woman who has learned all the prayers and songs must never attempt to go into trance for the first time when on the roof of the longhouse during a ceremony called *moginum*, as she would surely fall over and have difficulty breathing.

Paraphernalia of the *Bobolizan*

There is a certain amount of ritual paraphernalia necessary for invoking one's spirit familiars (*rundukan mangambo*). In addition to the clapper (*gonding*), which is shaken as the *bobolizan* begins the process of dissociation, there is a miniature ceramic jar worn around the *bobolizan*'s neck on a cord. This jar is the receptacle for the souls as they are brought home from the *rogon* to be returned to the body of the patient.

The spirit medium also wears around her neck a collection of small pieces of efficacious wood and other materials with magical powers which have been sewn into a piece of cloth. This neckband is called a *pomudsu* (to be washed) and serves two purposes. It protects against the anger of any malicious *rogon* who may come close to the *bobolizan* during the *rundukan*. It also has elements which ensure the efficacy of her efforts to heal her patient, as well as preventing her from falling asleep during her arduous task. There are other types of *pomudsu* which are actually immersed in water that is used to rub on a sick person to remove illness. However, this is not the case with the *pomudsu* of a *bobolizan*.

In addition to the above items the *bobolizan* holds a small knife, *dazap*, while in trance. This is fashioned like the bush knife used to fell trees and brush in clearing for a new swidden. But this is a miniature knife, six to nine inches in length. The *dazap* is used for protection when her *luma'ag* is in face-to-face combat with the *rogon*, who see it not as a miniature but as a full-sized bush knife.

The *gonding* and jar are stored, along with the *dazap*, in the *sovion*, a basketry container with a cover. Also stored in the *sovion* is the *surud do luma'ag*, "the comb of *luma'ag*," which is used during the cleansing ceremonies to comb oil through the hair of the *bobolizan* as part of the cleansing process. These ritual objects are treated with circumspection and cannot be opened up in the longhouse at times other than ceremonies or going into trance to diagnose illness (see Illustrations 2 and 3).

The *Bobolizan* and her Various Ritual Activities

Ceremonies for Illness. The structure of the ceremonies for illness involve first ascertaining the type of *rogon* causing the misfortune, which may be discovered during an induced trance or the interpretation of dreams. These may be the *rogon* of sacred groves or the forest, as well as the *rusod*, who are at times fickle protectors of the household. While in trance the *bobolizan*, with the help of her spirit familiar, not only determines what *rogon* are involved but what sacrifices are required for return of the souls. Some *rogon* receive large pigs, others small ones and some *rogon* want red chickens and others white. At this time she is able to ask for mercy and bargain for a smaller sacrifice.

The performance of the ceremony itself includes recitation of the appropriate sacred texts for those *rogon* who are being addressed, the invoked trances to have the *luma'ag* obtain the return of the souls, and then the killing of the sacrifices and eating them by the domestic family.

The *rusod*, the *rogon* which dwell in every Rungus longhouse apartment, are responsible for the well-being of each family. When not angered they protect all family members, but it is not difficult to anger them inadvertently. Therefore, it is necessary from time to time to hold a *tumuron* ceremony to undo the anger of the *rusod*, which is represented by the illness of a family member. These *tumuron* are the ceremonies most frequently held throughout the year (see Illustration 3).

However, for major or lingering illness, a bargain will be struck with the *rusod* to hold a renewal ceremony, a *moginum*, at some point a year or two in the future, when the family has been able to raise a pig of sufficient size and collect the supplies for such a ceremony. It is hoped that this will alleviate the illness. And at the time of making this bargain, a piglet is designated to be raised for this ceremony.

The *moginum* is held infrequently, only once every five to ten years per family. It is the ultimate ceremony for illness, and the only one where rice wine is consumed. The term *moginum* is derived from the lexeme *minum*, "to drink." There is much festivity during this ceremony, rice wine is prepared and friends and relatives come from far and near to celebrate and dance and sing in honor of the *rusod*. More than one *bobolizan* is required for this ceremony as the prayers and songs go on for five days or longer. After many pigs and chickens have been offered and much feasting and drinking on the part of the assembled guests, the ceremony culminates with the *bobolizan* going into trance on a raised platform above the roof of the longhouse. At the end of her *rundukan* the *bobolizan* dances with the *rusod* as they celebrate the renewal of their relationship with the family (see Illustrations 4, 5, 6, and 7).

Marriage: The *bobolizan* also officiates at marriage ceremonies with the recitation of sacred texts over the chickens. The prayers that accompany this part of the marriage ritual are called *monogit*, "to cool" the union and thereby insure that the couple will be successful in raising a family, that their children will grow to adulthood, and that their gardens will be profitable. There are no trance activities involved in this (see Illustration 8).

Though not encouraged, first cousin marriage is permitted, except where a sister's daughter and a brother's son are involved, for this is an analog of incest. However, such a marriage must be accompanied by a *momitas*, which is much more elaborate than the regular cooling ceremony for unrelated, or distantly related persons. The word *pitas* is translated as "split off from," and *momitas* is the action to cause splitting off. In other words, the close relationship of first cousins is ritually nullified.

Death. The *bobolizan* also performs the ritual and offerings that accompany a death. After the death of a spouse, the widow or widower are considered *alasu*, "hot," and no one may talk to them until the next weekly market is held. After this a *bobolizan* will hold a ceremony to send away the lingering souls of the dead from the family apartment for fear they might try to lure the souls of the living to follow them to the afterworld.

At some point in the following year or two the surviving family members must hold a *lumuvas* ceremony, "to clear" the grave. This is a time when all kin from near and far are called to memorialize the dead. The grave site is cleared and tidied up, and a *bobolizan* performs prayers to insure that any souls lingering around the cemetery are sent on their way to the final resting place of souls of the dead, *Nabalu* (Mt. Kinabalu). A pig is sacrificed and offerings of food and rice wine are left on the grave to provide sustenance for the souls on their journey. Again there is no trance associated with these activities.

The Participation in the Curing Performance

The alleviation of affliction does not occur through the active participation of the afflicted one in the ceremony. The sick are essentially an audience to the ceremony, and may not even be present for certain aspects of it, such as the sacrifice of a pig to the *rogon* in the forest. Thus, there is no attempt to change the patient's mood, sentiment, or perception of his affliction by bringing him actively into the performance. The afflicted one, however, does obtain emotional relief from the identification of the cause of the illness, the perception that there is a cure being effected, and the social support of family through their activity and contributions of resources to the ceremony.

The curing ceremonies are also not part of a community performance that involves participation of a human audience, unlike the Bulusu'. Young men and women from other families will be sought out to help the family in the work of the ceremony, such as catching the sacrificial animals and preparing them for eating. And people may come to watch certain trance performances that are considered spectacular, such as the one done on a platform raised above the roof during the renewal ceremony for the family. But much of the singing is done in a tone so low that it can be heard clearly only if one is sitting or standing close to the priestess.

The primary audience instead are the *rogon* and the *osunduw*. It is to them the prayers and songs are addressed. It is to them the sacrifice is made, although the domestic family giving the sacrifice will eat the animals that have been offered. Thus, the ritual performances are not entertainment for the longhouse members or visitors.

The one exception to audience participation occurs in those trance performances, discussed above, during which questions are put to spirit mediums as to the cause of an affliction.

Recruitment to the Role of *Bobolizan*

To become a *bobolizan* there are two skills that must be learned. The first of these skills is the memorization of the ritual texts consisting of prayers and hymns to the gods and spirits. These accompany the sacrifice of pigs and chickens to both spirit familiars and the pathogenic spirits and are sung with tunes from a repertoire of music. And the second skill is the ability to go into trance to communicate with one's spirit familiars.

A *bobolizan* is not called to her profession, nor does she have a serious illness indicating the onset of her profession. Instead a girl will make a conscious decision to begin to learn the ritual texts at an early age prior to the onset of adolescence, and this learning process continues up through a *bobolizan*'s career until she becomes as skilled in the various ceremonies as she wants to be. Certain sacred texts are considered dangerous, and a *bobolizan* will not ask to be taught these until she has passed the age of childbearing.

The process of becoming a *bobolizan* begins at the age of about eight to nine years old when girls begin going off to the swidden houses with their mothers, grandmothers or aunts to learn the elaborate ritual texts. Teaching and learning cannot be carried out in the longhouse as the *rogon* of the domestic family (the *rusod*), if they heard ritual words being recited, would expect a sacrifice and become angry if there were none forthcoming. A young girl chooses as her tutor a woman in her family line who has a reputation of successful curing and who also has a line of trusted spirit familiars inherited from her ancestors. If her mother is not such a person, she may study with a grandmother, an aunt, her mother-in-law, even a nonrelative. There are many levels of ceremonies starting with the *tumuron*, the simplest and most frequently held ceremony for illness that lasts for two and a half days. This forms the nucleus of some of the more elaborate ceremonies. (See Illustration 10 on page 44 in Laura W. R. Appell 1991 in which a grandmother is tutoring two of her granddaughters.)

Thus, it takes many years to learn all these texts and the songs that accompany them. They form the basis of the oral literature of the Rungus and they recount the work of the gods and the activities of *rogon*. These, as well as the long myths and stories of the Rungus, make up a body of oral literature rich in description and metaphor, and are equal in their grandeur to the old Norse Sagas.

During her period of tutelage a young woman will assist *bobolizan* in ceremonies, reciting some of the repetitive sections, which helps her in the memorization. But a woman is not considered capable of performing a cure until she not only controls the texts but can also enter a trance state and communicate through her spirit familiar with the spirit world.

All Rungus females are potential *bobolizan*, if they want to put in the long hours learning the extended ritual texts. Some *bobolizan* have extensive repertoires of these texts. Others may only be able to perform the more elementary ceremonies. In a sample of 60 households in the village where we resided, 23 percent had *bobolizan* living in them. This represented 19 percent of the total of 73 adult women who were married, widowed or divorced. Many others knew some of the ritual texts, but did not develop the ability to enter into trance.

A *bobolizan* is thus not considered to be ill (e.g. an epileptic) or a social deviant.[10] There is no perception that a *bobolizan* might be fraudulent. Nor is she feared, as are trance practitioners in some societies. A Rungus woman does not become a *bobolizan* in an attempt to gain power or to right any perceived inequality between the sexes (contra Lewis's [1989] argument). One of the basic tenets of Rungus society is that while male and female roles are not identical, they are equivalent and of equal value. A *bobolizan* is thus the normal occupation of Rungus women.

Only rarely do men go into trance or perform the ritual texts for illness. We have been able to collect reports of only four men who could go into trance, during the last 75 to 100 years. One did not know any of the sacred texts of ceremonies, but could be in contact with his *luma'ag* and other *osunduw* to ascertain reasons for illness. Another controlled the sacred texts for the major renewal ceremony of the family apartment (*moginum*). This involves a trance performance on a platform above the roof of the longhouse where the *bobolizan* dances with the *rusod* of the family. In doing this he did not dress as a woman. He wore a man's ceremonial jacket in place of the female ceremonial blouse, and wore trousers. In addition he carried a woman's ceremonial skirt (*tinongkupan*) over his shoulder. The third man knew some of the sacred texts of this ceremony, could go into trance, and also performed on the raised platform. The fourth man, still alive, can perform the short ceremony held in the forest for the *rogon* of the sacred groves and forest. This sacred text is not sung as are the others. He will go into trance after performing it. The interesting point about these men is that they did not don the clothes of women to go into trance, with the one exception of the special trance on the roof platform. And all were married with children, performing all the aspects of the male role.

Perceived Efficacy of Various *Bobolizan*

Not all *bobolizan* are perceived as being equally effective. Some *bobolizan* get a name for themselves in curing, and they are more sought after. The competence of a *bobolizan* depends on several factors. The first is her knowledge of the ritual texts and hymns. If she is careless or lazy and omits certain portions, this will anger the *rogon* and they will not return the souls of the ill person.

Another factor that gives a *bobolizan* a reputation for competence is her skill at diagnosing an illness and its cause. Ceremonies for illness are costly. And the less a family has to expend in providing animals for sacrifices because of a successful cure and recovery of the patient, the more sought after a *bobolizan* will be.

The reputation of her *luma'ag* is another aspect of the efficacy of the work of a *bobolizan*. Certain *bobolizan* have a *luma'ag* who is oɬohis, "straight," i.e. direct and not devious. Such a *luma'ag* can handle the offending *rogon* with dispatch and quickly obtain the souls for return to the ill. A *bobolizan* who attains such a reputation will be sought after for cures and will bring in a certain amount of income to the family, while less trusted *bobolizan* will not be called on as often. Laura W. R. Appell has worked with two sisters who were both *bobolizan*. Both had learned from their mother, but one was called upon much more frequently than the other to perform curing ceremonies. A great deal of jealousy arose between these two sisters because of this. This jealousy was carried over to the next generation in that this less popular sister refused to help her niece (the daughter of her now deceased sister) learn the complex ritual weaving patterns.

Payment for Performing a Ceremony

For her mediation with the spirit world and her curing of illness a *bobolizan* receives a ritual payment consisting of plates, bowls, dyed yarn, knives, and a part of each of the animals sacrificed. This, in addition to the ritual payments she receives for tutoring prospective *bobolizan* and the sale of her weaving with the yarn from her payments, brings in considerable income for the family.

Weaving and the *Bobolizan*

Prior to *Pax Britannica* and the cessation of warfare, a particularly eminent *bobolizan* was not supposed to do any work, but had a room of her own, a *rorizan*, situated above the family quarters in the longhouse apartment. Here she would sit all day and weave the ritual clothes of the *bobolizan*, the elaborate skirts and blouses worn by women on special ceremonial occasions, as well as the ceremonial jackets worn by men. Food prepared by others was brought to her here.

Thus, weaving is closely associated with the role of *bobolizan*, but not all women who weave are *bobolizan*, nor are all *bobolizan* accomplished weavers. A woman who is both a *bobolizan* and a weaver of the ceremonial garments is very highly regarded. There is ritual associated with the weaving of these ceremonial pieces of clothing, and if it is not followed strictly it is dangerous to the weaver and she can become ill (see Illustration 11 on Page 45 in Laura W. R. Appell 1991).

CONCLUSIONS

The activities of the *bobolizan* provide a bridge between the objective world constructed by Rungus culture and the individual's subjective world, which is also constructed and interpreted by Rungus culture. And the experience of this subjective world is so mapped on to the objective world that there is no seam, even between the visible and the invisible.

But this subjective world is also modified by each individual's own life experiences and his interpretations of it, creating for each a uniquely structured unconscious. The Rungus spirit medium through her trances and her interpretation of dreams provides access to this unconscious world that would otherwise remain unexamined, that would otherwise cause psychological distress and through its processes would drive behavior in nonrational modes.

This subjective world, however, does not only include material from unconscious processes but also material arising from the cognitive dissonance of the apparent unexplainable misfortunes experienced by the individual. As a resolution of this dissonance, as a mediator of this projective energy, as a means of venting the unconscious conflicts, the *bobolizan* do indeed provide cures, do indeed relieve distress, and aid the processes whereby humans adapt effectively and obtain success in their exchanges with their environment.

But the explanations for misfortune and illness are not only based on events in dreams revealing unconscious motives and repressed emotions or the chance opportunities of the *rogon* to do harm to wandering souls. They are also based on the violation of the basic cultural rules. Thus, the interpretations of the *bobolizan* both explain the unexplainable and reaffirm the basic cultural principles, serving as a feedback mechanism which keeps the culture on course.

Those activities of the *bobolizan* reinforcing the cultural rules might suggest that they are part of a central morality religion as defined by Lewis. Yet Lewis (1989:152-59) argues that one of the characteristics of central morality cults is that illness is seen as a sin not merely an unkind stroke of fortune, which only partially approximates the Rungus explanation for affliction. Furthermore, he states that entrance into the religious elite is restricted; largely men are selected by the divine to participate in ecstatic performances. On the other hand, in peripheral cults ecstatic performances are controlled largely but not solely by women. The role is open to all participants, and the recruitment to this role is largely from individuals in disadvantaged social categories. They thus represent protest movements and play no direct part in upholding the moral code of the society (Lewis 1989:26-27).

But this does not apply to the Rungus. The role of the *bobolizan* in Rungus society is an important and honored role. It is not filled by the physical, social, or psychological deviant. It is not an indication of social or political deprivation. While *bobolizan* are female, they are hardly in rebellion against the dominant sex, for female roles are valued equally with those of males. It is the esteemed role for all females, although not all achieve it. Thus, the role is not filled by those who might be considered psychologically impaired. Nor is it an indication of psychological distress. In fact a female may be under more stress if she is not a spirit medium as she is not as highly valued as a female who is one.

Murphy makes the important distinction in this regard between behavior that is under the control of the individual and that which is not:

> This suggests that seeing, hearing, and believing things that are not seen, heard, and believed by all members of the group are

sometimes linked to insanity and sometimes not. The distinction appears to be the degree to which they are controlled and utilized for a specific social function. The inability to control these processes is what is meant by a mind out of order; when a mind is out of order it will not only fail to control sensory perception but will also fail to control behavior [1976:1022].

For the Rungus spirit medium control of trance behavior is one of the critical capacities for her to perform her role successfully. Furthermore, the induction of Rungus females into the role of spirit medium is not preceded by a traumatic experience, contrary to Lewis' (1989:162) claim that this is almost universal for such practitioners. Thus, understanding the nature of spirit mediumship in any society requires close examination of the behavioral environment in which it occurs. And this suggests that Lewis' hypotheses need further testing by detailed ethnographic research to determine their limitations and applicability.

The Rungus data also raises the larger issue of definitions and the problem of what possession consists of. There has been an unfortunate intermingling in terms and in conceptual analysis of two different, separate aspects of these religious activities: the role of practitioner and the form of trance behavior. The terms of "shaman" and "possession" are examples of this, and the Rungus materials illustrates their limited use. While Bourguignon in her studies of altered states of consciousness has made the important distinction between possession trance and nonpossession trance, this does not solve the problems with the use of the term "possession." And there remain other issues to be sorted out.

In 1968 she wrote: "We may consider that where spirit voices speak through the shaman in trance we are dealing with possession trance, and that where he, in trance, is heard to converse with spirits, we are dealing with non-possession trance." Then in 1973 she wrote that nonpossession trance:

> most typically...involves the experience of hallucinations or visions, interpreted in the particular society as experiences of the (or, a) soul of the person, its temporary absence, its journeys and adventures, and so on...[It] may involve the repetition of messages of spirits to an audience, the imitation of the actions of spirits, or the narration of the subject's spirit journey; or it may involve a private, isolated experience of the individual, as in...[a] vision quest...The experience is remembered by the trance, for the memory of the experience and often its report to others is of particular importance...[Possession trance], on the other hand, generally involves the impersonation of spirits--the acting out of

their speech or behavior. It does not involve hallucinations, and it is typically followed by amnesia...One might ask whether it is not this radical discontinuity of personal identity, which is so characteristic of [possession trance]...that accounts for the observation that it is typically followed by amnesia, an amnesia that is absent in the case of [nonpossession trance]...

Unfortunately, the behavior of Rungus spirit mediumship does not fit this classification. In Bourguignon's 1968 definition, the Rungus form of trance would be called possession trance as voices speak through her, as she acts out the speech of the gods and spirits. But they do not suffer post-trance amnesia. Nor do spirit familiars "possess" the body, consciousness, or soul of the spirit medium in any shape or fashion. Instead, it is the Rungus spirit medium who controls her spirit familiars.

In Bourguignon's 1973 definition, the Rungus spirit medium's trance would be considered as nonpossession trance. But to use this we have to extend Bourguignon's definition, for among the Rungus it is not the spirit medium's soul that goes on journeys or talks with the spirits and gods, it is her spirit familiar.

Rungus trance behavior is thus uniquely different. The essential aspect of it involves the splitting of the spirit medium's consciousness, part in communication with the spirit world, part still aware, although incompletely, of her social surroundings. One might call this splitting of the consciousness "lucid trance." Consciousness is not overwhelmed by the altered state so that full contact with the external world is lost, in a manner similar to lucid dreams where "the dreamer feels he has awakened and is conscious, but experientially remains located in a sensorially real dream world" (Tart 1983:361).

Thus, we would conclude that the term "possession" should be dropped from the general vocabulary so that finer distinctions can be made in detailing precisely the nature of the behavioral environment in the description of dissociative behavior. And as a consequence, we have suggested that the term "lucid trance" be used for the dissociative state of the Rungus spirit medium.

This analysis of the work of the Rungus *bobolizan* and her relationships with the spirit world and her clients makes amply clear the importance in ethnographic inquiries of carefully charting the social geography of the relationship between the individual and the spirit world, the temporal processes of this relationship, and the definition of the self in its behavioral environment. Such analysis reveals that although both Rungus and Bulusu' have spirit mediums, the Rungus spirit medium in trance deals with her familiars at a distance while, as we shall see, the Bulusu' form of trance involves a close, physical relationship with the spirit familiars. Furthermore, this delineation of the social geography and the temporal processes will not only make our cross-cultural comparisons more accurate and insightful, it will also produce a great deal of important information on the map of the mind and its contents when in a dissociative state. Thus, Winkelman's (1986) innovative and important psychophysiological model of trance states and the relationships of these to the structure and physiology of the brain might be built on and enlarged by this approach.

But to do a proper comparative analysis of the behavioral environments of supernaturally explained altered states of body or consciousness, a universal grid also needs to be constructed of what might be found. Lewis and Bourguignon have gathered the ethnographic details so that work on this can now be started. The materials on the Rungus and the Bulusu' (also in this volume) will add to this grid. However, for such a grid to be a productive source of ethnographic findings, an abstract analytical system should be devised to put the grid in the same relationship as the phonetic grid is to the phonemic model (see G. N. Appell 1973, 1974, 1980, 1981, n.d. for an illustration of this for the domain of property interests). We only have an adumbration of what such a system model for dissociative behavior might entail, but it should start with the social relations that pertain between the spirit medium, her audience, and their spirit world, and it must distinguish the practitioner's role from the form of trance involved.

In sum, we need new categories to deal with the nature of spirit mediumship and the role of the *bobolizan* as found among the Rungus and, we suspect, elsewhere in northern Borneo among the various Dusunic speakers.

ILLUSTRATION 1

A chicken being offered to a *rogon* that dwells in trees. This *rogon* is Muslim and, therefore, will not accept a pig.

ILLUSTRATION 2

The ritual paraphernalia of the *bobolizan* showing clockwise from center top: The *sovion*, or basketry container; the *pomudsu* to keep the *bobolizan* from harm as she deals with *rogon*; the *surud*, "comb" of *luma'ag*; the *gonding* or ritual clapper; the knife, *dazap*; and the jar for souls, *solungan*.

ILLUSTRATION 3

Itulina and her sister singing the ritual texts over a sacrificial pig tied against the wall of the longhouse apartment. Her sister holds a clapper (*gonding*) for this particular portion of the ritual. Her position and holding of the *gonding* is similar to that used when going into trance.

ILLUSTRATION 4

A *bobolizan* in trance during the family renewal ceremony (*moginum*). She is indicating to the *rogon* with her foot those items that have been brought into the apartment to please them.

ILLUSTRATION 5

Another aspect of the trance depicted in Illustration 4. It shows the *bobolizan* in trance now dancing with the *rusod*. Children stand around waving fan palm leaves to add to the excitement of the dance.

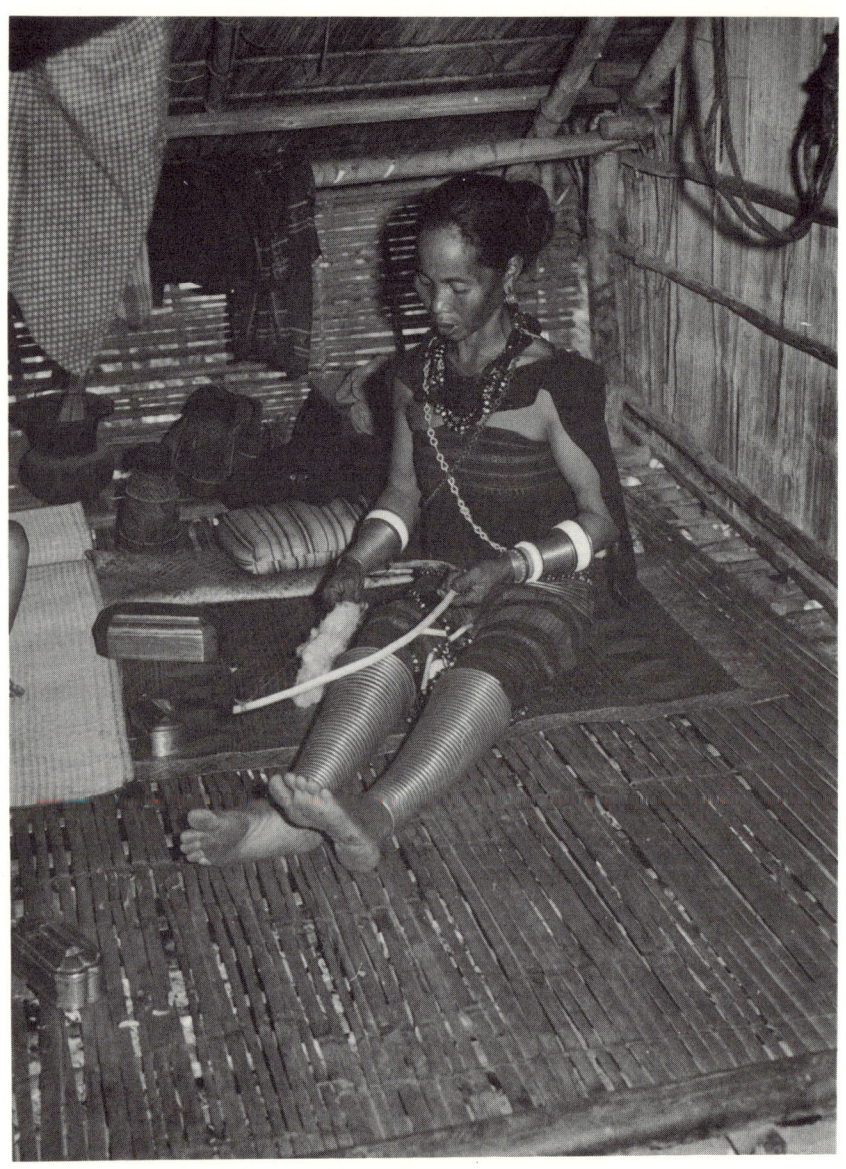

ILLUSTRATION 6

A portion of the ritual text for the family renewal ceremony (*moginum*) being sung by a *bobolizan* inside the longhouse apartment. She is wearing the woven ceremonial garments.

ILLUSTRATION 7

A *bobolizan* in trance as she dances with the *rusod* on a platform raised above the roof of the longhouse apartment during the family renewal ceremony.

ILLUSTRATION 8

A *bobolizan* performing the *monogit* texts for a marriage ceremony by the edge of the river.

ACKNOWLEDGEMENTS

Research among the Rungus 1959-60 and 1961-63 was under the auspices of the Department of Anthropology and Sociology, Research School of Pacific Studies, The Australian National University where G. N. Appell was a research scholar at that time. He wants to express his appreciation for the help provided by his supervisor, Professor J. Derek Freeman. Subsequent analysis of data was done under NFS Grant 923 and a grant from the SSRC-ACLU. Research in the summer of 1986 was funded by the Halcyon Foundation as was the work with two Rungus informants in the United States in 1987. Research in the summer of 1990 and the winter of 1992 was funded by the Wenner-Gren Foundation and the Halcyon Foundation. Laura W. R. Appell was primarily responsible for interviewing on those aspects of Rungus religion that were in the hands of the females. We want to acknowledge and thank the following respondents, sources, and collaborators for their help: Itulina, an eminent *bobolizan* who was the primary informant on religion and trance behavior for Laura W. R. Appell during our first field trips and who died in 1980 before we could complete our work on the religion; Orang Tua Majalu (deceased) and Orang Tua Mongimbal, who were G. N. Appell's informants on the jural realm and Rungus culture in general; Marajun Mongkurong who has helped us and facilitated our work from the beginning and who has provided immense help in sorting out difficult problems in understanding Rungus culture; Limpot Majalu, our original linguistic informant; Win Marajun, who has taken on the work of transcribing the oral literature being collected; Suruban Mabok, son of Itulina, who is continuing to collect oral literature and help in its interpretation and translation and who has helped us with his exceptional linguistic skills; Majukit Mongorib, who has provided materials in depth about the traditional Rungus culture; Govolong, a *bobolizan* who has provided us with further information on trance behavior and religious texts, permitting us to record the religious songs and texts; Magazas, the last of the *bobolizan*s to know some of the critically important old religious texts and who has cooperated in our tape recording of them; Monobidong, daughter-in-law of Itulina, who is carrying on her tradition and whose clear understanding of Rungus cosmology has been of inestimable value; Mabok (deceased), husband of Itulina, who provided us with data on the various ceremonies for the rice spirits and agricultural practices in general. We must also acknowledge with thanks those people too numerous to mention who have contributed their myths, stories, and ritual knowledge so that we have been able to record the fast dying oral literature of the Rungus, which helps elucidate the nature of the role of *bobolizan*. And finally as yet unmentioned is our friend Bolonok Banjiran, who as a young lady took care of our eldest daughter during much of our original work, and who now has six children of her own.

NOTES

1. For example, see G. N. Appell (1976) for a discussion of how the study of social structure has been biased by the failure to consider the Borneo ethnographic data on the nature of cognatic social systems.

2. Bourguignon (1965:56) makes a similar observation with regard to Haitian spirit possession.

3. Vinson H. Sutlive, Jr. (personal communication) notes that the concept of soul loss is fully as complex an idea as possession is, and also needs close examination and re-evaluation.

4. This ethnographic profile and the discussion of spirit mediums is in the ethnographic present of our first field sessions among the Rungus in 1959-60, 1960-63. Additional materials on the role of spirit mediums are incorporated from field sessions in 1986, 1990, and from working with two sets of informants in 1987 and 1992. However, this latter material also relates to the earlier time period of the traditional culture as by 1986 spirit mediumship, although still present, was fading fast before Christianity and modernization. In the Rungus orthography we have developed, /'/ transcribes a glottal stop and /w/ transcribes a glide with the movement of the tongue upward and backward accompanied by lip rounding. /ł/ represents a palatized [l] and contrasts with the alveolar /l/.

5. By the term "isoglot" G. N. Appell indicates a self-conscious speech community. That is, it refers to the speech of an ethnic group, the members of which consider their language or dialect to be significantly different from that of neighboring communities and thus have an indigenous name by which to identify it. G. N. Appell coined this term to avoid the problems involved in the terms "language" or "dialect," which imply a certain status in linguistic analysis. The term "isoglot" is neutral in this regard. But as it reflects the indigenous organization of their linguistic and ethnic environment, it has greater ethnographic validity (see G. N. Appell 1968).

6. A few families have experimented with wet rice over the past fifty years.

7. Head-taking must be distinguished from head-hunting. The Rungus never hunted specifically for heads. The goal of warfare was to kill the champion of an opposing group and then take his head, not just any head of a woman, child, or a man who was not a village champion.

8. *Lugu'* is also the term for heartwood. *Divato* is derived from the Sanskrit *devatā*, "godhead, divinity," and cognates of this are found widely throughout the indigenous languages of Insular Southeast Asia (Gonda 1973), including among the Tasaday.

9. However, this interpretation has been denied by all informants.

10. Winkelman (1986) raises the issue of the relationship of epilepsy to trance states. It is interesting that in the Rungus community of our study there was a woman who had rather frequent epileptic seizures but who never went into trance.

REFERENCES

Appell, G. N.
- 1965 The Nature of Social Groupings Among the Rungus Dusun of Sabah, Malaysia. Dissertation submitted for the degree of Ph.D., The Australian National University.

- 1966 Residence and Ties of Kinship in a Cognatic Society: The Rungus Dusun of Sabah, Malaysia. Southwestern Journal of Anthropology 22:280-301.

- 1967 Observational Procedures for Identifying Kindreds: Social Isolates Among the Rungus of Borneo. Southwestern Journal of Anthropology 23:192-207.

- 1968 The Dusun Languages of Northern Borneo: Rungus Dusun and Related Problems. Oceanic Linguistics 7:1-15.

- 1973 The Distinction Between Ethnography and Ethnology and Other Issues in Cognitive Structuralism. Bijdragen tot de Taal-, Land- en Volkenkunde 129:1-56.

Appell, G. N.
- 1974 The Analysis of Property Systems: The Creation and Devolution of Property Interests Among the Rungus of Borneo. Paper presented at the Conference of the Association of Social Anthropologists, University of Keele.

- 1976 The Rungus: Social Structure in a Cognatic Society and Its Symbolism. *In* The Societies of Borneo: Explorations in the Theory of Cognatic Social Structure, edited by G. N. Appell. Special Publication 6. Washington: American Anthropological Association.

- 1978 The Rungus of Sabah, Malaysia. *In* Essays on Borneo Societies, edited by Victor T. King. Hull Monograph on South-East Asia 7. Oxford: Oxford University Press.

- 1980 Epistemological Issues in Anthropological Inquiry: Social Structuralism, Cognitive Structuralism, Synthetic Structuralism and Opportunism. Part 1. Canberra Anthropology 3(2):1-27.

- 1981 Epistemological Issues in Anthropological Inquiry: Social Structuralism, Cognitive Structuralism, Synthetic Structuralism and Opportunism. Part 2. Canberra Anthropology 4(1):1-22.

- 1983 Methodological Problems with the Concept of Corporation, Corporate Social Grouping, and Cognatic Descent Group. American Ethnologist 10:302-11.

- 1984 Methodological issues in the Corporation Redux. American Ethnologist 11:815-17.

- 1985a Land Tenure and Development Among the Rungus of Sabah, Malaysia. *In* Modernization and the Emergence of a Landless Peasantry: Essays on the Integration of Peripheries to Socioeconomic Centers, edited by G. N. Appell. Studies in Third World Societies Publication No. 33. Studies in Third World Societies, College of William and Mary, Williamsburg,

Appell, G. N.
    1985b   The Bulusu' of East Kalimantan: The Consequences of Resettlement. *In* Modernization and the Emergence of a Landless Peasantry: Essays on the Integration of Peripheries to Socioeconomic Centers, edited by G. N. Appell. Studies in Third World Societies Publication No. 33. Studies in Third World Societies, College of William and Mary, Williamsburg, Virginia.

    1986   Kayan Land Tenure and the Distribution of Devolvable Usufruct in Borneo. Borneo Research Bulletin 18:175-82.

    1988   Emergent Structuralism: The Design of an Inquiry System to Delineate the Production and Reduction of Social Forms. *In* Choice and Morality: Essays in Honor of Professor Derek Freeman, edited by G. N. Appell and T. N. Madan. Buffalo: State University of New York Press.

    1991   Individuation of the Drives of Sex and Aggression in the Linguistic and Behavioral Repertoire of the Rungus. *In* Female and Male in Borneo: Contributions and Challenges to Gender Studies, edited by Vinson H. Sutlive, Jr. Borneo Research Council Monograph Series Volume One. Borneo Research Council, College of William and Mary, Williamsburg, Virginia.

    n.d.   Observational Procedures for Property Relations: Land Tenure and Tree Ownership in Borneo. Borneo Research Council Monograph Series. Forthcoming. College of William and Mary, Williamsburg, Virginia.

Appell, Laura W. R.
    1988   Menstruation Among the Rungus: An Unmarked Category. *In* Blood Magic: New Perspectives in the Anthropology of Menstruation, edited by Thomas Buckley and Alma Gottleib. Berkeley: University of California Press.

    1991   Sex Role Symmetry Among the Rungus of Sabah. *In* Female and Male in Borneo: Contributions and Challenges to Gender Studies, edited by Vinson H. Sutlive, Jr. Borneo Research Council Monograph Series Volume One. Borneo Research Council, College of William and Mary, Williamburg, Virginia.

Bourguignon, Erika
    1965   The Self, The Behavioral Environment, and the Theory of Spirit Possession. *In* Context and Meaning in Cultural Anthropology: In Honor of A. Irving Hallowell, edited by Melford E. Spiro. New York: The Free Press.

    1968   World Distribution and Patterns of Possession States. *In* Trance and Possession States, edited by Raymond Prince. Proceedings of the Second Annual Conference, R. M. Bucke Memorial Society 4-6 March 1966. Montreal: R. M. Bucke Memorial Society.

    1973   Introduction: A Framework for the Comparative Study of Altered States of Consciousness. *In* Religion, Altered States of Consciousness, and Social Change, edited by Erika Bourguignon. Columbus: Ohio State University Press.

    1976   Possession. San Francisco: Chandler & Sharp.

Crain, Jay B.
    1970   The Lun Dayeh of Sabah, East Malaysia: Aspects of Marriage and Social Exchange. Ph.D. Dissertation, Cornell University.

    1982   A Lun Dayeh Engagement Negotiation. Contributions to Southeast Asian Ethnography 1:142-87.

Doolittle, Amity Appell
    1991   *Latah* Behavior by Females Among the Rungus of Sabah. *In* Female and Male in Borneo: Contributions and Challenges to Gender Studies, edited by Vinson H. Sutlive, Jr. Borneo Research Council Monograph Series Volume One. Borneo Research Council, College of William and Mary, Williamsburg, Virginia.

Evans, I. N. H.
    1953   The Religion of the Tampasuk Dusuns of North Borneo. Cambridge: Cambridge University Press.

Firth, Raymond
    1964   Problem and Assumption in an Anthropological Study of Religion. The Huxley Memorial Lecture, 1959. *In* Essays on Social Organization and Values, by Raymond Firth. London School of Economics Monographs on Social Anthropology No. 28. London: The Athlone Press. (Reprinted from Journal of the Royal Anthropological Institute of Great Britain and Ireland 89(2):129-48, 1959).

Gonda, J.
    1973   Sanskrit in Indonesia. Second Edition. New Delhi: International Academy of Indian Culture.

Hallowell, A. Irving
    1954   The Self and Its Behavioural Environment. Exploration II, April. (Reprinted *in* Culture and Experience, by A. Irving Hallowell. Philadelphia: University of Pennsylvania Press).

Lewis, I. M.
    1986   Religion in Context: Cults and Charisma. Cambridge: Cambridge University Press.

    1989   Ecstatic Religion: A Study of Shamanism and Spirit Possession. Second Edition. London: Routledge.

Murphy, Jane
    1976   Psychiatric Labeling in Cross-cultural Perspective. Science 191:1019-28.

Tart, Charles T.
    1983   Lucid Dreaming. *In* The Encyclopedic Dictionary of Psychology, edited by Rom Harre and Roger Lamb. Cambridge: MIT Press.

Winkelman, Michael
    1986   Trance States: A Theoretical Model and Cross-Cultural Analysis. Ethos 14:174-3.

    1990   Shamans and Other "Magico-Religious" Healers: A Cross-Cultural Study of Their Origins, Nature, and Social Transformation. Ethos 18:308-53.

TO DO BATTLE WITH THE SPIRITS: BULUSU' SPIRIT MEDIUMS

LAURA W. R. APPELL
and
GEORGE N. APPELL
Brandeis University

Unlike dissociative behavior among the Rungus, trance behavior among the Bulusu' is explained as the result of the actual control of body and personality by various spirits. However, in describing the behavioral environment in which Bulusu' trance occurs, we shall avoid using the concept of possession. As we have pointed out in our discussion of Rungus spirit mediumship, the concept of possession is inadequate and actually hides critical distinctions in the nature of the social relationship between humans and the spirits, both divine and demonic. Instead we shall use the concept of occupation and control of parts of the spirit medium's persona, the exact nature of which has to be specified, including the source of the control, the locus of the control, and the mechanisms by which it is asserted.

It might be useful to point out here the degree to which the term possession is culturally contaminated and compromised as a scientific term. Possession entered the English language in the 16th century to refer to being inhabited, controlled, dominated, or actuated by a demon or spirit, usually evil. By the early 17th century it also referred to being demoniac, mad, crazy, lunatic (*Oxford English Dictionary*). It thus indicates certain states of mind and behavior that were observed and explained within the context of Christian theology. And in many instances these ethnocentric perceptions continue.

Finally, we shall avoid the term shaman. Lewis (1986:78-91) discusses how the term shaman is found more in American anthropological usage while the

Finally, we shall avoid the term shaman. Lewis (1986:78-91) discusses how the term shaman is found more in American anthropological usage while the term spirit medium is more commonly found in British anthropology. But he argues that it is a useful cross-cultural concept. Firth (1964:247-48; orig. 1959) on the other hand writes:

> **Spirit possession** is a form of trance in which behavior actions of a person are interpreted as evidence of a control of his behavior by a spirit normally external to him. **Spirit mediumship** is normally a form of possession in which the person is conceived as serving as an intermediary between spirits and men...The accent here is on communication; the actions and words of the medium must be translatable, which differentiates them from mere spirit possession or madness. **Shamanism** is a term I prefer to use in the limited North Asiatic sense, of a master of spirits. Normally himself a spirit medium, the shaman is thought to control spirits by ritual techniques, and in some societies...he may not himself be in a trance state when he does this...

Thus, in Firth's view shamanism involves mastery over spirits which may or may not involve dissociative states. And this is not the case among the Bulusu'. In returning the soul of the ill, Bulusu' spirit mediums go into trance to communicate with the spirit world. But Firth also views spirit mediumship as including possession. This represents a narrow definition of the term. We have found that among the Rungus the trance behaviors of women who serve as spirit mediums do not involve possession. Therefore, we believe it would be useful to expand the definition of the concept of spirit mediumship to include not only trance behavior with possession but also trance behavior without possession.

In addition, the position taken in the analysis of Rungus spirit mediumship is that the terms in use for the various types of dissociative states or interactive relations with the gods and spirits include behaviors that for ethnographic validity we must keep separate in any inquiry. Thus, Firth's distinction between spirit possession, spirit mediumship, and shamanism nicely demonstrates how concepts and terms for the role of the practitioner and concepts and terms for the nature of the trance itself frequently become intermingled with a loss of precision and a clouding of issues.

We shall thus use the term spirit medium to refer to those specialists who through dissociative states communicate with gods and spirits to solve human problems and who utilize spirit familiars in this process whether the spirit medium is under the control of or occupied by his or her spirit familiars or whether the spirit medium remains independent of occupation and control. It is our task then to delineate what exactly is the cultural explanation for each instance of trance. This will also alleviate the problem of the potential cultural contamination of ethnographic data arising from elevating cultural concepts from other regions, such as shamanship, to cross-cultural conceptual categories. But it does not yet resolve the problem of classifying types of trance behavior. This can only come about once the behavioral environment of trance behaviors in a number of cultures is adequately described.

ETHNOGRAPHIC PROFILE OF THE BULUSU'[1]

The Bulusu' are a self-conscious ethnic group of East Kalimantan. Traditionally they inhabited the lower and middle reaches of the Sekatak, Bengara, and Batayau Rivers and their tributaries. A few Bulusu' villages can be found on the south bank of the Mentarang River as well as some of its southern tributaries.

In the upper reaches of these rivers and on the height of land between watersheds, in the area G. N. Appell (1983a) has referred to as the Punan highlands, are found a number of Punan, who were originally hunters and gatherers. They now grow some crops, and a few have intermarried with the Bulusu', usually Punan men marrying Bulusu' women as part of the process of their learning agriculture and becoming Bulusu'.

Scattered Coastal Muslim settlements are also found along the estuaries of these rivers, but primarily at the height of tidal influences. The Coastal Muslim population is composed of members of both the Tidung and Bulungan ethnic groups as well as a few descendants of Arab traders. The Tidung and Bulungan languages are not mutually intelligible and are in fact highly divergent (see Amity C. P. Appell 1986; Appell-Warren 1986). At one time both these ethnic groups were organized in contending sultanates. However, these two groups are now heavily intermarried.

The Bulusu' are also known as "Berusu" or "Brusu." Their preferred autonym is, however, Bulusu' (see G. N. Appell 1991). They state that their closest linguistic affiliation is with the Tidung language.

Because of their intermediary position between the Punan and the Tidung and Bulungan, the Bulusu' culture occasionally shares traits with these three other groups. Traditionally they are longhouse dwellers and swidden agriculturalists.

They grow rice, cassava, taro, sweet potato, sago, and a variety of vegetables. When there is a year in which there is a good fruit tree crop, the swidden will also be planted with fruit trees. As a result, the Bulusu' own extensive fruit tree groves.

Travel to the fields and to other villages is by canoe, and the Bulusu' are skilled in navigating the various rapids that are found on their rivers. A considerable amount of time is devoted to fishing and the gathering of forest products for trading to the coast.

Pigs are kept in Bulusu' villages, but in the Sekatak River region they are raised primarily for sale in Tarakan, the district center, and to the Chinese but not for Bulusu' consumption. Chickens are also raised for sale, for use in ceremonies, and for eggs.

The kinship system is essentially of the Eskimo type.

Prenuptial Customs, Bride-Price, Marriage, and Post-nuptial Residence

Before marriage a young man will *moi dandu'*, literally "go to (visit) a young woman." It is very close to what is called "a date" in American culture, except there is no place to go but to the longhouse apartment of the young woman's family. A young man usually arranges with the young woman to call on her one evening. He brings small gifts, such as soap, perfume, etc., and she may reciprocate by preparing special leaves to insert into holes in his ear lobes. They talk, laugh, and giggle late into the night. If things progress, the young man may join the young woman in her sleeping sarong. Sexual foreplay may go on. If it leads to intercourse, the young woman is supposed to tell her father. This, or if they are discovered in the act, will result in jural action by the father. The father of the young woman receives a fine of several jars and a small pig from the young man's family. The ear of the pig is slit and the members of the longhouse, with the exception of the young woman, are wiped with the blood of the pig to eradicate the ritual jeopardy. Even if the two marry, there is still a fine of property and a pig, but the fine is smaller.

Fornication and particularly adultery will cause the village to become "dirty" (*rusam*). There will be floods, people will become sick with colds, and crops will be destroyed by forest animals. Some say that the woman becomes "hot" as a result of fornication. Occasionally a woman after marriage will tell her husband of previous fornication, and this requires a larger fine. She will reveal this if she fears ritual danger. However, in many cases of fornication it is said that neither party will mention it. After a young woman is engaged, with the proper jar being given to her father as an earnest of intentions, intercourse during *moi dandu'* of the groom does not precipitate a jural action or fine.

Marriage is normally monogamous. Rarely a wealthy man will have two or three wives. Traditionally, post-nuptial residence was usually uxorilocal for one to three years, followed by virilocal residence.

Since Indonesian Independence and the spread of Islam, temporary uxorilocal residence has become rare in the Sekatak River system. In other river systems it is reported that there is still temporary post-nuptial residence in the bride's village until there are children. Then residence is moved to the groom's village.

Virilocal residence is justified by the bride-price (*bumbung*) paid. It is denied that the bride-price is to pay for the sexual and reproductive services of the female as is stated among the Rungus. Yet the bride-price is lower for older women, women who can no longer bear children, or who have been divorced and have children. When asked what the purpose is for bride-price, it was also stated that the union would be considered fornication without it. There is no concept that the bride-price will vary according to the skills, industriousness, or beauty of the bride, or wealth of the father of the groom and father of the bride, as exists among the Rungus of Sabah.

Bride-price is measured in terms of jars (*tampaiyan*). Originally, all bride-prices were "thirty jars." Then, after the Japanese occupation during World War II, some families in the lower reaches of the Sekatak River began asking for "forty jars." The number of jars that can be asked for a daughter follows the amount that was paid for her mother. As a result, there have evolved two classes of families based on the female descent line: those who ask for "forty jars" and those who ask for "thirty."

The use of the term "jars" to indicate the size of a bride-price is a metaphor for the classes of property paid. That is, a bride-price is made up of gongs, cannon, brassware, and of course jars. A gong may equal one "jar." Also, some jars are so valuable as to count as the equivalent of "five jars." Thus, the arguments over bride-prices are not over the number of "jars," but as to what is to constitute the type and value of the thirty or forty items.

Bride-prices in Borneo may be divided into two types: corporate and redistributive. In Rungus society the bride-price is made up from the assets of the domestic family of the groom and paid to the domestic family of the bride, which adds the gongs and jars to its corporately held assets. This is what G. N. Appell has termed the "corporate" type (G. N. Appell 1971, 1974, 1983b, 1984). The Bulusu' bride-price is of the redistributive type. When a Bulusu' family puts together a bride-price for the wife of his son, they get help from their network of kin. Each kinsman who can offers to provide a jar, or gong, or a piece of brassware. This is repaid by the father at a later point when those who helped him need help for a similar prestation. The father of the bride takes the "jars" and redistributes them among his network of kin according to the help that they have given him in the past and the help that they have provided in the form of provisions for the wedding feast. Those who receive items from the bride-price then give to the bride a small gift of housewares, such as a plate or cooking pot, etc. As a result, Bulusu' society is composed of a vast, intricate network of debts and credits. And these may be recognized by descendants even though they were incurred over three generations ago.[2] Bride service (*tumulow*) may be substituted for the bride-price, but this occurs only occasionally.

Domestic Family Cycle: The Patrilocal Extended Family and the Nuclear Family

Following marriage the couple resides in the longhouse apartment (*lamin*) of the groom's father. They may stay there until they have several children. And this longhouse domestic unit may include more than one married sibling with children. On the other hand, some couples want to build their own longhouse apartment shortly after marriage.

Even if the son and his new wife join the apartment of his father, they still make their own swidden and swidden field house. The field house provides a place where the newly married couple can carry on their domestic life, if they wish. When they are sleeping and eating in the apartment of the husband's father, the cooking and providing of meals in this extended family apartment is the charge of the husband's mother, the senior female. Each nuclear family provides from their own swidden the necessary food stuffs to make a joint meal. But each nuclear family uses its swidden profits to buy its household necessities and invest in jars and other forms of nondepreciable property (*gama'*).

A son and his father, living in the same apartment, frequently will have adjoining swiddens. And they may share the same ritual structure and plot (*punsubon*), straddling the boundary between their swiddens, to ensure a good harvest.

Certainly by the time the second generation's children have reached marriageable age, the son of the founder of the apartment will have built his own separate apartment onto the longhouse of his father. However, the youngest son is expected to remain in the parental apartment to take care of his aged parents. If a widow has only daughters, and they marry into distant villages, the widow may stay with her siblings, keeping a separate apartment and swidden with the help of her brothers.

The Bulusu' Village

The inhabitants of a village live in one or more longhouses. The number of longhouses in a village depends on the developmental cycle of the village and whether the village is located near the coast or up in the interior. One informant from the lower reaches of the Sekatak River said that it was more usual to have one longhouse per village, although there were occasionally one or two more. An informant from upriver said that it was more usual to have two or three longhouses per village. And if a village is growing and splitting up into two, there may be two or more longhouses as part of this processes.

In addition, those cultivating swiddens far away from the village longhouse may construct a smaller version of the longhouse structure to live in during the agricultural season.

There is a village headman appointed by the government, and more recently the government has instituted the position of a village head of *adat*, "customary law." There are no hereditary social classes, such as are found among the Kayan and Kenyah. There are a number of female and male spirit mediums (*ulun gantu*), who are employed for curing illness.

The Bulusu' System of Land Tenure: Village Rights to Land and Rights to Swiddens

The land tenure system of the Bulusu' is similar to that of the Rungus. It is what G. N. Appell (1986) has termed "circulating usufruct." That is, once a swidden area has had all of its crops removed and it begins to revert to jungle, anyone else in the village may use that area again for a swidden. It reverts back to the village reserve, or what the Dutch *adat* law scholars called "the area of disposal" of the village. Thus, no permanent usufruct rights are established by clearing the forest, as occurs among the Iban, the Land Dayak, the Kayan, the Kenyah, and the Kantu' Dayak. Permanent rights so established among these groups may be devolved on others, through inheritance or through the partition of the *bilek* as among the Iban. G. N. Appell (1986) has called this latter system "devolvable usufruct."

However, if the swidden area is planted with fruit trees at the end of the swidden cycle, this removes that area from circulating usufruct. Rights over these fruit trees are usually devolved on all the heirs of the planter.

Village boundaries are marked by natural phenomena along a river, such as rapids, mouths of tributaries, or a large tree, and at the height of land between two river systems. Prior to the arrival of the Dutch boundaries were not well defined. However, if a stranger came into a village territory and took any produce from the forest or from the swiddens, he was liable to be killed. Therefore, it was customary when traveling to stop at each longhouse village and ask permission of the village headman to proceed. And it is still considered to be good form and a wise precaution against trouble to do so.

There are no rules on sharing with village members forest products that have been gathered by nonvillage members. This includes animals killed, honey gathered, fish taken, etc., as well as commercial products such as damar, rattan, etc. Nor is the village territory closed off at any point during ceremonies to increase its ritual goodwill. A longhouse that holds such a ceremony may be closed to outsiders visiting it, but not the village territory itself, contrary to the situation among the Rungus.

An individual may cut a swidden in a village area in which he is not resident as long as he notifies the village headman and gets his permission. He is not required to relocate his residence to that village. He also may plant the swidden with fruit trees at the end of the agricultural year, establishing a claim of long duration, without any jural liabilities. Seldom does a headman deny a nonresident the request to cut a swidden, unless he is known as a troublemaker. But when an individual wants to cut a swidden in another village it is usually because he or his spouse have relatives in that village, and they wish to join their swidden group.

Villages are interlinked by a network of kin, and as a result an individual may have rights to fruit trees in a number of closely related villages. Furthermore, population pressure on the land has not developed and land, therefore, is not scarce, certainly not as scarce as among the Rungus of Sabah. As a result, boundaries have not become as clearly delineated. The Dutch intervention did not produce any pressure on land in the Bulusu' area, and as a result it never became necessary to define more precisely village rights over specified tracts of land.

There is one exception to this, however. Two or three villages located up two small tributaries near the estuary of the Sekatak River are separated by a slight height of land, which could be easily crossed. One village became worried that outsiders from other villages might canoe up one river, cross over by foot to that part of its territory not reachable by canoe from its own river, and collect forest products for sale. As a result, this village established clearly its boundaries, identifying them by carving a hornbill-headed man or a crocodile on felled tree trunks. This was probably in response to a temporary increase in the value of rattan, damar, and other forest products. It was not adopted by any of the villages upcountry, and it apparently fell into disuse shortly afterwards. This is not generally known by our informants in the younger generation.

Thus, there has been little pressure on the resources of the village reserve to produce a further development of the jural personality of the village with regard to its assets. The defining feature of the jural personality of the village is not so much its relation to property as to the services of the headman in resolving disputes. One headman said that boundaries between villages represented in fact the division between the authority and power of headmen, and that the actual boundaries were very rough until the Dutch came.

Thus, the village was both a nexus of kin relations and a center of the power of an individual leader, who then, with the coming of the government, became the official village headman, less than being an explicit, well-defined territorial entity. The Bulusu' village represents the lower end of a continuum where the territorial nature of the village is ill-defined and which is found usually in remote areas. On the upper end of this continuum are found the well-developed jural personality of Borneo villages, such as among the Rungus and Kantu' Dayak. This development of jural personality arose in response to growing scarcity of land in order to protect both the village resources and its ritual goodwill.

BULUSU' COSMOLOGY: THE BULUSU' SELF AND ITS BEHAVIORAL ENVIRONMENT

The Bulusu' have a complex religion with a creator god and a variety of spirits, some of which inhabit the natural world and some of which inhabit an upperworld consisting of a number of levels. Explanations for illness include soul capture and torment by capricious spirits. Spirit mediums go into trance to negotiate with these for the return of the captured souls to cure the illness.

Traditionally, the Bulusu' raised pigs and chickens to sacrifice to these spirits and to cleanse a village after incest, and for rituals associated with headhunting. However, sometime, either right before or after the Japanese occupation, a number of people--primarily headmen and spirit mediums--who lived in scattered villages in the river system where we did our research dreamed that the blood of sacrificed pigs would attract the spirits to Bulusu' dwellings and a number of people would die. At that time the sacrifice of pigs ceased, and the killing of chickens in these ceremonies also dropped off. Thus, chickens presented to the spirits at ceremonies are let go afterwards. And where pigs once were sacrificed, an effigy of a pig is made of rice paste flavored with sesame which is consumed during one ceremony. For cleansing a village of incest, a pig is used, but its ear is slit to obtain the necessary blood, rather than it being killed.

Traditionally a pig was also sacrificed at marriage. But this ceased at least in the lower reaches of the Bulusu' region either at this time or before.

The prohibition on the sacrifice of pigs and chickens, however, appears to be confined only to the river system where we did our field work. In another, smaller river system, which is close by, the Bulusu' still sacrifice pigs in ceremonies for adultery and incest, according to an informant from that area.

The Bulusu' who have prohibited the killing of pigs will still eat pig meat if killed and cooked by some other ethnic group. And they still kill and eat wild pig.

The Bulusu' Self and Its Behavioral Environment[3]

The Bulusu' self is culturally constructed of the body (*kiring*), multiple *lingu*, which may be glossed as "souls," and a celestial counterpart that dwells on the mountain of the dead souls. The term *lingu* is also used to refer to the indwelling spirits of inanimate objects, such as jars, trees, etc., as well as animate objects such as animals and plants.

There is no unanimity on the number of souls. One informant said that there are four souls, one for both eyes, one for both ears, one for the body, and one for the heart, which goes to the "mountain of the souls" after death. On dreaming, the souls of the ears and heart go wandering. Another informant said that while people say that there are many souls, he does not believe it. He thinks there are only two, one for the eyes and one for the heart. He stated that when dreaming it is the soul of the eyes that wanders. A spirit medium stated that one soul became a "ghost," one soul became a *karaganan*, and another a *sunudun* (see below). These particular *karaganan* and *sunudun* may become spirit familiars of the spirit medium.

The soul that goes to the grave and stays there is called *'mburuow*, "ghost." The *'mburuow* feeds off the food that accompanies the corpse to the grave. While other souls go to the afterworld, where some may become spirit familiars, the ghost never becomes a spirit familiar. However, it is called upon for help when an individual is lost in a storm at sea and at the time of planting rice in order to gather all the family's "rice souls" (*lingu bilod*) to the swidden.

The celestial counterpart for males is called *yada*, and for females, *yadan*. These are not souls. They dwell on the "mountain (or hill) of dead souls" (*muruk lingu*), but die shortly before those on earth die, so that they can come down and guide the soul of their counterparts to the mountain of dead souls. The celestial counterpart of an individual plants a sago tree (*rimbiow*), which represents the life span of the individual. When a man and woman marry their sago plants come together and put out new shoots. If this celestial counterpart does not take care of the sago plant, spirits that cause illness (*karaganan mata'*) will cut the roots, resulting in its human counterpart falling ill.

The world is comprised of seven divisions, the earth and six sections of the upperworld. These are all joined together in an upward rising path with the mountain of the dead souls forming the first division of the upperworld. The earth and this upperworld are peopled by various classes of spirits that are collectively called *karaganan*. These contrast with the creator spirit (*yadu' lawang*), who is female, and *yaki bugang*, who is male and the keeper of the knotted strings, each one of which represents the life span of a human.

The *karaganan* are distinguished from human beings by being immortal. Thus, the general term for immortals is *patoi ngulan*--"die like the moon," which is reborn again, and that for mortals is *patoi yunti*--"die like a banana tree," which bears fruit once and is replaced by its offshoot.

The cover term *karaganan* is cognate with the Rungus lexeme *rogon*. However, the term *karaganan* refers to all gods and spirits, both helpful and capricious, while the Rungus term *rogon* refers primarily to those spirits who are irascible and therefore potentially dangerous.

The cover term *karaganan* has two subclasses, *karaganan* and *sunudun*, which are in turn divided into "helpful" (*hantu*) and a "bad" (*mata'*) classes. The latter cause illness by the capture and torment of wandering souls.

The *Karaganan Mata'*. These *karaganan* are one of the major sources of illness. In ordinary discourse the term *mata'* means "green," "uncooked," "unripe." The *karaganan mata'* are found both in the natural world and the upperworld. In the natural world they inhabit the earth, ravines, large trees, and boulders. But there does not seem to be as close an association of *karaganan mata'* with wet places in the earth such as springs and seeps as is found among the Rungus. Nor do the Bulusu' have "sacred groves" (*puru* in the Rungus language) that cannot be cut, as do the Rungus. This is perhaps because the Bulusu' region does not suffer from a marked dry season. However, some of the Bulusu' *karaganan* are found in damp places or rivers.

Jarong is a *karaganan mata'* that lives in the river and is like a dragon (*naga*). Indications of its presence are its feces, which look like hematite ooze and frequently appear after floods. This spirit causes intestinal and stomach illnesses. Offerings of bits of food or small coins are made to *jarong* when the Bulusu' go up the river from the estuary.

Then there are spirits that live in holes in the river bank where water seeps out, who are called *manan*. There is also the spirit that lives in the earth called *karakasi*. And every swidden has a household (*lamin*) of *karaganan*, who are called "spirits of the earth." Sacrifices are made to them when the swidden is prepared and when a household member becomes ill from them. Then, there are spirits that inhabit gullies, and since each hill has a gully, they are widespread as are the *karaganan* of the earth.

There are *karaganan* that live in large rocks, called "rock spirits." There are also *karaganan* that inhabit trees. The most important of these are the *karaganan* of the strangler figs (*Ficus* spp.), but there are also *karaganan* that inhabit trees with an enlargement of the trunk just above the roots. Such trees are called "pregnant" trees, and before being cut down, the indwelling spirit has to be appeased with an offering and asked to move away. In cases of strangler figs, a spirit medium must perform the ceremony and make the offering. A *karaganan* of the strangler fig can also become a spirit familiar of the spirit medium when propitiated, thereby becoming a *karaganan hantu*. And there are *karaganan* who live around the funerary houses that eat people and prevent stealing from these houses. The soul that stays at the grave, the *'mburuow*, becomes a *karaganan mata'* that causes headaches and dizziness.

There are also dangerous *karaganan* that wander about at the beginning of the fruiting season when the rains taper off. At this time there are heavy winds. So it is said that the wind gathers together all these capricious spirits. If the flowers do not form fruit, these spirits become angry and cause a lot of sickness at that time. Incest is given as one of the reasons that fruit do not form.

Also *karaganan* do not like fishing with poison or the pulling down of rattan. This makes them angry, and they cause people to get sick. Rainbows form the bridge between the upperworld and the earth for all spirits. But when there is a rainbow without rain, or a rainbow with just a drizzle, it is believed that it is an especially dangerous time for children to be on the ground, as the *karaganan mata'* and *sunudun mata'* use it to come to earth and wander about causing illness (see below). At that time people become quiet in the longhouse so as not to attract these spirits.

The *Karaganan Hantu*. The *karaganan hantu* are one of the classes of spirit familiars of the spirit mediums that help them cure illness. They are comprised mainly of souls of dead individuals. And during trance they bargain with the malicious spirits that have caused illness for the return of the lost soul(s) of the person who is ill. As such they will be discussed below.[4]

However, spirit familiars may also be spirits of crocodiles, monkeys, Punan, or the spirits of the strangler fig. There is one which appears to share characteristics of both this class and the class of *karaganan mata'*. These are the *'mbalid*, souls (*lingu*) of dead Punan. They live under wild sago trees. It is stated that they are like *karaganan mata'*, and can cause illness. But they are considered generally to be beneficial *karaganan*, and they appear in trance ceremonies as *karaganan hantu* (see below). The *'mbalid* are also guardian spirits of some of those Bulusu' who have Punan ancestry. They help in hunting, giving the hunter strength. And they also help in the swiddens and the accumulation of property. But if they are not placated frequently with sacrifices of wild pig meat, including parts of the heart and liver, they will cause illness.

Thus, after hunting, those who have an *'mbalid* will call it and give it some of the meat.[5] This spirit also watches out for the whole household of its client, so that if someone is ill in the client's household, he calls his guardian spirit for help and sacrifices to him. If the client dreams about this spirit, it can indicate that this spirit wants to be fed and if not he will make its client sick. Also the sacrifice of a pig or chicken to *'mbalid* will ensure an opportunity to buy a piece of heritable property at a low price.

The *Sunudun*. In addition to the *karaganan hantu* and the *karaganan mata'*, there is a class of spirits known as *sunudun*, who have the same division into *mata'*, who can cause illness, and *hantu*, who are helpful in the curing of illness. And like the *karaganan hantu* of the upperworld, the *sunudun hantu* are also derived from the souls of the dead. However, the *sunudun mata'* do not inhabit natural phenomena as do some of the varieties of *karaganan mata'*, but are only found in the upperworld. But the distinctions amond these four subclasses of *karaganan* are far from clear to us from our fieldnotes.

Explanations for Illness. There are three major explanations for illness. It may be caused by witchcraft, in which cases it is said the individual has been "struck down by a person." Or it may be the result of the capture and torture of one or more of the body's souls. In such cases it is said the person has been "struck down by *karaganan*." Finally, there is now a class of illnesses that are being treated at the local dispensary, as these are not considered to be caused by soul capture. They include malaria, tuberculosis, and other contagious diseases.

In instances of illness caused by soul capture by the *karaganan*, the sicker a person is the farther the soul has wandered away. Bulusu' *karaganan* are more capricious than most of the Rungus *rogon*. They do not usually make people ill in retaliation for wrongdoing either intentional or unintentional. Instead they arbitrarily pick on wandering souls of people and cause them to become ill just because they feel like it.

An alternative explanation of the illness caused by *karaganan* is a direct attack on the body itself rather than the soul. This includes the intrusion of animals into the body or stabbing the body with a pointed piece of wood, or beating the body with a stick. However, sucking or other techniques are not used to remove intrusions from the body.

Thus, in their definition of illness the Bulusu', like the Rungus, do not make clear-cut distinctions in their ordinary discourse about illness as to what parts of the self, body, or soul are involved. When they say that the body is attacked, it is in fact the *lingu* that has been captured, as all know. The use of the body as reference in this discourse is in effect a shorthand way of covering an elaborate etiology.

Individuals struck down by a *karaganan* are treated by the spirit mediums, or *ulun gantu*. When an individual is struck down by a person, by witchcraft, the individual consults a skilled practitioner in one of the Muslim groups, although the witchcraft attack may have originated from any of the indigenous groups.[6]

Also, threats to one's soul (*lingu*) makes one susceptible to illness, as it causes the soul to become *lami'*, "weak, soft," under certain conditions. For example, the soul of a man's wife will become weak if he dreams of intercourse with another woman, or if one's clothes are cut in anger, or if an individual is threatened with a knife. This will frighten one's soul away. Also a soul can become "hot" (*lasu'*), as, for example, if one's swidden boundaries are moved or if unfavorable omens are ignored. In these circumstances there are ritual steps to make one's soul "hard" (*kotog*) again. The individual can drink and wash his body with water in which heritable property has been washed, or one can wipe a knife, a betel chewing box, and a chicken over one's body. And for these rituals no special practitioner is used.

Semantics of Bulusu' Spirit Mediumship

The chants and songs used to placate the spirits are called *antu*. The spirit medium is an *ulun gantu*, "the person who uses chants and songs." The /g-/ prefix indicates that something is being used as in *gabag*, the wearing of an *abag*, or loincloth; or *gadagu-dagu*, "to converse," from *dagu*, "words."

The term for going into trance is *sumulod*. There are two explanations for trance behavior. The Bulusu' in explaining this trance state to us in everyday discourse used the term "to enter." Thus, in general, the folk explanation is that the *karaganan* enter the body. However, the exegesis by spirit mediums, *ulun gantu*, is that the *karaganan* only get close to the spirit mediums and control them from outside, as some say, hovering above them. Others state that the *karaganan* sit on the spirit mediums' shoulders. If the *karaganan* would actually enter the body, one spirit medium said, the *ulun gantu* would faint, would not regain consciousness, and would die.

The souls (*lingu*) of the *ulun gantu* also leave their bodies to go and help the *karaganan* search for wandering souls of those that are ill. It is unclear whether more than one soul is absent at one time helping in the search. The concept of soul absence is in contradistinction to the Rungus belief that if the soul of a spirit medium left her body while in trance she would become ill or die.

Function of Spirit Mediumship

Spirit mediums may be either female or male. Their primary function now is the curing of illness. There appears to be little involvement of the spirit mediums in maintaining the central morality of the society, as illness is largely adventitious and not attributable to a wrongdoing on the part of the individual, unless he cuts down trees where *karaganan* live.

However, the conclusion that spirit mediumship is not deeply involved in maintaining the morality of the community may be a distortion due to historical circumstances. During the period of headhunting, a new head, or an old head, or a head of a slave, was used in funeral ceremonies so that the soul of the dead would have a soul to look after him on his way to the afterworld. But heads were never used at a time of illness as the soul of a person killed in headtaking became a *karaganan mata'* and would cause illness.

Slaves were also killed in ceremonies to bring a bounty of fruit and honey and good omens for a river region, or to cleanse the village drainage area of the "heat" caused by death and the "filth" caused by illicit intercourse. At those times a spirit medium may have been used. And this certainly reflected the central morality of the village. But what part it played in maintaining it is not clear as we have little information on this.

Thus, the Bulusu' spirit mediums would at the most be involved in returning the village to a state of ritual goodwill following violations of community norm. But unlike those of the Kenyah (Whittier 1978), they do not engage in judging the moral life of the community during the year or suggest redressive measures to achieve a new harmony, thereby organizing responses of community to threat and social change. They also do not engage in acts to resolve disputes, unlike spirit mediums in some societies.

Recruitment to Spirit Mediumship

Prior to the arrival of effective Dutch rule, it is reported that the Bulusu' spirit mediums, *ulun gantu*, were primarily women. At that time there were fewer spirit mediums than now. And it was generally the old people who became spirit mediums.

It is reported that the ceremonies these female spirit mediums performed did not involve the aggressive attacks on the spirits that now occur in the ceremonies performed by male spirit mediums, which are accompanied by gonging and drumming. These female spirit mediums primarily divined illness and placated the spirits through prayers, chants, songs, and sacrifices of pigs and chickens for the return of souls and the removal of the agents of illness. It is also reported that these mediums used a hand clapper, similar to that of the Rungus, to divine causes of illness. The left hand was placed on the head of the ill person and the clapper was moved around over the body. When the seat of the illness was determined the spirit medium could tell by the sound of the bells and the feeling in her hand what the illness was. During the ceremonies performed by these female spirit mediums no drums or gongs were used, but instead the spirit medium plucked a *saranting kalid*. This looked like a miniature shield (*kalid*) with a brass wire strung on it. We have no further explanation for the term *saranting*.

With the decline of headhunting, men began to enter the role of spirit medium. Men at that time still used the *saranting kalid*. But the exact time period when this occurred is difficult to ascertain, as accounts of the cessation of headhunting range from approximately 1930 to around the time of the departure of the Japanese after World War II. With this change in role the ceremonies to cure illness became an active battle between the male spirit medium and the capricious *karaganan*, and the search for captured souls became an enactment of a frenzied journey in which swords and shields were used to threaten and chase away the spirits. At this time, it is reported, that the offering pole was introduced. This is erected in the longhouse, containing offerings of cloth and food to the *karaganan* helpers, and it has become the dramatic focus of the curing ceremony.

Now there are also more young people becoming spirit mediums as it is perceived that there is more sickness. One spirit medium stated that he could not travel far from the village for any length of time because he might be needed if anyone should become ill.

To become a Bulusu' spirit medium, as among the Rungus, the chants, songs, and prayers have to be learned and a spirit familiar obtained who can be communicated with in trance. However, among the Rungus the emphasis in curing ceremonies is much more on the hymns and chants and the sacrifice itself than the actual trance performance. For the Bulusu' the trance performance is the critical focus of the curing ceremony. Thus, the teaching of chants and songs is considerably less formal and structured than among the Rungus. Among the Bulusu' apprenticeship to older spirit mediums during ceremonies is one method used for memorizing the various prayers, chants, and songs (*antu*), as well as learning the ritual form of ceremonies, instead of formal instruction. In the process of learning to perform ceremonies, a pupil will assist a spirit medium by reciting the prayers, chants, and songs that he knows as the *karaganan hantu* are summoned to help. Thus, much of the instruction in the details of the form of the ceremony is carried on at this time, and the pupil acquires a lot of his learning by observation.

However, the critical skill for becoming a spirit medium is gaining the ability to enter a state of trance in order to communicate with one's spirit familiars. But trance is also experienced by many individuals without the acquisition of a spirit familiar as participants in curing ceremonies or as assistants to the spirit medium. Thus, many Bulusu', particularly females, are likely to have experienced trance and spirit control at a young age during the ceremonies as they follow the trance parade of the spirit medium as assistants (see section below on entering trance). While following the procession or parade, some of the spirits that are hovering around will control these young people. Though in trance the novice does not actually communicate with the spirit in control of his or her body but instead acts out the behavior of the spirit whose part he plays.

A Bulusu' spirit medium only acquires a spirit familiar following an illness, in contrast to the Rungus. After a severe illness, which the individual has recovered from, he or she may have a dream during which his or her spirit familiar appears. Sometimes a young person may become ill as the result of being controlled by a *karaganan* as an assistant in a trance performance. Following this the individual will have a dream in which he acquires a spirit familiar.

When a Bulusu' has acquired a spirit familiar, he or she is then considered to be a spirit medium and can conduct a healing ceremony. But before performance of a curing ceremony, the illness of the patient must be diagnosed, and the offending *karaganan* identified.

Divination for the Cause of Illness

Divination for the cause of an illness, *pata'id*, can be performed by a spirit medium, but not necessarily. There are other individuals who specialize in this. Trance is occasionally used in diagnosing illness, though this is rare.

In the process of divining the cause of illness, the body is felt to determine whether the sickness is from witchcraft or from soul capture, or whether it is a form of sickness that can be cured by the local dresser. A saucer of water is then inspected by the diviner to ascertain the exact source of illness, and if a stick appears he knows that it is witchcraft.

If witchcraft has been ruled out, there are then several techniques used to determine the location of a captured soul. First, a woman's beaded headdress (*ulos*) is used along with the root of the ritual plant, *kusur* (*Kaempferia galanga*), which has a soul (*lingu*). The *kusur* is first squeezed to release its aromatic oils and the root is then rubbed on the body of the patient. While quietly addressing the spirits, with the help of the soul of the *kusur*, the diviner suspends the beaded headdress over the body and allows it to swing. The direction of its movement indicates what *karaganan* are the source of the illness and where they are concealing the captured soul. A ritual stone, a small jar, or *damar* (resin) are also sometimes used in a similar way.[7]

Among some Bulusu' with Punan ancestry a blow pipe is used by a spirit medium to determine the source of illness. The blow pipe is held over the chest of the person who is ill, spear end down. The spirit medium stretches his arm to the farthest point up the blow pipe that he can reach and then measures a further length--the width of two fingers. As he talks with the *karaganan hantu* he moves his fingers up and down the blow pipe, asking the names of the various *karaganan mata'*. If the answer is negative his hand will move down, if getting close, his hand moves up. When he has correctly named the *karaganan* responsible, his finger tips will extend beyond the farthest point he has indicated in the initial measurements.

Types of Trance and Entering Trance

Bulusu' trance behavior is different from that of the Rungus in that the body of the Bulusu' spirit medium is actually controlled by the spirit familiars, while the Rungus spirit medium is only a conduit of communication with her spirit familiars. The purpose of trance for both Rungus and Bulusu' spirit mediums is, however, basically the same in that it involves the search for captured or wandering souls of the ill which must be returned to their owners before a cure can be effected.

The general term to go into trance is *sumulod*, and there are two types, "to go into dry trance" (*sumulod pua*) and "to go into wet trance" (*sumulod usa*). The term "dry trance" is used to refer to the state of trance that occurs when the spirit mediums evoke their spirit familiars (*karaganan hantu* and *sunudun hantu*) through prayers, chants, and songs or when they converse with them. Such a trance is not deep and is explained as a "half trance," in which the spirit medium is conscious of what is going on around him.

Sumulod usa, or "to go into wet trance," is entered into with the accompaniment of gonging and drumming. This is a much deeper form of trance than dry trance. It is facilitated by drinking copious amounts of rice wine or wine made from cassava. The trance involves very frenzied dancing and parading around with swords and shields as the spirit mediums and all their helpers run up and down the length of the longhouse circling the offering pole or chasing away harmful spirits that have been attracted to the ceremony. This aspect of the performance in which the spirit medium and his followers search for captured souls, and at the same time battle *karaganan mata'* that have come near, is referred to as *ningiang* (see Illustration 1).

During these trance performances wives and daughters of male spirit mediums will also go into trance and follow them. A male spirit medium may have some female familiars; however, he cannot be controlled by them while in trance. And it is for this reason that the assistants of a male spirit medium are predominantly women and young girls. A male spirit medium needs these additional women to take on the female spirit familiars who arrive to help. For example, the wife of a male spirit familiar will be passed on to the wife of the spirit medium he controls. Thus, female spirits will be handled by the spirit medium's wife and daughters as well as other women, both married and unmarried, who follow him as he parades and dances around after the *karaganan mata'*. However, females may also be controlled by male spirit familiars, and when they are they don items of male dress to indicate this (see Illustration 2).

Young girls often go into trance during these performances as it is said that the *karaganan* are fond of females. Unmarried men do not participate in these trance performances, as men are perceived to be less receptive to going into trance.

The arrival of the various types of *karaganan* is signalled by a change of rhythm played on the gongs and drums. Then, when the gongs stop and the various spirits have taken control, the spirit medium begins acting out the role of the *karaganan* who controls him.

Only a few young men are considered skilled in playing the gongs and drums and know the appropriate gonging that goes with each type of *karaganan*. Often it is necessary to go to a neighboring village to find people to play during a ceremony. Some young men from neighboring Muslim groups can also be recruited for this.

Spirit mediums state that when entering trance their chests feel tight as the spirit familiar arrives, and loosens as the familiar leaves. Shaking of the body and limbs is characteristic of someone going into wet trance. Spirit mediums say they perspire, though the skin becomes cold and goose flesh appears. At times when their own soul sees a captured soul their body hair stands on end.

Parents or spouse of a patient may be specifically "induced into trance" by the spirit medium during a ceremony. This is called *posulod*. The prefix /po-/

indicating causative action is added to the stem *sulod* from *sumulod*. The reason for inducing trance of these family members is so that spirit familiars of their ancestors can arrive and assist the spirit familiars of the spirit medium in effecting a cure (see Illustration 3). Spirit familiars of the family of the person who is ill will add strength to the bargaining powers of the spirit medium. These relatives who have been induced into trance join in the ceremony, parading and dancing along with the spirit medium and his assistants. There are occasions when these family members fail to go into trance, and at this point the spirit familiars of the spirit medium simply carry on without the help of the spirit familiars of the family of the person being cured. One informant estimated that only 50 percent of Bulusu' people were able to go into trance at such a time.

The experience of wet trance was explained to us by one of our informants as follows.

> Whatever is in my heart comes out.[8] I am not embarrassed by anything I do or say because I don't remember the silly things I do when in trance. You must drink rice wine before you start to make your heart 'big' so that the *karaganan* know you feel good towards them. When we are in trance we behave differently, we are not ourselves.

Sometimes the spirit mediums and their associates who have been in trance with the help of rice wine and brandy begin pressing drink on the assembled audience that have been observing the display. They can become very persistent in their efforts if a person refuses. At the same time they harass the audience, asking for donations of store-bought cigarettes, small change, sugar, salt, biscuits, perfume, and other belongings. If the donations are not forthcoming the performers will rifle through carrying baskets looking for what they want. During one ceremony L. W. R. Appell found a particularly favorite sarong missing from her basket. The next day the spirit medium "discovered" it with his paraphernalia hanging on the *singiang* and was astonished. He went around asking people where it had come from and when informed of the owner, he returned it. At these times those in trance may walk about addressing the audience and asking for things as if they had a frontal lobotomy. They appear empty of emotions, and they walk stiff-legged, with staring eyes.

Spirit Familiars

The spirit familiars of a spirit medium are subdivided into two groups, *karaganan hantu* and *sunudun hantu* and come from several sources. The primary spirit familiar is the one that arrives spontaneously during a dream following a severe illness. When a person is very ill and dreams that a soul has helped to make him well, it is said that he has been "adopted" by that soul.

Other familiars are derived from the souls of relatives or other people who have died that were close to the medium during their lives. One informant stated that there were two souls of each dead person that can become spirit familiars, one can become a *karaganan hantu* and the other a *sunudun hantu*. While not all souls become spirit familiars, all *karaganan hantu* and *sunudun hantu* are derived from souls.[9]

Those that are inherited from direct ancestors generally go as far back as three generations. Thus, a spirit medium may inherit the spirit familiars of his grandfather and his father. He can also receive spirit familiars from the souls of his dead children. All such spirit familiars received from family members are referred to as *karaganan muntuo*. *Muntuo* in everyday discourse is the term for "parents." It is said that these latter are more frequently men than women, as the men are more active in searching for captured souls. In trance *karaganan muntuo* will stay around longer and carry on longer discourse than other spirit familiars.

However, not all *karaganan muntuo* are from souls of the dead. The spirit medium may also inherit from his parent the familiars of the crocodile and monkey (see above). And rarely a spirit medium receives as a familiar the soul of one of the people he has ministered to during an illness even though they are still living.

Frequently, after the death of a child, a parent will become ill as a result of the parent's soul trying to follow the soul of the child to the mountain of the dead. During the ceremony for such an illness, if the parent enters trance and communicates with the soul of the dead child, it means that the soul has become a *karaganan hantu* or a *sunudun hantu*.

A spirit medium can have a relationship with one or more spirit familiars at the same time, but only one is in actual control at any one point. They may send one or more to be taken on by their helpers. Belching and yawning indicate the leaving of the familiar in command and the arrival of another.

Ethnicity of Peripheral Spirit Familiars

Some spirit familiars come from a neighboring ethnic group and exhibit the cultural characteristics of that group. The sources of these spirit familiars are

Tengkayu (Tidong and Bulungan), Punan Rama, and Punan Togung. The term "Tengkayu" is used by the Bulusu' to refer to both the Tidong and the Bulungan groups, and it is reported that many spirit familiars come from these groups. The ethnic group of Punan that the Punan spirit familiars come from varies depending on the location of the Bulusu' spirit medium. For spirit mediums in the Bengara River system, their Punan spirit familiars are from the Punan Rama, as the Punan Rama live close by. For spirit mediums in the Sekatak River system, it is the Punan Togung that provide spirit familiars, as souls (*lingu*) of the Punan Rama do not come there.

When controlled by a spirit familiar from another ethnic group than the Bulusu', the spirit medium or his assistants act out the salient behavioral characteristics or stereotypes of that group and at times wear the clothes attributed to that group.

There are, on the other hand, certain neighboring ethnic groups from which spirit familiars are not drawn. There are no spirit familiars drawn from the Chinese, Bugis, Timorese, Putok, or Tenggaran.

The Structure of Ceremonies

The preparations for a curing ceremony begin with the making of an offering pole. A small log is brought into the longhouse, peeled, carved, and topped with a decorated open box of carved wood, all of which is called a *singiang*. The *singiang* is erected and tied to a longhouse support. In the open box are placed various offerings for the *karaganan mata'* and *hantu*. These consist of freshly prepared coconut oil, rice colored with turmeric placed on a small saucer, small seed beads, small amounts of sugar and salt, etc. Cloths of various types and other objects pertinent to the ceremony are draped over the *singiang*. Offerings of cooked rice wrapped in leaves, as well as betel chewing supplies are placed on brass trays and containers which surround the base of the pole.

When everything is readied the spirit mediums arrive to open the ceremony. To please his spirit familiars the spirit medium must wear his best headcloth and loincloth, not his everyday clothes. It is said that his prayers will not reach his spirit familiars if he is not properly attired. Each spirit medium utters prayers over a handful of husked rice which has been colored yellow with turmeric. As the grains of rice are thrown out the open door of the longhouse the spirit mediums summon their spirit familiars to come near and assist them and their followers in searching for captured souls, removing the cause of illness, and restoring the patient to health. They ask the spirit familiars to assist them in communicating with the *karaganan mata'*, and at this time the *karaganan mata'* are alerted to the fact that there are to be offerings for them. And they are implored to behave and not cause any further illness as they assemble to receive these offerings.

Following these opening prayers, the ceremony begins on the verandah of the longhouse in front of the enclosed compartment where the offering pole has been placed along with the various offerings. The spirit medium with great care smells around the log post to see if the smell is sweet or bad. If the smell is sweet it means the ceremony will be efficacious. If it is a pungent or acrid smell it will not be efficacious. The spirit medium then spits on the post to cool it, and oil, which has had prayers, chants and songs said over it, is rubbed on the post to please the various spirits. The path the oil takes as it drips down the post is also used as an indication of how things will go in the curing. If the drip is straight and long, it indicates that the patient will quickly get well. If the path is angled or crooked, it is not a good sign. As the spirit mediums begin slowly circling the post, all the items offered are pointed out to the *karaganan* so that they will be aware that they are for them (see Illustration 4).

After this presentation of offerings the ceremony proceeds to the major aspect of the performance for the curing, which is the interaction between the spirit mediums and their spirit familiars as they negotiate with the *karaganan mata'*, who have taken a soul, or chase off others that have been attracted to the ceremony. Thus, a spirit medium when he is under the control of a spirit familiar can discern dangerous *karaganan* and must be on his guard to be sure they do no harm to the assembled people. When a spirit medium leaves the longhouse for any reason during a ceremony, he always carries his sword with him because it is said that there are always numerous *karaganan mata'* lurking around looking for an offering. Should they try to control the medium he would die, so he must fend them off.

At various points during these ceremonies all the participants dance and parade around with their swords and shields, wearing the appropriate clothing for the spirit familiar that controls them. At times this marching about is frenzied, as the parade charges around the longhouse in time to the gonging. The various spirit mediums and their helpers, under the control of their friendly spirit familiars, yelp as they fight and drive off with swords and shields the dangerous spirits that may have gathered at the ceremony (see Illustration 5). The spirit medium at various times approaches the person who is ill and swings his sword over his head to drive off spirits that might cause harm.

After a period of intense interaction with the *karaganan mata'*, a spirit medium will come out of trance and collapse, exhausted, and refresh and recharge himself with more drink. While resting he will again begin communication with his spirit familiars to determine how the search for souls is progressing. If he perceives that another *karagan mata'* has appeared, the spirit medium will suddenly jump up, landing on his feet at a run and resume his wet trance as he chases them away (see Illustration 1).

During one such rest period a spirit medium was seen to be peering in a mirror at something over his shoulder. When questioned as to what he was doing, he said that he was keeping his eye on the soul of the ill child for whom the ceremony was being held to make sure it was staying where it was supposed to be.

Smelling is a critical part of the ceremony to diagnose whether the person has been freed of pathogenic spirits. In addition to the log post, the body of the ill person is oiled and the spirit medium smells the joints of the individual. If the smell is sweet, it means a cure will be efficacious; if bitter or sour, it bodes ill. Or he will touch the sick person and then smell his own hand. Oil is also dripped on the back of the patient and a small coin stuck to the oil. The length of time the coin sticks to the skin and the path it takes as it slides down the oily skin also indicate the efficacy of the ceremony.

During the search for the wandering or captured souls the root of the *kusur* plant is again used. This root has a pleasing smell and its soul precedes the spirit familiars of the spirit medium as they travel, riding the wind on his shield, in search of souls. The search for souls begins on the ground around the longhouse. From the longhouse the search extends outward up and down hills, in gullies and wet places, crisscrossing rivers and streams, and farther and farther away from the longhouse. During the search for souls the spirit familiars ask for help from the souls of dead relatives of the person who is sick because it is said that their souls will recognize each other.

If a soul cannot be located there is always the fear that it might have crossed over to the land of the souls of the dead. If this is the case, the medium enters trance again to find out where the soul has been hidden. The soul of a living person can actually arrive at the resting place of souls of the dead, and can be retrieved by a spirit medium. It is said that in a section of the upperworld there is but one tree, the *kasian*, growing. To the souls of people who have died and entered the upperworld the taste of the fruit of the *kasian* is sweet and delicious. However, if eaten by the soul of a person still living who by mistake enters this upperworld, it is tasteless and unappetizing.

A spirit medium in trance may occasionally encounter the souls of another person along the way as he searches for the souls of the person for whom the ceremony is being held. If this happens he will send that soul back and return it to its owner. The owner is then notified and may himself want to hold a ceremony.

When the spirit familiars along with the soul of the spirit medium arrive in the house of a capricious *karaganan*, they search it for souls. They search in baskets, in trunks, in betel supply baskets, cooking pots, chicken nesting baskets, rolled up in sleeping mats, etc. The spirit medium while in trance acts this out in the longhouse itself, running around and peering into boxes and baskets and under belongings stacked on the floor of the longhouse in search of the soul.

When the souls have been collected they are brought back in a small container made from the dried fruit of a small bottle gourd such as that used to hold the plugs for blow pipe darts. Unlike the Rungus practice, in which the spirit medium wears a small jar suspended from a cord around her neck while in search of lost souls, the Bulusu' spirit medium does not actually have this container with him when looking for souls. It is merely stated that this is the method by which they are transported back to the ill person.

The spirit medium then ritually "drills" a hole in the skull of the patient to allow egress for any poisonous effects of the illness (see Illustration 6). Through this hole, when all the missing souls have been gathered up, the spirit medium puts the souls back into the ill person with his hand. With children the soul is returned through the fontanelle. He holds his hand down on the patient's head for a minute or so to be sure re-entry has been effected and no souls have escaped. After this the illness is swept away from the patient by dragging a yellow cloth over his head and shaking it out the door. Yellow cloth is used as it is said that *karaganan mata'* are particularly frightened by this color. After the soul has been returned to its owner, the spirit familiar who retrieved it keep watch over the patient until he is well again. While doing this, they feed on the remains of the offerings from the ceremony.

One method used for children to determine whether all the souls have been returned occurs during the closing part of the ceremony. Oil, in which seven seed beads have been immersed, is poured over the child's head. Then there is a search for the beads to recover them and count the number, with any less than seven indicating that the ceremony has not been entirely successful and that the child will not be cured completely. In such a case, this is repeated with seven additional beads and the ceremony is extended with additional performances. When a set of seven beads is finally recovered, all are strung and tied around the neck of the child. This necklace stays on until it breaks. The longer it stays intact the better the prognosis for a cure. It is said that the seven beads do not represent the souls of the child. If it is necessary to make a pact with the *karaganan mata'* for a further ceremony in the future because of missing beads, it is done at this time.

During such a ceremony anyone who is sick is invited to come and ask for help from the spirit familiars of the spirit medium (see Illustration 7). The spirit medium takes care of the sickest first. This usually involves anointing with oil and, by watching the course of the oil as it drips down the back of the patient, ascertaining how long it will be before they are well. At this time a spirit medium will also tell the family of such a person what ceremony they should hold to effect a cure. The price for the services of the spirit medium in cases such as this is small. A sarong or a shirt is given by the person who has been administered to. In addition to this all members of a longhouse where a ceremony is being held, whether or not they are sick, can ask to be anointed with oil which will help insure good health.

In addition to serving at the ceremonies for people who are ill, Bulusu' spirit mediums also officiate at ceremonies ending the various ritual prohibitions following a death. Some time after a death, when enough rice has been set aside to feed many people, there is a memorial ceremony held for the person who has died. This ceremony is to make sure the souls of the dead arrive at their resting place and no souls of the living follow. The harmful aspects surrounding a death are cleansed away at this time. Friends and relatives are invited from outlying longhouses, and the souls of the dead are called from the afterworld and fed. A similar ceremony is held several years later for the spirit familiars of the spirit mediums who ministered to the dead person in his last illness.

The Ceremony as Performance

A ceremony is also a performance to entertain the assembled members of the community in addition to returning the souls to the persons who are ill. For example, when a spirit medium or his assistant are controlled by a *karaganan* from a Coastal Muslim group, they may dress up in the clothes of the Coastal Muslim. He or she may put on trousers, in contrast to a loincloth, or he or she may wear a sarong. Sometimes the spirit medium who is controlled by such a spirit will tear off a piece of rattan as a fishing line and drop it down through the floor boards to fish. In this case he is "fishing" for lost souls. Or he or she may also sit as if in a boat and paddle with a stick.

A female controlled by a male spirit wears a headcloth and carries a sword and shield as she aggressively assists in the trance performance (see Illustrations 2 and 8). One female who was controlled by a male *karaganan* came up to our youngest daughter and had the audience howling as "he" engaged in ribald suggestions to her.

A parent or a sibling in the family holding a curing ceremony may go into trance and be controlled by the soul of a dead child. And when this happens the individual in trance acts out the behavior of that child. He speaks to the family to say how much he misses them, plays as he used to, kicks his toys, and performs all sorts of familiar actions that the child is remembered for. He starts crying for his parents and siblings, and the members of the family may break down and start crying when they see this behavior.

In addition to the various types of spirit familiars described above certain spirit mediums have inherited familiars that take on unusual forms, such as the crocodile. When controlled by this spirit, the spirit medium begins to crawl on the floor like a crocodile, in an amazing caricature of it. The lick of the crocodile's tongue on a member of the audience is thought to be particularly good luck and to provide protection from harmful *karaganan*. This is likened to an injection from a doctor. Because of the crocodile's reputation for many successful cures, people will prostrate themselves before him in order to receive the lick of his tongue.

Then there are Punan *karaganan*, which appear on the scene dirty, itchy, and covered with leech bites, pig licks, chiggers in the crotch, and ring worm and sores, which the controlled spirit medium scratches and rubs. But these are good *karaganan*. They help with animals, gardens, and property. There are many of these, and two or more people can be controlled by these at the same time.

Thus, the trance performance of the Bulusu' spirit medium does not only serve the purpose of curing the ill by returning the captured souls and placating the *karaganan* responsible for causing illness. In addition it provides much humor and elicits participation of the onlookers in the process of curing. The whole ceremony in providing explanation for illness and in its entertainment thus has therapeutic value.

Conclusion of the Ceremony

As the ceremony is ending the main spirit medium is controlled by a monkey, the pet of one group of *karaganan*. And he runs around the longhouse, swinging from the rafters just like a monkey to great gales of laughter and the amusement of onlookers.

The final scene of the ceremony involves a jumping match between the soul of the ill person and a *karaganan mata'* as the latter tries to lure the soul over an imaginary line and back under his control. However, the spirit medium and the family of the person who is sick stand by to assure that this does not happen.

After the ceremony there is a feast. At this feast all the offerings to the *karagan mata'* are displayed and pointed out to the *karagan mata'* by the spirit mediums as they parade around the offering pole (see Illustration 4). These may include the effigy of a pig made out of flour, which is cut up and eaten by those attending the ceremony. Also a white chicken is offered to the capricious spirits, who have promised not to repeat their delicts against humans. The chicken is not sacrificed, but is placed on the *singiang*. When this chicken flies out the door of the longhouse, it is followed by the *karaganan mata'* that have assembled. As they leave these *karaganan* are implored not to return and to refrain from making anyone ill in the future.

The spirit mediums must spend the night after the conclusion of the ceremony in the longhouse where it was held. The morning after the ceremony the spirit mediums and their helpers go to the river to bathe and wash their clothes. The illness can stick to their bodies and clothes. But by washing the illness is sent down the river ensuring that it will follow the current away from the village.

Payment of Spirit Mediums

A spirit medium receives a significant payment in return for his services. The major portion of this payment is a small to medium sized ceramic jar. He also receives a long piece of iron and a bush knife, both of which make him "hard," a woven mat, seven seed beads, some coins used during the time of Dutch rule, a blow pipe, and a length of brass chain.

CONCLUSIONS

The trance performances of the Bulusu' spirit medium have many of the characteristics of what in the past has been called shamanistic performances. Thus, as with the Haitian spirit control (Bourguignon 1965), there is postdissociational amnesia at least in the Bulusu' wet trances. There is also no responsibility taken by the postdissociational self for the behaviors while in trance. Bourguignon concludes that this represents a discontinuity in personal identity. We disagree. It represents only a discontinuity of parts of personal identity, that of cognition and behavior. For personal identity must surely include the capacity for dissociational states.

The Bulusu' explanations for illness and the curing ceremonies do not appear to be part of a central morality religion inasmuch as the explanations for illness are not primarily based on violations of normal behavior. Nor are they, on the other hand, in opposition to any central morality religion. They are instead a critical extension of the shared world view of the Bulusu' and form an integral part of it.

In the curing performances, the everyday world of the Bulusu' and the invisible world are brought into conjunction. Much of the invisible is made visible. And spirit mediums act out the cultural characteristics and the personalities of their familiars. Thus, this invisible world now made visible is a restatement of the relations of the Bulusu' to their phenomenal world of existence, which includes not only the natural world but also their social world which stretches out from the present into the historical past, to their remembrances of their past social worlds.

Punan spirit familiars behave through their spirit medium as Punan are characterized. Coastal Muslim groups are portrayed as continuing their traditional occupations of fishing. And the spirit medium when controlled by animal spirit familiars, like the crocodile, turns into a crocodile, and he slithers across the floor, acting out the crocodile's behavior.

The past is brought into conjunction with the present as the dead become alive when their souls take control of the spirit mediums and the participants in the ceremonies. A dead child reappears, and the grieving process is reawakened again, discharging unfulfilled emotions. And the souls of dead ancestors become the spirit familiar of the spirit medium, thus linking up the present with significant personages in the past.

But in bringing together the spirit world and the phenomenal world in these performances, it is more than just a mere interlinkage. The phenomenal world for a time actually becomes the spirit world. Thus, the spirit medium in searching for lost souls in the houses of those spirits who have taken souls, acts out these searches in the trunks, or other hiding places, in the household of the person who is ill. And the soul of the dead child re-enacts its human existence.

The trance performances of the spirit medium are highly athletic performances involving prancing, parading, and very aggressive acts of sword waving and threatening to chase away the dangerous spirits. But these performances represent a change from the curing performances that were used prior to World War II. And this change and its causes is of considerable interest. Prior to the interdiction of warfare by the Dutch colonial government, which may have been as late as the early 1900s in this area, curing ceremonies had certain similarities to those by the Rungus. There were female spirit mediums, and there was the use of a clapper similar to that of the Rungus as an aid to entering trance.

But with the end of warfare, men became more active in the performances to cure illness, and the performances then became more aggressive. It appears that these performances became an arena in which the men could discharge their aggressive impulses that were thwarted by the Netherlands colonial government.

Of considerable interest is the contrast in explanations for trance between the Rungus and the Bulusu' and the differences in the structure of the self and its many transformations in its behavioral environment. The spirit familiars for the Bulusu' come much closer physically to the spirit medium, some say even riding on his shoulder. And during trance a soul of the spirit medium leaves his body and travels with his spirit familiars to find the wandering and captured souls of the person who is ill.

Also, in contrast to the Rungus, the Bulusu' patient is much more intimately involved in his curing ceremonies. He is the focus of all the activities. He watches as the spirit mediums and their helpers fight off the dangerous spirits. His body is touched, manipulated, smelled, and oiled to make a prognosis of his illness. And there are tests to see how successful the ceremony will be, as for example, the counting of beads anointed with oil on the head of an ill child to determine if all his souls have been returned.

All aspects of the ceremony are such as to encourage self-healing. It has been found that social support, the giving of attention, the use of humor, explanations for causes of disease, and assurances of being cured are all psychobiologically active in the promotion of health.

ILLUSTRATION 1

An *ulun gantu* in deep trance, *sumulod usa* running around, stamping his feet and brandishing his sword as he does battle with the *karaganan mata'*.

ILLUSTRATION 2

The wife of a spirit medium who shares with him the burden of communicating with his many spirit familiars. The women seated in the background illustrate the dress of Bulusu' women, including the *ulos*. The woman in trance is wearing clothing of a Malay male.

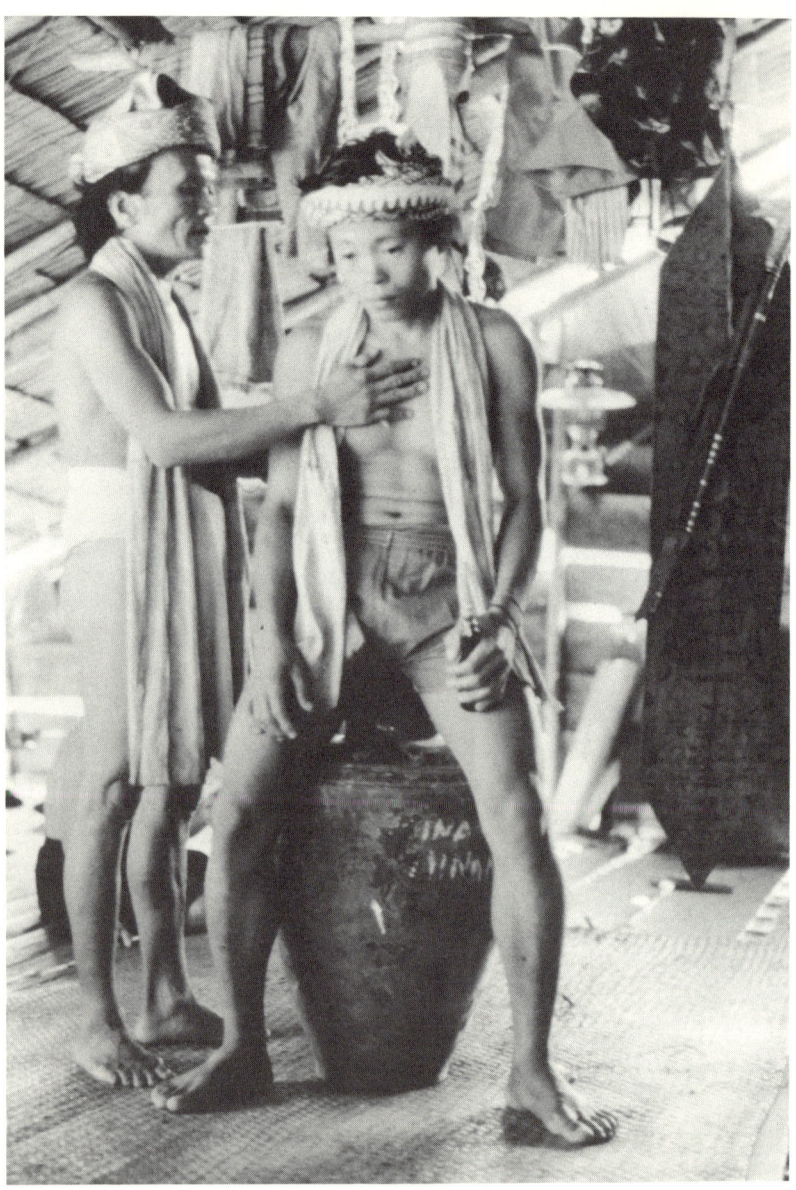

ILLUSTRATION 3

The father of an ill child sitting atop a valuable jar
as the *ulan gantu* puts him into trance, *posulod*.

ILLUSTRATION 4

Two spirit mediums at the end of a ceremony pointing out the various items which are offered to the *karaganan*.

ILLUSTRATION 5

Two spirit mediums charging around the longhouse with swords and shields doing battle with the *karagaran* as they search for the wandering souls of the ill.

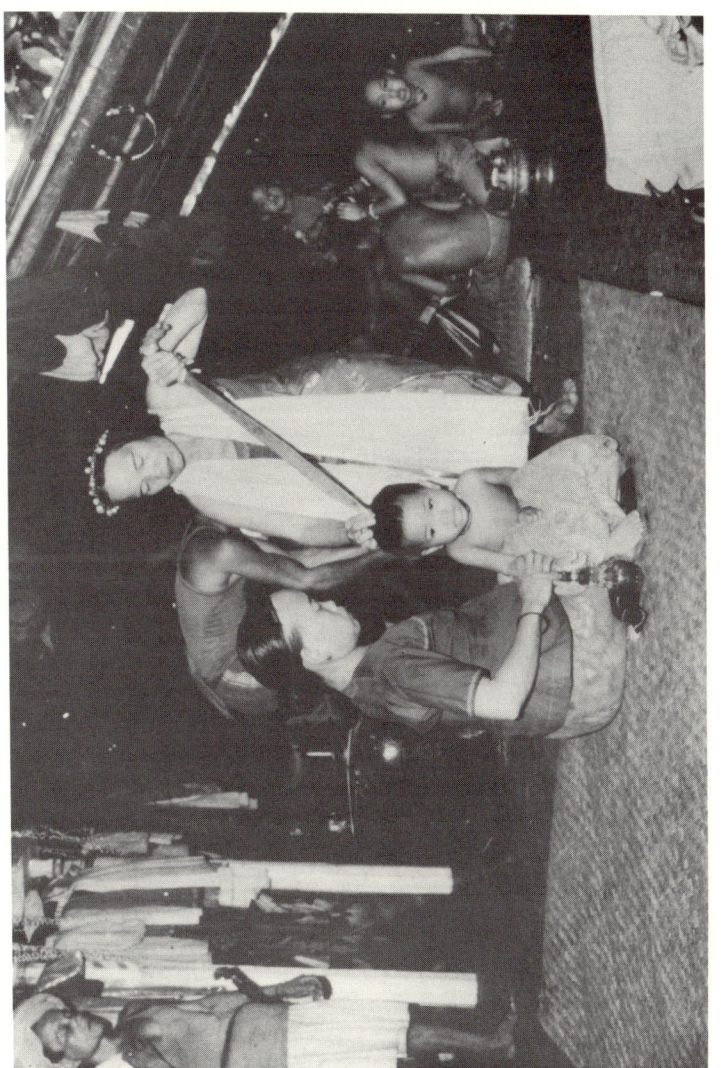

ILLUSTRATION 6

The helper of a spirit medium, his wife, "drilling" a hole in the skull of an ill child to allow any lingering illness to escape. In the background can be seen two posts with offering boxes (*singiang*).

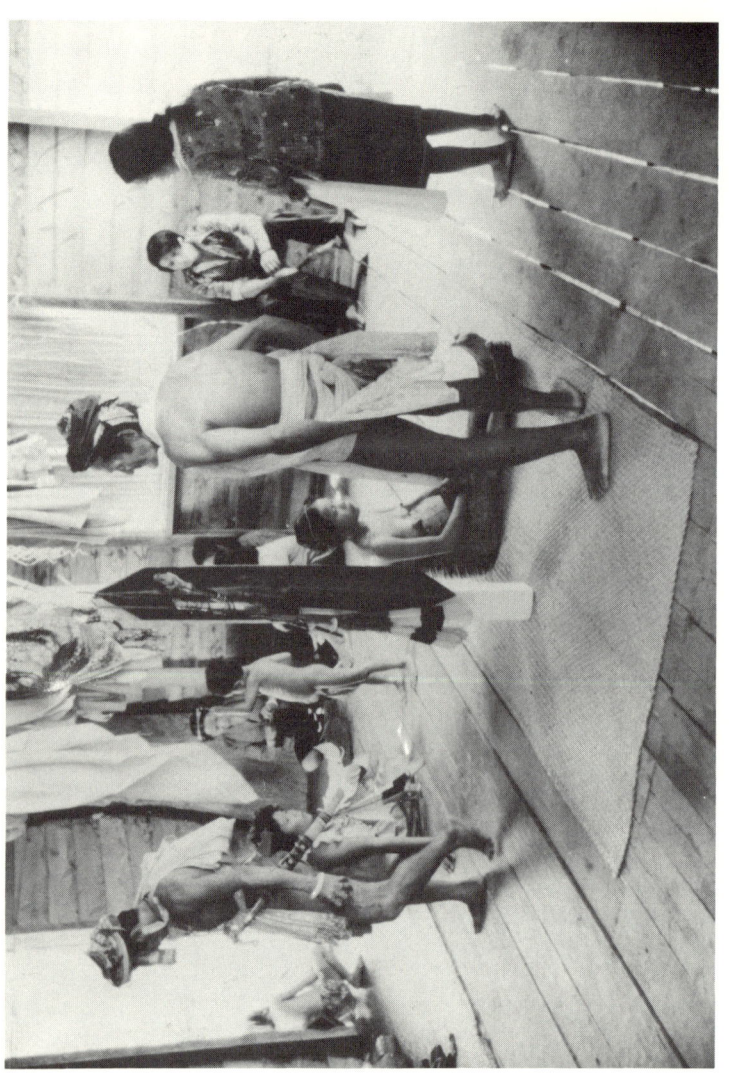

ILLUSTRATION 7

A person visiting a ceremony who is waiting for a diagnosis of her illness from an *ulun gantu*.

ILLUSTRATION 8

Two female spirit mediums possessed by male *karaganan* as they dance around the longhouse wearing male headcloths and brandishing swords.

ACKNOWLEDGEMENTS

Research among the Bulusu' of East Kalimantan was undertaken in 1980-81. G. N. Appell gratefully acknowledges support of this research from the National Science Foundation (Grant No. BNS-7915343), the Ford Foundation, and the Halcyon Fund, which has most generously supported his research over the years. We want to thank the Lembaga Ilmu Pengetahuan Indonesia for their help and approval of this research and particularly Dr. Masri Singarimbun, then Director, Population Study Centre, Gadjah Mada University, for his valuable advice and sponsorship. We are also indebted to Dr. Soetrisno Hadi, Rektor, Universitas Mulawarman, and Bupati Soetadji of Bulungan for their many kindnesses and help. Our daughters participated in this research, for which we are eternally thankful. Laura Appell worked on the Bulusu' religion with a particularly fine individual and an accomplished spirit medium. Laura Parker, our eldest daughter, studied child rearing and play, mapped the various Bulusu' settlements, and inquired into the history of the attempts at resettlement in the region. Our middle daughter, Amity, made a thorough linguistic inquiry into the Bulusu' lexicon and helped both run our field station and collect Bulusu' and Punan material culture. And our youngest daughter, Charity, made a collection of myths and folktales and also helped run the field station and collected examples of material culture. We also owe a great debt of gratitude to the many friends that we and our daughters made and who helped in this research. G. N. Appell worked intensively with two informants, one of whom we became fast friends with and now miss. We owe them a particular debt of gratitude, but they must remain anonymous according to their wishes.

NOTES

1. Our research was undertaken in 1980-81. It should be noted that at that time the Bulusu' were in the process of being forcibly moved into a government resettlement area so that their traditional culture was being disrupted (see G. N. Appell 1985a, 1985b). We were able to observe most aspects of the traditional culture, as not all had moved into the resettlement center. Consequently, the ethnographic present that we use throughout this first section on traditional Bulusu' society represents that period of Bulusu' culture just prior to this disruption. In the Bulusu' orthography /'/ transcribes as a glottal stop.

2. According to Crain (1970, 1982), the Lun Dayeh have a system of brideprice payments that is similar to that of the Bulusu'. And he provides a very detailed analysis of this type of system including an account of an engagement negotiation and the type of payments made and their redistribution.

3. We are indebted to Hallowell (1954) in this analysis and his critical delineation of the behavioral environment. His article reaches far beyond its time to influence today's theory construction.

4. The lexeme *hantu* presents some problems. The only lexemes with an initial /h/ in the Bulusu' language are loan words from the Indonesian language. Therefore, it is not clear whether this is a loan word from Indonesian, i.e. *hantu* meaning "ghost, evil spirit," or it is a phonetic modification of the Bulusu' lexeme *antu* (chants and songs for the *karaganan hantu*) in the direction of Indonesian, as the Bulusu' language is being strongly influenced by Indonesian. Occasionally the term *hantu* is replaced by the term *buntu*, which in Bulusu' is equivalent to the Indonesian lexeme *suruh*. In this context it might be translated to mean "messenger," or "sent." If *buntu* were the standard lexeme historically, the Indonesian *hantu* may be replacing it due to its phonetic similarity to *antu*.

5. We are using the third person pronoun for spirits and gods when their sex is unknown. If we used the male third person pronoun, as is usual in such instances, it might indicate falsely the sex of the supernatural.

6. There are also instances in which a member of a Muslim group will seek help from a Bulusu' spirit medium if their own practices have not been effective.

7. *Kaempferia galanga* is a widely used ritual plant in Borneo and the Philippine Islands (for example see Demetrio y Radaza 1973). Bulusu' plant it first in swiddens and along with *Derris elliptica* (*tuba*, Indonesian) at the foot of strangler figs (*Ficus* spp.) to make peace with the indwelling *karaganan* after firing a swidden with a strangler fig tree in it or beside it. It is also rubbed on a blowpipe to make it accurate. And a leaf is bitten to obtain good luck at marriage ceremonies and when making a swidden. Its spirit (*lingu*) is female.

8. The informant used the Indonesian term *hati* for what we have translated as "heart" in this context.

9. *Sunudun* are said to be stronger than *karaganan* at finding and returning souls. Also, there is the role for a man called *ulun sunudun*. *Ulun* means "person," and he tells stories of the work of the *sunudun* and the *karaganan* as a form of entertainment. Other than that the distinction between *sunudun*, both *mata'* and *hantu*, and the *karaganan*, both *mata'* and *hantu*, is perplexing. In our early interviewing we thought that the term *karaganan* contrasted with *sunudun*. But later we learned that *karaganan* is also a cover term for both of these, so that in our notes it is not always clear which variety of spirit is being discussed. And we suspect that in the discourse of individuals other than spirit mediums this distinction is not carefully made.

REFERENCES

Appell, Amity C. P.
    1986   The Bulusu' Language of East Kalimantan. Borneo Research Bulletin 18:166-74.

Appell, G. N.
    1971   Observational Procedures for Land Tenure and Kin Groupings in the Cognatic Societies of Borneo. (Prepared for distribution.)

    1974   The Analysis of Property Systems: The Creation and Devolution of Property Interests Among the Rungus of Borneo. Paper presented at the Conference of the Association of Social Anthropologists, University of Keele, 1974.

    1983a   Ethnic Groups in the Northeast Region of Indonesian Borneo and Their Social Organizations. Borneo Research Bulletin 15:38-45.

    1983b   Methodological Problems with the Concept of Corporation, Corporate Social Grouping, and Cognatic Descent Group. American Ethnologist 10:302-11.

    1984   Methodological Issues in the Corporation Redux. American Ethnologist 11:815-17.

    1985a   Land Tenure and Development Among the Rungus of Sabah, Malaysia. *In* Modernization and the Emergence of a Landless Peasantry: Essays on the Integration of Peripheries to Socioeconomic Centers, edited by G. N. Appell. Studies in Third World Societies Publication No. 33. Studies in Third World Societies, College of William and Mary, Williamsburg, Virginia.

    1985b   The Bulusu' of East Kalimantan: The Consequences of Resettlement. *In* Modernization and the Emergence of a Landless Peasantry: Essays on the Integration of Peripheries to Socioeconomic Centers, edited by G. N. Appell. Studies in Third World Societies Publication No. 33. Studies in Third World Societies, College of William and Mary, Williamsburg, Virginia.

    1986   Kayan Land Tenure and the Distribution of Devolvable Usufruct in Borneo. Borneo Research Bulletin 18:119-30.

Appell, G. N.
    1991   Errors in Borneo Ethnography: Part I. Borneo Research Bulletin 23:85-99.

Appell-Warren, Laura P.
    1986   The Tarakan Dialect of the Tidong Language of East Kalimantan: Distribution and Basic Vocabulary. Borneo Research Bulletin 18:148-66.

Bourguignon, Erika
    1965   The Self, the Behavioral Environment, and the Theory of Spirit Position. *In* Context and Meaning in Cultural Anthropology: In Honor of A. Irving Hallowell, edited by Melford E. Spiro. New York: The Free Press.

Crain, Jay B.
    1970   The Lun Dayeh of Sabah, East Malaysia: Aspects of Marriage and Social Exchange. Ph.D. Dissertation, Cornell University.

    1982   A Lun Dayeh Engagement Negotiation. Contributions to Southeast Asian Ethnography 1:142-87.

Demetrio y Radaza, Francisco
    1973   Philippine Shamanism and Southeast Asian Parallels. Paper prepared for the IXth International Congress of Anthropological and Ethnological Sciences, Chicago, August-September, 1973.

Firth, Raymond
    1959   Problem and Assumption in an Anthropological Study of Religion. The Huxley Memorial Lecture, 1959. Journal of the Royal Anthropological Institute of Great Britain and Ireland 89, 2:129-48. (Reprinted *In* Essays on Social Organization and Values, by Raymond Firth. London School of Economics Monographs on Social Anthropology No. 28. London: The Athlone Press. 1964.)

Hallowell, A. Irving
    1954   The Self and Its Behavioural Environment. Explorations II, April. (Reprinted *In* Culture and Experience, by A. Irving Hallowell. Philadelphia: University of Pennsylvania Press. 1955.)

Lewis, I. M.
    1986   Religion in Context: Cults and Charisma. Cambridge: Cambridge University Press.

Whittier, Herbert L.
    1978   Concepts of Adat and Cosmology Among the Kenyah Dayak of Borneo: Coping with the Changing Socio-cultural Milieu. Sarawak Museum Journal 26:103-13.

SHAMANISM AMONG THE OYA MELANAU

H. S. MORRIS
London School of Economics

The name Melanau is given to a culturally diverse set of peoples in Sarawak who inhabit the lower reaches of the River Rajang and the coastal areas to the north-east as far as Miri. In the Census of 1960 they numbered 44,661, of whom 31,770 were Muslim and approximately 10,000 pagan. Most of these people speak closely related languages, not all of which are mutually intelligible. Traditionally they practiced shifting cultivation and had similar types of social organization. Although it is probably legitimate to speak of a Melanau culture and a Melanau type of social structure, it is doubtful how far any one group can thereby be distinguished from another or from related groups in the interior who are not classified as Melanau.

THE VILLAGE

The Melanau of the Oya River inhabit some dozen villages on the banks of the river as it flows through the low-lying swamps between the hills and the coast. The upriver villagers mostly grow the sago palm as a cash crop, and those nearer the coast grow rubber and are fishermen. The majority are Muslim, though exactly how many is not known. Most of the pagans live in the upriver villages and it is with them that this paper is mainly concerned.

A Melanau village today forms a line of small rectangular wood and thatch houses on piles along both banks of the river, It usually stands on the site of a former longhouse settlement. Villages vary in size from 200 to 1,000 inhabitants and are separated from one another by three or four miles on the river, which is still the only practical route for travel. The swamp jungle on each side of it is dense and often dangerous; and for this reason the people of the different rivers have always tended to be culturally and politically distinct.

The earlier villages consisted of one or at most two longhouses. These were massively built fortresses, often thirty feet above ground, and situated at the confluence of a strategically important tributary stream and the main river. Each house was politically independent within its own territory, and was frequently on terms of active hostility with its Melanau neighbors and the Iban invaders who began to settle on the hills upstream during the nineteenth century. The investment of labor and capital in the longhouses was so great the they were rarely moved or completely rebuilt. When raiding was suppressed under Brooke rule in the latter part of the last century, and the houses became overcrowded, the people simply abandoned them and built separate dwellings on the edge of the river.

Although physically one structure, a longhouse was made up of separately built apartments, each owned and inhabited by one married couple and perhaps one married child. Longhouses were constructed in the form of a row of terrace houses with a common covered veranda like a gallery in front and behind, and they might house two hundred or more people. Much of the village life and ceremonial took place on the front veranda, which was fifteen to twenty feet wide and possibly up to three or four hundred feet long. When the houses were abandoned, no central meeting place replaced the veranda; and much of the culture, especially the performance of communal ceremonies, fell into disuse because the newer house were so small.

In longhouse days the political control of a village was in the hands of a small group of aristocratic elders (*a-nyat*), whose families usually owned the central apartments, and who were the descendants of the village founder. On each side of this core were apartments owned by freemen (*a-bumi*), and at each end of the house were the apartments of freed slaves (*a-dipen*). Most slaves were owned by aristocrats (*a-menteri*). An elaborate set of customary rules (*adet*) regulated the behavior of the ranks to one another and most other aspects of social life. The *adet*, one of the community's most valued possessions, was in the custody of the aristocratic elders. No single elder was superior to the others, though he might have special knowledge that fitted him for a particular tasks. A man with unusual abilities in war would be put in charge of raids, and another with knowledge of rituals might assume leadership on appropriate occasions. But leadership of this kind was not usually formalized as a permanent office, and there was no single political chief who ruled villages as of personal right.

Each household was economically independent. The members grew its rice and other crops and were primarily responsible for their own physical and supernatural safety and prosperity. There was little specialized division of labor, and a household normally could supply its own needs. Matters which affected other people in the longhouse fell either into the sphere of the *adet* and were therefore regulated by the elders, or, if they were concerned with the supernatural, were in the hands of ritual experts who might or might not be aristocrats.

Traditional Melanau society in the Oya River made use of three overlapping criteria in organizing social life. The first was that of local grouping; the second was that of kinship; and the third was that of hereditary rank. A Melanau thought of himself in each of these social dimensions. He was closely identified with a particular locality, especially with one longhouse whose inhabitants were thought to be, and often were peculiar and unique in matters of dialect and custom. As an individual, a man or woman was the focal point of a kindred with whom he shared a wide range of social and economic interests regulated by principles of bilateral descent. Lastly, he had by virtue of birth a rank status. In any context the behavior of one man towards another was largely determined by the fact that the two men were neighbors or strangers, kinsmen or not, of equal or different rank. Within the social order his behavior was regulated by the *adet*; with the symbolic order similar principles governed his ritual behavior (Morris 1953).

THE SYMBOLIC ORDER

For an Oya Melanau the longhouse (*lebu'*), or the modern village (*likou*), and the river on which it stands (*likou*) lie at the center of the social and symbolic worlds. Beyond the village are the forests, the hills, the sea, and other rivers, whose inhabitants, human, animal, and supernatural, are, or are believed to be, at best indifferent to humans and at worst really dangerous. Every creature in this the middle world (*likou dagan duah*) has his own proper place. Above this world is the overworld (*likou langit* or *likou bah bau*), and below is the underworld (*likou bah iba'*). The over- and the underworlds each consist of seven superimposed and named worlds, most of which are replicas of the middle world, with rivers, forests, hills, animals, spirits (*tou*), and villages thought to be inhabited by human beings (*tenawan*). When these "worlds" are thought of as countries like the Oya River they are called *likou*; but when they are discussed as parts of the cosmos they may be called *susun* (layers) or *lapih* (strata) to draw attention to the way in which they are laid one on top of the other. These fifteen "worlds" constitute the *dunia* or the whole World.

Different informants give different accounts of the *dunia*, but all agree that it is roughly egg-shaped. According to some it is balanced between the horns of a buffalo standing on a long thin fish (*jikan papa*) which swims in an ocean that surrounds everything. Others think that it is held in the hand of a spirit (*tou gerachi*). The sun and the moon revolve around the World, and day in the overworld is night below. Each world (*lapih*) is divided from the others by barriers (*pegar*), though in mythological times, before an impatient woman baking sago biscuits and worried by the close heat of the sun pushed up the sky with a pole, visits to the other worlds by heroes, shamans, and even ordinary people were not uncommon. But even then visits to other worlds often turned out to be dangerous to both the visitors and the visited.

Few people still remember the details of the cosmology. None know any myths of creation. The World and everything in it was created by Alatala; and though spirits have powers that are unlike and often greater than those of human beings, they are not thought of as gods, but merely as being different from men. Certain spirits, which are nevertheless still called *tou*, differ from most. Some live in the moon, and their leader, a female called Biliong, is especially concerned with the preservation of the proper natural order of things. Any human who disrespects it by mocking or teasing animals, for example, arouses her anger, and she summons thunder and lightning and hail to petrify the offenders (*baliyu*). For most Melanau today *baliyu* is a principle built into the scheme of things by Alatala, and they know nothing of Biliong. For them the World is the middle world, the sky, the world below, and the land of the dead, which some believe is a part of the underworld and others think is completely elsewhere.

The Inhabitants of the World

Men and women inhabit the middle word, but they share it with its vegetation, the animals, and the spirits. Each member of these different types of being has its own proper place; and if any being gratuitously or accidentally interferes with or obtrudes on another, the correct order of things is disturbed and trouble is likely to follow. The proper place of men and women is the village. In it they are relatively safe among friends and kinsmen; it is crowded and companionable (*ramai*); and the risk of meeting hostile humans or of encountering other alien beings is less than anywhere else. At home a man is guided and supported by the social order; only if he flouts the *adet* does he put himself in social or supernatural danger. But a man is everywhere and always in danger from mistakes and malignance.

All human beings are made up of four separate elements: the body (*bieh* or *badan*); the soul (*bedua*), which is thought to be a vaporous replica of the body; the emotions (*naseng*); and a principle of life (*nyawa*). For a man to be alive and healthy these four elements must be joined and undisturbed. The body is subject to accidents and illness, most of which can be attributed to breaches of the social *adet* or proper behavior generally, or to attack by spirits, or even by shamans. At the onset of an attack the *nasang* is upset, and may become so disorganized that the *bedua* begins its journey to the land of the dead, leaving only the *bieh* and *nyawa*. If it does not return, death is inevitable.

The word *bedua* would perhaps be better translated as "double" (which is its literal meaning) than soul; but it is convenient to speak of the soul because it is the element which is thought to survive death and make the canoe journey to the land of the dead (*likou a-matai* or *likou pengamou*). At the entrance to this land of the dead, the soul is directed to its appropriate place by a female, Balou Adet, who, as there is no other word in the Melanau language to describe her godlike attributes, is called a "spirit," though with some hesitation. A few souls fail to pass the barrier and haunt the middle world as ghosts (*amou*), where they attempt to steal the souls of the living. To ensure the safe arrival of a dead person at the house of Balou adet, mortuary rites enacting the journey used to be performed. Once the soul is established in the underworld it is not permitted to repass the barrier and gradually relinquishes interest in the living, except to welcome newly arrived kin.

No Melanau doubts the existence of spirits, but if asked about them says, "They are things which cannot be seen; how can we be sure what they are like?" Even so, almost everybody knows of a large number of them and their attributes. Many people who are not experts have sufficient knowledge of their forms and the afflictions they are thought to cause to be able to carve a few of their images for use in curing illness. An expert image maker may have iconographical knowledge of more than a hundred.

The most general classification of spirits is by the region they inhabit; for all, like men have their proper homes and settings. In the middle world are found air or sky spirits, forest, and river, and sea spirits; the upper and underworlds also have the same types, and all can move from one world to another in a way that humans usually cannot. Spirits are male and female and most are anthropomorphic. Some people think that like the Melanau they are hierarchically ranked within their categories, each of which has its own leader, who has authority over all his kind, whatever world he inhabits. According to one shaman:

Spirits do not worry humans if their lives are comfortable. If they are poor and cannot find enough to eat, they become dangerous and eat men. A strong *tou*, such as is useful to a shaman, is rich; and can if he wishes keep the poor ones in order. Some of the worst spirits are slaves.

Although people tell stories of marriages between humans and spirits and of men becoming spirits, others deny that this is possible. But all agree the animals, plants, human, and spirits are distinct orders of beings who happen to share the same environment--a fact which entails ordered rules of behavior. A Muslim, who had been a pagan as a child, explained the matter thus:

> A powerful man once met an angel (*melaikat*) and asked for immortality.[1] The angel called a meeting of all trees, animals, and other living things. The trees spoke first. If men did not die, they said, all the trees would be felled to make farms. The animals spoke next and said that if men did not die and all the trees were felled, there would be no shelter from the sun and the hunters and all the animals would be killed. The animals therefore asked the angel to bring 160 types of illness to kill men, and the trees asked for 112 kinds of remedy for the illnesses. Everybody except the man agreed to this. He asked that he and his wife should be turned into rainbows, and his wish was granted. Since then men have had to know what spirits caused illness and what herbs or other remedies will cure them.

The Melanaus' technical equipment gave them little control over the natural forces of their environment, and by personifying these forces and placing them in a system of relationships, stated in much the same terms as they used in handling the social order, and backed by the same kinds of moral sanction, they were helped to comprehend the environment and live in it with a greater sense of security.

Relations Among the Inhabitants of the World

The ideal of behavior implicit in the myth set out in the last section does not imply that the quality of all relationships ought to be the same. Within a village, relations, however formal, were expected to be basically friendly; whereas those between neighboring longhouses or with foreign peoples, such as the Iban or the Kayan, were thought to be potentially always hostile and at times actively dangerous unless treated with caution. Similarly, relations between humans and spirits were those of co-existence rather than of friendly cooperation. Unguarded behavior always carried the risk of misfortune or deprivation on one side or the other.

In one story a man found a woman and her daughter stealing fish from his traps in the forest. He seized them, and even though they were spirits, insisted on being taken to their longhouse, access to which was by a ladder that to human eyes appeared to be a large tree. He married the daughter, and after a child was born took them both to his own longhouse. Their arrival caused much trouble and the ultimate destruction of the village and scattering of its inhabitants.

This myth is placed in historical times, but another refers to the days before barriers were erected between the different "layers" of the World. A fisherman caught his hook on a snag and dived in to free it. He found it in the roof of a longhouse built in a country just like his own. The leader of the house, who was the ruler of that "world" (*likou yang*) allowed him to stay. He was given rice to eat--a food which no human had then seen. He lived there the best part of a year and helped cultivate the farms and harvest the crops. Eventually he was permitted to return to his family on condition that he took no rice seed with him; but when he went he concealed five grains in his foreskin. He planted them on the river bank by his own house, and from them comes all the rice in this "world." When the people of the underworld saw the roots, their ruler was so angry that he closed his kingdom; and no humans, except shamans, have ever again been able to visit it.

Most people believe that although human beings may become ghosts they cannot become spirits. In certain myths, however, they do, usually in consequence of disregarding the rules of proper behavior. A hunter wounded a pig in a forest, and when he caught up with it found that a hunting spirit (*tou gerachi*) was holding it up and drinking the blood. Instead of wisely going away, even though the spirit was at fault in taking another's pig, the hunter foolishly demanded some of the blood and refused to leave until he had some to drink as well. Eventually the spirit gave him some and he was at once transformed into a hunting spirit. When he returned home his wife sent him back to his proper place in the forest.

The lesson in these and similar stories is usually the same. Generally it is the human who suffers the more seriously for overstepping the boundaries of correct behavior, but sometimes it is an animal or spirit. The suffering may be regarded as a punishment, or it may be looked on as warning that an offence has been committed and that expiation is required to restore the proper order of things. According to the shaman quoted in the last section, spirits do not transgress the moral order and attack men unless hunger or poor control of their nature drives them. If they do, they can be brought to order by their fellows and rulers. To help men there are techniques for avoiding danger, and experts who know how to restore the balance when it has been upset, how to cure the harm caused by wrong or mistaken behavior.

MEDIATION AND MEDIATORS

The safest way of keeping out of trouble is to observe the *adet*, both in its social sense and in the extended meaning of proper behavior towards the symbolic order. But there are additional safeguards. A man about to embark on a risky project may make a vow (*niat*) to give a feast of thanksgiving if he accomplishes it safely; or he may, particularly if he is old, promise to give the most important of the shamanistic ceremonies (*aiyun*) for the enjoyment of the spirits in return for good health in the coming year.

Impending disaster or foolish behavior may also be averted by a warning dream (*nupei*) for dreams are one of the most important links between men and the symbolic order, and the correct understanding and interpretation of them is a serious matter. They may be conventional warnings whose meaning everybody knows (for example, to dream of a loose tooth in the right jaw foretells the probable death of somebody in the household), or they may be addressed personally to the dreamer, when they usually take the form of a benevolent old man or woman who gives warning or confers a favor. Nobody is quite sure who these persons are; they are not ancestors and everybody hesitates to call them spirits (*tou*), unless the dreamer is a shaman or a potential shaman and the spirit is instructing him. Similarly, the flight of birds and the behavior of certain animals carry warnings to prevent foolish behavior; but for whom or exactly why they are sent is no longer known, though few disbelieve their efficacy.

If in spite of the guidance of the *adet* and common sense combined with other warnings, a man does get into trouble and is not immediately killed, he is likely to suffer an illness of greater or lesser severity. He will then resort to mediators who are expert in diagnosing the cause of the trouble and prescribing the correct expiation or remedy for restoring the balance of nature and right relations among the different orders of being.

A man who has met with an accident or incurred an illness may first go to a herbalist magician (*dukum*) in the hope that his trouble is not serious; but he will soon, if not at the same time, also consult a carver of sickness images. From the symptoms of the illness the image maker decides what spirit may be attacking the soul (*bedua*) of the man. He then carves a likeness (*bilum*) of the spirit and spits betel nut juice at it, commanding the spirit to enter it. He holds the image over the sick person and pours water over it on to him, after which the image is taken to its appropriate place, that is, the dwelling place of the spirit in the forest or elsewhere. If the diagnosis is correct, the spirit is compelled to enter its image for three days and refrain from attacking the sick person. Both men and women may become *dukun* or *bilum* makers. These experts are not likely to be shamans, but if they are, they will not normally prescribe medicines or carve images if they are active shamans.

SHAMANISM AND SHAMANIST CEREMONIES

A man does not usually go to shamans (*a-bayuh*) for guidance in correct behavior until misfortune has overtaken him, because the shaman's principal task is to repair damage caused by spirits, not avert it. A shaman is a man or woman who is "a master of spirits." Normally himself a spirit-medium, the shaman is thought to control spirits by ritual techniques (Firth 1959:141).[2] Because of his familiarity with spirits and their habits, a shaman's advice about avoiding their attentions carries weight, but is seldom sought until it is needed for diagnosis and cure. At the same time he is potentially as dangerous as the spirits which possess him, and he must therefore be treated with circumspection.

No Oya Melanau myth explicitly tells of the origin of shamans; but the following is a summary of an episode in the Mueh Rejang, a series of versified stories formerly sung on ceremonial occasions:

> A man, Bunga Lawan, lived in a house on the bank of the very wide river, Ngam Pusan. On an island in it was a large tree, at the top of which Balou Belian and her sister Urip Raman lived in a house. A rattan (*sega' wai*) ladder led to the ground. One day Bunga Lawan fell from the ladder and lay seriously injured at the foot of the tree. His four friends, Juga, Sedawa, Panglima, and Ntala, found him and did not know what to do for they could not see the ladder. They therefore fetched four threads--Juga, a white one, Sedawa black, Panglima red, and Ntala yellow. All tried to throw their threads up and round the floor posts of the house, but only Ntala's yellow one reached. He then climbed up

to the house, followed by Juga and Sedawa. Panglima remained on the ground. All this took one month.

Balou Belian enquired the reason for the visit and Ntala told of Bunga Lawan's accident and death while they were trying to ascend the tree. He asked her to restore Bunga Lawan to life. The three men and the two women descended by way of the yellow thread, and Balau Belian picked up the bones of Bunga Lawan--all that remained of him--and wrapped them in a rich red cloth. They then crossed the river to Bunga Lawan's house. Balou Belian asked the men to make preparations for an *aiyun* ceremony, and to hand up a swing or cradle of *wai sega'* rattan. She placed the bundle of bones wrapped up in the cloth on it and began to rock the swing backwards and forwards. After six nights the bones again became flesh; but it was not until the seventh night that Bunga Lawan was able to speak. He at once asked Balou Belian to bathe him in coconut milk, after which he was completely restored to life and sense.

For her service Bunga Lawan gave her seven beads, one spearhead, one brass bowl, and one piece of gold. He escorted her and her sister home and later married Balou Belian.[3]

Unlike the herbalist magician and image maker, a shaman does not determine the cause of misfortune or illness by reference to symptoms, using his own judgement and experience; but he speaks in trance as the vehicle of his familiar spirit who makes the diagnosis. Because the shaman is, so to speak, the meeting place of men and spirits, he is a man set apart in some respects from other men; and because, too, of his special position, his relationships with spirits and men alike require care in their handling. His "public" relations with spirits occur mainly in curative ceremonies and mortuary rites; but if his moral nature is not upright, or if he lacks the strength to control the ill-nature of his familiars, he may, it is thought, prey on other men in private and act as a witch.

A shaman is able to approach the symbolic world with safety only if he can rely on spirit friends who have chosen him and taught him their names and the correct modes of calling them to him. A spirit, in the words of one shaman, may not be casually summoned: "He is not just called; if his name is not known he will not come; it is like making unintelligible noises at people." When the spirit arrives it uses the shaman's body, surrounding it, most people think, like a garment.

The incantation to the spirit is accompanied by beating a rhythm, peculiar to shamans, on the drum which the shaman acquired on becoming a full practitioner. He covers his head with a cloth, and when the spirit arrives he hisses loudly and shakes his head violently from side to side, so that in a female shaman her long, unbound hair swings round and round. One man described the taking of possession in these words:

> It is like being hit on the head; you fall sideways. You have to shake your head from side to side and hiss. The eyes are hot as when you smell onion (Another shaman described the approach of the spirit as being swallowed in a ball of fire, so that she was burned up in the heat.) The nature of a spirit is like a madman, and when a spirit is in me my nature is fierce and my talk angry. Spirits are all bad, and if the shaman is bad he will eat humans.

In addition to his drum and headcloth, a shaman must also have iron, usually in the shape of a spearhead, to bite for strength whenever he summons spirits. It is also needed for the patient and any assistant who may come into close proximity with the shaman and his familiars. Finally he will need water and certain kinds of foliage for washing and brushing the sickness out of the patient. These elements are the minimum essential equipment needed in any of the shamanistic curative ceremonies, which, because many of the spirits called up live in the underworld where night is day, are always held after dark.

The ostensible reason for a shamanistic ceremony is the private need of one individual, but it may have other functions. Matters concerning the village as a whole are often raised by the spirits at a seance; and controversial subjects can then be discussed openly or indirectly in ways not always possible elsewhere. The opinions of a spirit may carry weight because his sources of knowledge are thought to be greater than those of the villagers; but they can be ignored, too, either because the information is judged to be irrelevant, or because people are skeptical about that particular shaman and his familiars, or about the reality of his possession on that special occasion. For the Oya Melanau, however, shamanistic ceremonies do have a considerable significance; they are certainly more than merely minor mechanisms in helping to form public opinion. An *aiyun* (see below), for example, involves a large part of the neighborhood and draws together many people in social and religious activity. Whatever opinions people may hold of the principal shaman, the occasion is sacred, permeated by a sense of danger, awe, and mystery, and is one of the greatest affirmations of pagan beliefs.

Curative Ceremonies

In marked contrast with the proper distance that ought to be maintained between the different orders of being, the shaman's relationship with his familiar spirits is one of friendship; but in some senses it is always improper and attended by risk. He therefore does not call on them frivolously. Like human beings, spirits are busy creatures and resent unnecessary interruptions to their daily affairs. Like humans, too, they enjoy entertainment, good food, sweet scents, music, dancing, and good talk; so that if anybody through a shaman wishes to invite them to help him, he must provide a suitable reception, as he would were he to invite his friends and relatives to help him at a work party. For this reason shamanistic curing ceremonies are regarded as a series of entertainments, as it were, which ranges from a private domestic séance, where the shaman calls up a few of his more reliable spirits (like close friends visiting the family) to help in a household crisis, to the important and prolonged *aiyun* ceremony, which, though sponsored by one household, invites most of the village to attend (as at a wedding or mourning) and a large concourse of spirits as well. The equipment and ceremonial are consequently more elaborate.

The simplest routine ceremony to diagnose and cure illness is the *minget a-pedih*. It usually lasts one evening only. The shaman and his equipment must be fetched by a member of the household while the patient is made ready by a spouse or a parent. He is placed with his head to the east on a sleeping mat, visible to but apart from visitors. When all is prepared, the shaman and the patient bite a spearhead, and the shaman pours water or possibly coconut juice over the patient, who is now ready for treatment. He has been put into a ritual condition which separates him and also the assistant (spouse or parent) from the rest of the household, who, unless it is absolutely necessary, do not approach them until the ceremony in completed.

After the preparation the patient is taken back to his sleeping mat, and the shaman covers his own head and face in a cloth and begins an incantation to one of his familiars. On the spirit's arrival the shaman removes his headcloth, and the spirit asks why he has been summoned. The assistant shows him the patient, whom the shaman then examines. He may hold up his drum, which is open at one end, and place a lighted candle between the skin on the other end and the patient, and look through it into the patient's body to discover the cause of the illness. If the inspection is successful, the spirit through the shaman tells the assistant and the audience what is wrong; and they ask him to help. If he refuses he immediately departs, and the shaman hisses violently and shakes his head until the spirit has gone. The shaman then yawns several times and asks the assistant what happened. After discussing the matter, he summons up another familiar.

But if the first spirit does diagnose the cause of the illness, he will usually help cure it, though he may temporarily have to leave the shaman, still in trance, to fetch another spirit, who may not be a familiar, to assist him. When diagnosis and treatment are both agreed on, the shaman holds up his right hand and sings, asking for *pijer* from the sky spirits. *Pijer* are minute transparent stones and flowers from the overworld. At the end of the chant he shuts his hand, catching the gift, and rubs both palms together. He then presses the *pijer* into the crown of the patient's head. More are asked for and are pressed into the base of the throat, the belly, the back, and other places that are sore. The *pijer* are to strengthen the patient and help drive out the sickness.

The next step is to clean out the sickness and repair the damage it has done, so that the soul, if it has departed, may return in safety. First the shaman puts his lips on the places where the *pijer* were inserted and sucks out the sickness, at the same time silently bidding it depart. He then takes a bunch of leaves (*daun tebawan* [*Premna foetida Reinw.*]) and sweeps the patient from head to foot, sometimes singing aloud, but always bidding the sickness to go.

The treatment of the patient by this spirit is now complete, but before going he may stop to gossip and perhaps examine and treat other people. He may also advise further treatment of the patient by other spirits; for the cause of the illness may not be simple or single, and any one familiar's powers are limited. Moreover, if the "attack" has come from a spirit who has ill-will towards the patient, or who, on the contrary, has taken a liking for him and wishes to establish a permanent relationship of friendship, then the condition can be cured only by fetching the spirit concerned. The shaman's familiar may not be able to do this because he is not on good terms with the attacking spirit, or because the attacker intends the patient to undergo further ceremonies which will allow him to make his wishes known, and which may lead to the patient's full initiation as a spirit-medium and practicing shaman. But whether further treatment is advised or not, the shaman always summons other familiars, sometimes as many as fifteen to twenty in an evening.

The Melanau do not believe that all illnesses and deaths are caused by spirit attack. A common cold or other small ailment may be attributed to "wind" (*angin* or *pangai*)--an evil influence which floats in the air and affects human beings. Some animals, notably crocodiles, have the power to seize a man's soul, and if it not released by a shaman, the man will eventually be eaten by the animal. A very old person is thought to die naturally, but if he first suffers a long or sudden illness he is usually thought to be the victim of spirit attack. A man's soul may begin the journey to the land of the dead for many reasons, and if a herbalist or image maker cannot bring it back and restore a healthy balance, then the shaman and his familiars take over. It is the familiars who can find out whether the soul is being attacked by a witch, an animal, or another spirit. If the attack is by a hostile spirit, the man's recovery depends upon his making correct expiation; but if the illness is caused by a spirit's wanting the man's friendship, then the man must accept the fact, however unwelcome; for if he does not the spirit may kill him. He may resist for a time and continue in poor health, hoping that the spirit will desist; for the man's death will defeat the object of the attack, which is to establish a relationship with a human in this and no other world. It is this wish on the part of spirits to have friends in this world which makes it quite uncertain that a shaman will continue to be one in the land of the dead. It is thought that shamans undoubtedly exist there, but that they do not visit this world in order to make contact with human beings. When the ceremony of caring for the sick is over and the last spirit has gone, the patient may be de-sanctified by a further washing. This is not always thought necessary, but restrictions on the food he may eat and on undertaking ordinary work away from the house are usual. Sometimes the shaman and the assistant may also de-sanctify themselves by taking a special bath, though that is not often considered essential after a simple "caring for the sick."

In some respects caring for the sick is an informal ceremony, but the means it uses and the relationships it establishes between the social and the symbolic orders are not regarded casually. The space occupied by the shaman and his patient is sacred. It is a sanctuary in which men and spirits meet, it is also a small model of the World (*dunia*). In it the forces of good and evil are, so to say, more concentrated than in the ordinary world; and to enter it without rites of purification and strengthening is dangerous. Leaving it is also dangerous and requires further rites to adjust the humans to their normal life. The subsequent ceremonies of curing, which are also parts of the initiation of a shaman, attract a greater number of human and spirit guests, and therefore need a larger sanctuary, which is more fully furnished, and which, because of the greater number of beings present, is so to speak, more consistently sacred and must be treated with more formality.

Escorting the Spirits: *Menurun Tou* and *Beguda*[4]

When it becomes clear that the patient is not cured, or the illness recurs, he may decide to hold a *menurun tou* ceremony to ask the shamans's familiars to fetch the spirit who is causing the trouble, in the hope that the patient will be possessed by that spirit who will thus make his wishes known.

In this ceremony, which takes place on three successive evenings, the sacred area set aside for and the equipment used by the shaman, the assistant, the patient, and the spirits, are more carefully demarcated and more elaborate. There may be offerings of food; sweet-scented flowers are soaked in the water used for lustration; and instead of brushing the patient with leaves the shaman uses an unopened inflorescence of the *pinang* palm (*Areca catechu*), which must be taken from the eastern side of the tree. A larger number of spirits is summoned, and a lay drummer is employed so that the invited spirits may dance and sing on taking possession of the shaman or patient. In all other respects, however, the procedure is the same as in "caring for the sick."

A more elaborate form of the ceremony is known as *beguda*. It too lasts three evenings and has the same purpose as *menurun tou*, but is distinguished from it by the use of two *pinang* palm inflorescences and of woven decorations in the sanctuary. One inflorescence is wrapped in red cloth and hung from the roof (known as the sky) in the middle of a circlet of rattan (*sega' wai* [*Calamus* sp.]). The other inflorescence is used for brushing the patient.

The importance of this ceremony is that it is a necessary preliminary to the *aiyun*, and in it the "attacking" spirit is expected to take possession of the patient, who in turn is now expected to accept the perhaps unwelcome fact that he must enter a permanent and possibly dangerous association with a spirit. Exactly what the relationship will entail is slowly revealed by the spirit in dreams of instruction during the following months. Instead of waiting, however, the spirit may order the patient to undertake an immediate *aiyun* ceremony to confirm the friendship and complete his initiation as a spirit-medium in order to begin practice as a shaman with the least possible delay.

The Aiyun Ceremony[5]

The *aiyun* is the greatest of the shamanistic ceremonies, and the Melanau describe it as the "end of our remedies." A man who has agreed to *paiyun* knows that unless this ceremony appeases the spirit which is afflicting him, so that it takes possession of him, makes it wishes known, and allows him to recover his health, there is no more he can do except perform another *aiyun*. The purpose of the ceremony, then, is threefold: first to cure the patient; second, to restore the balance between the social and the symbolic orders; and third, to complete the patient's formal period of training as a shaman.

An *aiyun* may last five, seven, or even nine nights. Except for the annual ritual cleansing of the village (*kaul*) which is not a shamanistic ceremony, the *aiyun* is the most crowded and festive (*ramai*) occasion on which human beings and spirits meet. The preparations for it must be suitable and sumptuous. The material and ritual elements are basically those of the caring for the sick ceremony; but the sanctuary is larger, more carefully marked out, and more richly furnished. It is a large rectangle occupying as much as a third of the house's floor space, and is explicitly a model of the World. A white cloth is spread above the area to represent the sky, and a model house (*abun*) for the reception of the overworld spirits is placed on a rafter at the upstream end of the enclosure, close to one point of attachment of a rattan swing (*wai sega*) which is suspended right across the area. This swing is also called the *aiyun*, and it ought to be hung so that those who sit on it can swing east and west. It belongs to the officiating shaman and is the bridge that all spirits use to enter the sanctuary. Beside the *abun* is the end of a woven ladder (*taga yang*) which passes out of the building to a model boat (*rabong*) below--the place of reception for water and underworld spirits. From the center of the "sky" hangs one *pinang* inflorescence wrapped in red cloth, and in the sanctuary, below the *abun* and *taga yang*, is a bunch of bananas and a coconut. Food offerings are placed in the *abun*, the *rabong*, and on the floor of the sanctuary along with the rest of the essential equipment; the second *pinang* inflorescence for brushing the patients, a spearhead, a lighted candle, rice to feed the spirits, braziers and benzoin, and the shaman's drum. Outside the enclosure is a set of drums, brass gongs, Malay drums and tambourines, and even a violin, so that the orchestra may provide music appropriate to each spirit as it arrives.

The officiating shaman is known as the "father" or "mother" of the *aiyun*, and in addressing his or her familiars the shaman calls himself or herself their "grandfather" or "grandmother."[6] The shaman must have one lay assistant (*seladai*) even though other shamans may be helping. Assistant shamans are reluctant to participate fully because of the five days confinement to the house and the prohibitions of bathing, foods, and intercourse with spouses. The patient is known as the pupil (*murip*) and ever after remains in a kind of child relationship with the father or mother of his *aiyun*.

For the first three nights only the shaman, his assistants, and the patient may participate in the ceremony. Before entering the sanctuary they are purified;

pijer are pressed into the swing; the spirits are fed with rice; and the patient is treated by all the shamans present. At this stage these are the only people who may mount the swing in order to receive spirit visitors. During the third evening the shaman, holding his spearhead, leads the patient, followed by the assistant and participant shamans, to the edge of the river, where they scoop out water with their hands and catch fish and other water beasts, which are, however, visible only to the shamans. If the patient catches one that is dangerous or spiny, it is a sign that he will become a powerful and venomous (*bisa'*) shaman. The procession then returns to the sanctuary, and anybody who needs treatment may mount the swing. These are people who are ill and wishing to be cured, or who already have familiar spirits and wish to be possessed by them or by new familiars in order to learn their wishes.

At dawn, after the last evening's performance, three canoes in the river are lashed together and planks are laid across them to make a platform. Some of the decorations from the sanctuary are placed at each corner. The model boat (*rabong*) from below the house is put in the middle, and the shaman, the assistants, the patient, the orchestra, and paddlers go aboard. The three joined canoes are then paddled upstream to the head of the village and downstream again to a point on the bank well below it. The shaman stands at the prow calling spirits and casting rice for them to eat, and the orchestra plays. Other canoes, crowded with visitors, are lashed behind the three leading canoes, and the procession moves slowly through the village, gathering the spirits to it as it goes. At the chosen point on the river bank the model boat is raised onto a trestle and the decorations and offerings are placed in and around it. The patient and any others who wish, crouch beneath the trestle and the shaman and the helpers throw water over them. After much splashing and laughter, the procession returns to the house, where the sanctuary is dismantled under the supervision of the shaman. The participants in the ceremony are already partly de-sanctified by washing under the *rabong*, but the shaman, the lay assistant, the patient, and other helpers may sit on the swing once more; they are not, however, possessed by spirits, who are now supposed to have returned to their proper places after the purification below the village. The participants, unless they have received treatment which imposes taboos, are now free to return to normal life; but the return of the shaman and the patient from the sacred world of the sanctuary and the release of the patient from the special condition into which he entered when he began the series of *rites de passage*, beginning with the initial ceremony of caring for the sick and ending with the *aiyun*, are slower. Both shaman and patient are bound by restrictions on food, work, and movement for at least three days and sometimes until the next moon.

If the *aiyun* has been successful, the patient's formal initiation as a spirit-medium is now complete and he should regain his health. But he may still have to undergo a prolonged period of instruction in dreams before his new status is firmly established; and he is in some senses still in a transitional state. Before he ventures to practice as a shaman, even though invited to do so by other villagers, he must be secure in his relationship with his familiar; and he usually waits for more spirits to approach him in friendship, either in dreams or at *aiyun* ceremonies. This final training may be as difficult for the shaman and his household as any of the earlier stages when he was ill and emotionally unstable. The symptoms are still much the same as before, but the problem is now seen as a struggle between a human and spirits to set up an acceptable, though necessarily anomalous, relationship. With the help of his familiars, the shaman's soul at this time may visit different regions of the over- and underworlds; for to be effective he needs experience, powerful spirit friends, and a knowledge of their habits. It is, however, just such beings who are most dangerous. Failure to gain moral control over his familiars may cause him to become a witch and even to be executed by his fellow-villagers.

Mortuary Ceremonies

Traditionally a dead person is mourned for three, five, or seven nights. His body is then either buried in the ground or, if a first born infant son, or formerly if a person of rank and importance, is placed on a platform to await interment. During the wake, ceremonies are performed to see the soul safely on its journey to the underworld; but, except in one or two minor rites in which spirits are consulted to mark the progress of the journey, the services of shaman are not needed. When the soul arrives at the house of Balou Adet at the entrance to the land of the dead, a shaman is sent to take gifts and to bring back the souls of any living people who have accompanied the dead person. This task the shaman fulfills during the *platu* ceremony.[7]

A white mat known as the canoe is spread on the floor. Beside it is a woman's paddle and on it are three woven images of the spirits that guide a soul to the land of the dead, and also a pillow, a piece of gold, a spearhead, and the shaman's drum. Before beginning, the shaman tests one or two assistants who are to accompany him on the journey. These people have fasted all day, and in the test the shaman presses the carotid artery to render them temporarily unconscious and thus free their souls.

The shaman then sits on the mat and calls up a familiar to help him on his way. When it arrives, and if it agrees to go, he picks up the paddle, sits in the posture of a woman, and with the help of his paddlers sets off. On arrival he takes the gifts, some of which are for the relatives of the recently dead person who will come to Balou Adet's house to take him to his new home. Holding the gold and the spearhead, he steps off the mat and acts and talks as if he were going up into the house and were throwing food to the guardian dogs. The shaman and his assistants may go further into the land of the dead, if those he is sent to visit are no longer at the house. After he meets them, the living people at the ceremony, whose souls have made the journey with the dead person, are brought to him, and he presses *pijer* into their heads so that their souls may easily return. Sometimes the shaman himself brings them back; at other times he entrusts them to a fowl, which first has a few drops of blood taken from under the wing and is then thrown high over the heads of the assembly. His task completed, the shaman now returns home as fast as possible and in some apprehension because he and his assistants have tried to "steal" goods from the underworld.

The *platu* represents a journey and, unlike other shamanistic ceremonies, is not thought of as a festive meeting of men and spirits. Consequently music and elaborate preparations and decorations are not required; nevertheless, the "canoe" is a sanctuary, both sacred and dangerous.

THE SHAMAN

At any time the number of practicing shamans in the Oya River has always been small, and between 1948 and 1965 probably never exceeded a dozen. A man or woman needed to be seriously inconvenienced by prolonged ailments before undertaking the whole series of initiatory ceremonies. Moreover the illness had to be of a kind that did not leave him altogether unfit for an active life. All successful shamans have had histories of emotional disturbances and physical illness that go back several years, often to adolescence; most, too, are men and women of some imagination and intelligence. In addition to the practicing shamans there is also a much larger number of men and women who are spirit-mediums, in that they have preformed an *aiyun* and are fully possessed by familiars, but who are not compelled by them to practice as shamans, for the time being at any rate.

A shaman may be either a man or woman, but men, even more than women, are reluctant to assume the role. Correct Melanau etiquette, as prescribed by custom (*adet*), is contravened by the unseemly behavior of people under possession; and though illness may force a man into spirit-mediumship, most men strongly resist the further step of becoming an active shaman. A slave who attempted to practice might be thought presumptuous and unlikely to achieve an equal and satisfactory relationship with high ranking and therefore powerful spirits. Moreover, the role of a shaman is in many respects androgynous. There are stories of male shamans who lived as transvestites and of women who were unbecomingly masculine in the role; the possibility of such behavior is still today an element in the reluctance to become a full practitioner. Male shamans are seldom regarded with favor by the aristocrats and elders, who are the custodians of the social *adet*, and who fear that a shaman may use his knowledge of the symbolic *adet* to claim unwarranted authority. An aristocratic man in this position could be intolerable; and though it might be easier to resist a shaman of lower rank, there is always the fear of other-worldly retaliation. Such threats to entrenched rank are less from women, and most of the practicing shamans are in fact women. Of the men who take up practice most come from middle-ranking families. The male witches who are remembered from the past usually appear to have been men who were unduly ambitious, and who for one reason or another were unable to achieve secular honors, or who, like most of the women witches, had uncertain tempers and were unable to get on with their neighbors.

A method of resolving some of these difficulties would have been to confine shamanship to certain middle-ranking lines of descent, and if the ideal of endogamous marriage within the ranks had been observed, the threat to aristocratic interests would have been averted. A solution of this kind was in fact attempted, for it is said, "The spirits follow the blood," meaning that when a shaman dies his familiars are likely to establish an association with a close relative. But in a bilateral system of succession and inheritance, combined, as it is among the Oya Melanau, with a system of ranking in which an individual may use his pedigree in almost any way that is useful to claim position, and in which the ideal of rank endogamy is not strictly observed, a man can in fact aspire to almost any position in the society. To achieve high rank without the qualifications of birth he needs to be rich. He may, however, find his attempt resisted by the elders; consequently, an ambitious man who finds his opportunities for gaining power and prestige limited or blocked may, particularly if there is a history of spirit-mediumship in his family, try to realize his aims by becoming a shaman. But it is, and apparently always was, one of the last lines of endeavour.

The Melanau term *a-bayuh* refers principally to practicing shamans. It also applies to a spirit-medium who possess familiars but who does not practice as a shaman. Witches are always known as *a-bayuh bisa'* (venomous *bayuh*), but so also is a powerful and effective shaman. The only difference is that a witch has not mastered his familiars, and instead of acting as an intermediary preys on human beings. The victim is usually warned of this kind of attack by a dream of heads floating over his sleeping place. Sometimes another member of the household is warned in this way and not the victim himself. Illness or fatigue confirms the suspicion. It is said that a man in such circumstances first consults another shaman whose familiars attempt to dissuade the witch's spirits from continuing the attack; and that only if that fails does the victim or somebody else attack the witch physically. It is also believed that any human who has allowed his familiars to dominate him so completely is probably unable ever to control them again, though certain witches are said to have achieved this.

The dangers of being a shaman are reiterated in most conversations on the subject, and stories are told of men and women who, under the influence of familiar spirits, have turned rogue. Such stories are always set in the past. At night, it is said, such a shaman takes off his head and it flies to the sleeping place of its victim, where, according to some, it drinks his blood, or, according to others, eats his soul. In any event, illness and death are believed to follow.

There are many stories and some official records of the killing of such witches, though by no means all known witches died violently. One woman, whose husband had died not long before, reported in 1950 that she had divorced him many years earlier because he was a witch. She discovered the fact, she said, when she woke one night and found his headless body beside her. She was afraid to remain married to him, because the nature of such a man is completely under the control of his familiars; and he is therefore extremely dangerous. He takes offence at the slightest rebuff and does not spare the lives of even his own children. In another story the execution of a female witch did not end the matter, for her head continued to prey on the villagers from the grave, and was not stopped until the head was disinterred and reburied at a greater distance from the body and the village.

The social position which a man, or a woman, can hope to achieve as a shaman depends on a number of factors. The economic rewards are small and consist mainly of ritual gifts--spears, small amounts of gold, food, fowls, clothes, and a little money. Shamans therefore need other forms of economic support and practice part-time only. They do not participate in the administration of the *adet* or even act as leaders in the major communal rituals, unless they also have the proper secular qualifications and the confidence of the elders. Some reported witches seem to have exacted economic toll for a time, but the enterprise always was insecure and usually ended in failure.

Although the shaman's role as a mediator provokes ambivalent feelings, it is nonetheless recognized as a necessary service to the community. Some of his familiars are publicly known because they have consorted with his predecessors; but most are private, and their names and attributes remain unknown until he chooses to reveal them. His familiars are also appropriate in some ways to his position in life and his experience: a man who is widely travelled, for example, is likely to have Kayan and other foreign spirits for familiars. This fact adds to his reputation, so that Malays and even Chinese traders may send for him from distant places. Today women and the younger male mediums are more likely to be possessed by Malay (i.e., Muslim) spirits than by the older "traditional" type of spirit. Everybody now has some knowledge of the Malay language, and Malay customs are increasingly widespread. The orthodox Muslim ban on all relations with any spirits is, however, either unknown or disregarded. To the shaman it makes little difference whether his spirits' attributes are publicly well-known or not, whether they are good or evil, so long as they are thought to be powerful and he is believed to be in control of them.

Two Shamans

The following brief histories of two shamans indicate some of the reasons that led them to take up practice.

In 1964 N. was a man of 50 to 60 years. He was a man of middle rank (*bangsa bumi*), who for nearly thirty years had a high reputation as a shaman in the Oya River. His grandmother and other relatives had also been shamans, and the friends and relatives among whom he had lived most of his life were ritual experts of various kinds, but none were of the highest social rank. When he was adolescent he was seriously ill and remained for many months covered with a painful skin eruption. Eventually he retired to a solitary hut in the forest where a spirit who was both a snake and a woman instructed him in dreams how to cure himself by bathing in mud. He returned home and married a woman of the same rank as himself who came from the same section of the village. They had little sago land and were forced to work for other people. Neither was physically strong and both were often ill. Several children died. In time he preformed an *aiyun* and was possessed by a well-known familiar of his grandmother. His wife and the neighbors refused to allow him not to practice, but at first he did so unobtrusively and reluctantly. He was afraid, he said, that his familiar would turn on him if he refused. After a time he became guardian of the *belisieng* of Medong, the ritual object housing spirits used in the annual cleansing of the village ceremony. This office, which did not require its holder to be a shaman, also came to him from his mother's line and brought him in close contact with the elders, who were unwilling, however, to accept him as a member of their circle in the administration of the *adet*. On several occasions he quarrelled with the headman and other elders over the arrangement of village ceremonies. He gradually extended his practice to other villages and gained a great reputation, but was pointedly excluded from the company of the elders. In the 1950s when the price of sago slumped, he and his wife were compelled to retire to the River Igan to cultivate rubber gardens in some isolation; but he was still constantly pressed to return for shamanistic ceremonies. As the economic rewards were little, he tended to refuse, but often accepted if he was asked to act as an elder at a wedding. In 1964 he had almost established a position as an elder in the river, but not that of one whose word carried much weight in secular matters.

In 1964 S. was a widow living with her son-in-law and grandchildren. She too was middle rank (*bumi*). Although none of her immediate forebears had been shamans, her family--her brother--had been guardians of the *blisieng*. In 1950 she was a spirit-medium, and had, she said, always been delicate from adolescence. She did not practice as a shaman, except domestically. In 1954 she and her husband were seriously ill and her husband died. The news was kept from her as long as possible, and her recovery was slow. She performed an *aiyun* to help, and began to practice curing in a small way. Being a modest and diffident woman, she did so reluctantly, and has never acquired a great reputation; but in 1964 was one of the three shamans (all female) who regularly practiced in the village.

SHAMANISM AND SOCIETY

The relationship between a system of religious beliefs and a social system has in the past been viewed in a number of different ways.[8] Since Durkheim's work on the subject at the beginning of the century many anthropologists have considered religious beliefs to be collective representations corresponding closely, if not always exactly, with the system of social groups in the society holding the beliefs. Melanau beliefs and practices, for example, may be regarded as "one way of describing certain types of human behavior; the anthropologist's jargon and his use of structural models are other devices for describing the same types of human behavior" (Leach 1954:14). Each "layer" of the Melanau World is thought to be constructed on principles that are the same everywhere, and the inhabitants are held to be related to one another in the same general ways. The behavior of a man of a particular locality and rank in this the middle world necessarily reveals his position in it; but the rules which govern his behavior to other Melanau are different from those which apply to foreigners, whether Iban, Kayan, or entities of a completely different kind, such as animals or spirits. Iban *adat*, for instance, is known to be different from Melanau *adet*, and it is assumed that other creatures also have their own peculiar *adet*; but whatever the customs of "foreign" beings may be, it is necessary for a Melanau to have rules for dealing with them. These rules may be simpler and fewer than those governing a man's own village, but to be ignorant of or to ignore them can only cause trouble. A Melanau undertaking an *aiyun* or the ceremony of giving his daughter in marriage can do so with safety and satisfaction to himself and others only if he has knowledge of the appropriate *adet*; and in doing so he can be thought of as "saying things about social status" (Leach 1954:279). He does it in a language, as it were, which he shares with other Oya Melanau; and in it he indicates aspects not only of his rank, wealth, age, sex, and religious affiliations, but he also tells of his relationship with the spirit world. As in all language, too, the full implications of such statements can be properly understood only in the actual context.

The Melanau, then, look on spirits and other non-humans beings as members of foreign societies, so to speak, all of which make up the World or cosmos. Every creature has its appropriate place and mode of life; so that every creature and each part of the World is governed by its own particular *adet*. Ideally the whole is permeated and regulated by a principle of order--a principle of *adet*, in contrast with particular and local *adet*.[9] Like Melanau or Iban people, the various members of the non-human order are governed by their own *adet*, and nobody supposes that these must closely resemble one another, but it is believed that every creature everywhere is subject to *adet* in general and to an *adet* in particular. It is as if the Melanau thought that the World and the different beings in it formed a kind of loose composite or "international" society knit together by a commonly held idea of a "rule of law" (*adet*), and by certain practical arrangements for avoiding or resolving conflicts that arise between beings subject to different *adet*.

The shaman is, as it were, a kind of diplomat who is on good terms with members of various non-human societies. His spirit friends instruct him in the appropriate *adet* in each case and protect him from the dangers of offending influential personalities. Because of his special relationship with them, they are willing to help him to manipulate circumstances for the benefit of his human principals. Nevertheless, the occupation, in spite of all safeguards, is hazardous. By definition the role of shaman places a human in a marginal position which is indicated by his ambiguous behavior under possession and by the transvestite characteristics displayed in certain circumstances, and less often, by some shamans permanently. The marginal nature of the role is reinforced, too, by the belief that he must possess unusual moral qualities if he is to control his familiars successfully and use his special knowledge in mediating between humans and non-humans.

A meeting between potentially hostile beings of any kind is necessarily dangerous; and when it occurs in a "charged" area such as a sanctuary, then the dangers are likely to be redoubled. The efficacy of the sanctuary and the truce observed in it derive in part from the belief that it is both a model of the larger World and in some sense a reproduction of an earlier stage of history when there were no barriers and all beings were able to mingle freely and safely. At the same time this "re-creation" exists in the present World where matters are differently ordered; moreover, the powers of all beings mingling in it are concentrated, so to say, in a small compass, and are consequently even more dangerous. Any human who enters it is in a greater or lesser degree contaminated by its "holiness;" and for his own sake and other people's safety he must be carefully prepared before submitting to such an ordeal. He also needs ritual purification and a period of isolated "decontamination" after being subjected to such dangers. The initiation of a shaman and every encounter with spirits under his guidance are therefore *rites de passage*, which subject him and other participants in them to all the conditions and limitations of such rituals.

Although many shamans and experts believe that spirits and other non-human beings have a "social" order that in some respects corresponds with that of the Melanau (for they speak of invisible longhouses, spirit *rajas*, and high and low ranking spirits), nevertheless nobody is dogmatic about it. These are "things not seen; how can we know?" Besides, the matter is not very important; nobody expects foreign villages and their *adet* to be replicas of Melanau villages. On the other hand, everybody does expect that the basic rules which govern a Melanau in his behavior to alien beings, whether human or not, shall be approximately of the same kind throughout the World. In this, and only in this sense can the social and the symbolic orders be said to correspond.

Any collectively held view of the symbolic order is, of course, among other things normative in purpose. There is therefore always likely to be a tendency for the social and symbolic orders to correspond. The Melanau of Sarawak live, and apparently always have lived, in a highly diversified social environment in which many cultural and linguistic groups are interspersed with and closely related to one another. In so far as this environment forms a system it is a composite or plural one. The model of the World which the Melanau use for thinking about themselves indicates this state of affairs. Furthermore, the view that all human and non-human societies constitute a field of diplomatic relations, so to speak, is one that they share with many of the other peoples of Borneo, and it may also be that it is an outlook more generally characteristic of multi-cultural situations of this kind, in which the constituent parts, though in the main politically and economically independent of one another, do nevertheless form one kind of loose composite or plural society.

ACKNOWLEDGEMENTS

The field work on which this article is based was made possible by grants from the Colonial Social Science Research Council and the Sarawak Government from 1948 to 1950, and from the London School of Economics and Political Science in 1963-64. My thanks are also due to many Government Departments and Administrative Officers in Sarawak. To the then Curator of the Sarawak Museum, the Mr. Tom Harrison, and his staff I owe a special debt of gratitude, in particular to Mr. Tuton Kaboy, who worked with me as an assistant in the field. I am also deeply in debt to Professor Sir Raymond Firth, the late Sir Edmund Leach, and my wife, the late Barbara E. Ward, who at different times have guided, commented on, and criticized all my work on the Melanau.

NOTES

1. *Melaikat*: a Malay word rarely used in 1950 by pagans in the Oya River.

2. The term *a-bayuh* denotes both spirit-medium and shaman, but the distinction made by Firth is well understood by the Melanau. "Spirit possession is a form of trance in which actions of a person are interpreted as evidence of a control of his behavior by a spirit normally external to him. Spirit-mediumship is normally a form of possession in which the

person is conceived as serving as an intermediary between spirits and men. The accent here is on communication; the actions and words of the medium must be translatable, which differentiates them from the behavior in mere spirit possession or madness" (Firth 1959:141).

3. In modern Melanau *balou* means widow, but *belian* has no significance except that of ironwood. Cf. Wilkinson 1959(1):

   Belian. I. Shaman, sorcerer, sorceress in touch with the spirit world . . . The word . . . is in use in Java, Bali, Borneo and Halmahera and is (etym.) the true word for shaman . . .

   Most of the elements of this myth can be paralleled in shamanistic cults elsewhere (cf. Eliade 1964:145-214).

4. Wilkinson 1959(1): *Guda; Goda*: Inciting; tempting; bringing pressure to bear; to rack. Entym., even of forcible pressure, but usually of seduction or temptation.

5. Wilkinson 1959(1): "*Ayun.* Swaying, swinging. . ." In Melanau *aiyun* is either a baby's cradle or the rattan swing on which the shaman and patients sit and rock backwards and forwards waiting for the spirits to take possession. The Sarawak Malay verb *beraiyun* (Melanau *paiyun*) is the term most commonly used for the ceremony in the literature.

6. The use of these kinship terms in the context of the sanctuary indicates that the shaman is for the time being indeed a master of spirits and men. The model of the World in which he is operating is of his construction and under his control. The terms indicate, too, that he is more than a mere intermediary; he is also a man of high position and power, the host of a varied collection of guests whose comfort and safety are in his keeping. In one aspect of his role he is a diplomat, so to speak, standing between the human and the non-human orders; but he is at the same time more than that, since he exercises power over the beings in "his World." It sometimes happens that on arrival a spirit is confused and alarmed, and he is reassured by the shaman himself or his lay assistant. The following words spoken at one *aiyun* by a lay assistant are typical: "Do not be afraid. You are invited by your grandfather. It is he who is in charge of this crowded and friendly (*ramai*) occasion."

7. The Melanau verb *pela* means to paddle a canoe. See also Buck 1933, and Jamuh 1951.

8. In this paper I am principally concerned with the examination of Melanau beliefs about shamanism as a functional part of the social system which validates norms of behavior, and I am not concerned with the study of their meaning as part of the Melanau system of classification and symbolism. In my opinion the two types of investigation are quite distinct and equally valid. The former approach, though derived from Durkheim, owes its development in England largely to Malinowski and his students.

"Myth fulfills in primitive culture an indispensable function: it expresses, enhances, and codifies belief; it safeguards and enforces morality; it vouches for the efficiency of ritual and contains practical rules for the guidance of man...it is...a pragmatic charter of primitive faith and moral wisdom" (Malinowski 1948:79).

Firth takes essentially the same view when he writes: "Religious belief helps to provide organizing principles for human existence. In its content, its form, and its expression it is related to the attempts of people to give coherence to their universe of relations, physical as well as social" (Firth 1951:225).

9. This interpretation of Melanau statements was formulated in the field, and when put to informants was agreed to by them. Accounts of views held by other peoples in Borneo were found at a later stage to be in substantial agreement with Melanau ideas. Cf. Schärer (1963:75): "It is not only humanity that possesses *hadat*, but also every creature or thing (animal, plant, river, etc.), every phenomenon (e.g. celestial phenomena), every period and every action, for the entire cosmos is ordered by the total godhead and every member and every part of the cosmos possesses its own place in this order, allocated by the total godhead, and has to live and act according to this ordained place."

Of the Iban in Sarawak, A. J. N. Richards writes: "By the proper conduct of ritual, from the major and minor 'festivals' (*gawai*) to the provision of offerings, the exercise of 'magic' and utterance of words of power, the people and their possessions must be kept in a satisfactory state of balance among themselves and in relation to the 'unseen powers.'" (Richards 1963:1)

REFERENCES

Buck, W. S. B.
    1933   Notes on the Oya Milanos. Sarawak Museum Journal 4(13):157-174.

Eliade, M.
    1964   Shamanism. Translated by Willard R. Trask. New York: Pantheon Books.

Firth, R.
    1959   Problem and Assumption in an Anthropological Study of Religion. Journal of the Royal Anthropological Institute 89(2):129-148.

Jamuh, G.
    1951   Some Melanau Pastimes. Sarawak Museum Journal 5(3):446-456.

Leach, E. R.
    1954   Political Systems of Highland Burma. London: London School of Economics and Political Science.

Malinowski, B.
    1948   Magic, Science and Religion and Other Essays. Boston: Beacon Press

Morris, H. S.
    1953   Report on a Melanau Sago Producing Community in Sarawak. London: Her Majesty's Stationery Office.

Richards, A. J. N.
    1963   Dayak Adat Law in the Second Division. Kuching.

Schärer, H.
    1963   Ngaju Religion. Translated from the Dutch by R. Needham. The Hague: Martinus Nijhoff.

Wilkinson, R. J.
    1959   A Malay-English Dictionary. 2 vols. London: MacMillan.

FROM SHAMANS TO PRIESTS:
TOWARDS THE PROFESSIONALIZATION
OF RELIGIOUS SPECIALISTS AMONG THE KAYAN

JÉRÔME ROUSSEAU
McGill University

The Baluy Kayan have two major categories of religious specialists: priests and shamans. In this context, priests are experts who are trained in the performance of established ritual procedures, while shamans are religious practitioners whose efficacy derives directly from possession by spirit helpers. We will see that, while the theological principles behind priesthood and shamanism are similar, priests have a more important religious role than shamans, and a higher social status. The distinction between priest and shaman is not general in central Borneo.[1] Indeed, everything suggests that their respective roles were originally performed by the same person, and that a differentiation followed the increasing use of religion as an ideological tool to support the traditional system of inequality.

The Kayan are a stratified society which emphasizes the contrast between hereditary leaders and their followers. Stratification has economic and political aspects: chiefs receive corvees from commoners and control the labor of their slaves; they are the undisputed leaders, who rule in an autocratic fashion (although commoners manage to influence and modify their decisions). The chiefs' power is based on their political role (Rousseau 1990:199-212), but they also rely on religion to justify their position (Rousseau 1990:183-187). Kayan religious beliefs establish that chiefs, and the ruling estate in general, are imbued with supernatural power, and this is a reason why lack of respect towards them can bring supernatural retribution as well as fines. Religion is also integrated to chiefship insofar as the chief sets the dates of the rituals of the annual cycle.

The institution of priesthood contributes further to bring religion within the ambit of political control, as it calls for trained religious specialists paid for their services. Unlike shamans, their religious efficacy is not justified primarily by the presence of spirit helpers, but by their correct performance of formally-established rituals. This can be contrasted to the inherent egalitarianism of shamanism, in which direct contact with the supernatural is the only qualification. Priests perform the rituals of the annual cycle, as well as other communal rituals, under the authority of the chief; furthermore, they are co-opted into the power structure by joining the select group of men who advise the chief. We will see that the revelatory aspects of religious specialization are still relevant to priesthood, but they are encapsulated in a more formal structure, while shamans, for whom direct contact with spirits remains fundamental, are marginalized within the religious system.

In the late 1940s, the Baluy Kayan replaced their traditional religion (*adat Dipuy*) with an indigenous reform, *adat Bungan*. After initial adjustments, this reform maintained the same belief system and most rituals of *adat Dipuy*, but these rituals were now less onerous and less time-consuming. Another benefit of the reform was the disappearance of the old taboos and omens. Because the rituals of the old religion have been kept in *adat Bungan*, the role of religious specialists has been relatively unchanged by the reform, and, except where otherwise specified, the following description applies equally to *adat Dipuy* and *adat Bungan*.[2]

While all Kayan have a role to play in their religion, there is a clear contrast between laity and religious specialists. Priests are called *dayong*, and shamans *dayong na'ah*. To make matters somewhat more complicated, "*dayong*" also refers to a), a specific kind of ritual performed by priests, but not by shamans, and b), a particular kind of spirit. Kayan terminology underlines the centrality of priests: priests (*dayong*) are those who perform the *dayong* ceremony, while shamans (*dayong na'ah*) are only a sub-category of *dayong*.[3]

SPIRIT HELPERS AND RELIGIOUS VOCATION

> The link between affliction and its cure as the royal road to the assumption of the shamanistic vocation is thus plain enough in those societies where shamans play the main or major role in religion and where possession is highly valued as a religious experience (Lewis 1971:70-71).

In religions "where shamans play the major role," the path to religious specialization comes through illness and cure by a spirit. This principle remains in Kayan religion, but it has been profoundly transformed: people with spirit helpers are not expected to become religious specialists. An automatic link between possession and religious authority would go against attempts to limit access to positions of power (Rousseau 1990:163-215); thus, it is not surprising that spirit possession has become only one factor in priesthood.

Most Kayan acquire spirit helpers. There are several categories of spirit familiars, some of which are called *dayong*. The relationship between human and spirit is established through a dream or an illness; in order to deal with the disturbance, the patient hires a priest, who performs a curing ritual (also called *dayong*); by means of divination, the priest identifies the spirit (or spirits), and reveals that these spirits wish to become the familiars of the person whom they have afflicted. During the ritual, the *dayong* spirits come to dwell within the patient, thus curing him or her and establishing a permanent bond.[4] The attitude towards spirit helpers is somewhat similar to the traditional Catholic belief in guardian angels. In the old religion, spirit helpers served as important intermediaries to the other world; they have lost some of their importance in *adat Bungan*, because most prayers are addressed directly to its central deity, Bungan.

In most cases, the association with a *dayong* spirit does not create the obligation to be a religious specialist. The requirement to become a priest or a shaman follows from possession by specific sub-categories of *dayong* spirits; some of them are priestly spirits, others shamanistic spirits, and their identity establishes the nature of the religious calling: each category of spirit has a set of distinctive skills which are transmitted to the human counterpart. Most religious specialists have several spirit helpers: there are so many rituals, and so many offerings to be conveyed to spirits, that a single *dayong* spirit would be inadequate for the task. The efficacy of priests and shamans is related to the number and power of their familiars. Spirit helpers of priests are all male, while those of priestesses are both male and female. During rituals, *dayong* spirits dwell within their human counterparts and are a source of their effectiveness. Possession takes the form of a trance in shamanistic performances, but entails no altered state of consciousness among priests.

In contrast with some Borneo groups (e.g. Mallinckrodt 1924:535, Jensen 1974:63, 143; Sutlive 1976), religious specialists are not recruited from among those who suffer physical or psychological handicaps, or are otherwise not "normal." Indeed, A. W. Nieuwenhuis (1904:111) specifically notes that while women with various kinds of nervous disorders, such as epilepsy, are not rare among the Kayan, they do not become religious specialists; the latter are staid and stable community members. Kayan religious practitioners thus do not play the sexual role of Barito priestesses, who were also prostitutes (cf. Mallinckrodt 1924:535).

While a supernatural calling is a common factor in priesthood and shamanism, priests and shamans have very different tasks, become specialists in different ways, and have distinct social characteristics.

Priests

Avun, the senior priest (*dayong aya'*) of Uma Bawang, turned to priesthood as a youth. He had recurring dreams in which he travelled with spirits; he became interested in priesthood and approached the senior priest of the time, who became his teacher; every time the latter performed a ritual, Avun sat by him to learn and imitate. In his passion for all things religious, Avun also memorized the myths of origin which his mentor had learnt from an aristocrat who had spent much of his adult life travelling through central Borneo to broaden his knowledge of religious practices and beliefs.

By contrast, Huring, an Uma Bawang woman, had manifested no particular interest in priesthood until she became ill and her ailment was diagnosed as a consequence of a *dayong* spirit's wish that she be a priest. She accepted the calling and was cured, but she performed her trade as rarely as possible, just enough to satisfy her familiar, because she was shy about being the center of attention. Huring's case exemplifies the fact that some people initially resist the spiritual summons, but they submit to it if the disturbance persists. For other priests, evidence of spirit possession (manifested in a dream, and confirmed by divination) follows a personal interest in priesthood.

While priesthood is the result of a supernatural calling, candidates to the priesthood must first spend several years learning the rituals, during which they perform parts of rituals under the direction of their mentor.[5] In private sessions, the young priest memorizes long orations. Postulants are recognized as priests only after a ritual which may be performed only by a senior priest during the harvest festival. In the same way that each individual has a "pole of life" (*tuken urip*) in the other world, whose fate affects health and survival, priests also have a "priestly pole" (*tuken dayong*), which is erected at the occasion of this ceremony.[6] Every few years, during the harvest festival, every priest should undergo an almost identical ceremony, in order to "repair the pole of the *dayong*" (*neme tuken dayong*). Priests who are much in demand undergo this ritual more frequently (e.g. every other year), to guarantee that they maintain their efficacy, and to protect them against supernatural dangers.[7]

Priests are in charge of all communal ceremonies, including the rituals of the agricultural cycle. They also perform most rites of passage, i.e. naming rituals, weddings, and funerals. Finally, they officiate at *dayong* ceremonies. Each domestic unit is expected to sponsor three *dayongs* every year as part of the ritual cycle; in addition, these also take place whenever needed as curing rituals, or to provide other supernatural blessings to the household.

The structure of calendrical and critical *dayong* rituals is the same: they are intercessions to the spirits, who are asked to help humans; priests seek their goodwill through prayers, flattery, and offerings. People commonly hire two priests for a *dayong*, although this is not a ritual requirement. When there are two priests, one is in charge, the other is an assistant. The ritual starts in the apartment, where offerings are laid out. The priest puts on a bead wristband (*leku dayong*); household members touch the offerings to indicate their participation, then the priest utters some introductory prayers. Household members narrate their dreams, the significance of which is tested through divination. The second phase takes place on the gallery, where the altar (*jok*) is set up; the sacrificial animal is placed beside it. The priest talks to the animal for about an hour, giving it messages to convey to the other world; after that, the animal is killed and household members are purified and protected with its blood and other ritual implements. Then there is a break in the ritual, during which the offerings are stored in the apartment and a meal is prepared, the *pièce de résistance* of which is the sacrificial pig or chicken; it is served to the priest and the household members, sometimes to guests as well. The ritual resumes on the gallery; the priest calls his/her *dayong* spirits and, with their help, travels to the other world to carry the offerings to Bungan and other spirits. Towards the end, the priest catches the household members's souls and returns them to their bodies. During the third phase of the *dayong* ritual, which lasts until 2 or even 5 a.m., the priest sings almost constantly, with men in the audience singing responses at the appropriate moments.

Priests who are good singers are particularly sought after: a *dayong* is an artistic performance as well as a religious event. After the end of the ritual, priests may be asked to sing extracts from epic poems. I was always impressed by their stamina, when, after a ten-hour ritual, they proceeded to sing for an hour or two. Indeed, some priests, who were hired in consecutive days by several households, were able to perform night after night.

The lengthy apprenticeship of priesthood is a consequence of the number and complexity of rituals which they have to learn. Few priests master all the rituals, and it is sometimes necessary to seek a religious specialist in another community, especially for unusual or dangerous procedures, such as counter-sorcery, rituals which strengthen the efficacy of priests, and some curing rituals.

For public ceremonies, the senior priest of the village may organize matters independently or at the chief's request. For *dayong* rituals and rites of passage, the sponsoring household visits the priest in his/her apartment (or farm house, as the case may be). At that occasion, the priest obtains preliminary information about the reasons for the ceremony, and may specify some ritual requirements and name his fee. When a priest is hired from another village, the sponsoring household is responsible for his transportation in both directions. If the priest is not ready to travel immediately, another trip may be necessary to pick him up at his convenience. Priests are not allowed to refuse to perform a *dayong*, otherwise their spirits will punish them with illnesses which can be cured only by an experienced priest. This is one reason why priests agree to officiate in other villages, despite the inconvenience.

In the old religion, the priesthood could provide significant material rewards (Nieuwenhuis 1904:110-111); fees (*tibah*) are now more modest, though still not inconsiderable. In some villages, priests are not paid for communal rituals, but fees are an essential requirement of other rituals, otherwise the spirit helpers would be offended and would punish the priest. For a *dayong* ritual, a priest must receive at least a wrist-band of beads (*leku dayong*) and two scoops of husked rice. Usually, priests also ask for a sword and money (mostly between M$5 and M$30 in 1970). There may be additional items, such as a tray or a gong, and two yards of unbleached cloth. The value of the fee depends on the nature of the ritual and the supernatural danger associated with it. If there is more than a single officiant, both may receive the same payment, but usually, the more experienced priest performs the most important parts of the ceremony and receives a higher fee.

The number of priests varies from village to village. In 1970-72, Uma Bawang and one other Kayan village of the middle Baluy each had four priests; two villages had three priests each, three villages had two priests, while one village had no priest at all. Accomplished priests are called *dayong aya'* (*aya'* = "big"). Some rituals are performed only by them: thus, only a *dayong aya'* would dare treat a patient affected with madness (*buling*).[8] This rank depends on seniority and religious knowledge, but is not an office; some villages have no *dayong aya'*, and a community may have more than one *dayong aya'*, although this is uncommon.

Shamans

Shamans (*dayong na'ah* or *dayong ngujut*) occupy a more marginal position in Kayan religion. Kayan shamans are curers, and their services are used primarily for treating women and children.

In theory, the same individual could be both priest and shaman, as long as he or she had the appropriate spirit helpers, but I know of no such case. Priestly rituals and shamanistic séances are distinct and take place at different times, but shamanistic spirits sometimes impinge on *dayong* rituals, especially the *dayongs* of the harvest festival. At a specific moment of the ritual, shamanistic spirits manifest themselves because they wish to play. They possess some women, especially older women, who dance around the altar (*jok*) in a trance. While this is a valid religious experience, it makes priests--and men in general-- uncomfortable, and if it shows no sign of rapidly coming to an end, men intervene, first verbally, then by gently constraining the movements of women who are flailing in an apparently uncontrolled fashion, so that they can come out of trance and the orderly performance of the *dayong* ritual may proceed. Priesthood and shamanism also cross paths when, at the occasion of *dayong* rituals, shamans make offerings to their spirit counterparts. It is also permissible for a shamanistic cure to take place during a lull in a *dayong* ritual, but this is uncommon.

As for priesthood, shamanhood is the result of a spiritual calling but, for shamans, it manifests itself through trances rather than dreams. At first, the trances are uncontrolled; the person "dies" (*mate*), and is revived with the noise of gongs. With time, the relationship between human and spirit is harmonized. We saw that some priests obtain the portents of their vocation after they have developed a personal interest in priesthood. I cannot say whether the same is true of shamans, because those whom I met were not very reflective about their vocation. While the efficacy of a shaman derives entirely from spirit helpers, and there are no standard procedures, would-be shamans learn their trade by imitating established colleagues, who also help them control their spirits. During séances, the mentor also provides encouragement: in the middle of a séance, a fledgling shaman expressed herself unable to treat a patient; her teacher egged her on, saying "If you cannot, who will?"

I attended a ritual in which the *dayong* spirits were made to possess the would-be shaman.[9] The woman was held by two persons (who were replaced by others when they became tired) who made her dance. Her eyes were closed, and she looked as if she was about to faint. Her helpers made it possible for her to lose control without hurting herself, so she could be receptive to spirits. Little by little, she danced more independently, and eventually her attendants moved away. She asked for a hornbill-feathers headdress (*lavong tingang*) and a sword, and danced for a long period. She sang, and the men made responses (*nyabe*). People blocked the stairs to prevent her from going out, which she tried to do a few times. Afterwards, she treated patients, thus performing her first shamanistic cure.

There may be several shamans in a village. In 1970-72 in Uma Bawang, there were two active shamans, both elderly women. While priests are treated with respect, people make fun of shamans; the more bizarre their antics during a séance, the better, as this is evidence of the spirits' presence. I noted earlier that religious specialists are not recruited from among those who suffer physical or psychological handicaps, or are otherwise not "normal." While this statement is entirely correct for priests, Kayan shamanism may sometimes be "an alternate route to normality" (Sutlive 1976). Shamans whose everyday behavior is considered peculiar tend to be seen as particularly effective (*bisa*) and are in great demand. Thus, a Kajang man who married into the Kayan village of Uma Juman had a wide reputation in the Baluy; he was intelligent, quick-witted, self-important, and unstable. He said that he actually saw spirits, a claim other shamans do not make. His performances were very theatrical, and he conversed with spirits in mysterious languages. To bolster his image, he tried, by reinterpreting genealogies, to demonstrate that he was a high aristocrat (*maren*), an absurd claim which commoners would normally never make for fear of supernatural sanction. In 1972, he had become Christian, but continued to perform shamanistic séances, in which he included prayers to God (*Tuhan*). On the other hand, most shamans are indistinguishable from their fellow villagers in terms of personality or life history (except of course for their spiritual calling).

While in trance, shamans extract a disease-causing object from the patient by sucking it out or pulling it out with the fingers. Some shamans produce a gob of wax or a small piece of string or wood, which they identify as the cause of the ailment. Unlike the dayong cure, the shamanistic cure is immediate. While a shamanistic séance is set up in order to treat one person in particular, the shaman also attends to other patients, who may not belong to the same domestic unit.

Séances take place at night in an apartment or on the gallery. The shaman first gets into a trance, so that spirits will come to dwell inside her. The first evidence of their presence is the shaman's stumbling and inner-directed look. Spirits speak with the shaman's mouth, their identity being made evident by their voice or by self-introduction. Within the course of the evening, the shaman is likely to be possessed by a number of spirits, and her voice and demeanor will change several times; at one moment, she may speak in a high falsetto, then in a gravelly voice. Through the shaman's mouth, spirits sometimes engage in a dialogue with each other, and members of the audience also converse with them. The antics of the spirits are an opportunity for men to make jokes about the shaman's behavior, but this does not mean that they doubt the shamans' efficacy or the reality of the trance.

The shamanistic séance is in a true sense a performance. Spirits act out their desires: they ask for rice beer and cigarettes, which the shaman consumes. Some spirits have sex on their mind, which the shaman manifests with obscene gestures, as when a female shaman mimicked a man copulating, to uproarious laughter. Spirits are encouraged to dance to the accompaniment of a repetitive tune played on a three stringed-instrument (*sape' dayong*). Shamans share the same basic procedures, but they each have their idiosyncrasies, dictated by their specific spirit helpers.

Like priests, shamans may be hired from other villages. The Kayan would not employ priests of other ethnic categories, such as the Kenyah or Kajang, because their rituals are very different, but there is no problem in using the services of non-Kayan shamans, given the absence of any standard shamanistic procedure. One may even hire nomadic shamans. I heard several accounts of this, and Charles Hose also mentions the practice (see also Pauwels 1935:350):

> The medicine men or *dayongs* of the Punans are distinguished for their knowledge and skill, and are in much request among the other tribes for the catching of souls and the extraction of pains and disease. They are therefore fairly numerous...Their methods do not differ widely from those of the Kayan and Kenyah *dayongs* (Hose and McDougall 1912 (2):190).

Compared to a *dayong* ritual, shamanistic séances are very inexpensive, and this is one of their attractions; a few renowned shamans may command high fees, but most of them receive only token payments. It is not uncommon for people to hire a shaman at first, and then turn to a priest for a *dayong* ritual if the patient does not improve. Also, while one usually hires two priests for a *dayong* ritual, people require the services of a single shaman. Unlike priests' fees, no specific items must be given to the shaman, except for a bracelet of cheap beads.

SOCIAL ASPECTS OF PRIESTHOOD AND SHAMANISM

The Kayan explanation of religious specialization is straightforward: people become religious specialists because spirits have so decided, and religious specialization is thus beyond human control. In fact, social factors are important in their selection and status.

Outside of religious contexts, religious specialists are not set apart from other people. Indeed, even during ceremonies, they wear no ceremonial dress (except for a bead wristband).[10] In daily life, the only marker which identifies some people as priests is their personal name. Through the *dayong* ritual, most people acquire a ritual name (*aran dayong*), which does not supersede their usual name: the ritual designation is used only in religious contexts. By contrast, priests are often known by their ritual name, rather than the name given at birth. Such names as Avun ("white cloud"), Lirong ("bay"), and Tening ("limpid") are reserved for priests (Rousseau 1983:253). To my knowledge, the shamans are never known by their ritual name. Thus, the use of ritual names for priests emphasizes their special position, but shamans are not singled out in this way.

In *dayong* rituals, only men are allowed to sing responses (*nyabe*) to the priest's chant. Nonetheless, both men and women may become priests and shamans. Some tasks, such as the journey to Ujet Bato'--the area of the other world where the souls of powerful people sometimes escape--are performed only by male priests. It would be dangerous (*parit*) for a priestess to attempt this journey.

In the Kayan villages of the middle Baluy area, I counted fourteen priests and eight priestesses (Rousseau 1974:430). While it may be rather audacious to speculate on the basis of such a small sample, I have the impression that there is a bias in favor of male priests; by contrast, there are many more female than male shamans. In other words, men predominate in the most prestigious category of religious specialists, while shamans, who rarely gain status because of their specialization, are mostly women. This distribution is also congruent with Kayan ideas about human nature: men have stronger souls than women and can engage in activities which would be dangerous to women, especially coming into contact with powerful spirits or handling potent rituals and practices. Women are more liable than men to be possessed by shamanistic spirits. The priesthood involves controlling, or at least influencing, the supernatural world, while shamanism is a surrender to the spirits.[11]

Women priests have a somewhat lower status than male priests; they are thought to have less supernatural power than their male counterparts, although a woman can become a senior priest (*dayong aya'*). On the other hand, priesthood improves a woman's status, at least in men's eyes. Thus, priestesses are more likely than other women to participate actively in public discussions.[12]

In terms of personal characteristics, Kayan priests are not markedly different from the population at large, but I derived the impression that priesthood tends to attract people who are intelligent, as well as knowledgeable about and interested in their culture, including non-religious matters. The senior priest of Uma Bawang was a case in point: religious knowledge was a central focus of his life; he pondered myths of origin, to which he referred in everyday conversation. He was also interested in traditional arts: for several years, he persevered in trying to make a good reed organ (*keledi*), a musical instrument which has fallen into disuse, and whose sound he wished to hear again.

However, the ability to sing, an interest in traditional songs, and superior intelligence are not necessary requirements for priesthood. Some people who wish to become priests, and sing beautifully, are frustrated in their ambitions if they do not receive the supernatural calling; by contrast, one Uma Bawang priest generally considered to be dull-witted, and who sang terribly, was very effective because of the help of the Thunder, one of his spirit familiars.

I mentioned earlier that priesthood is not "an alternate route to normality," but can note here an apparent exception. I heard of one instance of a transvestite priest, who was active some time before the second World War: Lake' La'ing *jok* Doh[13] of Uma Nyaving. He was already adult by the time he took on a female social identity. He wore women's clothes, had long hair like a woman, had a husband (and he was apparently a jealous man, fearing that his husband would sleep with other women) and he did women's work. However, he was not tattooed on arms and legs as women normally are. He was deemed to have great supernatural power, and he was paid accordingly. The significance of this transvestite priest must be understood in its social context: I was told that most villages had at least one berdache, and these men took on a female social identity *without* becoming priests;[14] Lake' La'ing *jok* Doh was the only example which my informants knew of. From my informants' comments, I cannot assume that priesthood was for Lake' La'ing *jok* Doh an alternate route to normality, because he was perceived as a freak.

Like priests, shamans are not, on the whole, significantly different from the population at large, but a few of them are socially marginal. Shamanism may occasionally be a refuge for misfits, but this is not the norm for the Kayan. Most shamans are women, especially post-menopausal women. Most of the shamans

I knew were less verbally gifted than the average, in a society which values verbal communication; they usually had little social standing.

Although shamans have a lower status than priests, and shamanistic cures are regarded as being less effective than *dayong* cures, these are not competing systems. Priests have no hesitation in acknowledging the efficacy of shamanistic rites, or in accepting the fact of spirit possession, but they do consider the shamanistic séance to be rather ridiculous, and they show little interest in learning about the details of the shaman's art. I never saw or heard of a priest being treated by a shaman, although the reverse is common. As we saw, the fees for a shamanistic cure are much smaller than for a *dayong* ritual; while the Kayan appreciate the bargain, they also agree that you get what you pay for, and they think that shamanistic cures aren't worth all that much.

The higher status of priests is linked in part to their more onerous religious duties. As we saw, they are in charge of all communal and familial rituals as well as rites of passage. One has to study to become a priest, and the position is an achievement. Priesthood is an enviable social identity; priests are treated with respect and are seen as repositories of Kayan culture and art; they are protagonists in maintaining the ritual balance of the community. Priests also have religious authority. Thus, if someone desecrates a ritual, the culprit must pay for a purification and/or a second ritual. In the instance I observed, the offender paid without demurral, but if necessary, the chief, backed by public opinion, would exact compliance.

Those who play a prominent role in decision-making are collectively called "elders" (*kelunan aya'*). The reference to age is metaphorical because age is neither necessary nor sufficient for political prominence. All adult members of the ruling estate (*maren*) belong to this elite, as do a few commoners who establish a reputation by their economic success, their knowledge of customary law and precedents, and their participation in public discussions (Rousseau 1990:194-196). Most established priests are also part of this group of decision-makers, whose preeminence is justified in religious terms: they are powerful and worthy because they have strong souls and powerful spirit helpers. The role of shaman is not an avenue to membership in this political circle.

The lesser status of shamans is also marked by their clientele. They routinely perform cures for members of their own household, an informal approach which is not copied by priests. The latter almost always hire a colleague, even if they choose to participate in the ceremony; thus, there is greater formality in a *dayong* than in a shamanistic cure. Women are much more likely than men or boys to seek the help of a shaman; young boys are shy while being treated by a shaman, unlike girls who take the cure matter-of-factly. The Kayan do not overtly associate shamanism with women, but the link is there.

According to the principles of Kayan religion, the stratum ascription of a religious specialist should be irrelevant, because religious specialization is based on a supernatural calling. While no Kayan informant ever suggested that stratification was a factor, I never encountered or heard of a shaman who was a high aristocrat, nor a priest who was a slave (*dipen*).

While priests and shamans are differentially valued, each category is also internally ranked.[15] Not surprisingly, the prestige of religious specialists is related to the frequency with which their services are required. It is not unusual for priests to be hired by neighboring villages. This is indeed inescapable when the latter have few or no priests. But, even in a village such as Uma Bawang, with its four priests, some households hire priests from other communities, either for variety, or because they wish to bask in the glory of having brought a well-known specialist.[16] Thus, the chief of Uma Bawang hired either the foremost priest *dayong aya'* of the village (also an aristocrat), or well-known priests of other communities; he rarely called upon the services of other Uma Bawang priests. The highest achievement for a priest is to have officiated in every village of the area. Indeed, to fully deserve the title of *dayong aya'*, one should have performed *dayongs* in several communities. Priests from other villages are generally hired at the end-of-year festival, as this is a time for display, but they may be called upon at any time of the year. In 1970-74, one priest, Lake' Huluy, was in great demand, and he was recognized as the best priest in the area. In 1988, he was still popular, and I had the pleasure of attending a *dayong* in Uma Bawang where he officiated.

CONCLUSION

In the Kayan world, humans and spirits live side by side and interact on a daily basis; however, this direct relationship is eroded by other beliefs and practices. As the spirit world is considered dangerous and incomprehensible, people must use religious specialists as intermediaries. This parallels a fundamental feature of Kayan society: commoners feel unable to manage political relations between communities, so they rely on their chiefs to play this role (Rousseau 1990:188-191); this social reality provides a model for the relationship with the spiritual world. In Kayan religion, the supernatural is immanent but outside the control of ordinary human beings. A feeling of helplessness was particularly evident in *adat Dipuy*, under which humans were burdened by hundreds of taboos and thwarted in their endeavors by capricious omens. The *Bungan* religious reform provided a more cheerful alternative when it toppled *Dipuy*, the deity responsible for the burdensome taboos, omens, and long periods of religious inactivity. *Dipuy* was replaced by a benevolent goddess but, like her predecessor, *Bungan* is all-powerful, and she must be approached through the proper channels. More evidence of the distance between humans and spirits is provided by the very proliferation of specialists, not only priests and shamans, but also herbalists, funeral specialists, and so on. Even among priests, there is a division of labor: there are so many rituals that each priest does not master them all. From this follows a priestly hierarchy which further narrows the access to the supernatural.

Kayan religion (both the old *adat Dipuy* and the current *adat Bungan*) occupies an intermediate position in the hypothetical continuum between "pure" shamanism (in which supernatural revelation is open to anyone), and ritualistic-authoritarian religions (in which religious specialists are part of a social system which validates their role, and are skilled practitioners of a formalized ritual system which forms the necessary conduit to the supernatural). On the one hand, Kayan religion still leaves a place for shamans who experience an immediate contact with their spirit helpers. On the other hand, while spirit guides remain a prerequisite to priesthood, the relationship between human and spirit is less personal: priests find out through divination that they have acquired spirit helpers, while shamans need no other validation than their trances to recognize a supernatural presence. Finally, while Kayan priesthood depends on a supernatural calling, extensive training is necessary in order for them to perform the various rituals correctly.

ACKNOWLEDGEMENTS

I wish to thank Madeleine Palmer for her comments.

NOTES

1. A. W. Nieuwenhuis does not differentiate priests and shamans, and his descriptions imply that the same individuals perform all the rituals which in the Baluy are divided between two kinds of specialists (e.g. Nieuwenhuis 1904:110). The differentiation between priest and shaman is also not evident in the writings of Hose and Sombroek and, until additional ethnographic material demonstrates otherwise, I assume that it is a peculiarity of the Baluy Kayan. If this differentiation between priest and shaman exists only among the Baluy Kayan, then, almost by definition, it is not a fundamental feature of Kayan religion. Nonetheless, it helps to reveal some of its general characteristics. In other words, the distinction between priest and shaman is **one** solution to a general problem of Kayan religion, namely the relationship between religion and political authority. Chapter 2 of Hoek (1949) deals with religious specialists in Central Borneo. It is based almost entirely on Nieuwenhuis (1900, 1904) and Hose and McDougall (1912). For an early account of Bahau priests (*behabei*), see Tromp (1888:89-90).

2. This paper is based on fieldwork carried out among the Baluy Kayan in 1970-72 and 1974, especially in the village of Uma Bawang. The beliefs and rituals of *adat Dipuy* and *adat Bungan* will be described in a forthcoming book. This paper limits itself to priests and shamans, but there are also herbalists and magicians/sorcerers, who receive fees for their services. In *adat Dipuy*, the person who looked after the deceased before their interment also received a fee. Other religious specializations are not renumerated: the person who observes the *gnomon* to determine the date of the ceremonial sowing, or, in the old religion, omen specialists. I will not deal here with Christianity, which had very limited impact in the Baluy at the time of fieldwork. A fundamentalist missionary organization, Sidang Injil Borneo, was present in the area, but except for one village, Uma Kahai, it had made only a few converts. Roman Catholic missionaries started proselytization towards the end of my first fieldwork, and their impact has been relatively modest so far.

3. In answer to the question "*Hi aleng kelunan dayong halem uma anih?*," "Who are the *dayongs* in this village?," an informant might list only priests, or priests as well as shamans. Hence, "*dayong*" encompasses both priest and shaman, with the priest being the typical referent of the term. If there were a need to clarify the ambiguity, priests can be called "*dayong duan*" ("*dayong* who speak"), or "*dayong nevek uting* ("*dayong* who kill domesticated pigs"); both expressions refer to the fact that, during the *dayong*

ritual, priests utter long prayers and sacrifice pigs or chickens. Shamans are called "*dayong na'ah*" or "*dayong ngujut*" ("*dayong*" who pick with their fingers'); this refers to the way in which they cure patients: they extract the illness by pulling it out with their fingers, or by sucking it out. Kayan informants are not comfortable in describing a shaman simply as "*dayong*." Thus, if I asked whether X (a shaman) were a *dayong*, a typical answer would be "Yeesss, he/she is a *dayong na'ah*," while, if I asked the same question of a priest, the answer would be an unqualified "Yes." Yet another name for "shaman" is *dayong Kajang*. The Kajang are an ethnic category represented by several villages of the lower Baluy area and one village in the middle Baluy. By calling their own shamans "*Kajang dayongs*," the Kayan are marginalizing them further by suggesting that they are not really part of Kayan culture.

      At the risk of totally confusing the reader, I will add a few terminological notes: First, while, like previous ethnographers (Hose, Nieuwenhuis), I use "*dayong*" as a noun to refer to religious specialists and to a ritual, in many contexts it is a verb. If we say of someone "*Iha' dayong*," this might be translated as "he is a *dayong*," but also "he performs dayongs." In the same way, the common expression "*kelunan aleng dayong*" could be translated as "a person who is a *dayong*," but it seems more correct to translate it literally as "a person who performs *dayongs*." Second, in Kenyah, *dayong* also refers both to the religious specialist and the spirit helper (Whittier 1978:105; see also Elshout 1926:23 on *bali dayong*). Among the Ngaju, according to Mallinckrodt (1924:538), "*balian*" refers both to a religious specialist and to a ritual.

4. People with dayong spirit helpers are called *hnda' dayong* ("*dayong* counterparts"), or *putam dayong* ("entered by *dayong* spirits"). People who have dayong spirits but are not priests or shamans are called "*dayong tua*" ("*tua*":"only"), while religious specialists are described as *dayong lan* ("real priests"). This suggests that the primary meaning of "*dayong*" is now "religious specialist." Most Kayan have *dayong* spirits, as a consequence of having at some point undergone a *dayong* curing ritual.

5. Nieuwenhuis (1904:110) says that candidates had to undergo trials, such as eating dirt, but I have not heard of this.

6. The ritual is called *negreng kayo'* (or *tuken*, or *jok*) *dayong* ("to erect the staff [or pole, or altar] of priesthood"). In the old religion, the new priest received a pillow (*hlen lali*), which was used during the sowing ritual; an armband (*leku dayong*) was placed on the pillow of the oldest priest

(Nieuwenhuis 1904:124). Sombroek (Ms.) notes that, upon acceding to the priesthood, the *dayongs* received a staff (*tawei*) which they kept for their whole life. The foremost priests had two staffs.

7. This is almost identical to the curing ritual which restores the pole of life (*neme tuken urip*). It may be performed only by a senior priest (*dayong aya'*), who takes special ritual precautions. Another name for this restorative ritual is *meju yong kayo' dayong* ("to lift the pole of the priest").

8. In the old religion, only the *dayong aya'* practiced divination with bamboos (*neng'ap bulu*), because bamboo is used to curse (*pesupa*), and is thus very dangerous; ordinary priests used banana leaves for divination. A priest who is not a *dayong aya'* is a *dayong ok*, a "small dayong."

9. This was called *masok dayong*, "to insert the *dayong* spirits." Trances (*dayong nesun*) are an intrinsic part of the shamanistic performance, but they affect other people who are not shamans. By itself, spirit possession does not make one a shaman. Women are more likely to undergo trances, but some men are subject to them.

10. Shamans may dress up during a séance, but in doing so they are merely acting on the desires of their spirits helpers.

11. I lack precise figures on the gender distribution of shamans: during my survey of the middle Baluy area, I did not succeed in making an adequate list of shamans: informants had no problem in identifying priests, but usually ignored shamans (see also endnote 2). I met only one male shaman during my fieldwork; he was considered to be more powerful than any of his female counterparts.

The predominance of male priests is apparently not a pan-Kayan phenomenon. Nieuwenhuis (1904:110) says that Kayan-speaking religious specialists are usually women and reports that Tanjong Karang, a Mendalam Kayan village with fifty apartments, had twelve priestesses and two priests (Nieuwenhuis 1900(1):150). However, it seems that, in the Mendalam as in other Kayan areas, male priests played an important role in some ceremonies: a Mendalam Kayan who made drawings for L. von Römer (1913:146) specifically identified a male *dayong* (*dajoeng lakei*) in relation to the *dangei* ritual.

In marked contrast with secular life (Rousseau, in press), Kayan religion emphasizes gender differentiation. While this is speculative, I suspect that the continued relevance of gender differentiation in religious contexts is a survival from a previous social system in which hereditary stratification linked to a system of political domination and economic exploitation had not yet developed. In order to explore this issue further, one would need more data about the gender distribution of religious specialists in other Kayan areas, as well as ideas about the significance of gender in priesthood and in society in general.

12. A number of priestesses have had either a low fertility, or lost most of their children; it is difficult to say whether this is significant, because this was the lot of many Kayan women.

13. *Lake'* is the gerontonym for men of grandparental generation ("*doh*":"woman"). La'ing *jok* was the man's name. While *Lake'* is a title of respect, there was an element of irony in its use here.

14. Most Kayan men interpreted the assumption of a female identity as a trick in order to shirk men's work. Some transvestites were homosexuals, others attempted to have heterosexual (extra-marital) relations; few of them were married like Lake' La'ing *jok* Doh.

15. According to Mallinckrodt (1924:537-538), among the Ngaju, another stratified society of Borneo, there were three ranks of priests.

16. There may also be a religious motivation; I was told that priests from another village are more powerful (possibly because they are different).

REFERENCES

Elshout, Jacob M.
    1926   De Kenja-Dajaks uit het Apo-Kajangebied: Bijdragen tot de kennis van Centraal-Borneo. 's-Gravenhage: Nijhoff.

Hoek, Jan
    1949   Dajakpriesters: Een bijdrage tot de analyse van de religie der Dajaks. Doctoral dissertation, Amsterdam [no publisher].

Hose, Charles and William McDougall
    1912   The Pagan Tribes of Borneo: A Description of Their Physical, Moral and Intellectual Condition with Some Discussion of Their Ethnic Relations. 2 vols. London: MacMillan.

Jensen, Erik
    1974   The Iban and Their Religion. Oxford: Clarendon Press.

Lewis, I. M.
    1971   Ecstatic Religion: An Anthropological Study of Spirit Possession and Shamanism. Harmondsworth: Penguin Books.

Mallinckrodt, J.
    1924-25   Ethnografische mededeelingen over de Dajaks in de afdeeling Koealakapoeas (Res. Zuider- en Oosterafd. van Borneo). Bijdragen tot de Taal-, Land- en Volkenkunde 80:397-446, 521-600; 81:61-115, 165-310.

Nieuwenhuis, A. W.
    1900   In Centraal Borneo: Reis van Pontianak naar Samarinda. 2 vols. Leiden: Brill.

    1904   Quer durch Borneo: Ergebnisse seiner Reisen in den Jahren 1894, 1896-97 und 1898-1900. Vol.1. Leiden: Brill.

Pauwels, P. C.
    1935   Poenan's in de onderafdeeling Boeloengan. Koloniaal Tijdschrift 24:342-53.

Römer, L. S. A. M. von
    1913   Das Leben eines Kajan: Zeichnungen von Ngo Ping, Sohn des Mendalam-Häuptlings Akam Djoan. Internationales Archiv für Ethnographie 21:137-47.

Rousseau, Jérôme
    1974   The Social Organization of the Baluy Kayan. Ph.D. dissertation, University of Cambridge.

    1983   Kayan Personal Names. Sarawak Museum Journal 32: 251-72.

    1990   Central Borneo: Ethnic Identity and Social Life in a Stratified Society. Oxford: Clarendon Press.

    1991   Gender and Class in Central Borneo. *In* Female and Male in Borneo: Contributions and Challenges to Gender Studies, edited by Vinson H. Sutlive, 403-13. Borneo Research Council Monograph Series Volume 1. The Borneo Research Council, The College of William and Mary, Williamsburg, Virginia.

Sombroek, H.
    n.d.   Algemene opmerkingen. (Ms.)

Sutlive, Vinson H., Jr.
    1976   The Iban Manang: An Alternate Route to Normality. *In* Studies in Borneo societies: Social process and Anthropological Explanation, edited by G. N. Appell, 64-71. Center for Southeast Asian Studies, Northern Illinois University, Special report no. 12.

Tromp, S. W.
    1888   Uit de Salasila van Koetei. Bijdragen tot de Taal-, Land- en Volkenkunde 37:1-108.

Whittier, Herbert L.
    1978   Concepts of *Adat* and Cosmology Among the Kenyah Dayak of Borneo: Coping with the Changing Sociocultural Milieu. Sarawak Museum Journal 26:103-13.

CANOES FOR THE SPIRITS:
TWO TYPES OF SPIRIT MEDIUMSHIP IN CENTRAL KALIMANTAN

SIAN E. JAY

It is nearly fifty years since Hans Schärer (1946) wrote *Die Gottesidee der Ngadju Dayak in Süd Borneo*, in which he described the religious functionaries, *basir* and *balain*, at some length, referring to them as "priests" and "priestesses" respectively. Although Schärer used these terms, he appeared to be describing inspired shamans who lend their bodies to the spirits, and who send their own souls on a journey to the supernatural world. This paper attempts to rediscover these shamans and examine the changes that have taken place since the publication of Schärer's work. The *balain*[1] are no longer to be found officiating at religious ceremonies. However, there are women called *tukang sangiang* (lit. "masters/adept [at summoning] the spirits"), who lend their bodies to supernatural beings who then use their powers to cure sick people. Spontaneous possession also occurs, but space precludes its coverage here. This paper examines the *tukang sangiang* and *basir*, and attempts to relate their role behavior to Ngaju cosmological concepts. It also attempts to relate the roles to gender distinctions, and change.

The term *ngaju*, meaning "upriver," is a general appellation applied to those Dayak in Central Kalimantan living in the middle and lower reaches of the Mentaya, Katingan, Kahayan, Kapuas and Barito rivers and their tributaries (see map 1). More precisely, the Ngaju designate themselves according to the rivers on which they live, e.g. *ulun* Katingan, ("Katingan person"). The data described here are based on research from the Kahayan river and its tributary, the Rungan (see map 2).[2]

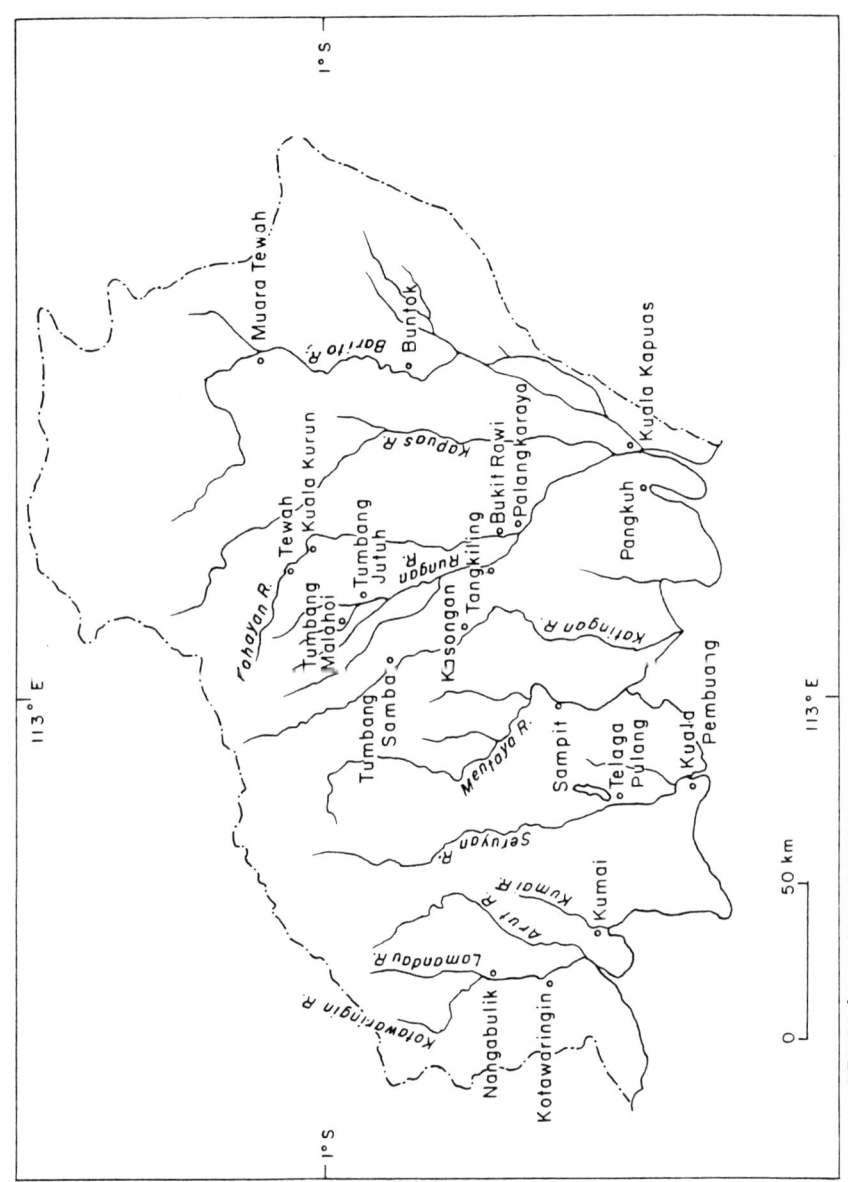

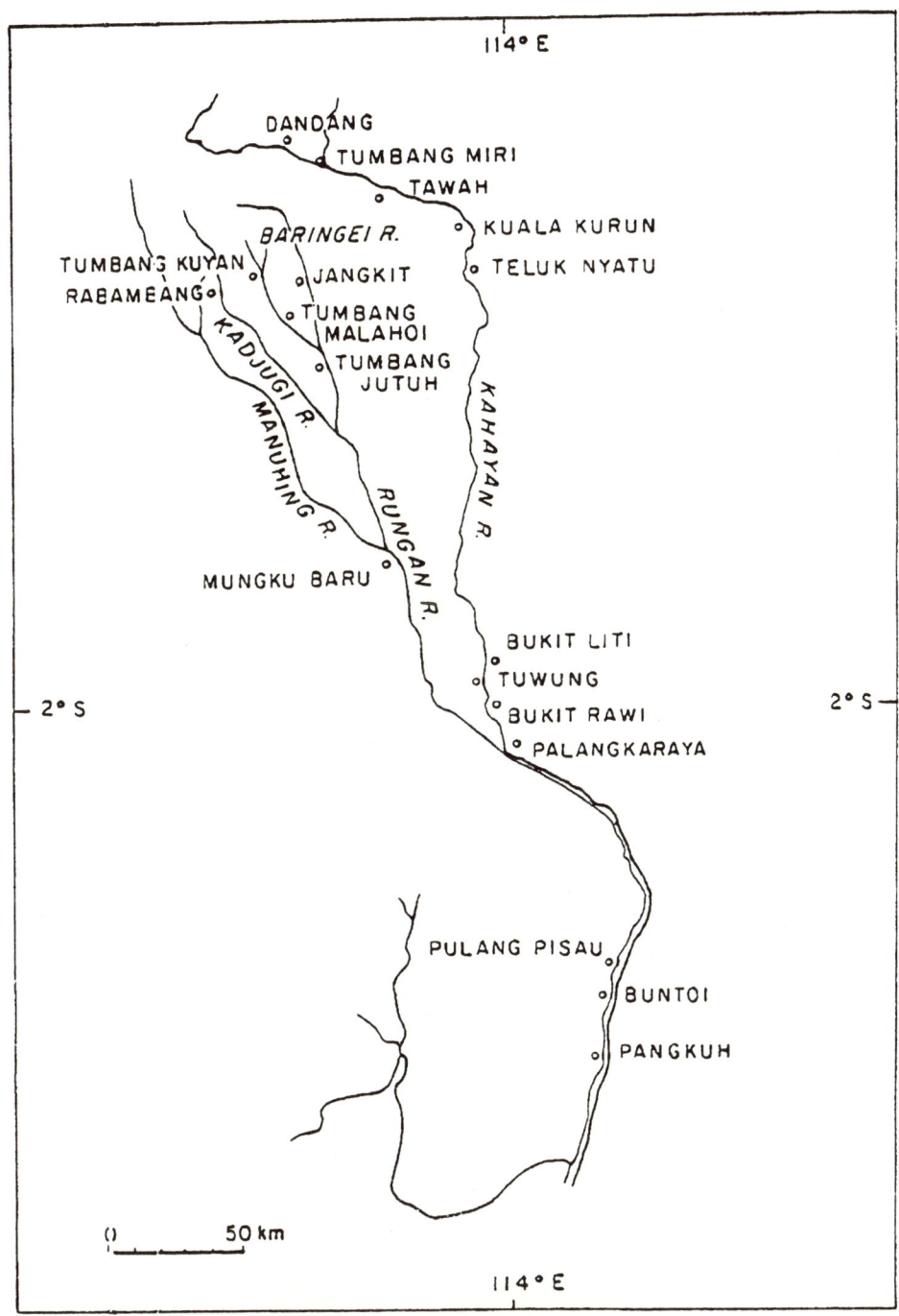

KAHAYAN and RUNGAN RIVERS

Most Ngaju live in rural settlements scattered along these rivers. They are swidden farmers, also fishermen and hunters when not attending to their fields, and may supplement their income by collecting rubber for sale. In the provincial capital of Palangkaraya, a vast government bureaucracy has provided many minor clerical jobs for those Ngaju with a good basic education. The more senior posts are generally filled by Javanese, as well as Sumatrans and Balinese, who have been relocated to Central Kalimantan by the Indonesian government. While happy to fill government posts, the Ngaju still regard themselves primarily as farmers, hunters and fishermen, and scorn any kind of trading. This they regard as being the role of the Banjarese and other Muslims who dominate the market place. A few Ngaju run small village stores, though many of these are run by Banjarese families who have settled in the interior.

KAHARINGAN

Traditionally, the Ngaju adhered to a religion they referred to as *agama helu*, "original religion," but which more recently has acquired the official title of Hindu-Kaharingan. Approximately 208,000 Ngaju are estimated to follow Kaharingan. A large number of Ngaju are Christian (approximately 209,000 though these figures also include Christian Chinese and others, as government statistics do not break religious affiliation up ethnically). A much smaller number of Ngaju have become Muslim. Whereas most Muslim Ngaju completely withdraw from their Dayak roots, Christian Ngaju do not. Those Christians in rural villages live in close proximity to their Kaharingan neighbors, and often a single household will consist of both Kaharingan and Christian adherents, who will commonly participate in each other's religious celebrations. They are more likely, moreover, to be first-generation converts. Those Christians living in Palangkaraya are more likely to be second- or third-generation converts, and have little or no knowledge of or contact with Kaharingan practice and belief. Pressures to convert to Christianity are greatest among Kaharingan believers living in Palangkaraya and, generally speaking, there is a conscious association of Christianity with advancement and better access to wealth through opportunity.

Those Ngaju adhering to Kaharingan posit a universe consisting of an Underworld and a seven-layered Upperworld, with the human world in between. The waters of the Underworld are presided over by a feminine deity named Jata Balawang Bulau ("Jata with the golden door"), who is sometimes represented as a watersnake (*tambun*). The Upperworld is presided over be a masculine deity named Raying Hatala Langit, apparently not his original title which was Raja

Tuntung Matanandau ("Prince of the Sun"). He resides in the Uppermost heaven on Gold Mountain, and is sometimes represented as a hornbill (*tingang*). These two deities also form a unity referred to as *tambun haruei bungai* ("the watersnake which is united with the hornbill"). Many *basir*, in keeping with the Indonesian state philosophy (the Pancasila), which defines a religion as the belief in one supreme God (see Indonesia 1985:2), insist that Jata and Ranying Hatala, or Jatatala, are one and the same; they are male, but Jata represents the feminine, Underworld aspect of God (see Jay 1992). The Underworld/Upperworld division is conceptualized in terms of sea and mountain, and downstream and upstream. The supernatural and natural beings that inhabit specific realms within this cosmos are placed within a hierarchy, the relationships and transactions between them being morally evaluated. Spirit mediums have access to different levels of the cosmos, and from this follow certain consequences which "infect and mould ritual action, which has for its objective the communication with and mediation between these culturally distinguished agents, levels, domains and events which compose the cosmology" (Tambiah 1981:122).

The creation myth of the Ngaju, called the Panaturan, describes the creation of the natural beings encountered by the Ngaju, and the various supernatural beings that the mediums deal with in different ritual contexts. The first man and woman created by Ranying Hatala and Jata initially cohabited without marriage, but each pregnancy ended in miscarriage. The blood from the first four miscarriages was thrown into the river and drifted downstream where the World Snake (*Naga hai*), often associated with Jata, blew upon it changing it into the *Rajas* ("rulers, kings") of the various illnesses that afflict mankind, and the evil spirits who taunt or harm mankind in other ways. These are, generally, the spirits that the *tukang sangiang* are called upon to deal with. The couple moved farther upstream and founded the first village, but continued to cohabit without marriage. The bood from the subsequent miscarriages fell on the ground and Ranying Hatalla's voice (represented by thunder), turned it into the useful plants and domestic animals that are to be found in and around most Ngaju villages. The last miscarrage was changed into the ancestor of the *patahu*, supernatural beings who guard particular villages. A small shrine (*pasah patahu*) containing an unusual stone that represents the *patahu* is found in every village, and offerings are made to it.

Following these miscarriages, Ranying Hatala sent seven heavenly shamanesses, the Kasampangan Bawin Balian ("female auxiliaries [who perform] the recitations"), to perform the first marriage ceremony. They were accompanied by the Raja Uju Hakanduang ("seven kings who are brothers," and their wives the Bawi Sintung Uju ("the women who number seven"), who live at the mouth of the river in the seventh heaven leading to Ranying Hatala's abode. They act as intermediaries between humanity and Ranying Hatala. Following the sanction of legal marriage, three sons were born to the first couple. The first two became the ancestors ot the *sangiang*, the mythical "cousins" of the Ngaju who live in the third and fifth heavens, and who, when summoned by the *basir*, must come to the aid of the Ngaju, during the ceremonies presided over by the *basir*. The third son became the ancestor of humans, the Ngaju themselves.

All these supernatural beings created from the first couple may be divided into two categories: *taluh je papa* (evil spirits), and *taluh je bahalap* (good spirits). Ngaju mythology posits a structural motif consisting of the opposition between the Underworld, downstream and the sea, all of which are associated with evil spirits; and the Upperworld, upstream and the mountains, all of which are associated with good spirits. The beings derived from the blood that fell on the ground in the primeval village (in contrast with the water) may be regarded as an intermediate category in that they are necessary and useful to the Ngaju. At another level one may construct an opposition between village and forest, which may be added to the Upperworld, Underworld opposition (see also Endicott 1981:96-124). The village is the domain of humans, domesticated plants and animals, and of guardian spirits such as the *patahu* and crocodile spirits (*jata*; not to be confused with Jata). The forest is the domain of wild animals and plants, and of ill-disposed spirits, although well-disposed and amoral spirits may also be found here. The village and forest represent the human world occupying the marginal areas between Upper- and Underworlds. All the beings created by Ranying Hatala and Jata occupy specific locations within the cosmic hierarchy, and as long as they remain in their allotted places, the universe is stable and harmonious. But at certain times the balance is upset--people die, they become sick or break taboos, for example--and evil spirits encroach on the human domain, bringing the threat of suffering and death. Good spirits are called upon to help persuade the evil spirits to leave their victims alone and to return to their own abode, thus restoring the cosmic balance. These are the times when the *tukang sangiang* and *basir* are called upon to mediate between the human and spirit worlds.

TUKANG SANGIANG

The *tukang sangiang* are called to their vocation by divine, or supernatural, means. With few exceptions, the women concerned had suffered some kind of mental disturbance (*kahaban gila*) or confusion (*kalayau, nyanayau*) before becoming *tukang sangiang*. This confusion or insanity is described in various ways: *gila awi daha* (lit. "insane because of blood"), meaning hereditary, taking the mother's tainted blood at birth; *gila awi mandaur taluh papa*, ("disturbance by an evil spirit");

or *gila hantuen kuyang* ("crazy because of vampires"). All three descriptions are related. The Ngaju claim that a child takes its flesh and blood from its mother, and its bones from its father, so only a mother may pass insanity down, though both sons and daughters may inherit it. It is further claimed that an unmarried woman who has a sexual relationship with a man may become insane, and may pass her affliction on to her children. This belief is closely related to the creation myth in which the incomplete or imperfect offspring who became evil spirits were the result of an unlawful union. Insanity or confusion may also occur when the blood is disturbed by an evil spirit, causing sensory abnormalities in its victim. For example, one woman saw people as monkeys, another noticed a rotten smell all the time. It is not clear whether only those individuals who have inherited this unstable disposition are disturbed by an evil spirit, or whether anyone may be a victim, but the evil spirits who cause the disturbance are the rejected, incomplete "cousins" of their human victims.

Ngaju vampires or *hantuen*, also *kuyang* (Banjarese) are described as "humans who are not human" because they feed on the blood of the newly deceased, the newly born, or of pregnant women. There are, furthermore, clear parallels between the supposed origins of *hantuen* and the origins of inherited insanity. One version of the *hantuen's* origins says that they were the offspring of a union between human and animal, consumers of raw flesh and blood like their animal forebears. Just as people who had unlawfully cohabited with animals produced *hantuen*, so women who had an unlawful sexual relationship passed insanity down to their children. Victims of insanity or confusion, however, are not regarded as bad or sinful by the Ngaju, for it is recognized that they cannot help their condition.

If an individual exhibits such abnormal behavior that she is diagnosed by a proficient *tukang sangiang* as being disturbed by an evil spirit,[3] she must undergo a major ceremony called Balian Mampendang Lunuk ("recitation to raise the *lunuk* tree") to cure her. The *lunuk* (*Ficus religiosa*) grows by the river's edge, often with its roots in the water, and it is said to be a pathway for good spirits to descend to earth. Ill-disposed, red-haired tricksters called *nyaring*, derived from the shed blood of the first woman, are said to live at the foot of such trees. The tree may be regarded as a symbolic axis between Upper- and Underworld, and branches of it are put up in the center of the room where the curing ceremony for a confused woman is to take place.

When an individual is disturbed by an evil spirit it is said to cause a surfeit of red blood (in contrast with white blood) which upsets the nerves, causing the sensory abnormalities experienced by its victim. At the curing ceremony the officiating *tukang sangiang* draws the disturbed blood of the patient to the top of the head and appears to remove it in the form of congealed and hardened blood that resembles a stone, and is called a *batu sambalik* ("fever stone"). *Sambalik* is defined as a "high fever caused by hantuen" (Hardeland 1859:498), again expressing a link between *hantuen* and blood. The patient is then referred to as *bawin lawang*, "female of the door," for there is now an invisible aperture, a door or path left by the stone, through which a good spirit may now descend to possess her.[4] Only by allowing her body to be used by the benign spirit, thereby becoming a *tukang sangiang*, can an insane or confused woman be cured. She will usually first become possessed by the main possessing spirit of her *tukang sangiang*. This spirit is referred to as her *batang sangiang* ("spirit guide"), the first who "travelled the spirit path" (*manajun jalan sangiang*), the spirit path being the *lunuk* tree. Having once been possessed, the patient has to be persuaded to invite other spirits to possess her until she finds one, or several, who are suited to her. She will be invited to accompany proficient *tukang sangiang* at curing ceremonies until she is able to officiate at such ceremonies herself. Her *batang sangiang* might never possess her again, having served to open the way for other spirits. This curing ceremony appears to be the only time that the new *tukang sangiang* are possessed through the head; thereafter the spirits use the right leg.

The *tukang sangiang* always begins a curing ceremony by calling upon her possessing spirit, and entering a trance state. The physical and emotional experiences of the individual mediums vary during the onset and progress of possession. Some are aware of what is going on but cannot control what they do. Many say they feel cold, their vision may blur momentarily, the voices of people around them fade, and for some moments they feel unwell. Their possessing spirits enter via the right foot, and up the right leg. (Evil spirits possess people via the left leg.) When the spirit enters the pit of the stomach, where it is said to lodge during possession, many *tukang sangiang* say they feed nauseated, and may make the motions of retching. These feelings disappear once the spirit has taken over the body. The notion of struggle is often expressed as *gawi je manangkiae* (lit. "process for winning, gaining, taking control"). The cold feelings and nausea are the human desire to reject the spirit that is not truly part of them. But because the human has an agreement with the spirit, made during her own curing ceremony, and because the spirits are stronger, it will always gain control. Having become possessed, the *tukang sangiang* takes on the personality of the possessing spirit.

It is generally agreed that a person may remain possessed for a certain period only; half an hour to an hour seems usual. If the spirit possesses the woman for too long, she may become weak, tired, or even ill; and when a ceremony lasts for a long time, the *tukang sangiang* invariably has short breaks when she comes out of trance. It is claimed that after a while the person begins to expel (*manolak*) the spirit, and again a struggle takes place. Often a *tukang sangiang* has several possessing spirits, and may cast one out only to find that another has taken its place. The struggle for control of the human host by the two spirits may be so violent that another person must dab perfumed water with a leaf brush (*tampung tawar*) on the shoulders of the *tukang sangiang* to remind the spirits that they are inhabiting a human body and must depart peacefully. The verb *manawar* means "to administer an antidote," or "to render ineffective, neutralize, or exorcise and thereby cure." The *tampung tawar* may also be used by the *tukang sangiang* on her patient as part of the ceremony to expel the evil spirit.[5]

The process of calling these spirits and being possessed by them is termed *manyangiang* or *nyangiang*, which may be glossed as "to have a *sangiang* as a helper," or "to be possessed by a spirit." Paradoxically, the spirits who are called by the *tukang sangiang* are not the true *sangiang*, i.e. those referred to in the creation myth, and who, as will shortly be discussed, are called upon by the *basir*; here the term is used generically, to refer to any good or helpful spirit which may be called upon to render assistance in certain circumstances. The good spirits called upon by the *tukang sangiang* may dwell on earth, or in the first heaven and, more rarely in the third heaven. This class of spirits is sometimes referred to as the *sangiang Bandar* after one of their number who lives in the third heaven. All these spirits are classified as inferior to the true *sangiang* (who live in the third and fifth heavens) who are called upon by the *basir*, and they do not have the same powers. They form a hierarchy: those lesser, good spirits that dwell in the third and first heavens are more powerful than those that dwell on earth. Those that dwell in the mountains are more powerful than those in the forest, and so on. It is generally known which *tukang sangiang* are able to call upon the more powerful spirits, and depending on the circumstances in which they are needed, a particular *tukang sangiang* will be called. Consequently, a person suffering from a bad headache, for example, may be treated by most *tukang sangiang*, but for a Balian Mampendeng Lunuk, only a very experienced *tukang sangiang* with a powerful spirit may officiate.

The cases that the *tukang sangiang* are called upon to deal with typically involve the curing of a person made ill by an evil spirit, because they have ignored an omen, transgressed a prohibition, or simply had their *hambaruan* (life soul) led astray while in a physically weakened state. I have briefly described a typical curing ceremony elsewhere (Jay 1991:5-6). The attacking spirits always originate from the forest, the river, downstream or the Underworld, having used their victims transgressions to cross the boundaries and encroach on the human world. The spirit possessing the *tukang sangiang* has the task of politely persuading the evil spirits to return to their own domain by making an offering. The Ngaju point out that the evil spirits are, after all, their own non-human "cousins" who are understandably envious of the favor shown by Ranying Hatala towards the Ngaju. They feel aggrieved that they have been cast aside, and that they lack a body.

The *tukang sangiang* is compelled to invite her spirits to possess her whenever asked to do so, and the spirits will always come when summoned. A *tukang sangiang* may become confused or insane again if she refuses to summon her spirits. The relationship between spirit and host is an intimate one. It is described as *mangumpang*, "to enter," and is derived from the noun *kumpang* meaning "sheath." In Ngaju mythology, men are referred to as *dohong* (daggers) and woman as *kumpang* (sheaths), a reference to the fact that by joining together in the sexual act they are like a sword and sheath. The relationship between *tukang sangiang* and spirit is like that of husband and wife. Most of the possessing spirits appear to be male. While entranced, the *tukang sangiang* may refer to herself as *bandung lasang* which in the sacred language means "canoe" (Baier et al. 1987:9), suggesting that the *tukang sangiang* is a canoe in which the spirit sits. But *bandung* may also mean "someone with whom one commits or has committed fornication" (Hardeland 1859:39), which suggests that the *tukang sangiang* is like a lover whom the spirits take by force.

BASIR

The *basir* (now almost exclusively men)[6] are religious mediators, specialists who function mainly, but not exclusively, during Kaharingan ceremonies, which may be divided into two categories: *gawi belum* (life celebrations), such as weddings, and *gawi matei* (death celebrations). Only the *basir* may mediate between humans and the true *sangiang* (i.e. the descendants of the children of the first couple). They may also communicate with the various Rajas who dwell in the Upperworld and who are charged with overseeing and safeguarding the affairs of mankind. All these supernatural beings may be considered to occupy the highest levels of the heararchy of supernatural beings. They are, futhermore, well-disposed towards mandind.

To become a *basir*, a man apprentices himself to an older, experienced *basir*. The decision to become a *basir* is one of individual choice. An alternative means is now available, as the Hindu-Kaharingan school in Palangkaraya (the provincial capital) also enables students to study to become *basir*.[7] The more usual method in interior villages, though, is through apprenticeship. A man may become an apprentice at any age, but must first fulfill several requirements. He must give his teacher gold and silver, symbolizing lasting value. The imputed purity of these metals further symbolizes the purity of the *basir*; they are also present at every Kaharingan ceremony. The novice also gives the *basir* a piece of iron representing strength (*kuasae*) and hardness (*batekeng*). The novice will have to acquire these qualities if he is to be able to endure many nights of drumming and chanting during Kaharingan ceremonies, and to go witout adequate sleep and not fall ill during a ceremony. He must also present his teacher with a new set of clothes to symbolize that the pupil will cast off his old body. Everything he learns will make him a new person. Finally, the novice must give the *basir* betel for chewing. At ceremonies the *basir* chew betel as a stimulant to help them remember the chants and drum rhythms. The novice similarly chews betel during training and to aid memory. Betel is also the food of the *sangiang*.

The *basir* will not only teach all the chants and drum rhythms, but also will pass on the secret names of the *sangiang*, the Seven Rajas, and of Ranying Hatala. These are secret (*basilim*) names that differ from those used by the layman, and they can never be divulged to anyone else, or spoken out loud in anyone's presence. The knowledge of these names, and whom they really denote, is what give the *basir* his efficacy during the ritual. It is the power inherent in this knowledge that gives the *basir* his ability to be entered by the *sangiang*.

When a group of *basir* officiate at a ceremony, the most experienced and knowledgeable is selected to act as leader (*upu*). He sits in the middle of the bench (*katil*) with the other *basir* to either side of him. Depending on the importance of the ceremony, either three, five, or seven and occasionally nine *basir* will officate. Generally, the more important the ceremony, the more *basir* are required. It is also generally the case that the greater the power of the supernatural beings required, and the higher the level of the heaven to be mediated with, the more *basir* are required. The *basir* to either side of the *upu* are referred to as *pengapit gantau* ("[*basir*] of the highest grade [seated to] the right") and *pengapit sambil* ("[*basir*] of the highest grade [seated to] the left"). The grade refers to the proficiency of the *basir*, those immediately to the right and left of the *upu* being the most experienced. The *basir* farthest away from the *upu* are called the *lawin katil* ("end of the bench") and are the most junior and inexperienced *basir*, often still undergoing their apprenticeship.

Unlike the curing ceremonies performed by the *tukang sangiang*, which are highly individual, the course and action being dictated by the possessing spirit, the Kaharingan ceremonies conducted by the *basir* have a set form. A *Balaku Untung* ("asking for good fortune") will make use of the same chants, drum rhythms and equipment wherever it is held. All Kaharingan ceremonies, furthermore, follow the same basic form, whether they are simple ceremonies lasting one night, or more complex ceremonies taking place over several weeks.

They begin with the strewing (*manawur*) of uncooked rice by the *upu*. The soul of the rice is said to change into seven beings who will make the journey to the Upperworld to fetch the *sangiang* who are requied to take part in the ceremony. Different *sangiang* have different roles in different Kaharingan ceremonies. The *basir* begin to drum and chant in order to "make a path for the spirits of the rice," their words describing the journey of the rice spirits, the celestial rivers along which they travel from earth, upwards to the third heaven to their destination, the village of the *sangiang*. The drum beats and the words are said to possess their own spirit or *gana* which carries the rice on its journey. Because the *basir* know the route to the Upperworld, their words can guide the rice spirits to their destination. At the *sangiang* village the rice spirits again become rice, and the spirit of the voice of the *upu* informs the *sangiang* when they have been summoned. The *sangiang* then prepare their celestial ships and everything required for the ceremony and then descend to the earth where the ceremony is being held, while the *basirs'* chants describe the return journey to the assembled audience. The *sangiang* enter the house where the *basir* are performing, and take their place in little baskets made from plaited coconut leaves that are suspended above the head of each *basir*. These are called *balai saling kambungan* ("meeting hall of plaited work"), and represent a resting house (*balai*) for the *sangiang*. They contain a quid of betel and a cigarette for the *sangiang* to enjoy after their journey.

The *sangiang* are then invited to enter the *basir*. There are two chief *sangiang*, one for life celebrations and one for death celebrations, and it is one of these who takes his place within the *upu*. The *sangiang* helpers use the bodies of the other *basir*. The *sangiang* enter the *basir* via the head, not the feet, as with the *tukang sangiang*. Once the *sangiang* have entered the *basir*, their hosts don headscarves to signify that a spirit is within them, and from this point onwards, everything the *basir* do and say is deemed to be due to the will of the *sangiang*.

The *basir* possess the knowledge that enables them to control the supernatural world during religious rituals, unlike the *tukang sangiang* who are controlled by the supernatural during curing ceremonies. The power of the *basir* is acquired through training, and lies in the potency of the drumming and chants. They do not merely describe what is taking place; the drumming and chanting make it happen, setting in motion a sequence of described and enacted events that bring about the descent of the *sangiang* to earth to create and fulfill the ceremoney. The *basir* have created a two-way channel between the human and supernatural worlds, merging the two so that whatever is taking place on the supernatural plane is paralleled on the physical, earthly plane, and is given meaning and potency.

Because they create this line of communication between human beings and the supernatural, and enable otherwise, meaningless actions to become meaningful ritual and, above all, because they give the actions potency and efficacy through the mediation of the *sangiang*, the *basir* may be regarded as shamans. Unlike true shamans, though, the *basir* do not regard themselves as possessed or entered (*ngumpang*), although the *sangiang* are deemed to be within the *basir*. The *basir* remain in control, and describe themselves as *lasang sangiang* ("spirit canoes"), their bodies being compared to boats. The *sangiang* disembark from their celestial ship and enter another boat (i.e., the *basir*) from where they may preform their tasks. Although the *basir* say that their bodies are spirit canoes because they are where the *sangiang* descend to, it is not the physical body that is the boat. The body is only a bridge between the celestial ship and the *ganan lasang sangiang* ("the spirit [*ganan*] of the *sangiang* canoe") which is located within the body. When the *basir* begin chanting and drumming, they wake up the spirit of the ceremony, the *ganan balian*, which is called *ganan tandak lasang sangiang*, "the spirit of the singing, the *sangiang* canoe," and it is this which is located within the *basir*, and in which the *sangiang* take their place. The ability to "wake up" this spirit is acquired during the *basir's* apprenticeship. When he is considered to have mastered this power he may be allowed to perform at simple Kaharingan ceremonies.

After the *sangiang* have entered the *basir*, the ceremony may entail a return journey to the higher heavens by the *sangiang*. The *basir* often say that they make this journey with the *sangiang*, though on closer examination it becomes apparent that it is the spirit of the singing conjured from within them that makes this journey. According to both J. Mallinckrodt (1924:536-537) and Schärer (1966:441), it is the *basir's* soul, by which they appear to mean the *hambaruan* (life soul), that ascends to the Upperworld. The present-day *basir* all insist that their soul remains within them, pointing out that a loss of soul (*hambaruan*) would lead to illness. The *basir* also refute Schärer's claim (1966:441) that they take on the personalities of the *sangiang* who enter them. They insist that unlike the possessed *tukang sangiang*, their personalities are not displaced. Nor does their behavior differ from their usual behavior. They are fully conscious and aware of their actions. However, they are accorded due deference and respect, and treated as though they were the *sangiang* curing the ceremony.

The *basir* also claim to experience a change of feeling when the *sangiang* descend to their bodies. They frequently say that they feel cold, and that after a while they feel light-headed. One *basir* said that at the moment the *sangiang* entered, his tongue began to tremble, and he felt that the was no longer making the words come out, or controlling the beating of the drum. Indeed, many *basir* said that they found it easier to remember the chants and rhythms once the *sangiang* were inside them.

CHANGES IN RITUAL ROLES AND GENDER

There have undoubtedly been many changes in the role and behavior of the *basir*, the most noticeable being the disappearance of women *basir*. Formerly women dominated the role, and somewhat surprisingly seem to have held a lowly and somewhat despised position in Ngaju society. They were said to have originated from the slave class, beautiful slave women being chosen to train as *basir*. They were also said to serve as prostitutes, being hired out as such by their masters, and to have had sexual intercourse with men in the audience during ceremonies. Schärer appears to have been the only writer to have regarded the practice in terms of sacred prostitution, with the *basir* representing the divine. However, as Mallinckrodt (1925:718) pointed out, in religious affairs these women had considerable influence, with scarcely a day going by without some form of exorcism being conducted by them. This reference to exorcism suggests that they served the community much as the *tukang sangiang* do today.

The idea that *basir* would act as prostitutes both horrifies and disgusts the present-day *basir*, many categorically denying that such acts took place. They resent this image of their religion, claiming that because many of these women were uncultured due to their slave origins, they behaved inappropriately. This was, the *basir* claimed, the main reason why fewer women took up the role of *basir*. Furthermore, such behavior insulted the *sangiang* who were present, and who chose to distance themselves form the *basir*. Previously the *basir* had been possessed, just as Schärer and others have claimed, but now they simply act as canoes for the *sangiang*.

However, other, more far-reaching changes have taken place, and these too have affected the *basir*. Christian missionaries have been active in the area for over 100 years, and have had a profound, though subtle, influence on indigenous religious belief. It may well have been Christian moral attitudes that led to Ngaju disapproval of, and the decline in, sacred prostitution. More recently, the Indonesian state recognizes as a religion only those beliefs that acknowledge a single, supreme God. Rather then being regarded as animistic and backward, the Ngaju have responded, with the support of Balinese Hindu organizations. The *basir* have codified their religion, and organized themselves into an official body, the Majelis Besar Agama Hindu-Kaharingan, "Great Council for the Hindu-Kaharingan Religion," an organization recognized by the government. This has lead to Kaharingan taking its place alongside Christianity and Islam as a central religion recognized by the state. Ceremonies are presided over by *basir*, who are officially recognized religious leaders, and the ceremonies follow an organized codified form. Curing ceremonies presided over by *tukang sangiang* have become marginalized, and do not follow any codified form, being more *ad hoc* in their performance. Although there are many similarities between Kaharingan ceremonies and curing ceremonies, the Ngaju describe the former as "religious ceremonies" (Indonesian *upacara agama*), and the latter as "cultural ceremonies" (Indonesian *upacara kebudayaan*).

Kaharingan religious ceremonies are thus controlled and organized by men who have access to the superior, well-disposed spirits in the pantheon. They choose their profession, and must, moreover, be deemed worthy of the position by the *basir* who train them. A *basir* may refuse to train someone he considers unsuitable. The spirits they mediate with belong to the Upperworld, masculine, upstream end of the cosmological spectrum. It is recognized and accepted that the *sangiang* use their bodies as canoes, but possession, if indeed it may be so called, is notional and controlled; the *basir* control the ceremony. Furthermore, as I have argued elsewhere (Jay 1989:42), the control and organization of the Kaharingan Council is male dominated, women remaining in the background. Those women who are involved tend the be the wives of Council officials, and their position and status reflect those of their husbands.

The *tukang sangiang* are women who achieved their position by transcending a relationship with inferior, ill-disposed spirits belonging to the Underworld, feminine, downstream end of the cosmological spectrum. This very fact precludes their becoming *basir*. Denied access to superior, officially sanctioned spirits recognized by the controlling religious organization, the *tukang sangiang* instead exert some control over the supernatural world by cooperating with an infinite number of well-disposed spirits who use their bodies as canoes. Possession, however, is total and uncontrolled, and it is the spirits who control their hosts and the ceremonies.

NOTES

1. Along the Kahayan and Rungan rivers, the word *balain* is a verb referring to the process of chanting by the *basir* during a religious ceremony. It is also used as a noun in reference to a particular ceremony, and may be glossed as "recitation." It was more usual to refer to the priestess as *basir bawi*, "female priests" in the area in which fieldwork was conducted.

2. Field-work in Central Kalimantan was conducted between 1987 and 1988, with the support of the Indonesian Institute of Sciences (LIPI). The data published here was collected primarily from the Kahayan and Rungan river areas, and forms part of my doctoral thesis entitled "Shamans, Priests, and the Cosmology of the Ngaju Dayak of Central Kalimantan."

3. The diagnosis is made at a simple ceremony at which a proficient *tukang sangiang* calls upon her helper spirit to enter and examine the confused woman. The possessing spirit will confirm or deny the presence of an evil being. It will also assess whether it (i.e. the *tukang sangiang's* spirit) can expel the evil spirit, or whether the services of a *tukang sangiang* with a more powerful possessing spirit must be sought.

4. A surfeit of red blood may simply make some individuals quick to anger or argumentative, or prone to frequent and severe headaches. A *tukang sangiang* may also cure this by removing the *batu sambalik*. Once the fever stone has been removed, the cured sufferer must wear some kind of head covering until the "hole" has closed up, so that the disturbing spirit cannot re-enter.

5. In addition to insanity, any illness not diagnosed as medical is regarded as being due to an evil spirit disturbing the person, and will require the services of a *tukang sangiang*.

6. I was told of two elderly female *basir* at the village of Tumbang Mangga on the Upper Katingan river who still officiated at ceremonies.

7. Some young women have now started training as *basir* at the Hindu-Kaharingan school.

REFERENCES

Baier, M., A. Hardeland and H. Schärer
    1987   Wörterbuch der Priestersprache de Ngaju-Dayak. Verhandeling van het Koninklijk Instituut voor Taal-, Land- en Volkenkunde 128. Dordrecht: Forus Publications.

Endicott, Kirk. M.
    1981   An Analysis of Malay Magic. Kuala Lumpur: Oxford University Press.

Hardeland, A.
    1859   Dajak-Deutsches Wörterbuch. Amsterdam: Frederick Muller.

Indonesia
    1985   Indonesia 1985. Jakarta: Department of Information.

Jay, Sian. E.
    1989   The Basir and Tukang Sangiang: Two Kinds of Shaman Among the Ngaju Dayak. Indonesia Circle 49:31-44.

    1991   Medicine and Magic. Patient Voice 54:5-6.

    1992   The Water of Life: Mythological and Cosmological Concepts of the Ngaju Dayak of Central Kalimantan. *In* The Gift of Water: Irrigation and Water Supply in South East Asia, edited by J. Rigg. London: School of Oriental and African Studies (in press).

Mallinckrodt, J.
    1924   Ethnographisches Mededeelingen over de Dajaks in de Onderafdeeling Kapuas. Bijdragen tot de Taal-, Land- en Volkenkunde 80:397-446, 521-600.

    1925   Het Priesterwezen bij de Dajaks van Kotawaringan. De Indische Gids 47:588-602, 708-722.

Schärer, Hans
    1946   Die Gottesidees der Njagu Dajak in Süd-Borneo. Leiden: E. J. Brill.

    1963   Ngaju Religion: The Conception of God Among a South Borneo People. Translated by Rodney Needham. The Hague: Martinus Nijhoff.

    1966   De Totenkult der Ngaju Dajak in Süd-Borneo. 2 Vols. 's-Gravenhage: Martinus Nijhoff.

Tambiah, S. J.
    1981   A Performance Approach to Ritual. The Proceedings of the British Academy 64. Oxford: Oxford University Press.

PART TWO

THE SHAMAN'S DESTINY: SYMPTOMS, AFFLICTION, AND THE RE-INTERPRETATION OF ILLNESS AMONG THE TAMAN

JAY BERNSTEIN
University of Kent at Canterbury

In every society there is a concept of malaise--a loss of well-being, as that is culturally defined. In malaise, or illness, we "experience ourselves as failing with respect to an implicit norm of physiological or psychological function, or form or grace, or of freedom from pain" (Engelhardt 1982:144). This individual experience of illness ultimately is structured by cultural paradigms of disease pathology. What counts as illness, or a symptom of illness, is defined by cultural standards or concepts. Culture, in effect, shapes the interpretation of illness (see Frake 1980). The following study will show how the interpretation of illness is related to the interpretation of dreams and fantasy and to the organization of a social institution, namely shamanism, among the Taman people of Indonesian Borneo.

The shaman's role among the Taman is one of curing sick people using a range of supernatural techniques. Shamans are drawn into this role because of an experience considered by them to be an illness, an affliction, and a victimization by a spirit-being. In this essay I shall discuss the nature of illnesses predisposing a person to become a shaman *(balien)*, and interpret the meaning of this phenomenon within the context of Taman society and Borneo more generally. I shall relate the data on these predisposing illnesses to psychiatric theories of hysterical illness. Finally, I shall consider the implications of the notion that illness is a sign of destiny for a healing role. Illness may be used to express unconscious or disavowed desires relating to social adaptation.

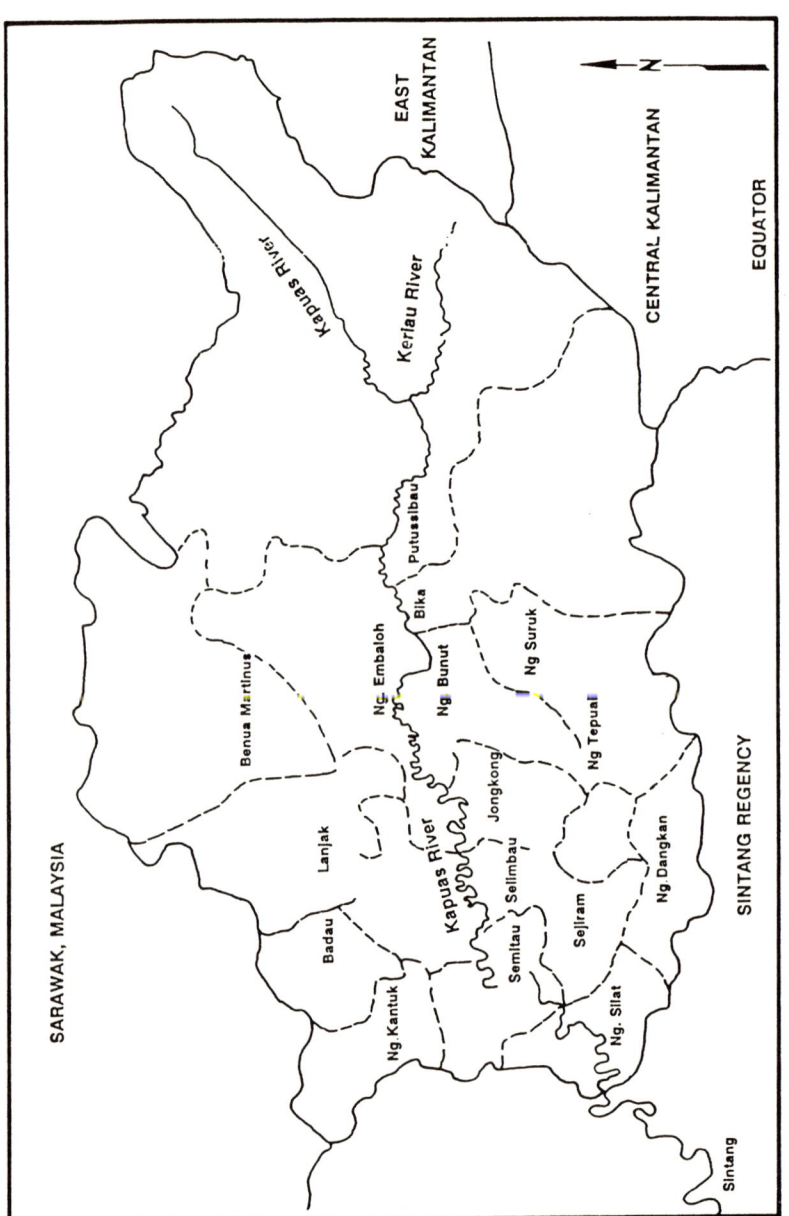

MAP 1

The Interior of West Kalimantan

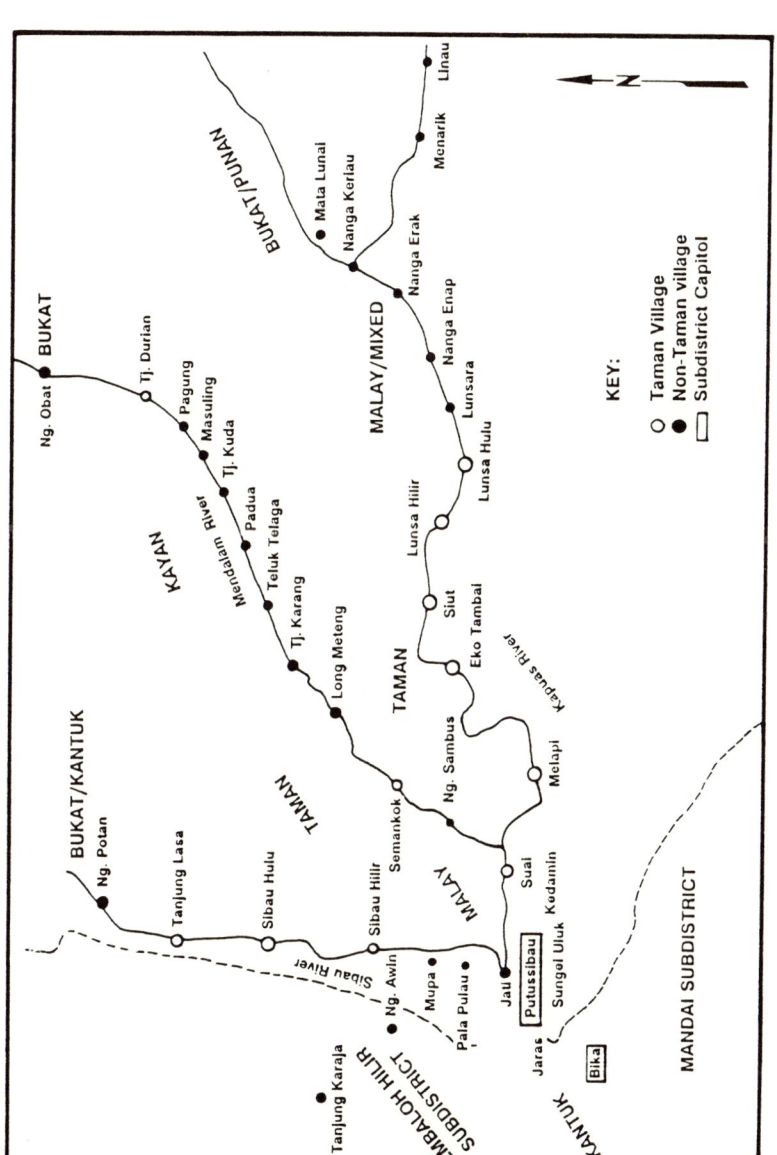

MAP 2

Putussibau Subdistrict, showing locations of villages on the Taman and neighboring ethnic groups. Certain remote Punan and Bukat villages are not shown.

THE TAMAN PEOPLE

The Taman, along with the nearby Embaloh and Kalis, are part of a larger ethnolinguistic entity known to outsiders as "Maloh." All of these groups are indigenous to the Upper Kapuas regency of West Kalimantan, Indonesia, shown on the accompanying maps. The Taman live in ten villages located several kilometers upstream of Putussibau, the uppermost Malay town on the Kapuas river and the capital of the Upper Kapuas regency (*Kabupaten Kapuas Hulu*). Further upstream of the Taman are scattered Punan and Bukat settlements; to the north is the Upper Kapuas mountain range forming West Kalimantan's border with Sarawak, and to the east is the Müller mountain range and the border with East Kalimantan.

Besides the Malays, with whom the Taman live in close association, other nearby neighbors include the Kantuk, the Kayan, and the Bukat. The Chinese are also a minority group in the area, and some Iban also live in one village among the Taman as a minority. Some people from farther distances such as Sulawesi and Nusa Tenggara Timur also live both in the Putussibau area and among the Taman. Many Taman people have themselves migrated to Sarawak, and an undetermined number have established themselves in various parts of the Second and Third Divisions of that state.

Taman society is composed of three ranked strata: *samagat* (nobility), *pabiring* (middle rank), and *banua* (freemen/commoners). A fourth rank, slaves (*pangkam*) existed perhaps as recently as 1920.[1] Traditionally, rank was essential to leadership; however, its significance has waned as other indicators of status have ascended, and it is now associated mainly with marriage payments and fines associated with divorce and adultery: twice the usual payments are made to parties of *samagat* rank.[2] These differences do not carry over to fines associated with delicts pertaining to death or disputes over land or property; nor are fines for people of *samagat* status lightened in deference to their noble pedigree. Finally, there is no discernable relationship between the system of rank and shamanism.

Taman social structure is characterized by cognatic kinship, ambilocal residence, and stem family household system. About half the Taman villagers live in longhouses while the remainder live in individual houses. Village units under the leadership of headmen may consist of a combination of a longhouse and single residences. The Taman economy is organized around shifting rice cultivation, which requires the mobilization of cooperative work groups based on kin and local ties. The other major source of income in this area is rubber tapping. But a large fraction of income is brought in by men who leave the area to work in timber areas in Sarawak and in remote areas of Kalimantan. All the Taman villages have schools, and while even elementary school education is not universal, most Taman people born after 1950 have had at least some education, and increasing numbers have gone on to junior high school, high school, and even higher education.

THE MEANING OF SHAMANISM

The Taman have been under the influence of the Catholic church since the 1930s, and a majority are now officially adherents of Catholicism, with a smaller number of Protestants. A small fraction (somewhat under five percent) identify themselves as Muslim, and the remainder have never been converted to a world religion. Shamanism and other forms of spirit propitiation persist despite the acknowledgment that such practices go against the teachings of religion and the inference that they may be associated with satanism.

Shamanism is a kind of magical healing common in many tribal and band societies, including the peoples of Borneo. It has often been characterized as the earliest religion or the most primitive kind of medicine, but shamanism is not in itself either a medical or a religious system; rather it is part of a comprehensive system of beliefs and practices relating the mundane human world to what is conceived to be a realm of spirits. Many of the magical and esoteric aspects of the shaman's craft cannot be known or perceived by laymen. Shamanism relies on the experiences of practitioners while they are in an altered state of consciousness that is represented as an encounter with a spirit. It differs, in this respect, from spirit possession and spirit mediumship in that spirits are not seen to occupy or control the shaman's body as they are in possession and mediumship. Raymond Firth (1967:296) defines spirit possession as abnormal behavior interpreted by others as "evidence that a spirit is controlling the person's actions and probably inhabiting his body." Shamanism, in contrast, is characterized by a "mastery" over spirits (Firth 1967, Lewis 1971)--the shaman controls the situation and works actively with certain spirit familiars. Mircea Eliade (1964:5) has stated that shamans specialize in ceremonies in which their souls are believed to leave their bodies "and ascend to the sky or descend to the underworld." Another essential characteristic of shamanism, noted by Åke Hultkrantz (1978), is that the shaman labors on behalf of a human interest through mediation between humans and spirits. Finally, Arthur E. Hippler (1976) views the shaman as creatively integrating psychosexual concerns. The content of these concerns varies "from culture to culture and according to the degree of [the individual shaman's] ability to 'regress in the service of the ego'" (Hippler 1976:112).

THE TAMAN *BALIEN* SYSTEM

Shamanism does not always involve the cure of disease, and in many societies shamans lead non-medical ceremonies of divination or propitiation. Among the Taman, too, the range of cures performed by shamans suggests that a purely medical definition of their role is too narrow and ethnocentric. Their principal task is to secure the recovery or safety of souls. While this mainly involves curing those illnesses caused by spirits and ghosts, it also requires them on occasion to perform ceremonies to assure the safe arrival of souls of the newly dead to their final resting place. Furthermore, the shaman, in recovering the souls of patients, also performs a ritual collectively redeeming the souls of the patients' entire family.

Shamanism among the Taman is loosely organized as a cult whose members execute their simple cures individually, but work together to perform their more advanced ceremonies. For their labor they receive compensation in goods such as cloth, bowls, and rice, as prescribed by custom.

The Taman shamanic complex involves a transformation of patients into healers. This process begins when an ailment is no longer identified as mere illness but as an affliction resulting from spiritual victimization, and curable only by exorcism. The person is next identified as a candidate for shamanic induction. Finally, having mastered the spirits, this person, previously defined as ill, becomes proficient at curing the illnesses of others.

All the illnesses curable by the shaman (*balien*) are attributable to spirits or ghosts. The simplest cure of the *balien* involves stroking the patient's body with stones that have been dipped in a medicinal decoction, the purpose of which is to bring the disease to the surface. The *balien* catches in a bowl a small pebble or splinter, that object purportedly being the disease: either a spirit or an object injected by a spirit. This very common ceremony is performed to cure simple bodily aches and pains, as well as a more complex illness called *najam* or *badet*. *Najam* is a cramp-like pain in the abdomen or chest which may "travel" to different parts of the torso, and cause shortness of breath. This respiratory or gastrointestinal disorder may be treated further by another ceremony if it persists. The more advanced *balien* ceremonies involve calling back, recapturing, and replacing the soul of a patient that has been taken hostage by a spirit.

Other circumstances surrounding the illness may call for a re-interpretation of the illness. Dreams or waking fantasies may be viewed as signs that pre-existing illnesses such as *najam* are due to a more deeply entrenched involvement by a spirit with the victim's soul. This illness can be treated by exorcism, but it could require the person to reorient his or her life by being initiated as a *balien*. A diagnosis of *pais layu-layu* ("pining away illness") or *dawawa jalu* ("capture by a 'being'") totally recasts the meaning of illness.

The decision to go through with the full initiation depends on the weighing of several factors, including oracles, the recurrence of symptoms, and consensus within the family (Bernstein 1990). Even so, there may be no interest in the *balien's* vocation. Becoming a *balien* involves a reorganization of identity. People do not voluntarily become *baliens*; on the contrary, they tend to dismiss suggestions that they be initiated into this cult. Some are even skeptical about the validity of the *balien's* cure. It is through a process of practicing cures and experiencing success as curers that they finally become adapted to this role.

Virtually all *baliens* are middle-aged or elderly women. Women's illnesses are more commonly reinterpreted as signs of shamanic destiny than are men's, and the recommendation to advance toward shamanic initiation is more often followed by women, due to the pattern in which their illness responds to treatment. Men and women appear to have the same motivations in becoming shamans, although the social forces bearing on the decision tend to propel women into *balien* candidacy while dissuading men from it. The *balien*, whether male or female, is above all a person who has been cured by coming to terms with the repressed unconscious by projecting threatening thoughts onto external agents who can be related to as friend on an esoteric plane of reality. Young people, too, are not prone to become shamans. The issues of psycho-sexual adaptation of young adulthood rarely cause concerns leading to shamanistic intervention. Rather, it is the mature adult, who already has a family, who is liable to be plagued by these issues and to suffer the illnesses that are viewed as symptomatic of spiritual affliction.

Comparison with Iban Shamanism

The best-described Bornean system of shamanism is that of the Iban people (Freeman 1967, Graham 1987, Sutlive 1976). Taman shamanism is very different from Iban shamanism in its techniques, despite the fact that the use of stones is integral to both. The Iban shaman (*manang*) holds quartz crystals (*batu ilau*) to the light to diagnose the cause of disease, while the Taman shaman rubs stones over the patient's body. These stones are thought of not only as "gifts" to the shaman, as they are among the Iban; they also are believed to be concrescences of spirit beings caught from the air during ceremonies. In communicating with the spirit world the Iban and many other Bornean peoples rock on a swing to induce semi-consciousness; the Taman shaman on the other hand crouches under a blanket while grasping a hook-tipped pole to conjure the spirits.[3] In Taman shamanism the lost soul of the patient is located and recaptured, and in some cases the disturbing spirits are neutralized by being caught and turned to stone. Derek Freeman (1967) has described a ceremony wherein an Iban shaman (*manang*) kills a spirit with his spear; Freeman maintains that this is a very rare procedure of which few shamans are capable. I know of no case of a Taman shaman ever killing a spirit in this way, though I cannot say definitively that it never happens among the Taman. The spirits turned to stone in the exorcism ceremonies are neutralized but potent.

Even more important than these technical differences between Iban and Taman shamanism are the differences in the character and motives of persons inducted into this healing vocation. Shamanism among the Iban is often the occupation of males who are ill-adapted to normal male pursuits, and it has been suggested by scholars that some Iban shamans are homosexuals, transvestites, hermaphrodites, or transsexuals. In fact, the highest degree of Iban shamanism is the "transformed" shaman (*manang bali*)--that is, one who has changed from a man into a woman. Vinson Sutlive (1976) has even pointed out that among the Iban becoming a shaman functions as an "alternate route to normality" for effeminate males.[4] And Valerie Mashman (1991:240) writes, "The manang has no gender and both genders at the same time. He apparently gets his superhuman power from this initial position, outside of the conventional notion of masculinity."

These issues of sexual identity are not pertinent in Taman shamans. While sexual conflicts and preoccupations are highly significant symptoms of the Taman shaman's predisposing condition, as shall be described below, I know of no evidence of deviations such as those that have been reported among the Iban.

Among the Taman, as among some Ibanic peoples, the calling for a shamanic vocation may indeed be associated with misfortune in the person's life. For instance, a Kantuk shaman whom I interviewed had suffered the loss of all his children before becoming inaugurated as a *manang*.[5] But in such instances the prospective shaman feels a vocation to heal. By contrast, the Taman patient facing shamanic initiation views becoming a *balien* as undesirable but necessary. It is undesirable because it involves close encounters with spirits that are uncomfortable and frightening to anyone but an initiated *balien*. It is also undesirable because the initiation ceremony involves a large expense and is complicated to prepare. The ceremony requires the labor of as many as ten *baliens*, including at least one male *balien*, and lasts for five days and nights (including a day-long pause after three days). The total expense, estimated during the time of my research to be between Rp.150,000 and Rp.200,000, was equal to an average family's income from all sources in as much as six months.[6]

The *balien's* initiation, in short, is viewed not only as a person's ceremonial inauguration as a member of a cult, but also as training for an occupation, and as the continuation and climax of a cycle of therapy.

Dreams as Symptoms

The syndromes of *pais layu-layu* and *dawawa jalu* that signify a shamanic destiny, cannot be understood except in the context of Taman concepts of the soul and the meaning of dreams. The Taman believe that each person has eight souls, seven of which are capable of leaving the body without causing death.[7] Illness can occur, however, if these souls do not return within one to two days. The wandering of the soul is considered a normal phenomenon the existence of which is proven by dreams. It is thought to cause illness only when a ghost (*antu*) or demon (*sai*) is encountered, because that being captures the soul or leads it astray, confusing the person.

Dreams are believed to be what the soul sees in its travels outside the body during sleep. They are thought of as harbingers of a person's fate, but normally not considered in themselves to signify illness. However, sexual dreams, as well as dreams in which one is offered food, are rarely taken by the Taman to be ordinary dreams, or to reflect a dreamer's pre-occupations; instead they are thought to be the result of a spirit's romantic attachment to the dreamer, and a pathogenic disturbance of the dreamer's soul.

One woman, Samarai, whom I interviewed when she was preparing to be exorcised as treatment for headaches and *najam*, had experienced erotic dreams that she said were very realistic. She said her dreams seemed as if a person actually slept with her, only the person was a spirit and not a human. She gave the following statement about the erotic ideal in her fantasy that she attributed to spirits:

> If one has already had sex with the devil after being treated by a *manang* one cannot get well. The dream is the same each night. He's like a beloved person. Like a former lover. If the dream is just once, it's nothing. If I sleep in the daytime the dream is the same. It is not one man but several. It is like a foreigner. People call this a *bayangan* ("vision," "apparition," "reflection," "shadow").[8] That's the most dangerous thing. If

you've made love to the ghost it is as if your spirit has been sold, there is no cure.

My informants gave a range of statements as to the meaning of sexual dreams. One said they meant something bad would happen. Another said that they were meetings with spirits. Another said that they meant the dreamer would become ill. Yet another said they were no problem (though he denied ever having them), and that

> if it is every night the result is that you will become a *balien*. All the more so if you dream a woman always wants you, loves you, gives you food. That's not a person, you know, but a *sai*, very beautiful.

This man apparently held the view that dreams about things in ordinary village life represented normal psychological functioning. He claims that there is no such thing as not dreaming. Asked about his own dreams, he reported that he dreamed every night, and that his dreams were ordinary ones of being with people in the village. He also admitted that an erotic dream could be the product of the imagination. But extraordinary dreams, with personages too ideal to come from real life, he attributes to bona fide spirit encounters. For more than two decades he has suffered from constipation, an affliction that has in others been resolved in shamanistic healing and initiation. For his sickness he has been treated by *baliens* "to his heart's content" (*sudah puas*) but to no effect. Asked whether he too would have to become a *balien* if he did feel cured after being cured by a *balien*, he replied only that he would not want to. He said his sickness is the same as that of a woman, Bolom, who did become a *balien*. Bolom, he said, was suited to be shamanized. Bolom's illness "has a time," while his does not. That is, her illness had a clear pattern and corresponded to certain relevant events, and has a definite pattern of its own, indicating that it is not an ordinary illness. They both suffer from the same sickness, he said, but their dreams are different. My informant knew Bolom's dreams, and Bolom herself verified his account.

In her dreams other people are given cooked food, but she is given raw food. This is a "test" by the demons. Bolom after awhile did not want her husband anymore, since she had a better lover in her dreams. If such a sickness is not quickly resolved, a person can go crazy, running in the forest. Banting (a male *balien*) also had dreams of women more beautiful than his wife. He was sick too, didn't want to eat, and was depressed. There is no other explanation than a shamanistic calling in such cases. How many years was he sick?

Bolom, when first exorcised, explained that her first problem was stomach ache, vomiting, and nausea;[9] she felt as if there was a baby in her belly. In Taman terms, her illness was *najam*. She said her problem had begun four or five months before. She went first to a doctor at the Military Public Health Center who gave her an injection and some pills, at the cost of Rp.3000. She was treated next by two Malay healers in succession, the first in another village and the second in town. They interpreted her illness as a kind of *najam* known in their terminology as *dugal*. Their attempted cures were unsuccessful. Only after these avenues had been tried did she seek advanced treatment by a *balien*. At this point, relevant dreams became pertinent to the explanation that a spirit had caused the sickness. In the dream she met an unknown man who asked to make love to her and tried to kill her with a knife when she refused. According to Bolom's original account she was frightened by the dream, and when she reported it to her husband they realized that she was being disturbed by a spirit. But I later learned that she was seduced by the dreamed figure, since she reportedly did not want her husband anymore, since she had a better lover in her dreams. Besides the sexual dreams, Bolom repeatedly dreamed that she, among many people, was offered raw food, while the others were served cooked food. This dream was interpreted as a "test" by the spirits. Bolom's husband talked to several *baliens* and found four to perform the *mengadengi* ceremony, a night-long exorcism in which spirits are called and neutralized by being caught and turned into stone. After the ceremony, the couple were not certain of whether she would herself be initiated as a *balien*. It depended, they said, on the sign from the areca blossom. At the conclusion of the *mengadengi* ceremony, a frond is split open and the young blossom examined and hung up. If the tips are hooked it is a sign or "proof" that the person will be cured by the ceremony. The woman had danced with the *baliens* but said she had no interest in becoming one herself. She said she felt somewhat better and thought that maybe she was cured.

Three and a half months later Bolom was initiated as a *balien*. The decision to go ahead with this ceremony was made one month in advance of the ceremony, and it is a tribute to her husband's resources that it was completed so promptly. According to him, if the person is briefly cured, then relapses, it is a sign that the sickness is from the spirits and the person must be initiated with all possible speed. He said that many cases of lingering illness may be attributed to the fact that these reappearing symptoms following a successful *mengadengi* ceremony are ignored.

Long after her initiation, Bolom still suffered occasionally from constipation, but she felt, and her family agreed, that she had been cured of spiritual disturbance inasmuch as she had regained her appetite and ceased having dreams indicative of that illness. The "real" illness, it was perceived, had disappeared as she adapted, both psychologically and socially, to the role of the shaman.

Bolom's case, far from being unique, fits into a pattern that is culturally recognized. It appears that this "illness," at least in part, is the projection of one's own desire for a tabooed love object onto a spirit being who lives on a different plane of reality, and with this scenario the illness is re-interpreted as victimization by the spirit, with the subject as an unwilling participant.

Pais Layu-layu

Pais layu-layu is a label given to illnesses previously considered "ordinary" that have been re-interpreted. It has strong implications of spirit involvement and the shamanistic cure. The term refers to an illness that comes and goes inexplicably. It is undefinable at first; however, as the person complains and behaves in an uncharacteristic way, his or her fellows make a hypothetical diagnosis in the search for a resolution. The term *layu-layu* means "wilting, fading away, withering, weak, or drooping." The term *pais layu-layu* can be translated as "pining-away illness." It is the quintessential affliction of the prospective *balien*. A man who had recently undergone a one-night exorcism for *pais layu-layu* said:

> When one is sick one doesn't know what it is. For example, you can't eat, but you don't know what is wrong. But other people notice the difference. Someone who is destined to become a *balien* can't be treated by other medicine.

Generally, it is the *longing* for the person in the dreams that signals that the dream is part of a larger pattern of *pais layu-layu*. The influence of ghosts and demons is deduced from the coexistence of "sickness" and a dream. The illness itself may not be oppressive and the person may still be able to work. But the illness is considered highly perilous because the person's soul has been taken by a spirit or the ghost of a dead person, and may be difficult to extricate from the place of the dead. Another part of the pattern of those destined to become *baliens*, say some informants, is their sense of melancholy: they sometimes sit quietly, just pondering, and are sad for no reason.

Most of the *baliens* interviewed indicated that they had experienced sexual dreams before initiation, and felt a longing for the fantasized figure. Some women characterized their dreams as ones in which they were the objects of affection by an aggressive suitor, thus denying that they themselves had played an active role in the fantasy; one woman added that in her dreams her soul was submerged in water. The husband of a *balien* chronicled his wife's *pais layu-layu* as follows:

> Before she was initiated as a *manang* her sickness was normal, but she got thin, didn't want to eat, dreamed of meeting a man who wanted to take her away; in the daytime she remembered him.[10] She didn't want me anymore. She'd be in bed with me, and then say, "he has arrived." After she was initiated, these dreams never came again. (The spirits) had all been caught and turned into stones. The stones resembled (two men in the village).

When the apparition resembles living acquaintances, as in this case, those persons appearing in the vision are not held responsible for any role in the seduction.[11] Rather, the entire fantasy is considered to be the work of one or more spirits.

A girl about the age of puberty also suffered from *pais layu-layu*. She had a number of peculiar ailments, became thin, and lost her hair. The doctor in town was unable to cure her or to comprehend one of her symptoms, a wound on the abdomen. She also had dreams, which might have been considered insignificant were it not for the prevailing illness. In the dreams she met children who asked her to come with them to fish or capture fruit. In the context of the illness such dreams are taken as a sign of being chosen by a spirit as an object of interest, and a ruse to capture the person's soul. Consistent with the theme of *pais layu-layu* is the fresh fruit. Regular daily food for the Taman is rice with dried fish and boiled vegetables. Furthermore, she had a craving to drink palm wine and was constantly asking her father to bring her some. Not only is this an extremely unusual craving for a young girl under any circumstances, but the ceremonial use of palm wine by *baliens*, and the fact that it must be offered to spirits, signifies an obvious connection to the spirit world and to *balienism*. The *balien* in the village considered her sickness to be "different" from ordinary illness, and a night-long exorcism was performed. The cut on the abdomen disappeared, as did the dreams and cravings. The girl and her family were also told that she needed to be inducted as a *balien* to rid her of the illness, but because of her age she was advised to continue with the initiation after she reached adulthood.

Dawawa Jalu

A closely related but diagnostically distinct illness is called *dawawa jalu* ("capture by a 'being'"). Unlike *pais layu-layu*, it is not a dream, nor is there necessarily an implication of sexual longing. A male informant said that an example of *dawawa jalu* would be if he walked in the forest and, seeing an image of a person he knew, followed it.

My informants considered this syndrome to be different from *pais layu-layu*, or at least a special category of it. It is specifically a *balien's* sickness. There are several symptoms: seeing imaginary persons, loss of appetite, and weakness. In the case mentioned above, Bolom's family denied that she had *dawawa jalu* even though she did suffer disorientation *(hilang pemikiran*, "lost thinking") and sexual dreams:

> If she was in the forest and went to an area where there were certain large trees *(kayu ara*--possibly banyan), she was unable to pass. She would stop. She heard 'people' talking--the man in her dreams.

In *dawawa jalu* there are visions in waking life as well, and this seems to be the main distinction. While most informants mentioned the longing for a seducer who appeared in visions as the most salient symptoms of *dawawa jalu*, one recently-initiated *balien* denied having these. She told the following story:

> It wasn't that I wanted to become a *manang*, but when I walked in the forest I saw an imaginary person. This started two or three years ago. At first I didn't believe it. Then I told my family. They said maybe there was a ghost or 'being' *(jalu)*. The 'being' resembled a number of real people--my child, friends, male and female. After that when I saw rice it looked like ants to me and I didn't want to eat it. I was afraid of vines, thinking they were snakes. I frequently fainted.

A male *balien's* story was also typical:

> I did not know what sickness I had but was confused and saw (an apparition of) a girl. The girl was like a lover. I would often cry because I could not catch the spirit. When I was sick, I would notice that I had rattan cuts all over, but did not feel it, because a demon had entered me.

Many of the *baliens* I interviewed said their sickness was *dawawa jalu* rather than *pais layu-layu*. In one case I interviewed a *balien* and her family during her inauguration. Her family said that her *dawawa jalu* was from a spirit who resembled her husband. The first time she was sick, she was just sitting, and she fainted. The woman herself was very unspecific about the kind of spirit bothering her. Although she had seen it, she was unable to describe it at all, other than to say that it looked black. Another *balien* said that her soul had been taken by a demon who was her husband's double. This spirit, whom she loved, had the same name as her husband and looked like him, "only better." She felt an uncontrollable love for this apparition and stated that her heart was always going to him.

The narrative of a man who had just been exorcised days earlier exemplifies clearly the dissociation of one's own will from fantasy so characteristic in this illness:

> Prior to the exorcism ceremony I was disturbed by apparitions of three or four different girls whom I longed for. These images, not the actual girls they resembled, were the objects of my love. I would often faint when I was alone, walking or at home.
>
> Before I became sick I frequently dreamed of one particular girl, but when I saw her in real life I felt nothing toward her. This is because I was falling in love with a spirit rather than an actual person. This is typical of someone who is destined to become a *balien*. She could touch me but I could not touch her. I would see the apparition and want to follow it instead of my wife. The first time I was sick I was in my dry rice field planting something, about ten meters ahead of my wife. Then I saw the same girl who had been in my dreams. She wrapped her arms around me, but when I tried to return the embrace she was gone and I saw her somewhere else. I followed her and tried to catch up with her, but she disappeared again only to reappear somewhere else. My wife called attention to my odd habit of going off and asked, "Where are you going?" Only then did I realize that I had been distracted from my work, and I returned to my wife. After this I longed for the girl. That night she came again. According to other people I began dancing, but I was not aware of this. My wife and children began noticing my peculiar behavior. They took me to the Public Health Center for an injection, and also to an Islamic *dukun* who gave me an

amulet (*jimat*), but these treatments had no effect. Thus I was forced to find a *balien* in the village. Then the girl was caught by the *balien*.[12] I wanted to find the girl, and was given a choice. If I wanted to become a *balien* I could catch her myself. I tried to catch her with the leaf of the *suri* (*Cordyline fructicosa*) bush, according to the procedure of the *baliens*. But I did not tap her in quite the right way, and she "punched" me, striking me down, causing me to faint momentarily.

Dawawa jalu conforms to the phenomenon Price-Williams identifies as the "waking dream"--strikingly realistic imaginary scenes over which the subject feels no sense of control. These waking dreams, unlike active imagination, "are usually spontaneous and characteristically burst into an individual's ordinary consciousness" (Price-Williams 1987:251). Price-Williams comments further: "It has long been our habit to associate this frame of mind with passivity and sleep so that the possibility of an imaginative behavior expressed in action has escaped us--except on the theatrical stage, where it is generally conceived as being 'put on'" (1987:257-258). Erika Bourguignon (1972:415), however, cautions against accepting at face value informants' reports of dreams as compared to apparitions. She points out that not only the reporting of dreams and apparitions, but the subjective experience of these states, may be influenced by what she calls "cultural dogma."

In any case, in all of these instances of *dawawa jalu* a person's reference group notices the person's disorientation and distraction and puts pressure on the person to resolve it. The behavior patterns communicate to the group that the person is not living in the ordinary world.

BALIENS' ILLNESSES AS HYSTERIA

The Taman distinguish between *pais layu-layu*, which involves meeting a spirit-being in dreams, and *dawawa jalu*, which involves meeting the spirit-being in waking life. The underlying similarity, however, is far more significant than the difference. In both syndromes there is withdrawal, confusion, and a distaste for food. Sexual fantasy and its disavowal are often at the root of these symptoms that do not permanently cease upon being medicated. Pain and illness become associated with conflicts resulting from desires that the subject denies as originating in his or her own mind.

In both *pais layu-layu* and *dawawa jalu*, chronic disorders involving senseless suffering begin to make sense existentially when looked at as being the result of victimization. Both of these syndromes can be comprehended as hysterical illnesses. In fact, the entire *balien* cult, including the characteristic preoccupation and association with stones (projections of one's own self) appears to be a hysterical complex.[13]

Hysteria refers to psychoneurotic disorders that may include either dissociation (alteration in consciousness and personal identity) or conversion (somatic and sensory disturbances), or some combination of the two. Interestingly, the American Psychiatric Association has abolished the category of "hysteria" in the most recent editions of its Diagnostic and Statistical Manual of Mental Disorders, DSM III and DSM III-R (American Psychiatric Association 1980, 1987). Without denying the validity of hysteria as an etiology, the editors of the new manuals have dispersed hysterical illnesses into the unrelated diagnostic categories of "somatoform disorder" (previously labelled "conversion disorder") and "dissociative disorder." John C. Nemiah is critical of recent editions of *DSM*, noting, among other things, that "patients frequently manifest a mixture of both 'dissociative' and 'conversion' phenomena" (Nemiah 1988:246).

Psychoanalytic theory holds that hysteria involves the expression of repressed wishes first in fantasy and then in bodily symptoms. Clinical symptoms of hysteria include episodic disturbances in which "an ego-alien homogeneous constellation of ideas and emotions occupies the field of consciousness" (Abse 1959:274). The hysteric presents him or herself as weak and passive. While sexual relationships are disturbed, the person is often able to function normally in a work situation.

It is possible to express through fantasy desires about prohibited relationships. According to psychoanalytic theory (Fenichel 1945, Krohn 1978) the secret object of these fantasies is actually a parent. Alan Krohn, summarizing the psychoanalytic interpretation of hysteria typified by the work of Otto Fenichel, writes that hysteria is a sign of "forbidden wishes toward tabooed objects. The conflict...revolves...around the wish to establish a prohibited Oedipal relationship, (namely) a romance with a parent" (Krohn 1978:57). One theorist has written that "when traced to its roots, hysteria in all its forms is predominantly related to the climax of infantile sexuality, the Oedipus situation, with the struggle to surmount incestuous genital wishes" (Abse 1959:283). This interpretation of hysteria may need to be revised in applying depth psychology to the Taman folk syndromes, but it does appear that **some** tabooed relationship is fantasized.

The psychological prerequisite for hysterical symptoms is "a tendency to turn from reality to fantasy, to replace real sexual objects [with] fantasy representatives of infantile objects." Hysterics "retreat from disappointing reality to magical, wish-fulfilling daydreams." But if the daydreams are connected to repressed material, they too must be repressed, and the resulting repression yields somatic symptoms (Krohn 1978:59-60).

In hysteria, symptoms indirectly communicate wants and needs when direct expression is impossible. The expression of these symptoms must also meet with sympathy. Psychoanalysis posits that hysterics achieve through their illness both a "primary gain"--by keeping an internal conflict or need out of awareness--and a "secondary gain"--avoiding an unpleasant activity and getting support and relief from others (American Psychiatric Association 1987:257). Slavney (1990) has noted that this concept of secondary gain is closely related to what sociologists have called the "sick role," which involves exemption from ordinary duties (cf. Parsons 1964).

As to the etiology of hysterical personality, Blacker and Tupin have suggested that the hysteric is one whose mother has not allowed the overt expression of assertive behavior, but fosters dependency, encouraging illness by giving the child special care when he or she is sick. They write that:

> The hysteric experiences a period of early maternal deprivation. The more severe that is, the more the adult personality is seen as oral, dependent, infantile, pregenital, or reactive to the threat of narcissistic injury [Blacker and Tupin 1977:132].

Indeed, a craving for love is a characteristic part of the hysterical personality.

In applying these psychiatric interpretations of hysteria to the Taman ethnographic data one should ask whether any desires or motives may unconsciously be expressed by symptoms. What are the possible sources of the dreams, apparitions, and other symptoms of the prospective *balien*? What are the uses or purposes of the illness?

In clinical cases of hysteria, as in the Taman folk syndromes, patients commonly attribute their outbursts not to their own feelings but to alien forces (Shapiro 1965:128). Is it possible to understand complaints of spirit interference in the context of Taman values regarding sexuality?

Sexuality in Taman culture is viewed as the "disturbance" of a person, and marriage as "stealing" a woman, whose family must be compensated. Sexual behavior is highly regulated by customary law. But it appears that sexual fantasy is institutionalized in illness, spirit beliefs, and shamanism. Fantasies about forbidden sexual relationships are projected onto spirit beings. The person may then think of him- or herself as the "victim" of these externalized desires.

The inhibition of appetite characteristic of these syndromes may be the result of the eroticization of oral aggressive and receptive tendencies, resulting in the association of the hunger drive with threatening ego-alien sexual impulses (Alexander 1950:92). The dreams of being offered uncooked food may also evince a desire for a tabooed encounter. Fenichel (1945:145-147) has written of the inhibition of appetite and delusions about food as resulting from the repression of oral instincts, in which the food reminds the person of a desired object. However, Fenichel notes that eating disorders can be symptomatic of any number of mental disturbances:

> Orality, as the oldest field of instinctual conflicts, can be used later on to express any other instinctual conflicts, especially if experiences in infancy have left an oral fixation that facilitates a displacement from subsequent frustrations (primal scenes, birth of siblings) to oral conflicts. Any conflict between activity and receptivity may result in eating disturbances [1945:176].

The person suffering from *pais layu-layu* and *dawawa jalu* often experiences repulsion at normal nutrition, which should be a source of pleasure. However, in dreams the person is entreated to eat raw food. In waking life as well there may be a desire for unusual food and drink. At the same time, sexual relations with the usual partner are inhibited while the person longs for an envisioned perfect lover. The cultural associations of uncooked food may be related to an idea that the victim is afflicted by animal rather than human spirits, and that animals eat uncooked food. The spirits' preference for raw food may also reflect the theme of the spirit world being opposite to the human world.

Further insight into Taman values regarding food and orality can be gained by looking at their belief in, and practices surrounding, *kempunan*, a concept found in parts of Borneo and elsewhere in Southeast Asia (Geddes 1954:54; Howell 1984; Maxwell 1988; Tsing 1988). *Kempunan* refers to danger created by failing to complete an intended action or an expected one. A spirit, displeased at a person who has not acted properly, sets that person up for a disaster, usually in the form of an animal bite or other accidental mishap. The victim has, in essence, brought about his or her own misfortune because of a transgression. The victim has been negligent, in the view of the spirit, and suffers the consequences. This may be so even though the actions of a person other than the affected person may have been the cause of harm.

Kempunan is set off most often by neglecting to satisfy a desire to eat a certain food. Many illnesses are attributed to *kempunan*, and are diagnosed and treated as such by *baliens*. The belief in *kempunan* results in a system of etiquette by which a person may not eat without offering his or her food to everyone in the vicinity, even if that requires passing a spoonful of rice around a room. Not doing so exposes the others to *kempunan*. Also, food may not be declined outright, but must be symbolically accepted (Bernstein 1990:112-115). In psychological terms, oral frustration is seen by the Taman as extremely dangerous, with the potential of incurring the anger of spirits, thereby causing disaster or the accidental death not only of oneself but of others. This belief has resulted in norms that underlie the Taman etiquette system.

THE *BALIEN* VOCATION AS DESTINY

Having noted the importance of unconscious forces as factors in the shaman's predisposing illness, let us turn finally to the question of whether a person presents signs of illness **in order to** become a *balien*. Such an aspiration is culturally unacceptable. A person who admitted to having become a *balien* voluntarily, out of personal interest, would be considered a fraud. For the Taman, the idea of someone wanting to become a *balien* defies the prevailing belief that authentic *baliens* acquire their vocation as a result of being victimized by a spirit being. Not only is *balien* status not sought, but people **avoid** the prospect of becoming a *balien* even if they have been told that they must do so.[14] The issue of "choosing" to become a *balien* is often put as a matter of saving one's own life.

This attitude was expressed in a case in which two *baliens* performed an exorcism for a young woman who refused to consider the prospect that she might have to become a *balien* herself. The two *baliens*, talking between themselves, spoke of the futility of avoiding the inescapable call to the *balien's* profession. They remembered how they had both tried to avoid becoming *baliens* by seeking cures from Malay *dukun* (curers). One did not eat pork for twelve years because it was a prohibition attached to an amulet (*jimat*) given to her by the *dukun*. Finally she threw out the amulet and became a *balien* because the spirit kept returning to disturb her. The other woman said that she kept a *jimat* in her mosquito net on orders of a *dukun*, but the demon came in nonetheless. If a demon targets a person ("has their address") there is no way to keep it out, she said. So she threw away the *jimat*.

Having noted the hysterical qualities of the *baliens'* illnesses, we can apply to the Taman a hypothesis developed by Theodore Schwartz (1976) to explain the behavior of members of cargo cults in Melanesia. Noticing that the leaders of these cults often appear to experience epileptic-like seizures, Schwartz proposed that such behavior, in the context of cult organizations, is rarely truly pathogenic; more often it would better be described as **pathomimetic**. As Schwartz (1976:184) writes, "Some of the extreme behaviors observed in cults are **modeled** on pathogenic behaviors that occur under other circumstances." Among the pathogenic forms of ego-dissociation in such cases is the "conscious or unconscious acting-out of culturally defined cult behavior, as in acting-out under 'possession'." While certain illnesses may be significant as signs of authentic membership in a cult, a person who is self-selected or group-selected for such a role, "as an expression and perhaps resolution of other neurotic or psychotic tendencies" may imitate that pathological behavior. Thus it can be seen that certain needs pertaining to social adaptation may be expressed in the symptoms of *pais layu-layu* and *dawawa jalu*. There may also be an unconscious or unspeakable desire to join the *balien* cult as an initiate.

This does not necessarily mean that the people who suffer from these symptoms desire in any way to become healers. Rather, the *balien* system provides a socially acceptable and culturally meaningful way of repressing sexually disturbing material by projecting it onto a world of supernatural beings. Exorcism is the social process of recognizing and coming to deal with these feelings, while the *balien's* initiation is the process for curing the person, in part by formally altering the person's status from that of a victim to one who can heal others with the help of spirit intimates with whom he or she has made peace. Successfully initiated *baliens* are, in effect, cured: their delusions and psychosomatic disorders disappear, and they are liable to harness their imaginative powers in performing healing ceremonies. Previously ill-adapted in Taman society, they are well-adapted because of the specialized role now available to them.

CONCLUSION

It may be concluded from this study that people are not motivated to become *baliens* because of a vocation for healing, an interest in helping people, a desire for wealth, social position, or power from possessing a relationship with or esoteric knowledge of the supernatural. The cultural explanation of initiation into the *baliens'* cult is that it is a response to a situation of being targeted by a spirit. A condition of general malaise is prone to be labelled as a illness, and blamed on the machinations of a spirit seducer, if the sufferer experiences longing, melancholia, or loss of appetite in connection with a recurring fantasy or dream. This connection may require initiation into the *balien's* cult, depending on how the illness responds to ceremonial cure as well as augurs made during the initial exorcism. Whether the treatment works and the person goes on to become an effective *balien*, or the initiate does not recover, but sickens and dies, is considered in terms of fate, and not the quality of the ceremony or the motivation of the initiate.

The Taman syndromes I have described in this essay are not unique culture-bound disorders. They clearly fit a pattern of hysterical illness. But the forms hysteria takes depends very much on cultural and social circumstances. This investigation of two Taman folk syndromes suggests that culture molds the recognition, definition, and interpretation of illness.

ACKNOWLEDGEMENTS

My research in West Kalimantan (1985-1988) was made possible by fellowships from the National Institute of Mental Health and the Social Science Research Council. I am also grateful to the Indonesian Institute of Sciences (Lembaga Ilmu Pengetahuan Indonesia) and the Center for Environmental Studies of the Gadjah Mada State University for sponsoring my research. An earlier version of this paper, which was presented at the Annual Meeting of the American Anthropological Association in 1989, benefited from critical readings by Burton Benedict, Jeanne Bergman, George De Vos, Marco Jacquemet, Ondina Fachel Leal, Lyn Lowry, Roland Moore, Maria Olujic, Mary Porter, Bob Priest, Lesley Sharp, and Nick Townsend.

Of course, I am most deeply indebted to my Taman hosts and informants. In the interest of protecting their confidentiality I have substituted pseudonyms for their real proper names in this essay and all other reports on my research.

ILLUSTRATION 1

Baliens dancing in initiation ceremony.

ILLUSTRATION 2

Baliens dance with bowls on their heads, in which stones are to be captured.

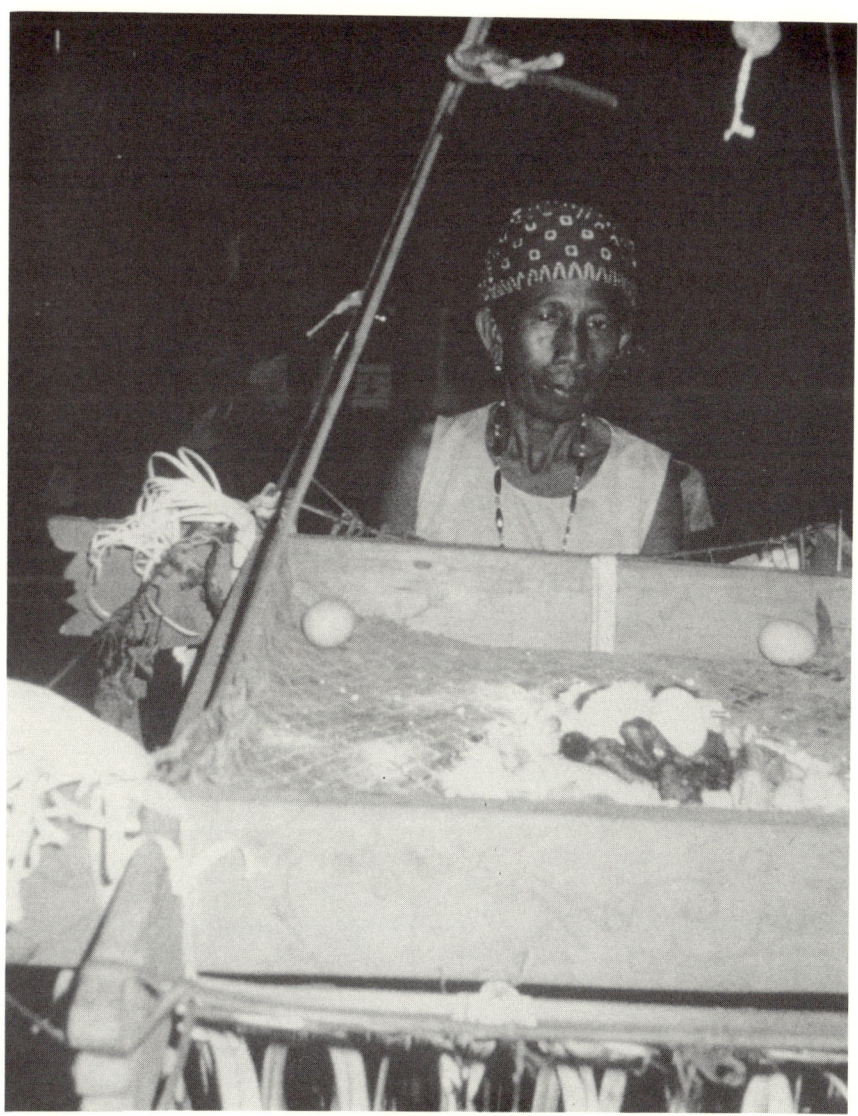

ILLUSTRATION 3

Balien prepares offering tray atop a structure called a *kalanqkang* to be used in the exorcism ceremony.

ILLUSTRATION 4

Leader of initiation ceremony strokes a young areca blossom with the herb *tantamu* as an augury to indicate the candidate's fate.

ILLUSTRATION 5

Display of the opened areca blossom.

ILLUSTRATION 6

A *balien* and her husband posed with a bowl containing their stone-doubles (*tamang*).

199

ILLUSTRATION 7

Balien prepares food in cracked bowls to be offered to spirits in a healing ceremony.

NOTES

1. Victor T. King (1985) has provided an outstanding study of the rank system as it existed in traditional Maloh society. See also Rousseau 1990 for further information on the context of inequality in traditional, pre-colonial Borneo.

2. See Anyang (1985) for a detailed account of Taman customary law pertaining to marriage, and Siong (1984) on divorce among the Taman.

3. Compare Gell's (1980) analysis of rocking as autistic behavior, and other forms of behavior used to induce trance. Gell draws a useful distinction between passive and active trance states.

4. Morris (1967) has written that Melanau men strongly resist the shamanic vocation precisely because of the shaman's reputation for androgyny. On the association of shamanism with sexual inversion see also Bogoras 1953.

5. A group culturally and linguistically similar to the Iban, but traditionally an enemy of both the Iban and the Taman; the Kantu' have been described by Michael Dove (see Dove 1985).

6. Equivalent to US$132.00 to $176.00 prior to a 32 percent devaluation of the *rupiah* on September 12, 1976.

7. Some believe that a person has sixteen souls, that is, two-times-eight. See Bernstein 1990:90.

8. *Bayangan* is an Indonesian word, and this informant in speaking to me may have been "switching codes" (Gumperz and Hymes 1972). However, other informants also used the word *bayangan* to describe their visions.

9. She used the Dutch word *maag*, which is commonly used in Indonesia to refer to gastritis.

10. This use of the Iban word to refer to the Taman shaman is very common.

11. People can try to force others to fall in love with them through the use of magical oils called *iayau*. See Bernstein n.d.(b).

12. That is, a stone was caught. The spirit being is turned into stone when the *balien* catches him or her.

13. Bernstein n.d.(a).

14. On resistance to becoming a shaman see also Morris 1967, Krader 1978.

REFERENCES

Abse, D. Wilfred
    1959   Hysteria. *In* American Handbook of Psychiatry, edited by Silvano Arieti, vol. 1, 272-92. New York: Basic Books.

Alexander, Franz
    1950   Psychosomatic Medicine. New York: W. W. Norton.

American Psychiatric Association
    1980   Diagnostic and Statistical Manual of Mental Disorders. 2d. ed. Washington.

    1987   Diagnostic and Statistical Manual of Mental Disorders. 3d. ed., rev. Washington.

Anyang, Y. C. Thambun
    1985   Hukum Adat Perkawinan Daya Taman Di Kecamatan Putussibau. Banda Aceh: Fakultas Hukum, Universitas Syiah Kuala Darussalam.

Bernstein, Jay H.
    1990   Taman Ethnomedicine: The Social Organization of Sickness and Medical Knowledge in the Upper Kapuas. Ph.D. dissertation, University of California, Berkeley.

    In Press(a) Stones in Taman Culture. *In* The Realm of the Sacred in Southeast Asia, edited by Robert R. Reed and Eric Crystal. In Press. Center for South and Southeast Asian Studies, University of California, Berkeley.

Bernstein, Jay H.
   In Press(b) Poisons and Antidotes among the Taman of West Kalimantan, Indonesia. (Ms.)

Blacker, Kay and Joe P. Tupin
   1977   Hysteria and Hysterical Structures: Developmental and Social Theories. *In* Hysterical Personality, edited by Mardi J. Horowitz, 97-141. New York: Jason Aronson.

Bogoras, Waldemar
   1900   The Invert as Shaman. *In* Primitive Heritage: An Anthropological Anthology, edited by Margaret Mead and Nicholas Calas, 425-8. New York: Random House.

Bourguignon, Erika.
   1972   Dreams and Altered States of Consciousness in Anthropological Research. *In* Psychological Anthropology, edited by Francis L. K. Hsu, 403-34. Cambridge, Mass.: Schenkman.

Dove, Michael R.
   1985   Swidden Agriculture in Indonesia: The Subsistance Strategies of the Kalimantan Kantu'. Berlin: Mouton.

Eliade, Mircea.
   1964   Shamanism: Archaic Techniques of Ecstasy. Translated by William R. Trask. Princeton: Princeton University Press.

Engelhardt, Tristam H., Jr.
   1982   Illnesses, Diseases, and Sicknesses. *In* The Humanity of the Ill: Phenomenological Perspectives, edited by Victor Kestenbaum, 142-56. Knoxville: University of Tennessee Press.

Fenichel, Otto.
   1945   The Psychoanalytic Theory of Neurosis. New York: W. W. Norton.

Firth, Raymond
   1967   Tikopia Ritual and Belief. Boston: Beacon Press.

Frake, Charles O.
1980   Interpretations of Illness: An Ethnographic Perspective on Events and Their Causes. *In* Language and Cultural Description: Selected Papers of Charles O. Frake, edited by Anwar S. Dil, 61-82. Stanford: Stanford University Press.

Freeman, Derek
1967   Shaman and Incubus. Psychoanalytic Study of Society 4:315-343.

Geddes, W. R.
1954   The Land Dayaks of Sarawak: A Report on a Social Economic Survey of the Land Dayaks of Sarawak Presented to the Colonial Research Council. London: Her Majesty's Stationery Office.

Gell, Alfred
1980   The Gods at Play: Vertigo and Possession in Muria Religion. Man 15:219-248.

Graham, Penelope
1987   Iban Shamanism: An Analysis of the Ethnographic Literature. An Occasional Paper of the Department of Anthropology, Australian National University, Canberra.

Gumperz, John J. and Dell H. Hymes, eds.
1972   Directions in Sociolinguistics. New York: Holt, Rinehart, and Winston.

Hippler, Arthur E.
1976   Shamans, Curers, and Personality: Suggestions Toward a Theoretical Model. *In* Culture-Bound Syndromes, Ethno-psychiatry, and Alternate Therapies: Volume IV of Mental Health Research in Asia and the Pacific, edited by William P. Lebra, 103-114. Honolulu: University Press of Hawaii.

Howell, Signe
1984   Society and Cosmos: Che Wong of Peninsular Malaysia. Singapore: Oxford University Press.

Hultkrantz, Åke
1978 Ecological and Phenomenological Aspects of Shamanism. *In* Shamanism in Siberia, edited by V. Diószegi and M. Hoppál, 27-58. Budapest: Akadémiai Kiadó.

King, Victor T.
1985 The Maloh of West Kalimantan: An Ethnographic Study of Social Inequality and Social Change among an Indonesian Borneo People. Dordecht: Foris Publications.

Krader, L.
1978 Shamanism: Theory and History in Buryat Society. *In* Shamanism in Siberia, edited by V. Diószegi and M. Hoppál, 181-236. Budapest: Akadémiai Kiadó.

Krohn, Alan
1978 Hysteria: The Elusive Neurosis. New York: International Universities Press. (Psychological Issues 12[1/2], monograph 45/46).

Lewis, I. M.
1971 Ecstatic Religion: A Study of Shamanism and Spirit Possession. Harmondsworth: Penguin.

Mashman, Valerie
1991 Warriors and Weavers: A Study of Gender Relations Among the Iban of Sarawak. *In* Female and Male in Borneo: Contributions and Challenges to Gender Studies, edited by Vinson H. Sutlive, 231-70. Monograph Series of the Borneo Research Council, No. 1. College of William and Mary, Williamsburg, Virginia, Williamsburg: Borneo Research Council.

Maxwell, Allen R.
1988 The Cultural Construction of Danger in Brunei. Paper presented at the 87th Annual Meeting of the American Anthropological Association, Phoenix.

Morris, H. S.
1967 Shamanism among the Oya Melanau. *In* Social Organization: Essays Presented to Raymond Firth, edited by Maurice Freedman, 189-216. London: Frank Cass & Co.

Nemiah, John C.
1988   Psychoneurotic Disorders. *In* The New Harvard Guide to Psychiatry, edited by Armand M. Nicholas, Jr., 234-258. Cambridge: Harvard University Press.

Parsons, Talcott
1964   Social Structure and Personality. New York: Free Press.

Price-Williams, Douglass
1987   The Waking Dream in Ethnographic Perspective. *In* Dreaming: Anthropological and Psychological Interpretations, edited by B. Tedlock, 246-262. Cambridge: Cambridge University Press.

Rousseau, Jérôme
1990   Central Borneo: Ethnic Identity and Social Life in a Stratified Society. Oxford: Clarendon Press.

Schwartz, Theodore
1976   The Cargo Cult: a Melanesian Type-Response to Change. *In* Responses to Change: Society, Culture, and Personality, edited by George A. De Vos, 157-206. New York: D. Van Nostrand Reinhold. Co.

Shapiro, David
1965   Neurotic Styles. New York: Basic Books.

Siong, Bartholomeus Moses
1984   Berberapa Faktor Sosial Budaya Yang Ikut Berperan Dalam Terjadinya Perceraian Dikalangan Suku Dayak Taman Kristen Di Sibau Hilir. Sarjana [Master's] thesis, Fakultas Theologia, Universitas Kristen Satya Wacana.

Slavney, Phillip R.
1990   Perspectives on Hysteria. Baltimore: Johns Hopkins University Press.

Sutlive, Vinson H., Jr.
1976   The Iban *manang*: An Alternate Route to Normality. *In* Studies in Borneo Societies: Social Processes and Anthropological Explanation, edited by G. N. Appell, 64-71. Center for Southeast Asian Studies, Special Report no. 12. Northern Illinois University, Dekalb.

Tsing, Anna
1988   Healing Boundaries in South Kalimantan. Social Science and Medicine 27:829-839.

SPIRIT POSSESSION AS EXCULPATION, WITH EXAMPLES FROM THE SARAWAK CHINESE

RICHARD C. FIDLER
Rhode Island College

Nearly a third of the inhabitants of Sarawak are ethnic Chinese. Only the Iban outnumber them. Although the Chinese of Sarawak can be found in every part of the state, in every kind of physical environment, occupying every variety of resource nitch and occupational mode, they are best known as urban professionals and middle-man entrepôt traders (*towkay*) in the hundreds of bazaars and market towns that dot the banks of Sarawak's rivers.[1] There they purchase the jungle products collected from the interior by the indigenous peoples and export those products to the world. They also provide the imported manufactured goods, including steel and the heirlooms (*pesaka*) and their modern equivalents, that the interior communities cannot produce for themselves. Often, too, they are providers of skills and services and conduits of communication and contact linking their local community to the outside world.

Virtually all Sarawak Chinese today are locally-born citizens, often three, four, or more generations removed from the original immigrants. They do, however, retain the use of the southeastern Chinese "dialects," the mutually unintelligible languages that distinguish Hokkiens, Cantonese, Foochows, Hakkas, Teochiews, and the score of other regional variations originating in Guangdong and Fujian Provinces of China. They communicate with each other (and their non-Chinese neighbors) by being multilingual. In addition, **written** Chinese, being ideographic, is identical for all dialects and therefore communicates across these divisions. Remnants of the history of Chinese immigration in Sarawak can be seen in the concentrations of certain dialect groups in certain parts of the state--Hakka in the First (now Kuching) Division, Foochow near Sibu, etc.--but these distinctions are beginning to fade as the younger generations move, intermix, and intermarry. Much the same is true of other cultural traits and traditions of the different dialect groups--they have certainly not yet vanished into a homogenized "Chinese" culture, but the movement in that direction is inexorable. The religious beliefs of the Sarawak Chinese exemplify this trend; they were not so different from each other to begin with (especially regarding demons and spirit possession) and they cross dialect boundaries quite easily today.

Although the historical, linguistic, and cultural origins of the Chinese could not be more different or more remote from those of the interior indigenous peoples or the lowland, coastal Malay speakers of Borneo, they all **do** share one cultural concept in common--a basic "animistic" belief in the existence of spirits (*antu*, *hantu*, or *kwei*), the belief that such spirits can and do cause illness and distress, and the use of a talented practitioner, an exorcist, to combat them. Therefore, the observations and conclusions that follow, though drawn from my research in the small market towns of the Rajang Valley, apply not only to their residents but to all people everywhere who are subject to spirit possession.

THEORETICAL BACKGROUND

In his classic essay "The Self and Its Behavioral Environment," A. Irving Hallowell (1955) reminds us that self-awareness is a generic human trait, one of the features that distinguishes us from animals lower on the evolutionary scale. "Everyone, with the possible exception of infants, some philosophers, and some psychopaths, is aware of one's self" (Chien 1944:305 quoted in Hallowell 1955:75). **Self**-awareness leads to the distinction between "self" and "other;" one thinks of one's self with reference to the sociocultural world in which the self must function. A person's concepts of his/her own self cannot be divorced from the characteristics of the society that socialized that self, and the society's ideals regarding the relations between the self and others in the group. Other animals can function in groups without self-orientation, but humans cannot; a common function of culture is to provide these self-orientations (Hallowell 1955:76). Hallowell suggests (1955:89) that culture provides five basic orientations for the self: to the self, to objects, to space and time, to needs and motivations, and to social norms.

Normative orientation inculcates in the self a set of values, ideals, and standards; self-awareness becomes self-appraisal of one's conduct with reference to these social norms. The individual is motivated to consider whether his/her actions are good or bad, right or wrong, socially acceptable or normatively "abnormal." This constant self-appraisal is the source of one's feelings of self-esteem and self-respect. "Implicit in moral appraisal is the concomitant assumption that the individual has volitional control over his own acts" (Hallowell 1955:106). Being capable of doing good means being capable of also doing evil; doing the right thing means you can also do wrong. If fulfilling the norms brings positive self-esteem and respect, failing them brings the negative--embarrassment, shame, **guilt**. Hallowell (1955:106) states that in other animals, anxiety can cause feelings of fear and apprehension, but not of guilt. In spite of the common children's joke, you will never see an embarrassed zebra, to feel responsible for the actions of one's self one must have the solely-human awareness of self. Self-deprecation and negative esteem are counter productive to self-maintenance and social interaction, yet self-evaluation is inescapable. "This imposes a characteristic psychological burden upon the human being," since it is not always possible to reconcile the individual's needs with the demands imposed by society's norms. "Unconscious mechanisms that operate at a psychological level that does not involve self-awareness may be viewed as an adaptive means that permits some measure of compromise between conflicting forces" (Hallowell 1955:106). These unconscious mechanisms can alleviate the stress caused by this conflict, relieve the psycho-burden of guilt, and bolster self-esteem. Hallowell (1955:107) even includes "self-deception" among these mechanisms; aspects of the self that are disapproved are disguised, for the needs of self-image are primal.

The role of religion in the amelioration of anxiety and relief of social and personal stress is so well documented in the literature that it need not be repeated here. In Melford Spiro's essay, "Religious Systems as Culturally Constituted Defense Mechanisms" (1965:100-113), the title by itself makes this point. He states that Burmese men who become Theraveda Buddhist monks would be insecure, abnormal types in society at large, but the very nature of their psycho-social defects makes them ideal members of the monastic community. Religion not only relieves them, and society, of the trauma of their deviance, but staffs a vital social institution in the process. Since religion, as Tylor said, is "belief in spiritual beings," spirit-possession is an aspect of religion and is quite frequently used as a mechanism for the relief of anxiety and stress. Listing the uses made of spirit possession ethnographically, Vincent Crapanzano (1977:20) includes "an escape from an unpleasant situation." I. M. Lewis (1971) elaborates these uses in detail while Crapanzano and Vivian Garrison (1977) provide ethnographic examples. These authors and others mention a variety of ways that spirit possession can be employed regarding anxiety, stress, insecurity and uncertainty--divination and augury, decision making, preparation of charms and prophylactics, curing, confession, sanctification, salvation, and various combinations and synthesis of these elements. I believe that one important mechanism has so far been overlooked: exculpation--to free from blame.

It is my thesis that by ascribing the causes of one's actions to involuntary possession by supernatural spirits, the self not only avoids the penalties for those actions but, most importantly, obviates any feelings of blame, shame, self-deprecation, or guilt: "It wasn't my fault; the Devil made me do it." Thus in any arena in which the self comes into conflict with its normative orientations, regarding self or others, thoughts or actions, commissions or omissions, self-esteem and -respect can be maintained by exculpation. I disagree with Anthony Wallace (1966:140-41) when he says that while the possession theory "may be intellectually satisfying to the victim as an explanation for his condition, [it] will not bring relief, and the search for exorcism becomes a search for the path to salvation itself." Exculpation makes salvation unnecessary, irrelevant, for the **victim** has committed no breach of norms and has done nothing to be saved from. Exculpation is even better than witchcraft for transferring fault, for witchcraft requires that the responsibility for the negative behavior be assigned to some other person, some fellow human being (see Lewis 1971:118). With exculpation, no **one**, that is, no fellow human, need be accused; the blame lies beyond the realm of human responsibility.

This process can work even in societies where illness is seen as a punishment for sins: if you're ill you must have sinned and you deserve it. But if spirits caused the illness, no sin is needed. "Possession by a peripheral spirit thus provides an explanation of sickness which does not carry this implication of guilt" (Lewis 1971:87n); Lewis cites the example of Job. Benjamin Paul (1967:163-64) describes a case from Guatemala, where suffering from mental illness connotes personal inadequacy, lowering self-esteem so that the victim feels at fault for being disturbed. Bad behavior may have caused the spirits to send this curse, but **whose** bad behavior? Not necessarily the victim's. "It is likely that in her own mind, Maria [the victim] was only an innocent bystander who fell victim to ghostly vengeance directed at someone else in the household." Even in societies where these illness-causing sins must be confessed before curing is possible (e.g. Clive Kessler's [1977:299] Kelantan Malays and Hallowell's [1955:256] Saulteaux) the spirit possession excuse can provide some measure of exculpation "since it permits reference of virtually all serious problems to the 'powers' for solution. Thereby the individual is to some degree freed of responsibility for controlling and directing his own life" (Mischel & Mischel 1958:257). This is done, in Crapanzano's (1977:170) terms, "by casting out the tensions and hostilities, the resentment and anger, the acceptance and projection of guilt...onto the demonic stage."

It should be noted here that exculpative possessions are most often the "involuntary" kind that can strike anyone at any time without being sought-after, induced, or desired by the victim, rather than the "voluntary" possessions used by spirit mediums or shamans who wish to put themselves into a trance state or to be possessed, as part of practicing their mediumship. (An exception to this is described later in this paper.) Therefore, the treatment for these possessions is usually to attempt to exorcise the offending spirit with the goal of permanent expulsion--get rid of it forever--rather than seeking to establish a continuing symbiosis with the spirit that might be utilized in future supernatural communications, as a medium might have with his "familiar" (Crapanzano 1977:15).

Some Examples from the Literature

Research to find cross-cultural examples of exculpative possession has not been easy. Murdock's Outline of Cultural Materials (1967) has no category number for "sin." His index directs you to "Wrongs" (673), which are violations of **legal** norms, "Religious Offenses" (688), largely blasphemy and impiety, and "Purification and Expiation" (783), which at least includes "sense of guilt" and "riddance of sin." Actual ethnographic material filed under this heading in the Human Relations Area Files, however, usually turns out to be of the "what to do with menstrual blood" variety.

Reading ethnographic case studies of spirit possession can be equally frustrating; so many authors dwell entirely on the voluntarily possessed, such as the medium, rather than on the involuntary victims who need the exorcism. Walter Skeat (1972[1900]:436-444), for example, devotes eight pages to describing the exorcism of a man "ill of some slight ailment" that he observed in Selangor in 1896. Though the detail of the ritual is vast, complete with chants and a floor-plan, he never tells us what had caused the ailment **or what happened to the patient**. Kessler (1977:303) tantalizes us by mentioning that he has data on nine cases of *main puteri* for Kelantan Malay men suffering from stress-related illnesses. The younger men had all returned reluctantly to the village after failing to succeed in the outer world; the older men had all lost their jobs on fishing boats to younger, stronger men and were retired to a life among the women--prime subjects for exculpative possessions. But since Kessler's purpose is to support Lewis' (1971) thesis that possession is used by weak, down-trodden **women** to gain personal status and respect, he tells us no more about these cases of male possession. Finding societies where it is believed that "evil spirits" cause illness and misfortune is easy, both around the world and in Borneo, where Iban, Bidayuh, Malays, and Chinese all qualify. Finding examples of exculpation is more difficult.

Some evidence of exculpation can be derived from the ethnographic literature by reading in the negative. The Ifaluk, as described by Spiro (1952:497-503), live on a Pacific Ocean atoll so small that interpersonal violence simply cannot be tolerated. They believe that all humans are born good and normal. All abnormalities, including aggression, are termed *malebush* and are caused by being possessed by an *alus* spirit. "The people could not remember one instance of antisocial behavior, **aside from the** *malebush*, nor were any examples of it observed in the course of this investigation," reports Spiro (1952:498, emphasis mine). So there **is** violence among the Ifaluk after all, in the form of *malebush*, but is so thoroughly exculpated to the spirits that it is thought not to exist among **people**. Spiro's purpose in presenting this case is to describe how aggression is rechanneled, so he does not examine the exculpative aspects that we can extract from his data.

To take another example, the Oglala Sioux as described by Paul Radin share the Ifaluk view that humans are naturally, normally good. "Jealousy, maliciousness, etc., are not conceived of as caused by any soul or entity residing within but are regarded as due to discarnate *sicun*" (1957:268). *Sicun* are souls unworthy of a contented afterlife; they wander the earth, communicate with mankind, and are a cause of trouble. This concept of the Sioux, says Radin "throws infinitely more of the responsibility for our actions upon the gods."

Some references in the literature are not so oblique: Wallace (1966:141) reports that among the Iroquois, abnormal people who walked on all fours were regarded as possessed by the bear spirit and received the cathartic rituals of the Bear Society, while "kleptomaniacs were, by analogous reasoning, subjected to the rituals of the Chipmunk Society."

When Ruth and Stanley Freed (1967:295-320) report the primary and secondary gains that can result from spirit possession, they do not include exculpation of blame, but it can be seen in the ethnographic case study upon which their analysis is based. A teen-age bride in North India suffered repeated attacks of spirit possession for the first time in her life shortly after her permanent move into her husband's extended family household. She was alternately teased and dominated by her new in-laws, greatly missed her supportive natal family, and had an enduring fear and dread of sexual intercourse and its consequences, even with a marital spouse. As a result of her attacks, she became the center of attention in the household, aroused sympathy and concern among both her parents and her affines, and "her husband reduced his sexual demands" (Freed and Freed 1967:315). In the eyes of her society, it was the evil, possessing spirits, not the reluctant bride, who got the blame.

Douglas Raybeck (1974:225-242) describes a quarrel between two brothers-in-law in a Kelantan Malay village where the prime offender actually used--successfully--the Malay equivalent of the "the Devil made me do it" excuse. Ali and Ismail had been quarrelling for some time about many disagreements when Ismail lost his temper and hit Ali with a *parang* knife, sending him to the hospital and alerting the police and courts to the altercation. In his letter to the court, Ismail "stated that he was not fully responsible for his actions as he had been invaded by the spirit of Satan in a moment of weakness." Since it is "common knowledge in Kelantan that spirits (*hantu*, *jinn*, etc.) can in certain circumstances possess a man's body and direct his actions...Ismail's excuse provided a means for Kampong Pura-Pura villagers, especially members of Ali's *waris* [kindred] to rationalize his actions...A portion of the blame, and responsibility for a normally unacceptable act, was displaced to the spirit world" (Raybeck 1974:230-231). Other examples can be found in the literature that illustrate the exculpative utility of spirit possession, including Crapanzano (1977), Firth (1974), Garrison (1977), and Lewis (1971), though none of these scholars uses this label to identify it as such.

There is a variation of the exculpative process in spirit possession that appears so frequently in the literature that it must be noted here, even though it is not directly related to my thesis that being possessed can alleviate the social and psychological guilt that comes from failure to adhere to cultural norms. This other form is that of people doing things while in a possession trance that they couldn't get away with normally. Breaches of sexual mores or gender behavior, violence, swearing and vulgar language and acts, verbal abuse and confrontation are among the examples found in the case study literature. Walter Mischel and Frances Mischel (1958:254) thus "hypothesize that the practice of spirit possession permits the sanctioned expression of behaviors which are otherwise socially unacceptable or unavailable." Although at first glance this appears to be identical to my thesis, an examination of the case histories and the **sequence of possessive, exculpative events** in these histories, demonstrates the inherent differences in utilization. For example, a woman patient, "down-trodden and seeking status" in Lewis' terms, becomes possessed by a spirit during a public trance performance. She acts a male role, performing exclusively-male behaviors, and uses the opportunity to blatantly "tell off" the gathered audience, openly expressing the nature of her discontent (see Kessler [1977:306-312] regarding a Kelantan Malay instance; see also Crapanzano concerning Morocco [1977:141-176]).

Several common features occur in this form of exculpative possession: 1) The person goes into a possession trance **voluntarily**, rather then being a "victim" struck or attacked **involuntarily** against his/her own will or desire. 2) The possession usually occurs in public before a large local audience; it does not strike privately while alone or with close family. 3) Perhaps most notably, it is the actions during this specific, induced, voluntary possession that are "exculpated" from standard normative sanctions--"the things I'm doing right now here in front of you all," rather than any past or previous infractions of the norms or social rules. This form of exculpative possession can certainly preform a variety of very useful social and psychological functions for the group, the patient, and even the attending medium or shaman. It can instruct the community regarding appropriate behaviors, release tensions, both group and individual, provide a catharsis for the patient, display the power and prowess of the medium, even entertain the crowd. (See Jack Potter's [1978:321-345] account of a medium at work in a Cantonese village in Hong Kong for a variety of these behaviors.) It must certainly be included in any analysis of exculpative possession, and may even overlap with or intertwine with the form of exculpation that is the focus of my observations and concern. How this form differs form "my kind" of exculpation is best illustrated by presenting two cases I have personally observed and recorded.

CHINESE RELIGION IN SARAWAK

It will be easier to understand these cases and place them in the context of our concerns regarding spirit possession if I first present some brief orientation to the religious beliefs and practices of the Chinese community of Sarawak.

In an earlier article (1978:179) I introduced the religious beliefs of the Chinese by stating that Chinese religion, wherever it is practiced, has three major foci of orientation: 1) the organized theologies of Buddhism, Taoism, and the non-religious moral philosophy of Confucius; 2) the "folk religion" of supernatural powers, gods, spirits, demons, and deities; and 3) the cult of family ancestors. These three foci are not mutually exclusive; in fact, they are rarely embodied in independent ritual practices. Whichever of the three is dominant in any specific ritual, belief, or function, the other two are integral subsystems supporting it. These three aspects of belief operate, as all Chinese relationships should, in harmony with each other. In a temple, at permanent or temporary shrines, in the home, at the graveyard, all three orientations mutually reinforce the fundamental relationship of the individual to his universe.

Of these three, it is "folk religion" that is most salient in a discussion of spirit possession among the Chinese of Sarawak, but the other two cannot be ignored completely. The cosmology of "folk religion" is so similar to, and historically intertwined with, the fundamentals of Taoism that these are inseparable concepts. None of the participants in the rituals or events I describe below would identify themselves as "Taoists," nor even consider themselves to be especially knowledgeable about its precepts, yet all have absorbed and inculcated the Taoist beliefs regarding the nature of the universe and its supernatural powers as part of their heritage. To them, this is "Chinese culture." The same can be said for the "cult of the ancestors." In Sarawak today it is quite unusual to observe any semblance of the "traditional" ancestor homage (altars, tablets, lineage temples and the like) outside of the immediate (usually nuclear) family household. In the smaller towns and bazaars, clan temples and ancestor tablets simply do not appear. In their place, and serving the same social/structural functions, is the regard for the "family" and respect for the earlier members of **all** descent lines who established it in Sarawak. As with the Taoist cosmology, the *hsiao* (filial piety) of the ancestor cult has become ordinary "Chinese culture."

"Folk Religion" has no formal name in the Chinese languages. The scholars and literati who invented and utilized the ideographic characters considered it to be foolish peasant superstition, not worth writing about, and did not deign to recognize it nor dignify it with a proper character name. "The Master [Confucius] did not speak on these matters." Yet for millennia it has been the most common and widespread belief system among the Chinese. Chinese folk religion is basically a form of animism, but animism that has had so many thousands of years to develop that its fundamentally-simple roots have been enormously elaborated by myth and legend. Underneath all this cultural trim two alternating cosmic powers, *yang* and *yin*, generate the vital forces that animate the universe, drive the dynamo of existence, and influence its course. These vital forces, often symbolized by the eight trigrams of solid and/or broken lines, direct earthly events, but can also **be** directed and channeled. Dealing with the universe of existence is a constant balancing of these supernatural forces to maximize beneficial effects and minimize detrimental ones.

Overseeing, interacting, and constantly tinkering with these forces is a vast multitude of supernatural entities, "gods" and "demons" of all sorts and persuasions--a giant bureaucracy of spiritual beings. Most fall into one of two basic categories: *shen* ("gods"), often personified with names and biographies, such as The King of Heaven, Kwan Yin, Goddess of Mercy, or the popular local favorite in Sarawak, Tua Peh Kung, Patron of Prosperity; and *kwei* ("demons"), wily, sly characters that are constant sources of trouble wherever they appear. Obviously, in addition to prophylactic charms and rituals to repel them, one way to counter the negative effects of *kwei* contamination is to harness a more powerful *shen* spirit to drive them away--exorcism. This requires the use of a shaman or medium, an individual who can release his or her own soul from the body in order to allow a familiar *shen* spirit to take its place and utilize this borrowed human form to exercise its powers on earth (among the Chinese both males and females can be equally accomplished mediums).

Spirit mediums can be found in most Chinese communities in Sarawak, though not all individuals are acknowledged as being equally adept or practiced in the same abilities. It is not uncommon to seek out spiritual "specialists," as well as consulting the resident local practitioner or a visitor from outside the community. All can provide the two basic services of a medium--preparing charms and potions to **prevent** trouble from happening, and **exorcism** to get rid of it when it does. They may provide additional services as well, such as divination and fortune-telling, or *fung shui* geomancy. Some are full-time practitioners, some part-time; all expect to be paid for their skills. Generally throughout the Rajang Valley communities, and in the first case described below, the Hokkien term *dang ke* is used for this medium/exorcist. This usage is not identical, however, with this term as found in the literature regarding Taiwan and elsewhere.[2]

TWO CASES OF EXCULPATION

In my first case of spirit possession as exculpation, the honor of a family was at stake. The concept of *hsiao*, "filial piety," has always been the most salient of normative orientations in Chinese culture, and remains so among the Sarawak Chinese today. *Hsiao* means more that just "honor," "obedience," "respect"--it includes a sense of "worthiness," and obligation to meet or exceed the standards and behaviors expected of you. And *hsiao* does not apply just from sons to their fathers or children to their parents--it delineates the role of the individual within his/her defined social group--the institution, the community, the nation, and of course, most especially, the family. With *hsiao*, you, the self, are your "family writ small;" perceptions and evaluations of you epitomize the public image--the "face" of your family as a sociocultural entity. Another normative orientation deemed important by the Sarawak Chinese is the value placed on education; in fact, these two often become inextricably intertwined: "Our ancestors emigrated to these foreign lands so that they and their children--our family--could have more opportunities for a better life. Education optimizes opportunities. This is what we came for, this is what we've struggled and sacrificed for, this is what you **owe** us, owe the ancestors, owe the family."

Therefore it was doubly tragic when Yang Yu Hsi, teenage daughter in a *towkay* (shopkeeper) family, went "mad" just three weeks before her scheduled government exams. These exams were crucial to her academic future--they were the Sarawak Junior Secondary Exams, and without passing them she could continue no further in the educational system. She had already failed them once, the previous year, as a student at the local government secondary school. Her family had then enrolled her in a private school to prepare her to retake the exams as a Private Candidate (though the success rate of Private Candidates is low). This was her **last chance**, and now she was "mad."

"Mad" (in English) is the term that my local informants used to describe her condition. When she awoke that morning she was "cold," she could not move her body freely and normally, nor could she see or hear or speak or react normally. She wouldn't/couldn't eat; nor could she explain to anyone what was wrong. She just sat there, immobile, seemingly in a daze, with a blank stare in her eyes. (This is as it was reported to me--I did not see her personally at this stage.) She was apparently in good physical health otherwise, so there was no **natural** explanation for her being this way. Something **supernatural** must be involved.

The family did not consult a medical practitioner (there seemed no medical reason to do so), nor did they consult the community's own resident spirit medium. This woman was a part-time practitioner, handling only occasional, well-selected cases. She was very sensitive to skepticism and doubt, and allowed no one except the principals who had personally encountered the spirits in question to attend her rituals. She could be very effective, however; I have "kept tabs" on a shophouse from which she once expelled a ghost and there has been no further disturbance for more than twenty years. In the event, she was not brought into this case. The family had heard that a dynamic, young medium, Master of his own spirit cult, was temporarily in residence in Sibu. They called him, and from the description of the symptoms he heard on the phone, he said that he suspected the dirty of work of a tree spirit. He agreed to come to town that very day for an examination, and, if necessary, an exorcism.

The Master arrived with a small retinue of followers on the afternoon boat and was conducted to the home of the patient. Word spread throughout the town that he would perform his rituals in a large room upstairs in the family's shophouse, and that the public was invited to attend. The Master was male, about 30, a Hakka from First Division where his cult had its home. He also spoke Hokkien, which he used to communicate with the patient, her family, and the townspeople in general. He said he was not able to speak either English or Mandarin Chinese. (On later occasion, while possessed by the great Immortal, Li Tieh Kuai, he conversed with me in Mandarin; Li Tieh Kuai was a physician, an educated man--when **he** occupied the body of the Master, **he** could speak Mandarin.)

Activities began about eight o'clock in the evening, and the room was packed with retinue, family, and nearly a hundred townspeople (including some Ibans). A large table placed against the center of the back wall served as an altar. On it were several incense burners, several bowls of fruit and sweet cakes as offerings to the gods and spirits, several bowls of "holy water" with the leafy twigs used to sprinkle it, and other accouterments. Front and center were three "seals," carved wooden printing blocks, each three to four inches in diameter, and shallow bowls of vermillion ink for stamping spirit charms. The largest seal contained the hemispheres symbolic of the *yang-yin* forces surrounded by the eight trigrams--the standard symbol for representing the Chinese cosmology and its animating powers. The other two seals, containing unrecognizable (to my informants) designs and glyphs, were the personal charm symbols of the Master's familiar and the Master's familiar *shen* spirit. (Both of these familiars were named for me, but were neither recognizable nor memorable to me or any of my informants; both were minor *shen*, generally-benevolent deities.) Laid in front of these seals was the focus of everyone's attention--a thin silver spike nearly two feet long.

The Master prepared for his ritual by donning a bright red jacket and binding a long red sash very tightly around his waist; (red is an especially effective prophylactic color for repelling or containing spirits). When all was ready, he went into a trance, allowing his body to be possessed by his familiar. His body was rigid, his movements stiff; a low-pitched, guttural, teeth-grinding noise issued from his throat, (evidence of his possession), which continued throughout the trance, even when he spoke. After introductory offerings of incense and prayers, he engaged in a long discussion with his chief assistant (a man in his fifties) concerning the specifics of this case. The familiar, now using the Master's body, spoke a special "spirit language" intelligible only to the chief assistant, who served as translator and moderator of the proceedings. (My informants told me that they could not understand the spirit language, but it sounded "something like Hakka.") After about twenty minutes of this analytical dialogue, the patient, Yu Hsi, was brought out from a rear bedroom. She was wearing a long white robe-like dress, and displayed the stupor previously described. Through the translator-assistant, the familiar conducted a gentle interrogation of the patient, so quietly it could not be overheard. At its conclusion, Yu Hsi, who was accompanied by her mother and other relatives, retired to the bedroom. The Master released his familiar and came out of his trance, announcing that indeed possession by a tree spirit was the cause of the "madness," and that the offending *kwei* (demon) resided in a large tree almost directly behind the shophouse. The Master was exhausted by the strain of possession, and a short break was called, during which the Master rested and chatted with members of the audience.

When the ritual resumed, the Master again tightened his sash and entered into a possessive trance, again marked by the throat grinding noise. The familiar began by preparing a large number of paper spirit charms, using the seals previously mentioned. These were eagerly snatched up by members of the audience; even some of the skeptical young men of the town carried them around thereafter in their wallets--("Well," they said, "you never know.") The familiar then spent about fifteen minutes formulating special charms, potions, and powders from special, secret, ingredients provided by the chief assistant. Some were granular, the consistency of coarse salt, others were like baby powder; all were white. The granular ones were kept in small bowls, the powdery ones in paper packets. Yu Hsi and her companions were brought forth again. As she knelt before him, the familiar chanting incantations, sprinkled her (and the other women) with these potions and powders. White paper charms were stuck to her face and clothing. This time the familiar, in his spirit language, was quite aggressive, even violent, in his tone of voice, and these exactions were not translated into Hokkien for the girl or the crowd, for they were addressed solely to the offending demon. (He was being told, in effect, to "get the Hell out" of her.) At the conclusion, the cowering girl was again led away.

Then came the moment everyone was waiting for: the exorcism itself. Taking up the long silver spike, the familiar had the Master's body thrust it (seemingly) through both cheeks, in the right cheek, out the left.[3] Thus impaled, and throat-growling louder than ever, the Master's body began to quiver, then violently shake, often on one foot. The chief assistant handed him a bowl of "holy water" with its leafy sprinkler and, in the other hand, a bundle of paper packets and charms. This all took several minutes to complete, allowing the audience a good chance to appreciate the power of the trance and the imposing spike. Quivering, hopping on one foot, the familiar directed the Master's body down the staircase and out the back door of the shophouse. Only the retinue of assistants were permitted to join the familiar around the contaminated tree; the rest of us were instructed to stay well away. Dancing around the tree, sprinkling water and potions, the familiar cast the *kwei* spirit out of its arboreal abode. By the time he'd finished, the shophouse was empty of visitors. The weary Master, out of his trance, retreated through the back door and the ritual was ended. He returned to Sibu on the first boat the next morning. He was persuaded by the family to accept a monetary offering for the work of his cult, about M$400.

The exorcism worked; the *kwei* was driven out; the girl was cured. Recovery was not immediate--it took several weeks for her to gradually return to normal. By then she had missed so much school at such a crucial time that it was, unfortunately, just not possible for her to sit for the exams. To speed her recovery (and get her away from the offending tree?) she was sent to visit her aunt in Kuching. She eventually decided to stay there, found a job, and did not return to live at home.

Family honor was maintained; *hsiao* was satisfied all around. There was no unworthiness, no dereliction of duty, no shame, no blame. It was all just an unfortunate accident at an unfortunate time. She'd worked so hard to prepare for those exams; she'd done everything a dutiful daughter ought to do, all anyone could expect of her. Then that damned demon ruined her chances forever--**but it wasn't her fault**--it wasn't **anyone's** fault.

No further analysis is required; the case speaks for itself. It does raise several questions, however, similar to those raised by other observers of spirit possession and religious phenomena.

Was this girl "psychotic?" Melford Spiro (1965:109f) asked the same about the Theraveda Buddhist monks he studied in Burma--they were men whose psychological **mal**adjustment to the "normal" world made them **ideally** adjusted to the cloistered life of the monastery. If we take an appropriate quotation from Spiro's analysis where he addresses the question of these men's "psychosis," and change his word "monk" to "Yu Hsi," the girl who was "mad," we would read:

> The psychotic resolves his problems by means of idiosyncratic, private, defenses; [Yu Hsi] resolves [her] problems in an institutionalized manner, by utilizing elements of [her] religious heritage as a culturally constituted defense. The differences between these two types of defense accounts for the following differences between the psychotic patient, on the one hand, and the normal [Yu Hsi], on the other (Spiro 1965:109).

He further notes that "the behavior of the psychotic is incompatible with any normal social role within his society...the psychotic is **psychologically incapable** of performing social roles or complying with those cultural norms which he violates" (Spiro 1965:109, his emphasis). The behavior of the monk or Yu Hsi, on the other hand, is "entirely appropriate" within the context of the given society's normative orientations. No, she's **NOT** psychotic.

Was this girl faking it? Was this her premeditated plot to avoid her responsibilities and appear to be an innocent victim? Her family, the townspeople, and most of my informants seemed to accept her possession at face value. Benjamin Paul (1967:162), writing about the possession of "Maria" in a Guatemalan village, comments on cultural features that permit escape from guilt: "One is the fact that hallucinations are not culturally defined as products of fantasy.

Sights and sounds of ghosts are regarded by most normal people in Maria's [or Yu Hsi's] village not as fears or fancies but as real occurrences." Even if a large percentage of Sarawak Chinese today do not "really believe" that there are tree spirits, they can't prove that there **aren't**. In the event, it's completely irrelevant whether any of these people "really believed" in this possession, or whether the girl was "really" faking it. It worked! Even if total fiction, it was **culturally normative** fiction that provided a culturally acceptable solution. **All** culture is fiction in the sense that it only exists "made up" in our heads, yet it works nevertheless.

The second case of spirit possession as exculpation is not nearly so dramatic or ethnographically exciting as the first--there are no crowds of spectators, no growling and hopping, or two-foot long spikes through the cheeks. But in its quiet way it is probably a much more realistic, and indicative, example, for it illustrates how educated, urban, middle class Chinese have adapted their cultural heritage to provide new coping strategies for dealing with the pressures of complex modern life.

The life of a working mother is difficult enough in any culture--children to get off to school or day care, meals to plan and prepare, laundry, social responsibilities and social entertainments, a husband and family to please, all in addition to The Job. Making it even worse is that the husband's family--nearly all of them--have moved in, with no clear date for leaving. The brother and sister aren't much bother, but satisfying one's husband's parents is a challenge to **any** Chinese wife at any time. Doing all this when eight months pregnant with a third child is simply too much to bear. It would be enough to drive some people mad, but a woman who could normally handle such complexities with pride and self-assurance of her worth and abilities would see "madness" as a sign of personal weakness rather then a means of escape. On top of all this a foreign guest is coming to visit for several days. What has gone wrong? Why is everything so fouled-up?

Everything seemed perfect to me on my arrival. I could see nothing wrong, nothing out of place. The house was spotless, the meal delicious, even the children were quite well-behaved. I was astounded when I was invited to go along for an evening visit to a local spirit medium--not for my edification, but for the sake of the wife, who had become a frequent client ever since the house had become infested with demonic *kwei* spirits. The older child, a boy of about six, was taken along too, since the *kwei* had been making him very "naughty" recently. It was then that I noticed that every room of the house had several charm papers pasted to the walls.

The medium had a nice new townhouse in a residential neighborhood not unlike those of his clients, for he seemed to specialize in the plagues that strike the middle class. He was a man of late middle age with a female assistant slightly younger--apparently his wife. He did not do anything especially dramatic or memorable in his rituals, and seemed to drift into and out of his trance with great ease and frequency. He spent as much time in conversational banter as in spiritual trance, for both were his tools for diagnosis and treatment. In the course of the evening he said prayers and chants over the boy, using potions and holy water to repel the demons, and he prepared a whole new batch of charms and papers for the house. I saw the wife burning some of them in the upstairs hallway the next day, and she returned to the medium alone several times during my stay.

Did the charm papers and special prayers work? They certainly did. The blame for all imperfections, all deviations from the norm, all flaws and failures, was shifted away from this normally-quite-capable housewife and dumped onto the offending *kwei*. There were no "you should have...," "you **could** have...," "you **ought to** have..." recriminations for her failure to meet the standards of some self, or social, image of proper behavior. "The house was full of *kwei*; what else could I do?"

The visitor left, the baby was born, the in-laws eventually returned home or moved out, and life settled down to its usual manageable sub-chaotic level. The demons had been exorcised, for they were not needed there anymore.

CONCLUSION

I believe that exculpative possession is far more widespread than it appears to be from reading the literature. I don't believe that it is rare or unusual at all. And I don't think we have to "search for it anew," in Borneo or elsewhere to find it, but merely consider the material we already have in this context. After all, the idea of "exculpation" is certainly not foreign to us in American culture. Examples actually and literally claiming "spirit possession" abound: in the Son of Sam murders, Satan commanded David Berkowitz, using as a medium the neighbor's dog; a teenage murderer in Connecticut claimed possession in court (unsuccessfully); a police sergeant in Rhode Island addresses two or three audiences a week on the dangers of Satanic cult crime, and **he** really believes it. Exculpation (even possession) is common parlance in our contemporary language: "He's full of the old Nick;" "She acted like a woman possessed;" "Something's gotten into him;" or the old standby, in a case of murder or Flip Wilson's

Geraldine--"The Devil made me do it." We've developed our own modern-day "scientific" equivalents: alcohol (which we call "spirits")--Ol' Demon Rum. "It's not my fault, I was drunk;" killing someone while driving drunk is everywhere (in America) much less severely penalized than "culpable homicide." There are drugs, and of course our cultural favorite (so often linked with spirit possession by anthropologists)--insanity, dementia (to be "out of, away from, one's mind.") We normally excuse all sorts of behavior for this reason, even killing someone. On the streets of Washington D. C., John Hinckley Jr., possessed by whatever "demons of the mind," attempted to assassinate the President of the United States. Although, via television, millions saw him do it, he was exculpated as "Innocent Due to Insanity."

Every society must have norms that must be followed. Every society has some times when some individuals need to be released from those norms without destroying themselves or the social order in the process. Exculpation, by spirit possession or otherwise, allows a society to relax its rules while keeping them, to forgive without forgetting, and the norms themselves are reaffirmed.

ILLUSTRATION 1

The Master with the banner of his spirit cult.

ILLUSTRATION 2

The altar with its ritual paraphernalia for the exorcism of a tree spirit *kwei*. Left - a bowl of "holy water" with leaf sprinkler. Rear - offerings of fruit and incense. Center - wooden stamp blocks, stamp pad, and vermilion ink for printing spirit charms. Front - the spike The Master thrusts through his cheeks during his possession trance.

ILLUSTRATION 3

The Master recovering from his possession trance.

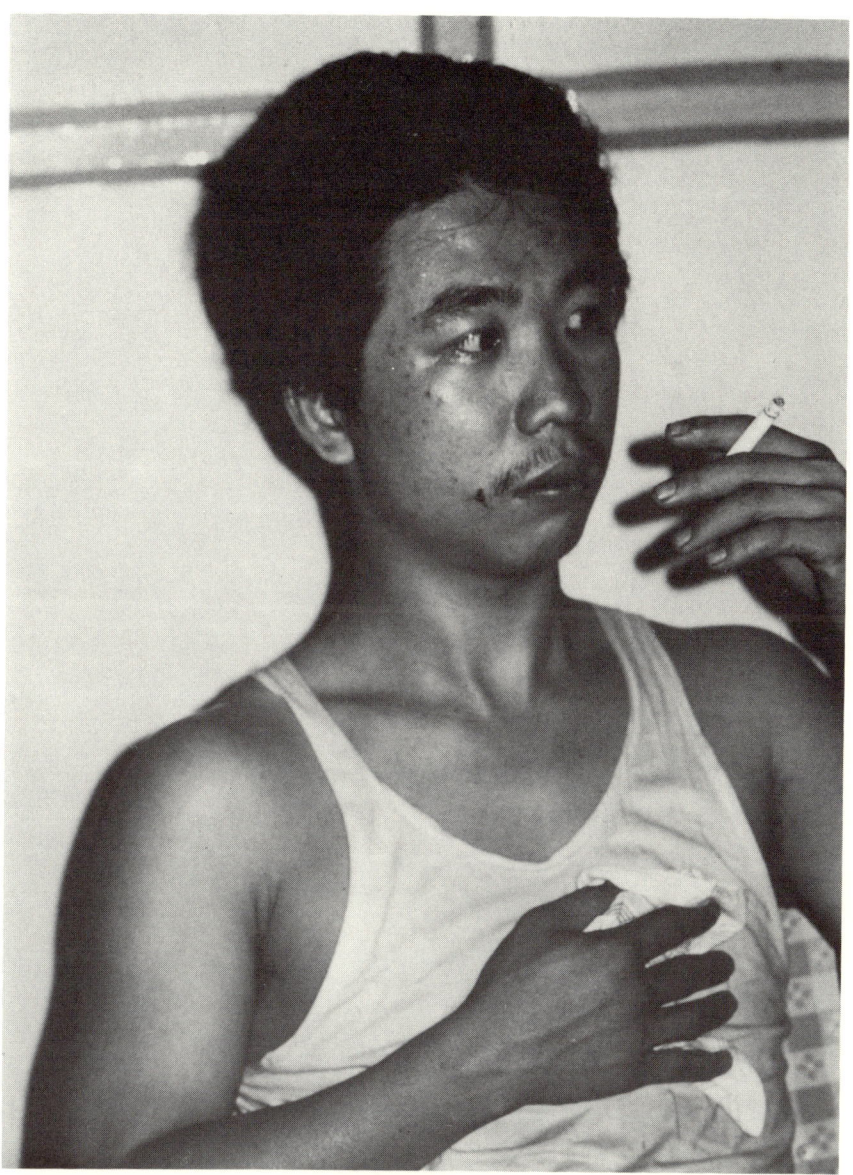

ILLUSTRATION 4

Close-up of The Master recovering from his trance, showing the mole on his right cheek that disguises the hole through which the spike was passed. He is dabbing small drops of blood from the hole with his handkerchief.

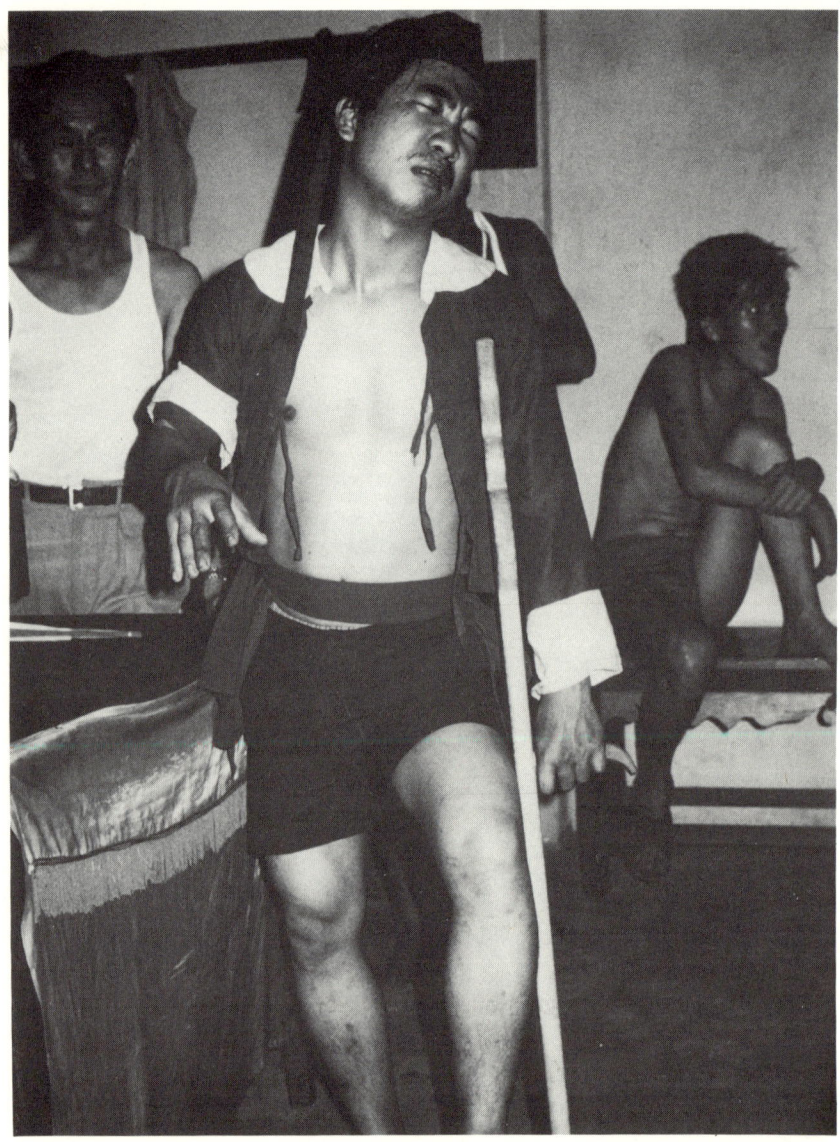

ILLUSTRATION 5

The Master being possessed by the spirit of Li T'ieh Kuai, one of the Pa Hsien ("Eight Immortals") of the Taoist (and Buddhist) pantheon. The occasion was a farewell meeting with his followers and apprentices in Sibu before returning to his home in Kuching, April 1971.

NOTES

1. An excellent account of the history and role of the Chinese in Sarawak, including an extensive bibliography, can be found in Daniel Chew's (1990) recent book.

2. Bernard Gallin (1966:241-6) describing the Hokkien-speaking agricultural village of Hsin Hsing, Taiwan uses the *Mandarin* terminology to make a major distinction between "...the Taoist priests known as *tao shih*...and the shamans known as *fa shih* and *t'iao t'ung*." The former functions only as a religious practitioner, but with no supernatural powers. Both the *fa shih* and the *t'iao t'ung*, however, "have definite supernatural powers." Only the former, however, has sufficient power to actually command the spirits and exorcise them. The *t'iao t'ung* has no such power, but is merely a conduit through which a spirit (often just one specific spirit) can speak; usually a *fa shih* must **also** be present to interpret what the spirit, through the *t'iao t'ung*, is saying. The latter are of little use alone. In his glossary Gallin (1966:310-311) defines *fa shih* (法 師) as "a powerful shaman who exorcises demons or negative spirits." *T'iao tung* (跳 童) is "a shaman (in Taiwanese, called a *dang ki*); one who is possessed by a god; a medium."

   In the Rajang Valley, the dichotomy is differently drawn: the *fa shih* is grouped with the *tao shih* into a class of priestly practitioners of ritual, ceremony and the scholarship of theology, that is of Taoist or Buddhist priests. The *dang ki* (Mandarin: *t'iao tung*) is both the "medium" or conduit for the priests *and* the "shaman" who can control and cajole them. When speaking English, the term "The Master" was used as a gloss for *dang ki* by the family and informants in the case described in this article.

3. The silver spike **seemed** to pierce both of the Master's cheeks, but close observation revealed that this was only half true. The Master has a hole permanently pierced through his right cheek, about two inches from the corner of his mouth. This hole is disguised by a natural mole, and is not noticeable in normal circumstances. On the night I saw him, the spike stretched the hole enough to cause a few drops of blood to form after it was withdrawn. The master blotted these with a handkerchief without comment as part of his "recovery." On the left side, however, the master "cheated;" the spike did not pierce his skin, but exited through the extreme far corner of his mouth, distended back to the molar teeth. A photograph of an almost identical piercing, taken by Ronni Pinsler, can

be found on page 25 of C. S. Wong's 1987 illustrated edition of his Chinese Festivities in Malaysia and Singapore.

REFERENCES

Chew, Daniel
    1990   Chinese Pioneers on the Sarawak Frontier 1841-1941. Singapore: Oxford University Press.

Crapanzano, Vincent
    1977   Mohammed and Dawia: Possession in Morocco. *In* Case Studies in Spirit Possession, edited by Vincent Crapanzano and Vivian Garrison, 141-76. New York: John Wiley.

Fidler, Richard C.
    1978   Religion and Festivals in a Multi-Cultural Bazaar Town. *In* Sarawak: Linguistics and Development Problems, 167-200. Studies in Third Word Societies, Publication Number 3. The College of William and Mary, Williamsburg, Virginia.

Firth, Raymond
    1974   Faith and Skepticism in Kelantan Village Magic. *In* Kelantan: Religion, Society and Politics in a Malay State, edited by William R. Roff, 190-224. Kuala Lumpur: Oxford University Press.

Freed, Stanley A. and Ruth S. Freed
    1967   Spirit Possession as Illness in a North Indian Village. *In* Magic, Witchcraft, and Curing, edited by J. Middleton, 295-320. New York, Natural History Press.

Gallin, Bernard
    1966   Hsin Hsing: A Chinese Village in Change. Berkeley: University of California Press.

Garrison, Vivian
    1977   The "Puerto Rican Syndrome" in Psychiatry and Espiritismo. *In* Case Studies in Spirit Possession, edited by Vincent Crapanzano and Vivian Garrison, 383-450. New York: John Wiley.

Hallowell, A. Irving
    1955   Culture and Experience. Philadelphia: University of Pennsylvania Press.

Kessler, Clive S.
    1977   Conflict and Sovereignty in Kelantanese Malay Spirit Seances. *In* Case Studies in Spirit Possession, edited by Vincent Crapanzano and Vivian Garrison, 295-332. New York: John Wiley.

Lewis, I. M.
    1971   Ecstatic Religion. Middlesex, England: Penguin Books.

Mischel, Walter and Frances Mischel
    1971   Psychological Aspects of Spirit Possession. American Anthropologist 60(2):249-260.

Murdock, George P.
    1967   Outline of Cultural Materials. New Haven: Human Relations Area Files Press.

Paul, Benjamin D.
    1967   Mental Disorder and Self-Regulating Processes in Culture: A Guatemalan Illustration. *In* Personalities and Cultures, edited by Robert Hunt, 150-165. New York: Natural History Press.

Potter, Jack M.
    1978   Cantonese Shamanism. *In* Studies in Chinese Society, edited by Arthur P. Wolf, 321-364. Stanford: Stanford University Press.

Radin, Paul
    1957   Primitive Man as Philosopher. 2nd. ed., rev. New York: Dover Publications.

Raybeck, Douglas A.
    1974   Social Stress and Social Structure in Kelantan Village Life. *In* Kelantan: Religion, Society and Politics in a Malay State, edited by William R. Roff, 225-42. Kuala Lumpur: Oxford University Press.

Sarawak Census
    1983   Sarawak: State Population Report, 1980. Kuala Lumpur, Department of Statistics, Malaysia.

Skeat, Walter W.
    1972   Malay Magic. (1900). New York: Benjamin Blom, Inc.

Spiro, Melford E.
    1952   Ghosts, Ifaluk, and Teleological Functionalism. American Anthropologist 54(4):497-503.

    1965   Religious Systems as Culturally Constituted Defense Mechanisms. *In* Context and Meaning in Cultural Anthropology, edited by Melford E. Spiro, 100-113. New York: The Free Press.

T'ien, Ju K'ang
    1953   The Chinese of Sarawak. London School of Economics, Monographs on Social Anthropology No. 12. The University of London.

Wallace, Anthony F. C.
    1966   Religion: An Anthropological View. New York: Random House.

Wong, C. S.
    1987   An Illustrated Cycle of Chinese Festivities in Malaysia and Singapore. Singapore: Jack Chia-MPH Ltd.

PART THREE

PERFORMANCE, EFFECTIVENESS AND THE IBAN *MANANG*

ROBERT J. BARRETT
University of Adelaide

The Iban consult *manang*, shaman healers who conduct rites known as *pelian*, for the purpose of curing illness, dealing with inauspicious dreams and effecting a proper separation of the dead from the living. They also speculate about shamanism, comparing the performance of one *manang* with another, discussing how *pelian* rites heal, and debating the question of whether or not *manang* deceive their audience. In this essay, I look at the *pelian* rites and the indigenous discourse which reflects on them, in order to explore ethnographically the nature of Iban ritual healing.

The concepts of performance and effectiveness, as developed recently in the anthropological literature, are examined. I argue that an operationally restricted definition of performance, one which does not fully integrate talk about ritual with performance of ritual acts, is unlikely to yield an understanding of the therapeutic effect, or of the therapist's social position. I propose that the current concepts of performance and effectiveness can be extended by viewing them as discursive categories; they are topics under which persons practicing the same culture engage in meta-commentary on the nature of ritual and, more basically, on issues of appearance, action and causality. By this I do not mean to reduce ritual to discourse but to argue for the importance of the talk that takes place in and around ritual action and incorporate this into the analysis of ritual effectiveness.

This approach allows for some anthropological ideas of effectiveness to be treated as yet additional instances of meta-commentary on ritual, instances which themselves reflect the secular definitions of reality that underpin academic anthropological discourse. For the Iban, discussions of ritual turn on the complex problem of how the appearance of an action and its consequences are related to the reality in which that action takes place. Deception is central to the nature of the *manang's* work, for he is engaged in transforming the basic coordinates of Iban lived experience, and defining the relation between phenomenon and noumenon.

The Problems of Effectiveness and Performance

Contemporary anthropology, largely in reaction to earlier structuralist approaches (Levi-Strauss 1967), has addressed the problem of the effectiveness of ritual by focusing on ritual performance. Bruce Kapferer's (1983) study of Sinhalese exorcism is an outstanding example. He begins from Victor Turner's view of performance as the dramatic expression of dominant, plurivocal symbols, organized in a processual order, that transforms the experience of patient and audience both at an individual, emotional level and at the level of shared cultural representations. For Kapferer, however, this perspective, like that of structuralism, is still locked within a model of performance as the enactment of text, or what he calls **the performance of structure**. His counterthesis is that meaning in ritual emerges in **the structure of performance**. Kapferer's ethnography stresses the transition from early phases of an exorcism, when the presentational symbolism of music, dance and trance embraces the subjectivity of the patient in a direct revelation of her/his subjugation by the demonic, to the final phase when the discursive medium of comic drama, essentially reflexive in nature, distances the patient from her/his subjectivity and invites her/him to stand outside and reflect upon her/his experience. He traces the shifting stand-points of the participants (patient, family, audience) in relation to the performance and each other. These transitions run parallel to the curative transition from subjective immersion in experience to objectification of that experience, culminating in the audience and exorcists enjoining the patient to laugh at the absurdity of the demons who had previously dominated her/him. Exorcisms work because the dynamic properties of the major aesthetic modes reorder the context of the patient's experience from that of being in the thrall of demonic illusion to the demons being themselves controlled and ridiculed by the exorcist's trickery. By these means, exorcisms effect a retypification of the patient's personal and public identity.

This is a powerful framework for the analysis of ritual forms in which the participants' senses are flooded by dancing, incense, drumming and music. It is applicable to the study of rituals in which the attentive focus of the patient is considered crucial and where the patient must understand the meaning of the rite for it to be effective. It is not as applicable to healing rites with a less vivid aesthetic, where the physical presence of the patient is not considered important or where the patient may be an infant and may not grasp what the rite means. The analytic framework does not transpose well to these situations for two reasons. First, Kapferer does not propose a general theory of performance that transcends the Sinhalese context. Second, he directly employs the social phenomenology of Schutz, McHugh and others in a manner that presupposes a quintessentially Western model of a person as a wide-awake, perceiving, unitary, subjective consciousness. For Kapferer, it is the apperceiving consciousness that is transformed by means of the oscillation between subjective involvement and objective distance. To impose a fully pre-formulated Western ethno-phenomenology on the data like this actually runs counter to a more rigorous phenomenological method, which should begin with the discovery of the informants' own taken-for-granted structures of time, space, causality and person and their culturally signified varieties of experience.

Other contemporary studies of ritual also sometimes get into trouble because of this problem. E. L. Schieffelin (1985), for example, has recently reinterpreted his earlier studies of Kaluli ritual within a social interactionist framework to argue that the meanings associated with illness are defined and transformed only through the active participation of audience and trance medium as they jointly create a performance reality. For the Kaluli, illness is caused by a person's invisible pig aspect having become injured by hunters within a spirit world. During the séance, the medium's spirit child searches for this pig aspect, releases it from a spirit trap and heals invisible bodily wounds. Through his various stylistic strategies, the trance medium engrosses members of the audience, drawing them in to decipher the riddle of his songs and thereby construct a conjoint definition of the patient's illness. How can such a rite transform the experience of the patient, asks Schieffelin, when the patient is usually not present at the séance and indeed should be asleep? Unless we posit "para-normal" effects, he answers, the rite cannot influence the patient in any normally understood way but instead it can shape community expectations of prognosis. "During the performance, the medium may form an assessment about the patient's condition and gear the level of success of his invisible curing efforts to correspond with his notion of the most probable outcome...The deciphering of the spirit's message is a cooperative construction of reality in the guise of a search for hidden meaning" (Schieffelin 1985:718-719).

This cynical conclusion dismisses Kaluli definitions of performative efficacy as "para-normal." It misunderstands Kaluli notions of personhood by insisting that the patient is not present in the ceremony, whereas the patient (in his pig aspect) is there all along (in the invisible domain). It also misconstrues Kaluli structures of phenomenal experience by failing to recognize that a sleeping person is also an experiencing subject. These problems in Schieffelin's work have arisen because he did not use social phenomenology as an ethnographic method so much as an analytic framework to reinterpret his earlier data. In a more sensitive use of phenomenology, sleeping experience would be treated with the same seriousness as waking experience and the perceiving soul might emerge as equally important as embodied consciousness.

The present discussion of Iban shaman healing draws from Kapferer the concept that it is through the structure of performance that reality is constructed, defined and transformed. But my analysis seeks to be grounded more carefully in Iban phenomenal reality and is therefore built on a discussion of Iban concepts of body, soul, waking, dreaming and perception. It also approaches the Iban as a people who formulate and debate concepts of performance and effectiveness.

At the same time, this paper works toward a more general understanding of performance and effectiveness which transcend the Iban context by proposing that they are, in themselves, categories of discourse that are systematically employed by members of a culture, to define the essential features of ritual. The discourse on performance and the discourse on effectiveness are reflexive. They enable cultural members to account for ritual, make sense of it, either defend it or attack it, but always imbue it with meaning. Indigenous notions of performance and effectiveness are indexical features of the logic of the ritual itself. This is to view ritual as a form of social action which reflects on itself, constantly providing for a meta-commentary on its own essential features. It treats performance and effectiveness as categories which, like hierarchy or person, are discoverable cross-culturally.

Theories of performance and effectiveness are always concerned with a single problem, the nature of social action and its meaningful relation to culturally-defined reality. If there is to be any distinction between the two aspects, the discourse on performance is more concerned with the relationship between appearance and reality and the discourse on effectiveness is more to do with the relationship between the consequences of action and reality.

The Iban *Manang*

The Iban are an indigenous people of north-western Borneo, the great majority (over 440,000) of whom live in Sarawak. In spite of increasing migration to towns and cities, they largely remain agriculturalists who live in longhouse communities along the rivers which flow from the central highlands out onto the coastal plains. The cognatic kin structure of the Iban has been extensively described (Freeman 1970), as has the architectural symbolism of the Iban longhouse. Enclosed family apartments (*bilik*) are arranged side by side. The Iban term "*bilik*" refers both to the physical space (*bilik*-apartment) and the domestic group who live within it (*bilik*-family). At the front, an enclosed gallery (*ruai*) runs the length of the house. Although each family owns and maintains that section of the *ruai* in front of its *bilik*-apartment, the *ruai* is nonetheless a public, unpartitioned space. If the *bilik*-apartment is the domestic space for the family as an independent, corporate group, then the *ruai* is the public space for the family as an integral member of the longhouse community.

This essay reports on field work carried out among the Saribas Iban between April 1988 and June 1989, as part of an ethnographic and psychiatric study of Iban concepts of illness and modes of dealing with psychiatric disorder. It is based on what I learned from fourteen *manang* mainly from the Rimbas and adjacent areas, and on observations of *pelian* ceremonies conducted by eight of them. I calculated that their average age lay approximately between sixty and sixty five (range 50-90). Only one of the fourteen was a woman. From a psychiatric point of view, these *manang* were mentally robust, neither psychotic nor pre-psychotic, neither effeminate nor hypermasculine. The only pattern I detected was a vulnerability to alcohol use, an occupational hazard which comes from being constantly plied with *arrack* spirit by young men in the audience as a waggish test of the *manang's* stamina.

The power of the *manang* is derived from spirits. Potential initiates are called in dreams usually in the fourth or fifth decade of life and, although it is common to put up a token resistance by pleading the excuse of domestic responsibilities, all eventually succumb to the insistent command, on pain of death or madness. The commanding being, or *yang* may be the spirit of an ancestral *manang*, Menjaya Raja, a principal deity of *manang* or, more commonly, an animal spirit, and it subsequently provides spirit assistance in the *manang's* ritual cure. Since effectiveness resides with the *yang*, *manang* make competitive claims, talking in hushed and reverent tones about the strength of their particular *yang*. One manang laid claim to *antu gerasi* himself, the most ferocious and feared of all spirits. In explaining the relative contributions to the spirit journey and the retrieval of a sick person's soul, a *manang* compared the *yang* to an aeroplane and the *manang's* soul to a mere passenger.

Genealogies I collected showed particular families with strong horizontal and vertical concentrations of *manang* as well as other ritual and healing experts and, even in the current generation, paramedical staff working in the government health service. This clustering was viewed as an extension of spirit power from one generation to the next (*tampong menampong*) rather than an inherited status (*purih*) because *manang* were called in dreams by the soul of their departed father or grandfather, himself a *manang*.

Curative power is materialized in charms (*ubat*). These small, powerful (*bisa*) objects have a peculiar appearance and a quality of transformation--a pig's tusk which continues over the months to close into a smaller circle, a deer's horn half turned to stone. They, too, derive from spirits, their location revealed to the *manang* in dreams.

Nowadays the most frequent reason to consult *manang* is to perform the *serará bunga* (separation of the flowers) ceremony. One of a series of mourning rites, its purpose is to achieve a clear-cut separation between dead and living, and there is some urgency to schedule this ceremony if the dead have returned to interfere with the living, as evidenced by illness, bad dreams or the mysterious disappearance of rice. The treatment of illness is the second most common reason to call *manang*, notwithstanding the advent of Western medicine to Sarawak and its rapid expansion since independence, for the Iban make a primary distinction between illnesses that can be cured by doctors and those that can be treated by traditional modes of cure. *Manang* also perform *pelian* to deal with bad dreams (*jai' mimpi*), as well as smaller scale rites to neutralize bad omens (*penabar burong*) or neutralize a breach of taboo (*penabar pemali*), whether or not this has resulted in illness.

Manang are specialists in dealing with disordered relations between living humans (*mensia*) on the one hand, and the dead (*sebayan*), spirits (*antu*) and gods (*petara*), on the other. Penelope Graham (1987) argues that the power to do this derives from their extraordinary status within Iban society. The term "*manang*" itself is used in contradistinction to the term "Iban," thereby defining them as a separate category of person. They are treated with an ambivalent mixture of skepticism and belief, derision and awe and, historically, could enter a transformed (*bali'*) status of assuming the opposite-gender identity. Thus, set apart from and transcending ordinary categories of Iban society, they occupy a powerful structural vantage from which to transform their own ontological status and cross basic divisions within the Iban cosmos. Men require personal intercourse with supernatural beings in order to maintain a sense of harmonious interaction with them, but at the same time they need protective distance from them. At times of malevolent interaction, *manang* intervene on behalf of men, first to connect the human and spirit domain, then to engage in transactions which restore a sense of reciprocity, and finally to create appropriate barriers between the two domains again (Graham 1987:148).[1]

However, I would contend that a major problem within the ethnographic literature on Iban society is that it characteristically posits a natural/supernatural dichotomy as the main division in the Iban cosmos, and a material (body)/spiritual (soul) dichotomy as the main division in Iban ideas of the person. This materialist interpretation can be seen, for example, in Freeman (1967:317), who misrepresents Iban thought by equating "natural" with "physical" and "real," in opposition to "supernatural," "spiritual," "phantasy" and ultimately, "imagined." To Iban, *antu* and *sebayan* are no less "natural" or real than *mensia*. The distinction between "visible" and "invisible" (see Sather, this volume) is more salient because it structures Iban notions of the cosmos and person, pervades Iban origin mythology, organizes Iban phenomenal experience and is the principle around which *manang* performance is oriented.

VISIBLE AND INVISIBLE ASPECTS OF IBAN PHENOMENAL EXPERIENCE

The difference between the body (*tuboh*) aspect of the Iban person and the soul (*semengat*) aspect, conventionally glossed in the literature as the physical and spiritual, are clarified using this indigenous distinction. The skin forms the visible surface boundary of the *tuboh* separating the outside environment from the inside body parts. The chest/abdomen and the head are two compartments whose interior spaces are normally invisible. The organs located within have to do with the core of the person, particularly the heart/liver complex (*ati/atau*), the seat of emotions and intentionality, and the brain, the locus of calculative ability or cleverness. With such a distinctive cultural valence, these spaces are the most frequent site of symptoms and the focus of *manang* treatment. Furthermore, since these two interior, invisible spaces are involved in thinking, there is a symptom/thought continuity which the *manang's* therapy addresses.

The boundary function of the skin is augmented by clothes which, insofar as they accumulate bodily smells, become invested with personal and sexual identity. However, the skin boundary is permeated by invisible openings in the palms of the hand, soles of the feet, hair follicles, and also the region of the anterior fontanelle, which allow entry of unseen substances causing illness. Air may enter (*sirang angin*) as may rain during sun showers, turning into small stones inside the head. Spirits leave invisible wounds (*pansa' utai*), depositing stones or other small objects inside. Conversely, it is through the anterior fontanelle that the *semengat* leaves the *tuboh* in dreams, illness and death. Thus, the Iban body comprises an invisible interior encapsulated by a visible integument, the latter breaking down in illness to allow passage of invisible substances back and forth.

Iban posit, in part, an embodied concept of the person, since the *tuboh* is a perceiving, communicating subject, imbued with intentionality and moral agency, whose province of reality is the everyday world of wakefulness, which in Iban culture is associated (though not exclusively) with daylight hours. Schutz (1962:222, 342) writes of the spatially and temporally delimited nature of this reality. It is spatially finite in that it extends to the objects within actual and potential scope of vision and range of hearing and it is temporally finite in that it is a social world in which the person is immersed with others in a shared present time frame.

Iban also posit a soul-theory of the person, because within dreams the soul thinks, feels a range of emotions, is capable of seeing, hearing, and smelling, and engages in speech and social interaction. It, too, possesses intentionality and is capable of certain moral actions such as choice and resistance. There is a correspondence between dreaming and everyday experience because within dreams, souls appear to be physically embodied. I observed a very mundane quality to dream reports--working with one's great grandfather in the field, living with one's deceased wife. Such experiences are endowed with the same accent of reality as waking experiences and have much the same evident value as an eye-witness account.

There is a continuity of moral agency expressed in causal attributions of illness. A moral infraction committed by the body aspect of a person (say a woman leaving her underwear on the clothes line at night or carelessly throwing it away in the jungle) leads to her *semengat* aspect being interfered with or seduced (*kachau antu, anu' antu*), or even possessed and betrothed (*tunang antu*)[2] by a spirit which, in turn, leads to bodily illness.

Dream reality is also the obverse of waking reality. It occurs during sleep and is associated with night time. The basic phenomenological categories of space and time are quite different. The soul is not fixed in space like the body but leaps geographical and cosmic distances to interact with far away people or the dead. Temporal coordinates are also fundamentally altered because dream experiences are fleeting and there is no sense of "growing old together," especially when it comes to being with the dead, who are experienced as being more or less the same age and appearance as they were just before they died. However to the Iban, the salient difference between the waking and dreaming reality is that beings who are invisible in the former (*semengat, antu* and *sebayan*) are visible within dream reality.

This does not exhaust Iban concepts of the person, for humans are also described as having a plant aspect (*ayu* or *bunga*), which thrives in health and becomes choked with weeds and wilts in illness. This botanomorphic metaphor also has a place within the visible/invisible dichotomy, for it is invisible to wide awake mortals but visible to mythic *manang* who clear around it, shade it, transplant it and tend it back to health.

Spirits and The Dead

Other beings and domains within Iban cosmology can be understood in terms of the same dichotomy, and in this essay we are chiefly concerned with spirits and the dead. In myth, spirits were originally the same as humans but became separated and estranged from men as a result of sibling conflict. It was at this point that spirits became invisible. Now they wander at large through the same cosmic region as men, though they congregate in uninhabited places such as jungle copses, hill tops midway between longhouse communities, or among unused equipment in seldom frequented spots in the longhouse loft or under the floor boards. They are seen or heard in these locations, usually at night, but this is only a fleeting appearance (*ayan*) for they disappear (*lesap*) when the viewer blinks the eyelids. Appearances are characteristic: a pair of red eyes high on a fig tree at night, a tall, black figure in the jungle with a high conical head, small figures flitting in the loft.

More often spirits are experienced by the soul in dreams, where appearances deceive, for they characteristically masquerade as animals or humans. There is a common theme of dangerous sexual encounter. Dreaming of an attractive person of the opposite sex is *prima facie* evidence that one's soul has been seduced by a spirit. Even dreaming of one's spouse may not be safe because it may be a spirit in disguise. Spirits are masters of deception. They are malevolent and cause illness or death, though the evil nature of spirits has been systematically overstated, especially within Christian commentaries on Iban culture. Spirits are also a source of benign power that are sought after to help in executing dangerous projects.

In contrast to spirits, the dead are the souls of Iban. The soul leaves the body shortly after death and travels to the land of the dead (*menoa sebayan*). This region bears a paradoxical relation to the world of the living. On the one hand, it has a this-world location in the Kapuas river basin within present-day Indonesia, associated in legend with the origin of the Iban people. There, the dead resemble the living, for they are fully embodied beings who lead a mundane and material existence in their longhouse, working their hill padi or sitting on the veranda talking. On the other hand, this region lies in a different cosmic domain on the other side of the mythic gate to the earth, where everything is the opposite to this world. Day here becomes night there, light becomes dark, bad becomes good and fish becomes fowl. Invisible to the waking eyes, the dead are visible to the soul. Direct experience of one's own dead relatives in dreams does not necessarily bode ill since they often wish to help. It is only when, in a state of want, they beckon one's soul to live with them that illness and death may result.

The Visible and Invisible in Health and Illness

The above sketch of Iban categories of phenomenal experience points to two equally paramount realities which are at once identical and opposite. This paradox lies at the heart of Iban cosmological thinking and is the basis on which *manang* healing practices are built. In one reality, the wide-awake body engages in the social world of living people. In the other, a dream reality, the soul interacts with other souls, spirits and ancestors. As I have shown, in some respects these realities are identical or at least analogous; every thing and every action in one has its counterpart in the other. However, they are also related by a principle of inversion. Iban contend that from the point of view of one reality, everything in the other is reversed, upside down or topsy-turvy (*tunsang*). The two realities are culturally signified in terms of polar opposite metaphors; day/night, waking/sleeping, light/dark and, most fundamentally, visible/invisible. The latter dichotomy is the most basic because it not only separates these two realities but it also subdivides each of them into smaller provinces. For example, within waking reality, the body has visible and invisible compartments and within dream reality, the soul is visible to other souls but normally invisible to spirits.

It is mainly in illness that these underlying schemata are raised to the level of explicit discourse. That is, Iban and ethnographer alike can fully articulate these categories only when they have broken down. In illness, the visible body boundary is punctured by invisible wounds. The soul becomes separated from the body just as in death. The soul now becomes visible (*tampak*) to spirits and the dead who, in turn, make their appearance to the soul. These encounters are not actively sought and, furthermore, both spirits and the dead behave in a greedy, lustful or grasping way to weaken and sicken that person. It is to rectify these categorical disruptions and inequitable transactions that Iban turn to the *manang*.

BODY AND SOUL DIAGNOSIS: RENDERING THE INVISIBLE VISIBLE

Brought to the longhouse by a male member of the family, the *manang* at first interacts as an ordinary Iban guest, engaging in mundane conversation which, as often as not, is a matter of catching up with news about relatives, thereby reaffirming the close kin links which always bind a *manang* to the family who have called him.

He relinquishes the role of Iban kinsman at twilight, performs through the night as *manang*, and returns at dawn to Iban status again. Starting within the *bilik* apartment, he sits near the sick person, with family and wider relations clustered around, and inquires into bodily symptoms and dreams. Reports of physical symptoms are brief, usually restricted to the location of pain or discomfort, which is characteristically the head or abdomen. Dream reports are more elaborate and narrated in a muted, intense tone that conveys a sense of danger. Other conversations lower as everyone strains to hear. The *manang*, too, focuses his concentration on the dream, nodding, commenting or seeking clarification from time to time. Dreams provide clues to the fate of the soul and indicate to the *manang* which *pelian* rites to perform. Hearing a dream of drowning, for example, he performs a *pelian* using a fishing net. Dreams of kin are also relevant, lending corroborative weight to the patient's dream evidence. *Manang* add their own dreams which have a special authority given their expertise within this reality.

As the enquiry proceeds, the focus shifts to the body of the patient, who now lies on the floor in front of him. *Manang* I observed began with firm, massaging movements of their fingers across the patient's forehead and scalp or abdomen (depending on the symptom location), drawing up and pinching the skin at the end of each pass. They would repeat these sweeping movements with a stone charm in their hand, or carefully hold one stone charm to the affected site and percuss it gently with a second, held in the other hand. Unlike ordinary Iban, they can see and feel invisible wounds in the skin and palpate evidence of illness that lies deep within the body--the deeper, the more serious the illness. *Manang* described this to me as a quivering sensation and they were not surprised that I was unable to feel these vibrations. Although similar to the medical physical examination (*peresa*), the technique differs in that it makes the illness within the body palpable at the surface. The term for this procedure, *begama'*, can be translated as groping and in common use means to feel one's way in the dark. So central is this skill that the power of the *manang* is located idiomatically in their hands (*sidi' jari*).

The groping captivates the audience because it often culminates in the removal of a small stone miraculously extracted from within the body. I was struck by the prolonged build-up of tension climaxing in the sudden display of the stone. One *manang* would crouch over the patient with increasing concentration, intently massaging and tapping closer and closer to the source of trouble, and when it seemed he was going on forever, he would abruptly sit upright triumphantly to display a little stone, held aloft between the thumb and forefinger of his right hand, before flicking it carelessly into the corner of the room where it would tinkle as it hit the floor, then fall between the boards to the ground below.

Finally, the *manang* closes the spirit wound through which he has extracted the stone using a covering or patching charm (*ubat penampal*), thereby reintegrating the integrity of the boundary. Strictly speaking, none of the procedures to this point constitutes shamanic healing since they are all routinely performed by non-shamanic Malay and Iban healers (*dukun*). But they are an essential precursor to the *pelian* because they define the *manang's* jurisdiction over the body and establish him as a practitioner who encompasses other modes of treatment. Unlike the *dukun* or the western doctor who are restricted to bodily treatments, the body is merely a point of departure for the *manang*. Moreover, these procedures demonstrate his ability to move beyond the scope of the Iban, to see and feel into the invisible, interior spaces of the body, to externalize illness and render it visible before the very eyes of the Iban.

Rendering the Soul Visible.

By now it is dark and the *manang* turns his gaze on the patient's soul by looking at a quartz crystal (*batu karas*) held at arm's length with a kerosene flame directly behind. Within the crystal he sees an image of the soul which Iban cannot see. The several terms for this technique refer again to the process of rendering the invisible visible. For example, the crystal itself is called a seeing stone (*batu ilau*), although the word *ilau* does not refer to everyday vision (*peda'*) but to the perception of spirits or people who have "visions" (Richards 1981:114). The stone is also named *penampak manang*, because it makes the soul visible, obvious or clear (*tampak*). The Malay term *terupong* or telescope is also used, since it confers distance vision. The process is termed *mandang* (to show, exhibit or expose) or *ninjau* (to scan from a high vantage).³ Height and distance are the crucial dimensions of the soul image that spell the severity of illness and the danger of treatment. The taller the soul, the more visible it is to spirits. The more distant the soul, the further along the road to the dead it has travelled. The *manang* formulates his assessment on this basis, as well as taking into account the physical symptoms, vibrations within the body and especially the dreams. The audience anticipation is therefore intense as the *manang* concentrates his vision on the crystal and finally pronounces on the severity of the situation, the fate of the soul and, most importantly, the particular choice and sequence of *pelian* he will use and the equipment he requires the family to provide.

Thus, the assessment process entails a transition from day to night and from body to soul. Points of heightened dramatic tension occur when the *manang* suddenly renders what is invisible (be it stones inside the body or the patient's soul) visible and thereby reveals the nature of the problem.

IBAN DISCOURSE ON EFFECTIVENESS AND PERFORMANCE

Iban actively debate about the nature of the *manang's* practice. Discussions among the audience take place offstage during lulls in the action. Skeptics argue that the *manang* could not possibly remove the stone from deep within the body, that he has cleverly concealed it beneath his fingernail. Believers argue that the stone is extracted from the body. The majority, agnostics, state that they do not know. Foremost among the ranks of disbelievers are younger Iban who have received schooling within the modern Malaysian state education system, but older Iban, too, both men and women, including those who hold political status (*tuai rumah*) and traditional ritual status (*lemambang*) are not reluctant to express their incredulity. The most admired *manang* in the Saribas, a tough-minded old pragmatist, would regularly poke fun at the false pretenses of *manang*, including himself. Early, colonial ethnographic accounts of the last century and early parts of this century derided the gullibility of the Iban, dismissing shamanic practice as little more than deceit, pretence and sleight-of-hand.⁴ Not only did these commentators fail to recognize that Iban themselves traditionally shared this skepticism, as shown by the earliest serious account of shamanism (Freeman 1967), but they also displayed a profound inability to grasp the cultural logic which lay beneath the *manang's* prestidigitation.

As the debate goes back and forth, the opinion is stated, before long, that it is the *yang* (commanding spirit) who actually performs the treatment, not the *manang* himself. Whether or not the *manang* actually extracts a stone, what happens is that as the *manang* enacts the treatment, the *yang* simultaneously removes the illness from the patient's body. From within a structure of skepticism emerges a reaffirmation of the effectiveness of the treatment. An experienced *manang* stated the conundrum by explaining that it was both sleight of hand (*silap mata*) and at the same time it was not sleight of hand, because it worked through the *yang*.

The Iban discourse on effectiveness proposes that ritual is a form of action which leads to actual consequences. It is cast within the cultural schema of twin realities and their paradoxical relationship. On the one hand, since there is a mirror-like correspondence between the two realities, it is axiomatic that action correctly carried out within a ritual frame in this world is paralleled by the same action within invisible reality. But on the other hand, in keeping with the principle that these realities are also obversely related, it is argued that what is merely simulation in this reality, is the opposite there; it has actual consequences. The corollary of this is that consequences effected by the *yang* in the invisible reality are mirrored by the same actual effects in this reality; hence, the patient undergoes physical improvement. By means of this oscillating reasoning (based on the paradox that a relation of identity can coincide with one of polar opposition), Iban construct a dualistic model of effectiveness which relates ritual action to its consequences within the visible and the invisible reality. Ultimately they assert that ritual action has practical consequences for the patient's soul and body. The bodily consequences are direct and occur when the *manang* and his *yang* manipulate the body. The effect on the soul is also direct and may be carried out in the absence of the patient's body. Therefore the patient's physical presence is not important when the soul is being manipulated and he may even be asleep at the time.

Since Iban do not use an ideas/action dichotomy to differentiate the two realities (both are equally pervaded by action and ideas), there is no place for a theory of ritual performance as working its effects by changing participants' minds. Such theories are commonly the preserve of anthropological analysis and work by means of a different dualism that pits body against mind; that the effect of ritual action is through symbolic manipulation of the patient's and audience's definition of their experience, which is then transformed through a psycho-somatic equation into physical changes in the patient's body.

Performance and the Construction of *Pelian* Reality

The Iban use the term "*main*" for performance. In common use the word refers to calculated action, either in the sense of "doing" things within the context of everyday life or competitive action within the setting of a game (Richards 1981:201). The word is usually translated into English as "play" and in fact it connotes a similar range of meanings as this word, for it can also mean idle action for amusement, or express a dramaturgical concept of enactment.[5]

In the context of shamanism, *main* refers to the performance of the *pelian* rite. Iban approach the *pelian* as a separate reality that is created by the *manang* through performance. While observing *pelian*, when I asked informants what was currently happening, they prefaced replies with "*Dalam main*" (within the ritual) or "*Dalam leka main*" (in the words of the chant). The pelian is treated as a third reality, distinct from everyday reality and also from that of the dead, spirits or gods. Through the media of chant and enactment the *manang* builds *pelian* reality by means of representations. Ritual objects represent or stand for (*ambi ka*) other objects and the *manang* himself employs mime or pretence (*ngaga' diri, ngelulu' ka*). However, "*main*" is differentiated from dramatic performance purely for entertainment. Iban resort to the Malay term *belakun* to describe the latter. To say of a *manang* that he is a good entertainer may imply criticism that he plays to the audience at the expense of concentrating on correct ritual performance.

Main is thus a term which, on the one hand, connotes a dramaturgical idea of ritual action as performance, that is, representation. On the other hand, *main* also connotes an instrumental notion of ritual action as performative, in the sense meant by J. L. Austin (1962). As in the above discussion of effectiveness, it asserts that enacting has actual consequences. Though *main* is drama, it is true (*amat*) not false (*bula'*).

TRANSFORMATION OF SPACE IN THE CONSTRUCTION OF *PELIAN* REALITY

The performance proper comprises several discrete *pelian* arranged in a sequence and separated by intervals during which the *manang* chats and drinks with members of the audience or joins them in a meal. In ten curing rituals I observed, the average and modal number of *pelian* per ritual was six (range two-ten). The duration of each was between ten minutes and an hour. *Pelian* are named by their central action (e.g. killing a spirit, **bebunoh antu**) or the scene at which the action takes place (e.g. the spirit's iron cage, *sankar besi*). The variety is rich and the data I collected on 54 different types by no means exhausted either the opus of the Saribas *manang* or the *pelian* recorded in the ethnographic literature.[6] The object of most *pelian* is to retrieve the soul of the sick person. The chant describes the retrieval and culminates with the *manang* enacting the recapture, then "fainting," during which his soul, accompanied by the *yang*, carries out the actual soul retrieval. The *manang* reawakens with the soul, substantiated as a small black seed, in the palm of his hand. He inserts the rescued soul back into the patient's head by placing the seed over the region of the anterior fontanelle.

Although a few small scale rites are performed entirely within the *bilik*-apartment, most shift from *bilik* to *ruai*, oscillate between these two spaces through the evening, and finally return to the *bilik* next morning. Through the ritual organization of space, the *pelian* makes explicit the crosscutting social and cosmic categories which structure Iban experience. The initial emergence onto the *ruai* (*pansut ka ruai*) is a sufficiently important juncture to be identified by name. It marks a change from diagnosis to treatment amid a change in focus from the family as a separate entity to the family as a constituent element of the longhouse community.

This transition from domestic to public is also a transition from women's to men's space, for although in everyday life these areas are used by both, within the ritual signification of longhouse space, *bilik* is to *ruai* as female is to male. A gender division of labor is evident in the transition. A senior female relative prepares an offering (*melah dekoh*) then carries it onto the *ruai*, along with *pua' kumbu'* weavings and other items that are the stock-in-trade of women's labor.

The *Pagar Api*

Men, meanwhile, erect a shrine (*pagar api*) on the *ruai* immediately in front of the *bilik*-apartment, contributing items (such as a banana leaf) from outside the longhouse and also items (such as a spear) that epitomize male pursuits and masculinity itself. They suspend a single, transverse, bamboo pole horizontally above head height, securing it at each end to longhouse pillars. Underneath they place a small rush mat. A jar on the mat forms a base in which to put a vertical spear (or blowpipe) that is secured near its tip to the mid-point of the bamboo horizontal. A banana frond is prepared by cutting away proximal parts of the leaf to expose more of the stem, where two series of notches are fashioned, one on each side, like rungs of a ladder. It is also placed in the jar, its stem secured to the spear with red thread. The women's contribution is added and the entire base wrapped in a *pua' kumbu'* weaving.

Table 1 sets out some referents of the main components of the *pagar api* and associated equipment at its base. They are transformative symbols with shifting referents: a banana leaf, the flag of the travelling *manang*, later becomes a tree where he meets spirits; the *pua' kumbu'* weaving in one moment is the *manang's* wing and in the next, a protective covering for his soul. Amid the profusion of referents, two symbolic themes display the central purpose of the *pelian*. One is a theme of protection from the malign influence of the dead or spirits, for example a plate bound with rattan becomes the *manang's* shield.

The other is a counter-theme of involvement with these beings.[7] It is expressed through the concept of a journey, an encounter and a return, relying on images of travel, itself a fundamental organizing motif within Iban symbolism. The *pagar api* is the point of departure and return for the journey and has been likened to a boat landing (Richards 1981:262). It is also the axis around which the journey takes place (the *manang* circumambulates it) as well as the means of travel (a ladder of ascent and descent or a boat with painter, flag and, according to Erik Jensen [1974:148], a paddle). Furthermore, the *pagar api* is the point of encounter where the *manang* meets with spirits and engages in transactions with them. This meaning is encoded in a legend (*cherita tuai*) I recorded concerning the origin of the *pagar api*, in which Jarai, one of the original *manang*, meets with the demon *antu gerasi* at a tree while out hunting. Both have killed female pig-tailed macaques (*nyumboh*) which they roast on a fire. Recognizing, however, that they have actually killed each other's wives, they agree to exchange corpses and each returns home with the body of his respective wife. For Jarai's part, as he gets closer to home, his wife's body becomes smaller and smaller until it transforms into her soul, as tiny as a millet seed within the palm of his hand. Arriving home, he first bathes in the stream so that the soul is cooled and does not stick to his palm. When he enters the longhouse he finds that while he was away hunting his wife died of a painful illness in the chest--the same place where the *antu gerasi* wounded the macaque--so he places the soul into his wife's body and she comes to life again. The *pagar api* is indeed the tree where *manang* and spirit encounter in a reciprocal killing and retrieval of wives.

TABLE 1

ELEMENTS OF THE *PAGAR API* AND THEIR SYMBOLIC REFERENTS

horizontal bamboo pole	scaffold only, no symbolic referent
rush mat (*tikai bemban*)	*manang's* boat
small jar (*kebok*)	base for the shrine/base or root of tree/container for the soul
spear (*sangkoh*)	path of *manang's* journey/path of return of soul/masculinity
banana leaf	flag of *manang's* boat/tree
notches in stem of banana leaf	ladder of ascent and descent
red thread (*ubong mansau*)	to bind the soul (*penanchang semengat*)
cloth	used to catch soul/protection for the *manang's* soul
white thread	the "stalk" of the soul (*tampok semengat*) where it becomes attached
duku sword	paddle/weapon/soul strengthener (*kering semengat*) because it is made of iron
plate bound in *rotan*	manang's shield (*terabai manang*)
pua' kumbu' weaving	*manang's* wings/protection for *manang's* soul/shade for patient's plant aspect

An intriguing aspect of this shrine is its name. Literally translated, *pagar* means fence or barrier and *api* means fire, though the meaning of the phrase has long since puzzled ethnographers and Iban informants alike. The *manang* with whom I worked were no exception for, although they were quite explicit about the symbolism of its component parts, they were not clear about the meaning of the name *pagar api*, as if the meaning of the whole was less than the sum of its individual parts. The informant who recounted the above myth said that *pagar api* referred to a barrier of fire, for it represented the fire on which the macaques were roasted. The fire formed a barrier for the *manang* against the *antu gerasi*, for Jarai heaped it with *lukai* wood, the smoke of which blinds, weakens and repels spirits.

The puzzle of the *pagar api* has prompted several ethnographers to take various speculative leaps in order to locate its "real" meaning, but in doing so, they ignore the very unintelligibility of the shrine and its name which is, in itself, one dominant meaning. Iban assert that they do not know what the name means because its meaning is too deep (*dalam*). Depth, in this usage, refers both to meaning which is not transparent and to a meaning which is buried within history, myth and the origin of Iban. Hence, it is the very mystery of the *pagar api* which captures the Iban imagination. In a cosmological system that is based on paradox, the *pagar api*, because of its inherent opacity, stands as one of the primary symbols which does not have that same paradoxical quality. It therefore becomes the lynch-pin of the Iban system of ideas, summating and organizing the different contradictory provinces of meaning.

The Social Organization of Space Encoded in the *Pelian* Sequence

The *pagar api* is one pivotal point of the performance. The audience encircle it; older men with interest and expertise in ritual sit closer, younger men and some of the women at a greater distance. The *manang* makes excursions away from the *pagar api* beyond the audience along the *ruai*, even sometimes out into the dark. If there were such a concept as a ritual stage, it would be one which filled the entire longhouse and beyond, enveloping the audience. The *pagar api* would be at the center of the stage.

Usually, the patient remains physically in the *bilik* (along with a great many of the women who also stay there) to form the other pivotal point of the performance. At the end of each *pelian* the *manang* returns to the *bilik*, soul in hand to replace it in the patient's head. Since several *pelian* are performed in the course of one night, the soul is returned several times and by morning, the path between *pagar api* and patient is well trod. There is a spatial axis of treatment which connects the *pagar api* on the *ruai* to the patient's body in the *bilik*. Thus the ritual repeatedly describes an open passage between *bilik* and *ruai*, between family and longhouse community, so much so that some *manang* regard it as ritually forbidden (*mali*) to close the door between *bilik* and *ruai* during a *pelian*.

In the breaks, when food and drink are served by the *bilik*-family to the longhouse audience, the open intercourse between *bilik*-apartment and *ruai* is again made explicit by the to-and-fro of young men who bring out a stream of food cooked by young women. Gender and age categories are formally displayed at these times. Moving from the back of the longhouse to the front, young women cook at the hearth near the back of the *bilik*, older women sit in the main *bilik* to eat, young men bring the food out and the empty plates back, and older men sit on the *ruai* to eat, the most senior among them at the front (*pantar*) section. Women are to men, as back is to front, as *bilik* is to *ruai*, as domestic space is to public space, as family group is to longhouse community. Similarly, young people are to old as preparers and servers are to consumers, as hosts are to guests, as family group is to longhouse community. The *pelian* not only transforms the entire longhouse into a ritual space but also employs this space to display age and gender categories in relationships of respect and deference.

The *pagar api*/patient dipole is also evident in the way *manang* join together a sequence of *pelian*. After the initial diagnostic work within the *bilik* during the early evening, the very first *pelian* is very often the *tali wa* (rope swing) performed on the *tempuan*, a transitional space between *bilik* and mid-*ruai*. Later into the night, subsequent *pelian* are enacted in the middle of the *ruai*, then out on the *tanju'* (outer veranda) or even right outside the longhouse, but the penultimate or terminal *pelian* (*pelepa*) is again performed on the *tempuan* and concludes with the *manang* hanging *pua' kumbu'* weavings over the front and back door of the *bilik*, a ritual barrier that reconstitutes the integrity of the *bilik*-family. The following morning, the final ritual (*adat*) payments and *ex gratia* payments are made within the confines of the *bilik* again, completing the night-long cycle from *bilik* to *ruai* to *bilik*.

Through the organization of performance space, the major categories of the Iban social world are revealed; gender, age and the *bilik*-family in its relation to the wider community. Performance space is structured processually. First the family is defined, then it is opened out into the longhouse community, articulated and integrated with them, then closed off again as a discrete entity. The *pagar api* stands at the center, synthesizing dichotomous categories. Built by male and female labor, it combines gender categories. Erected in the center of the *ruai*, it stands midway between the domestic and the exterior, becoming the interface between humans and spirits. Through the multivocal symbolism of its elements, it epitomizes transformation itself, and the problematic relationship between appearance and interpretation. At a most fundamental level it mediates between an absence of signification (people do not understand its name) and an over-abundance of signification (each element is polysemic) and in this regard represents the underlying logic of *manang* healing, which is to reveal what is invisible--to provide meaning where previously the situation was not understood.

The Symbolic Organization of Space Encoded in the Hierarchy of *Pelian*

Iban use several classificatory schemata to categorize *pelian*. Two important categories are related to this discussion. Their internal ordering illustrates how longhouse space is transformed from mundane reality to symbolize alternative realities.

The first category comprises a group of *pelian*, all directed at recovering the soul from spirits (*jalai ngagai antu*). The different *pelian* within this group can be thought of in terms of an hierarchy of increasing danger. At the lowest level, *manang* use stage props to represent the spirit's lair which, in actuality, is said to be located in the jungle not far from the longhouse. The *pelian sangkar besi*, for example, employs three swords arranged on the mid-*ruai* to resemble a spirit's iron cage from which the captive soul is sprung, whereas the *pelian luban batu* uses three stones arranged on the ruai floor in the shape of a rock cave to represent the lair of a tiger spirit. In the *pelian* entitled *kara penjuang*, which brings the *manang* closer to the offending spirit, two bamboo uprights erected outside on the outer veranda and tied together at their tips into an "A" shape, represent a well-known haunt of spirits, the upper branches of the parasite fig plant. Long wooden pestles hang down to represent its giant aerial roots. Within the performance, the *manang's* soul and *yang* beard the spirit in this tree top den. In a closer confrontation, *manang* may attract a spirit to the longhouse by food offerings in order to drive it away (*muru antu*), blind it using a blowpipe (*besumpit*) or ultimately slay it with a sword (*bepantap* or *bebunoh antu*).

The safest procedures, recovering a soul from an iron cage or stone cave when the spirit is not there, are enacted on the *ruai*. It is increasingly risky to confront a spirit out on the outer veranda, to drive it away from the longhouse or blind it with a dart. To engage the spirit in sword play is to run the risk of the *manang* being killed. The progression from the light of the *ruai* to the outside darkness, from the social space of the longhouse to the natural jungle space of malevolent spirits, signifies increasing danger. The more dangerous the patient's affliction and the more fearless the *manang*, the further out he ventures into the world of spirits. Within the *pelian* reality, the longhouse becomes a stage in which everyday social space fuses with spirit space.

The second category is an hierarchy of *pelian* in which the *manang* must travel toward the land of the dead to recapture the soul (*jalai nagagai sebayan*). As with the spirit category, the worse the illness, the further the *manang's* soul must travel into the heartland of the dead. In several *pelian*, the middle of the *ruai* represents an intermediate zone between the world of the living and the world of the dead. *Munggu tunggal* refers to a solitary hill in this no-man's land and is represented by a large upturned wooden mortar placed near the *pagar api* and covered with a *pua' kumbu'* weaving. In *tinting lanjan*, seven such mortars stand for a ridge of seven peaks, giving a sense of moving ever farther from this longhouse and this world toward the world of the dead. The adjective *lanjan* primarily means "lost" or "beyond recall" and can be used in reference to illnesses thought to be imminently fatal. I saw it performed for a woman who was obviously dying, the ridge of peaks extending along the *ruai* a graphic display of what could not be openly broached in conversation--the futility of any attempt to cure her.

Many of the landmarks of the *manang's* soul journey are described in the *sabak*, the funeral dirge which is a sort of mythic itinerary for the passage of the deceased's soul from the longhouse in the world of the living to the longhouse in the world of the dead. The major river there, the Mandai, is represented in the longhouse by the *tempuan*. In the *pelian titi rawan*, the *manang* recaptures the patient's soul at the "bridge of fear" which crosses this river and separates the living from the dead. The bridge is represented by a wooden pestle placed transversely across the *tempuan* from one upturned mortar to another. Scenes of succeeding *pelian* are set further toward the longhouse periphery to convey a sense of the increasing distance the *manang's* soul must travel. At the edge of the longhouse, the *manang*, seated on a large plate, slides down the ladder running from the door to the ground below (*belanchar ba' wong Limban*). This represents his soul slithering down the waterfall on the Limban river, deeper within the land of the dead. At the mid-point of the hierarchy within this series are *pelian* that are performed outside on the clearing below, at which stage the longhouse of the living comes to denote the longhouse of the dead. After this, in succeeding *pelian*, spatial progression still represents increasing proximity to the dead, but now in reverse direction. In the *ruai*, now the *ruai* of the longhouse of the dead, he enacts a tug of war with the dead (*belian bebatak lampong*). There are *pelian* which take the *manang's* soul right to the *bilik* of the dead, as in *bedagang bilang lawang*, where he walks from *bilik* to *bilik* pretending to trade, though he is actually searching for the sick person's soul. He might masquerade as a visitor (*nemuai*) entering each *bilik* in turn, though his true purpose is to locate the lost soul which comes into his *sintong* basket, attracted by the smell of the patient's clothes which have been hidden there. As in the spirit series, the closer the *manang* comes to confronting the dead, the more dangerous the *pelian*. Just as I described everyday space fusing with spirit space in that series, so in this series, the longhouse of the living becomes one with the longhouse of the dead.

Thus, within *pelian* reality longhouse space is signified to display explicitly the structures of Iban social life, and symbolically transformed to fuse the invisible reality of souls, spirits and the dead, with the visible reality of everyday life.

CHANT, DRAMA AND THE CONSTRUCTION OF *PELIAN* REALITY

Sitting by the *pagar api*, the *manang* first bites the sword to strengthen and protect his own soul, then begins to chant, quietly at first so that it is drowned out by the chatter of men sitting nearby, then in a gradual crescendo that emerges out of the conversation and finally dominates and suppresses it. It is a true chant, an adagio, in which the words are drawn out in long tones that oscillate between two or three notes just a semitone or a tone apart. Each line progresses into a characteristic quavering trill which is very difficult to execute, then comes to an emphatic and very abrupt end that accents the terminal rhyming syllable. Before long the *manang* rises and begins his slow, measured march, in time with the chant, moving the left foot forward, bringing the right foot up level with it, then moving the right foot forward and bringing the left foot up level, as he circles the *pagar api*.

The chant is composed of lines that contain runs of internal rhymes and ends with syllables that rhyme with the terminal syllables of adjacent lines. Lines are grouped into stanzas of varying size, each expressing a discrete set of ideas. The sequence of stanzas is highly structured, from the opening stanza used in all *pelian*, through an orderly progression of themes to the characteristic terminal stanza describing the return of the *manang* to Mount Rabong, the mythic home of shamans.

The language of the chant is *jako dalam* or "deep language," in contrast to everyday, obvious or shallow Iban (*jako mabu'*). "*Dalam*" refers to an historical sense of depth, just as it does in regard to the *pagar api*. The language is archaic, employing words and phrases of forebears rarely used nowadays and referring to equipment long since outdated, such as rattan door hinges instead of metal hinges. An informant likened the chant to a pool of water, explaining to me that the deeper the language, the more important the meaning you could extract from it, in the same way that the deeper you dive down into the pool, the bigger the fish you are likely to catch. The chant is also deep in the sense of being cryptic; a series of puzzles that the listener must decipher to make the meaning obvious. Of all the chants in the Iban opus, the *pelian* chants are recognized as being the hardest to understand. In some parts, the language is so deep that even expert interpreters cannot make sense of it. These sections are described as the language of spirits (*jako antu*) or the language of the dead (*jako sebayan*), since according to the principle of inversion, what is unintelligible to us makes sense to them. Finally, deep language is a register of respect which voices the *manang's* deference to these beings. Hence, the chant is a hybrid form that speaks partly to the living and partly to the dead or spirits. Through the control over language "depth," the *manang* creates a *pelian* reality which bridges visible and invisible realities.

He also becomes many different characters within this reality. At times he is self-reflexive, describing his own equipment and actions in the third person. At other times he takes on the part of the mythical *manang* seeking the soul, or the spirits of a series of fish species who attend the ceremony. He becomes the gods, their wives, and he even plays the part of the healing charm, personified as a child. He speaks in the voice of the spirit's lover, attracting her with his love song. Derek Freeman (1967:327) shows how, in the case of a male demon, the *manang* assumes the role of a female lover by simulating a female tone of voice. During the breaks between *pelian* he runs commentaries on the nature of the *pelian* itself. One *manang* would achieve an alienation effect by breaking off the chant momentarily to comment on the characters. After singing about one ancestor who tried in vain to move a large rock that blocked the gateway to the earth, the *manang* stopped for a few seconds to scoff at him saying that the gateway to the earth was no place to test one's strength. The *pelian* chant is thus a one-man show in which the *manang* moves from character to character and becomes all beings within the Iban cosmos, including an ordinary Iban. This establishes him as the being, par excellence, who can move back and forth across major boundaries which normally divide the cosmos--from mundane reality to *pelian* reality to invisible reality. Through the chant, the *manang* personifies the power of illusion. His performance breaks the nexus between appearances and what lies behind them. He demonstrates that the connection between phenomenon and noumenon is a function of the particular reality in which we are living.

Excursion to the Land of the Dead and Back--the *Pelian Nyembayan*.

The chant narrative relates an excursion which begins in the longhouse, journeys out into the reality of spirits, the dead or gods, and returns to the longhouse again. Early stanzas describe what is visibly apparent to the audience; the *manang's* equipment, his ritual action or the longhouse itself. There is frequent reference to time in poetic images of dusk, the depth of night, or whatever time it is when the chant begins. By these devices, the beginning of the text is anchored in the time, space and action of this-world reality.

The very concept of a cosmic journey is signified in the strict sequence of stanzas and the order of their thematic development. This can be appreciated in the *pelian nyembayan*, for retrieving souls from the dead--one of the six *pelian* I observed one night for the treatment of Dom,[8] an infant suffering from abdominal pain and crying at night. Before Manang Jimbau began the chant, Jantan, an old man who himself had some healing expertise, measured a cup of uncooked rice exactly level by passing a tightly rolled cigarette paper across the top. Pouring it out into a flat, woven sifting tray, he used the rice to fashion a model of a monitor lizard (*menarat*), a carnivorous animal of greedy habit and of little value to the Iban. This model of the lizard only had three legs. He draped the tray with a *pua' kumbu'* weaving and placed it near the *pagar api*.

Each stanza of the chant comprised two halves, a question and an answer. In the first half, Manang Jimbau played the part of several original ancestral *manang*, asking of birds whether they knew the whereabouts of Dom's soul. In the second half, he replied in the voice of the birds, who answered that they did not know, for they had been too busy with their normal daily activity to notice. In each stanza, different ancestral *manang* asked the question of different birds. Manang Lansu and Disit asked the Kunchit birds but they did not know, being too busy flitting from branch to branch. Manang Gendau and Jelapi asked the Kejira birds, but they were too busy making their nests in the ground left fallow from last year's crops. At first the puzzle, then the answer. This engaged members of the audience who, if they knew the characteristic habit of each bird as well as their significance as omen birds, could predict why each particular species did not know the whereabouts of Dom's soul before Manang Jimbau chanted the answer. An underlying logic was gradually revealed in the sequence of stanzas, for the birds' habitats progressed from domestic to wild: from the longhouse environs to fallow land with young growth, then older growth, then to jungle. The birds themselves were progressively bigger and wilder. The first five birds of the series were associated with the living, their calls being heard during the day, whereas subsequent ones were night--calling birds which Iban associated with the dead. The Semalau birds were too busy inspecting grave goods to see Dom, the Tiup Api birds, (which have special significance at funeral time), were singing in the deep of night, and the Kuong Kebat birds were preoccupied with tying up the bones of the dead. As the search for Dom became more frustrating, the forward momentum of the chant became agonizingly slow.

Time stood still. Descriptions of birds and their activities were elaborate but no progress was made. Finally the *manang* asked Bunsu Bubut, the coucal bird who stands near the bridge of fear that crosses into the land of the dead itself, singing her mournful cry whenever a soul crosses over. She had indeed seen a woman take Dom's soul across--she saw them hurry along the river of the dead.

By means of the progression farther and farther from the longhouse, the elongation of time, and the transition from domestic to wild, from day to night, from birds of the living to birds of the dead, the chant transported us to the very foot of the stairs of the longhouse of the dead where the dead themselves were gathering to see the monitor lizard, half-hidden under a log, looking sleek and satisfied. Dom was there among them, sitting down on the ground. Crowding closer to peer at the lizard, they were surprised and amused to see that this curious creature had one leg missing. Here lay the deception, for in the instant that the dead were caught off guard by their own curiosity, Manang Jimbau's *yang* snatched Dom's soul and spirited it back to the land of the living again at breakneck speed, condensing time so that the long return journey was compressed into a few stanzas. Each stanza line reworked three to four modal concepts: the name of an ancestral *manang*, his *yang*, the method of recapturing the soul, and the mode of return. Image was heaped upon image in a repetitive emphasis of the sudden snatching of the soul and the rapid journey back into this reality:

> The *yang* of Manang Guyak, a python, finds the soul and slithers home faster than a speeding bullet, the soul on its back.
> The *yang* of Manang Bidu, a crocodile, drags the soul back.
> The *yang* of Manang Gelanyang, a leopard with teeth bared, fetches the soul.
> The *yang* of Manang Jelapi, the fighting owl, ties a knot to fasten the soul.
> The *yang* of Manang Rechap, the demon Nading Gerasi, steals the soul away.
> The *yang* of Manang Emong, an orangutan, frees the soul by snatching it away.

The final leg of the journey was described in metaphors of bounty, health, coolness, generativity and long life. As they passed the old ruins of the former longhouse, the trees were flowering and fruiting profusely and when they bathed in the stream, the stones of the river bed turned miraculously into charms (*ubat penchelap*) that were as cool as large drops of rain, as cool as cucumbers. Toward the end, Manang Jimbau again employed devices to tie the text to everyday reality, accurately describing the three paths leading up from the river, and adding that the whetstone festival was only just over, thereby identifying the scene as this particular longhouse at this point in time.

At the end of the chant Manang Jimbau grasped the *duku'* sword in his right hand and suddenly lay down near the *pagar api*. The men covered him with a *pua' kumbu'* weaving. During this faint (*luput*) his soul and *yang* together performed the actions just described in the chant. After about 40 seconds, he emitted several queer, high-pitched moaning sounds and emerged from the faint, uncovering himself and sitting up with a dazed expression on his face. The soul clasped in his right hand, he returned to the *bilik*-apartment and placed it on Dom's head, repeating the same procedure for Dom's mother as well. Jantan carefully uncovered the image of the monitor lizard to the expectant audience, who crowded around to see if there were any slight depressions on its back, evidence of spirit wounds. He disassembled it, putting every last grain of rice back into the same cup. For the second time he measured the volume by passing a cigarette paper across the mouth of the cup and now there was more than before, for a few grains were swept onto the tray below. The fact that the cup overflowed with rice signified that the dead, instead of being in a state of want, in which they took souls, caused illness and mysteriously thieved rice, were now satisfied and bestowing bounty on the family. Although the excess rice is sometimes eaten, in this case it was placed on Dom's and his mother's head as provisions for the soul (*bekal semengat*).

Key elements of the *pelian* chant performance are the manipulation of time and space and the creation of another reality by sheer power of description. The chant is first tethered in time and space to mundane reality but then breaks loose. Viewed from the mundane perspective, *pelian* time appears to move slower and slower as the *pelian* reality converges with the world of the dead. Later, *pelian* time is compressed, bringing us back with a jolt to the longhouse again. Within this *pelian* reality, the *manang* makes the dead visible through the vividness of his description. He engages them in a characteristic exchange by first attracting and deceiving them with an offering, then suddenly snatching away the soul. The exchange is reciprocal and satisfying for both dead and living. At one level, rice grains are offered and returned in excess. At another level a soul is exchanged for a deformed monitor lizard. The latter, although of no value to the living, is highly valued by the dead (what is bad here is good there), and in fact is the embodiment of greed now satisfied. The *manang's* deception becomes, according to the principle of opposites, a solemnly measured exchange. Balanced reciprocity between living and dead is restored, according to the logic of ridding society of badness by passing it on to the dead, who perceive it as goodness and reply with bounteous fruitfulness, powerful charms and health. The *manang* thus achieves a double exchange; he exchanges lizard for soul and exchanges the meaning of the encounter from deception to reciprocal transaction. The poetic structure of the chant turns around this point of exchange. Leading up to it, there is a frustrating, slow outward journey of fruitless searching, but suddenly, the deception revealed and the soul snatched away, the momentum of the chant changes into an abundantly satisfying, speedy homeward journey.

Attracting a Spirit to the Longhouse--*Pelian Muru Antu*

Similar principles can be seen in the *pelian muru antu*, (driving away a spirit) performed by Manang Jimbau that same night, for it was additionally thought that Dom's soul had been seduced by a female *antu buyu*, who, in the Saribas, may be an old hag who lives either in the ruins of deserted longhouses, in the nearby jungle or in the loft among disused paddy bins. A food offering had been hung on a tree as a bait just outside the back door, half concealed with a palm frond. There was some great anticipation since Manang Jimbau had said he would kill the spirit and was now armed for combat with sword and a plate for a shield. At first he burned some *lemba* leaf to blind and weaken the spirit (*enkerabun*), then began the chant, in which he summoned the spirit from all her three usual locations. He implored her to show herself using the highly-refined language of respect and flattery. He called her by extravagant praise names and sang in adoration of her beautiful tattooed body, describing the patterns in elaborate poetic detail. The spirit was attracted to the longhouse through the language of courtship. It was by the spirit's seduction that Dom's soul had been led away in the first place and, accordingly, it was by means of flirtation that the *manang* began to rectify the situation.

Still chanting, he proceeded through the *bilik* and out through the back door. Other Iban were excluded. In the entire range of Iban ritual, spirit slaying was the only action I was not welcome to observe and photograph. Not only was it regarded as too dangerous for me, but my presence, particularly the illumination from the flashlight on my camera, could frighten the spirit and interfere with the central purpose of the rite, to entice the spirit to show itself, become visible and thereby amenable to being dealt with and controlled. By contrast, Manang Jimbau was happy for me to attach my remote microphone to his shirt, with a tiny radio transmitter that beamed the chant back to my receiver and cassette recorder. The transcription subsequently confirmed that he did not kill the spirit at all. Instead, he continued to attract her with bells and the *piring* offering, and when she finally appeared, his language suddenly changed from the adoring blandishments of seduction into the stern rebuke of an irritated teacher. She should leave this child alone and accept the food offering as fair exchange. She should be wishing the child success at school rather than taking his soul away. He slashed a banana leaf in warning to her that next time he would be forced to kill her. Once the spirit was taught how to behave (*ngajar antu*) and driven away, he returned to the polite style of respect and apologized profusely for dealing so harshly with her. This approach to spirits is typical of the Saribas *manang*, who eschew armed combat when it comes to conflict resolution. Instead, they value intellectual agility, the capacity to deceive, and verbal negotiation carried out in a tone of politeness and respect. My informant said that this was an acknowledgement that *manang* are half-spirits, half men, and reluctant to kill or be rude to their own kind. Since spirits, too, are bound by ritual obligations to eat food given them (*puni'*), the offering forced her into the sort of commensal (*semakai*) relationship with men that Iban associate with close kin. One *manang* said that this forced spirits to become like siblings with Iban again. The most powerful effect of the *pelian*, (more effective than killing her would have been), was to reverse the visibility dimension of this spirit. He made the sick child invisible to her by blinding her and at the same time made her visible by enticing her to show herself. These were the crucial procedures that ultimately neutralized her.

Enactment

In the above accounts are two examples of the brief enactment which brings the *pelian* to an end. This enactment is more like a sketch that is minimalist in style than a developing plot, and therein lies its dramatic force, for it has an abrupt and unanticipated quality which, when performed well, startles and astonishes the audience as it ushers in the denouement of the *pelian*. The unwary ethnographer or untutored among the audience can easily be caught off guard, gazing in the wrong direction for a brief while, and miss the crucial few moments of action.

Manang enact the recapture of the patient's soul with a sudden, grasping movement, as in the *pelian betansang* where the *manang* leaps to seize the soul from a spirit's nest (represented by a *sintong*-basket attached high on a longhouse upright) before falling to the floor in a faint. In the previously mentioned *pelian tinting lanjan*, after circling slowly so many times around the ridge of seven upturned mortars, the *manang* without notice jumps onto the ridge and leaps nimbly from peak to peak to the far end where he jumps down again and kicks over the last mortar. As it skids away, he scrambles around on the floor, his hands beneath the *pua' kumbu'*, grabbing at the soul as if it were darting this way and that. The Iban word *ngerampas* or snatching, conveys the sense of a sudden pouncing on the soul unawares.

The killing of an animal spirit, or rather the point where the spectators are allowed in to view the evidence, is one of the most gripping moments in the *manang's* repertoire. Though barred from viewing a slaying, I was invited by a *manang*, as he strode in, triumphant, from the dark, to inspect his *duku'* sword and the blood of the spirit on the blade. Freeman's (1967:330) vivid account captures the anticipation and excitement created by the *manang's* "superbly dramatic essay in the uncanny."

The faint, too, grips the audience, and as the chant draws near to this point, one of the men will call the women within the *bilik* to come out and look. Spectators often exclaim at this point, "*manang luput, manang luput!*" (the *manang* is fainting!). The faint is abrupt. The *manang* drops precipitously to a supine position. I was struck by the agility of these old men who, like professional tumblers, could fall to the floor without hurting themselves. The art of emerging from the faint is just as important. Onlookers are interested in the dazed expression on the *manang's* face as he uncovers himself and "comes to." The faint is simulated rather than a result of any altered state of consciousness (cf. Freeman 1967:316). Those who have spectacles usually take them off just before fainting. Novices must learn how to enter and emerge from a faint. While observing an initiation (*bebangun*) ceremony, I saw a young initiate emerge from under the sacred weaving with a sheepish grin on his face, to be greeted by gales of ridiculing laughter from the spectators who chided him, telling him to take the whole business more seriously. On the very next occasion he emerged in a "dazed" state. Nonetheless the faint is culturally defined as a dangerous state, analogous to death, in which the soul and *yang* are accomplishing what has just been chanted and enacted. On recovering from the faint, the *manang* has the patient's soul clasped in his hand. This, too, arouses curiosity when he displays it to them as a visible object (the tiny, black seed), washes and cools it down with water prior to placing it on the patient's head. Here, the *manang* is not only enacting the ritual chant but also the myth of Jarai, who washed his wife's soul before entering his longhouse.

Through this highly condensed form of theater, the *manang* represents various aspects of the invisible world; the myth of Jarai, the *manang's* soul journey and even small cameos depicting the patient's dreams. Unlike the chant, a discursive medium which relies on an extended stanza sequence, elaborated descriptions and the subtle transformation of time to achieve its effects, the drama is a medium whose abridged presentational form is a succinct expression of the essential purpose of the *pelian*. So sudden and abbreviated is the enactment, that the audience are caught off guard, paralleling the intention of the *manang*, to catch the dead or spirits unawares while he steals away the soul.

Audience Involvement Through Critique of the Performance

Members of the audience, especially near family, ritual experts and the more senior men, become engrossed in the ritual through their critical appraisal of the performance. They listen to the chant with a discerning ear and critique the quavering quality of the *manang's* voice. During the breaks between *pelian*, discussions between older men and *manang* regularly turn to matters of performance technique, often in the form of amusing accounts of *manang* they have known who made errors; one was so entranced by the beauty of his chanting that he ran over time and spoiled the entire ceremony, another did not know how to faint. *Manang* themselves use these discussions to promote their own reputation, often by humble self-disparagement that ultimately elicits statements of praise from the audience. The most accomplished *manang* I knew, the aforementioned skeptic, was adept at controlling the appraisal of his chant by making jokes at his own expense, to the amusement of his audience; for example, that he was not quavering his voice very well tonight because he was worried his false teeth would fall out.

The elements which attract critical commentary and which excite the greatest audience involvement are the essential elements associated with the effectiveness of the rite. In the chant, the foremost issue at stake is the *manang's* ability to sing a correct order of stanzas (*ripih*), a skill requiring extraordinary feats of memory. The cognoscenti are quick to point out (though not to the *manang's* face) any errors of sequence (*salah ator*). The most glaring of these errors involve singing stanzas in reverse order or repeating sections which have already been sung. Since the stanza sequence encodes a soul journey, these "backtracking" errors detract from the efficacy of the chant. The orderly progress of the journey into other cosmic domains and back is central to the cure.

The *manang's* power of description is the second area of critical attention which, I have argued, is intimately tied to efficacy because it is through chant imagery that *manang* create a separate *pelian* reality within which the mundane is brought into conjunction with the supra-mundane. On the one hand, audience members listen for descriptions of their longhouse, the different peaks of nearby hills, or other aspects of mundane reality, and may ejaculate "*betul!*" (exactly right!) or "*amat!*" (true!) when they are accurate. The *manang* thereby establishes the empirical validity of the *pelian* as it describes everyday life.

Listeners also appreciate the extravagant imagery, the indirect allusions, and the deep language of those parts of the chant which describe and thereby bring to light the invisible reality. In a *pelian* which employs an areca palm flower to represent the patient and his treatment (*betimang mayang*), the god

Sempandai and his wife are described in terms of extraordinary beauty. The yearning of his wife to come and help cure the child is likened to the yearnings of a beautiful virgin, sick with love for a young Malay king. In the *pelian betanam ayu*, the focus of the rite is a cordyline palm, which is planted near the longhouse at the end of the ceremony. The words of the *pelian* chant praise this tree using fabulous imagery, its branches laden with riches, reaching as far as Thailand and Singapore. In an extended series of subtly shifting metaphors, the palm transforms into the child-patient himself, his plant aspect, his subsequent thriving development, his longevity and his future travels to these far away cities from which he returns with gold and precious jars. One expert, on listening to such imagery, would exclaim with pleasure, "*Chukup dalam!*" (deep enough!). However, this is not merely a matter of poetic sensibility, for it is the very imagery of praise which empowers the treatment, transforming *piring* offerings into exemplary feasts that are suitable exchange for the patient's soul, the river bed stones into powerful cooling charms, the palm flower (*mayang pinang*) a potent form of medicine in itself. The words themselves are performatives, whose locutionary or propositional content coincides with their elocutionary force.[9]

In the overall structure of a chant performance, the crucial accomplishment is the juxtaposition of mundane reality, depicted in all its facticity, and invisible reality, conjured up through poetic hyperbole. Some *manang* develop this to a fine point by bringing together deep and shallow language, "traditional" and modern themes, within a single stanza, captivating the audience through the humor inherent in such an absurd conjunction of opposites. They sing of the existence of a new bus service within the land of the dead or describe the journey along the mythic River Mandai being made at breakneck speed with the help of a "Johnson" brand outboard motor. I found myself drawn into the performance by this technique since my presence was acknowledged in the chant by incorporating "Australia" into the rhyming structure and into the sequential order of territories on the *manang's* mythic itinerary. The structured juxtaposition of shallow and deep language allows *manang* to incorporate social and political themes into the chant and express some of the major contradictions within Iban society, particularly the contradiction between modern and traditional, between Christianity and the Iban religion, and between modern medicine and shamanic healing.

When discussing shamanism, Iban frequently compare the individual styles of different *manang*. Again, since Iban do not differentiate between aesthetic and effectiveness, appraisal of a *manang's* style implies an evaluation of his ability to cure. In fact, performance prowess is not attributed to the *manang* himself, but to power derived from the *yang*. Most *manang* carry charms given to them by their *yang* to assist in the performance, *ubat pengingat* for memory, *ubat pemanchal* for the courage to perform in front of an audience, and so on. An accomplished performance is treated as an indicator of the involvement of spirit forces. To the Iban, the aesthetic of performance is an index rather than a means of ritual effectiveness.

The points of dramatic intensity also occur at crucial junctures in the ritual enactment; a stone is produced from within the body, the location of the soul is revealed in the quartz crystal, the monitor lizard is uncovered, the *manang* suddenly faints then emerges from beneath the *pua' kumbu'*, the soul is made manifest, the *manang's* charms are displayed. As with the chant itself, there is a congruence between aesthetic and effectiveness, since the moments that captivate an audience are precisely the moments when he reveals the invisible reality, the very transformation which is crucial to the effectiveness of the rite. Just as ritual chant is doing things with words, so ritual drama is doing things with enactments.

CONCLUSION

As the *manang's pelian* rite unfolds, it uncovers what was hidden, reveals what was invisible and brings to the surface what was deep, working its effects at the level of person, society and cosmos. His preliminary gaze exposes several aspects of the Iban person--body, soul and plant--and their disordered relations with one another. The *manang* displays the boundaries as well as the deep and surface compartments of the body aspect; he displays the location and the moral state of the soul, and he displays the state of vigor of the plant aspect.

Through the processual organization of longhouse space within ritual, the major structures of Iban society are revealed. Gender and age categories become distinct. The relationship between the *bilik*-family and the longhouse community is defined and redefined, first as a discrete group, then opened out and articulated with the longhouse, then circumscribed as a discrete entity again. Within the reality of the *pelian*, the *manang* brings into relief the major categories of beings within the Iban cosmos--the living, the spirits, the dead and gods--and their various habitats. He exposes the disordered relations between these beings as a general state of unsated desire and greed, both sexual lust and rapacious hunger. Through the seductive guile of his chant, he entices spirits away so that they relinquish their passionate hold over the souls of men. By ritual exchanges of food for souls, the *manang* forces spirits and the dead into reciprocal relations with men again, relationships characterized by mutual satiety and harmony.

His skill, in this regard, is to create a performance reality within which the taken-for-granted structures of everyday lived experience are transformed. The longhouse space becomes a spirit lair or the longhouse of the dead. Everyday time is stretched and compressed. The *manang* examines the very phenomenal basis of Iban life, space, time and perception, especially visual perception. Within his performance reality, the relationship between appearances and things is made problematic. Phenomena are demonstrated to be expressions of alternative possible noumena, depending on the reality within which they are defined, the reality of spirits or the dead, or the reality of the living.

This is why deception underpins the ritual drama and chant. Without deception it would not be a *pelian*. When they see a *manang* drawing stones out of a head and producing souls in the palm of his hand, Iban theorize about the nature of deception and its relation to the visible and invisible realities, and conclude that what is deception here actually takes place within the invisible reality--the Iban "law of opposites." But the Iban "law of correspondence" states that it is also true that the *manang's* ability to deceive in this world corresponds to his ability to deceive in the invisible reality and thereby effect a cure. By pretending to be her lover, the *manang* induces the spirit to show herself. By masquerading as a visiting trader, the manang is able to gain entry into the very *bilik* of the dead. The monitor lizard is a grand hoax, to enable the *yang* to snatch the soul away from the dead. Simulation is the hallmark of the *manang's* action in this world and the curative force of his action in the other world. This is an entirely appropriate weapon to use against spirits who epitomize dangerous duplicity. In the end, the *manang* out-deceives the arch-deceiver by sheer artifice.[10]

Anthropological analysis has long paid lip-service to the idea that performance and effectiveness cannot be understood outside the terms of a ritual's specific cultural logic, yet its theory of performance is derived directly from Western dramaturgical assumptions about the nature of representation. Likewise, anthropological approaches to the effectiveness of ritual have always implied a Western psychologistic theory of mind as well as rationalist assumptions about the relationship between the natural and the supernatural. This essay has been concerned to treat cultural members as commentators and critics who engage in debate about the fundamental nature of ritual. Iban are highly articulate, as they are in most matters, when it comes to the issue of ritual performance and effectiveness. They argue that the relationship between the appearance of an action, the action itself, and the effects of this action, is problematic and can only be fully understood by taking into account the relationship between different realities within the Iban cosmos. Only by recognizing that the cosmos comprises two analogous but opposite worlds, can one begin to understand that the mere representation of a thing in the visible world (say, a seed) is indeed that thing in the invisible world (a soul) and that feigned effects in the former become real effects in the latter.

Ultimately they contend that ritual directly affects a patient's body, soul and plant. It has no indirect effect on the patient's mind by changing his perceptions. It does not work because we are moved by it; rather we are moved by what works. It works by exposing the spirits and the dead who covet and hunger for the person. Exposure neutralizes the harmful effects of these beings by making them visible and knowable. Thereby, harmonious and satisfied relationships are again restored. Iban also incline to a view which is not dissimilar to a structuralist stance, that ritual uncovers important (*berat*), hidden meanings that lie deep at the basis of their society, resolving and clarifying the complexity of these meanings in the same way that we would solve a riddle.

This paper takes the theorizing of cultural members seriously but at the same time it is not restricted to the specifics of one culture because it seeks to identify performance and effectiveness as categories of discourse, identifiable cross-culturally, through which members of a society reflect on the nature of ritual, phenomenal experience and cosmos. This perspective provides enough analytic distance to view successive anthropological analyses of performance and effectiveness in themselves, as indexes of the anthropologists' own definition of reality. Each wave of interpretations of ritual effectiveness, the functionalist, the psychoanalytic, the structuralist, and the social-phenomenological interpretation, are themselves reflections of different constructions of reality located within the various microcultures of Western academic discourse--small-scale schools which derive from the great anthropological tradition of discovering secular explanations for the effectiveness of religious ritual.

To treat the Iban thought as equivalent to, say, psychoanalytic or structuralist theory is to raise additional questions about the extent to which the Iban discourse on ritual is informed by a framework of what properly may be called theorizing. It could be tentatively suggested at this point, that in a society such as this, with an extended tradition of observing, criticizing and incorporating elements of Malay and Christian thought as well as Western technology and medicine, that ritual provides a context for abstract reasoning, accounting for facts in terms of general principles, generating hypotheses, comparing alternative models and testing propositions; in short, theorizing. This issue requires much more discussion than is possible within the scope of the present paper.

The approach I have proposed provides a stand-point from which to examine the quintessential features of ritual through the meta-commentary which surrounds it. While it is important to see ritual as a context in which performance by cultural experts transforms patient and audience, I have argued here that it is just as important to see the patient, his suffering and his disturbed social relations, as a social arena within which cultural experts can define and transform the nature of ritual, cosmology, and the basic parameters of lived experience. Through the discourse on performance, cultural members articulate phenomenological theories of appearances and their relation to the multiple realities defined by their culture. Through the discourse on effectiveness, members articulate causal theories of words as action and acting as action.

ACKNOWLEDGEMENTS

I am grateful to the Sarawak State Secretary, Y. B. Datuk Amar Bujang Nor and the Director of the State Planning Unit, Encik Mohd. Jamil bin Mukmin for permission to conduct this research. Mr. Lucas Chin and Dr. Peter Kedit of the Sarawak Museum provided me with valuable advice and encouragement as did Dr. Stalin Hardin, the Director of Medical Services. The research was supported by the Australian National Health and Medical Research Council (Project Grant No. 89/0317). I wish to thank the many Saribas *manang* who contributed to this paper, in particular, Manang Asun anak Janta and Manang Gudum anak Enteri. I am indebted to Aru anak Gundi and Nicholas Unggot anak Dee who provided crucial assistance in interpreting the ritual action and *pelian* chants. A number of people worked on earlier drafts of the paper. I am grateful to Rod Lucas, Clifford Sather, Issy Pilowsky, Roy Fitzhenry, Althea Leonard and especially Sanghamitra Guha.

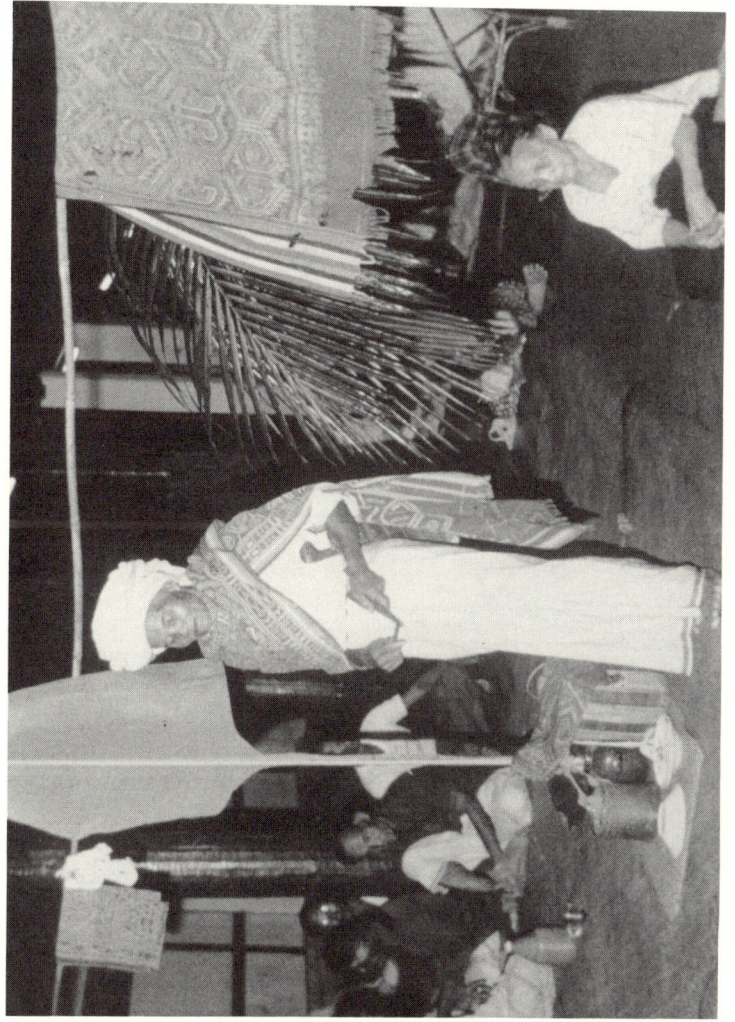

ILLUSTRATION 1

Pagar Api.
Manang Engkiong circumambulates the *pagar api* as he chants the *pelian*.

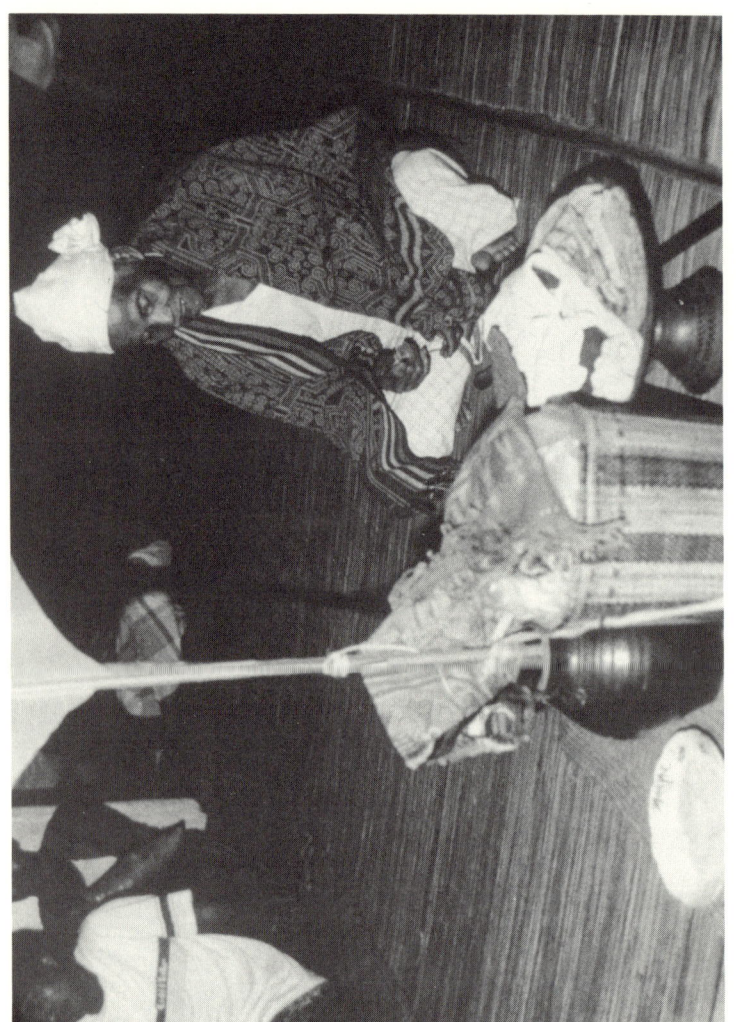

ILLUSTRATION 2

Close up of the base of a *Pagar Api*.
Manang Engkiong taps two pieces of iron to summon a spirit.

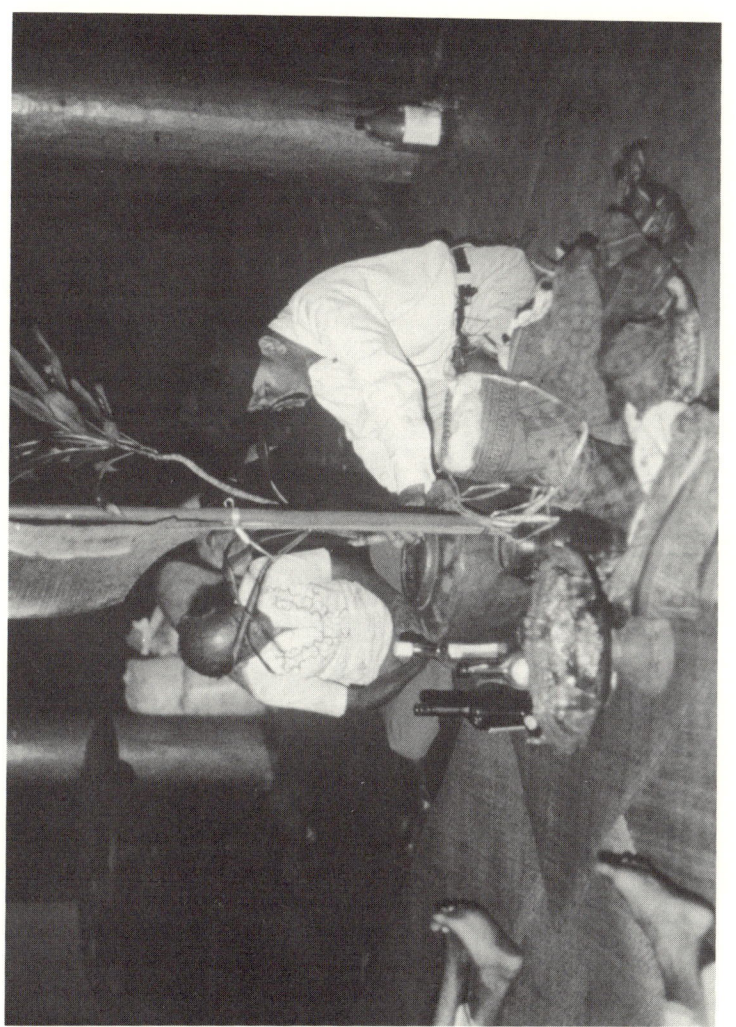

ILLUSTRATION 3

Pagar Api.
Manang Asun makes final adjustments to the *Pagar Api*

ILLUSTRATION 4

Batu Ilau diagnosis. Manang Asun gazes at a flame through the quartz crystal to discern the fate of the sick person's soul.

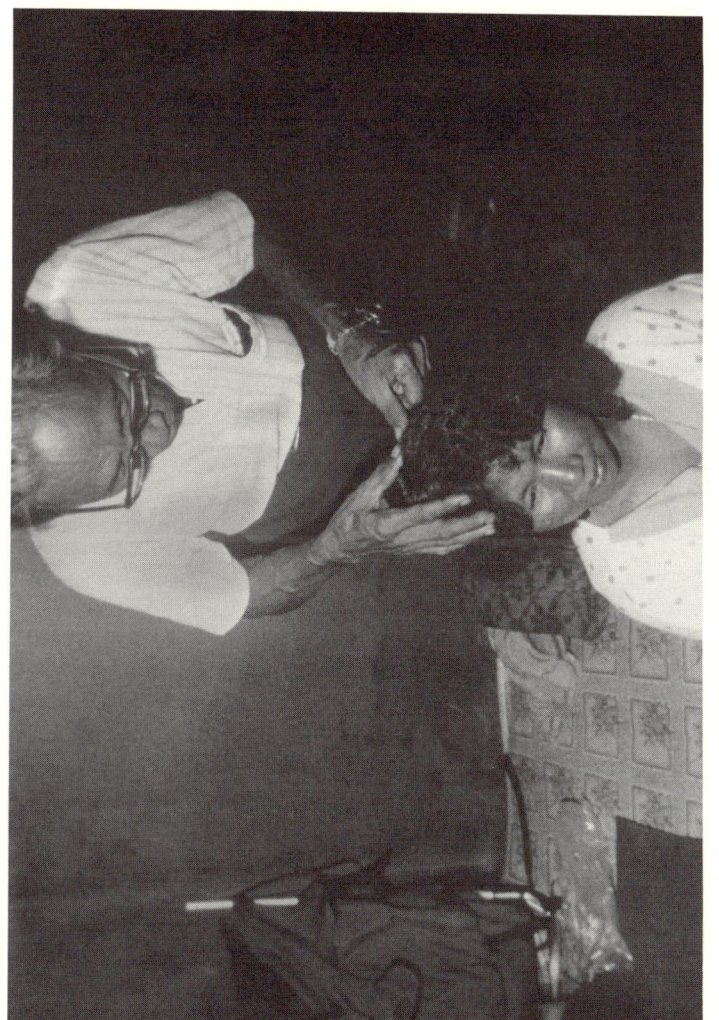

ILLUSTRATION 5

Nama ka Samengat. The soul is returned to the sick person through the anterior fontanella region of her head.

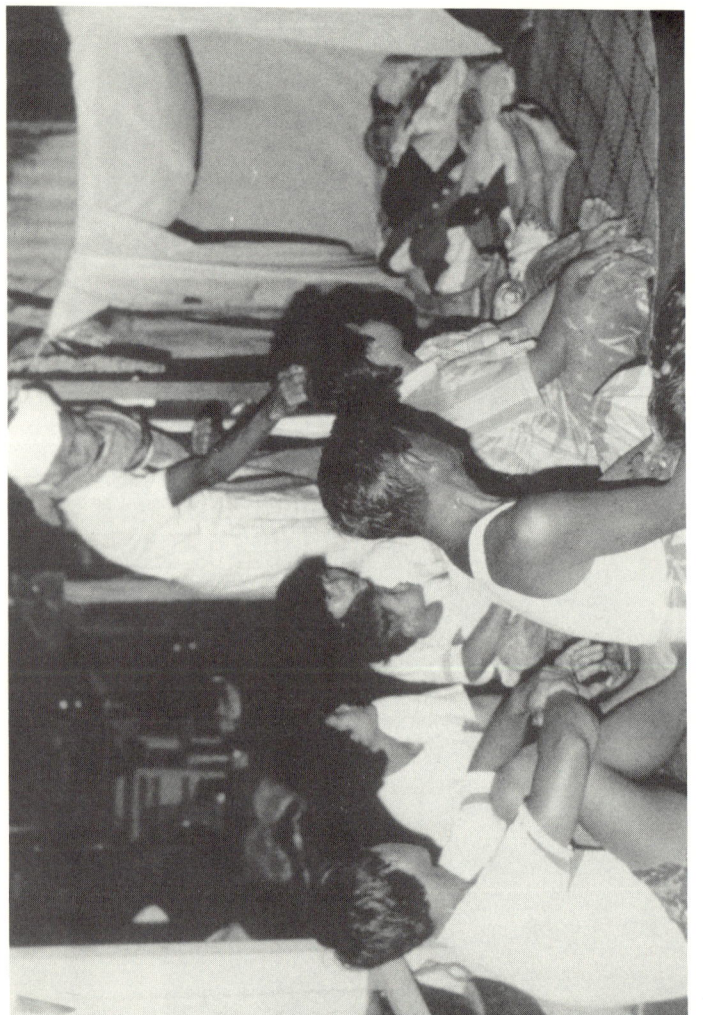

ILLUSTRATION 6

Returning souls to the family. In a *pelian* for a sick elderly woman (lying under the mosquito net) the *manang* returns souls to each family member.

NOTES

1. The power of Graham's analysis is that it locates shamanic intervention within a more pervasive set of cultural themes (that are also evident within kinship and political organization) related to the dialectical interplay between self and other and the limits of human autonomy in Iban society.

2. See Sather (1978) for a definitive discussion of the world of Iban spirits and "*tunang*-ship" in relation to concepts of sexual peril.

3. Saribas *manang* only used the crystal to visualize the soul, but Freeman (1967:323) reports that in the Baleh region, it is also used to visualize the plant aspect, to see if it is wilting, weed choked or vigorous.

4. See Graham's (1987:16) discussion of Brooke Low, Perham and Gomes's use of terms such as "charlatan," "trickeries," and "humbug." Freeman too (1967) comments on the "wiles," "artifice" and "duplicity" of the shaman, but does not analyze the central place of deceit in the effectiveness of his rite.

5. See Ehrmann (1968:31-57) for a typology of play as *ludus* (controlled, play), *paidia* (spontaneous play) and simulation.

6. Graham (1987:54-69) comprehensively reviews ethnographic accounts of pelian rites from the earliest reports to the more recent work of Sandin (1978).

7. This analysis complements Graham, who interprets the *pagar api* in terms of access to the supernatural and at the same time, protection from its malevolent aspects.

8. Pseudonyms and pseudo-nicknames are used.

9. For a discussion of the difference between locutionary, elocutionary and prelocutionary, aspects of a speech act, see Ricoeur (1979:76).

10. Kapferer, too, emphasizes that exorcists are masters of illusion and that artifice and deception are central to the logic of Sinhalese ritual. "Much of the skill of exorcists rests upon their ability to trick the demons, to trap them in their own morbid jest, to uncover the reality behind the demonic illusion and so revealing it, use this reality, dominated and controlled as

it is by the Buddha and the deities, to ensnare the demons, to dissolve them, as did Vishnu of Bashman Asura, and banish them to their own lowly plane of existence (Kapferer 1983:128)."

REFERENCES

Austin, J. L.
    1962   How to do Things with Words. Oxford: Oxford University Press.

Ehremann, J.
    1968   Games, Play and Literature. Boston: Beacon Press.

Freeman, Derek
    1967   Shaman and Incubus. The Psychoanalytic Study of Society 4:315-344.

    1970   Report on the Iban. London School of Economics. Monographs on Social Anthropology No 41. London: The Athlone Press.

Graham, Penelope
    1987   Iban Shamanism: An Analysis of the Ethnographic Literature. An Occasional Paper, Department of Anthropology, Research School of Pacific Studies, The Australian National University, Canberra.

Jensen, Eric.
    1974   The Iban and their Religion. Oxford: The Clarendon Press.

Kapferer, Bruce.
    1983   A Celebration of Demons: Exorcism and the Aesthetics of Healing in Sri Lanka. Bloomington: Indiana University Press.

Levi-Strauss, Claude
    1967   Structural Anthropology. New York: Anchor Books.

Richards, Anthony
    1981   An Iban-English Dictionary. Oxford: Clarendon Press.

Ricoeur, Paul
    1979   The Model of the Text: Meaningful Action Considered as a Text. *In* Interpretive Social Science: A Reader, edited by P. Rabinow and W. M. Sullivan, 73-101. Berkeley: University of California Press.

Sandin, B.
    1978   The Pelian Bejereki: Iban Rite of Spiritually Fencing an Expectant Mother. Sarawak Museum Journal 26:57-80.

Sather, C.
    1978   The Malevolent Koklir: Iban concepts of Sexual Peril and the Dangers of Childbirth. Bijdragen Tot De Taal-, Land- en Volkenkunde 134:310-355.

Schieffelin, E. L.
    1985   Performance and the Cultural Construction of Reality. American Ethnologist 12(4):707-724.

Schutz, A.
    1962   Collected Papers. Vol 1, The Problem of Social Reality. Edited by Maurice Natanson. The Hague: Martinus Nijhoff.

SHAMAN AND FOOL: REPRESENTATIONS OF THE SHAMAN IN IBAN COMIC FABLES

CLIFFORD SATHER
Australian National Univeristy

Comedy thrives on inconsistency...[It] lives in the discovery of alternative possibilities,...and attempts to falsify that which we take to be objectively true...(Kapferer 1983:210).

INTRODUCTION

Don Handelman (1977, 1979, 1981), in a series of stimulating essays, distinguishes play and ritual as symbolically framed domains which, within their demarcated parameters, "alter perception and experience."

> The passage to either is predicated upon a transformation of cognition, which is meta-communicative, and which bypasses paradoxes about the nature of reality which such alteration connotes (1979:185).

In communicative terms, the meta-message of play signals a transformation of cognition to one of "make-believe." Although modelled on ordinary experience, play, Handelman argues, inverts everyday reality and so communicates a sense of its arbitrariness and subjectivism. "By contrast, the bypass to ritual is predicated upon a premise of "let us believe." Thus communication within a ritual frame is sanctified...imbued with moral worth...made "true" and..."absolute" (1979:185; 1977).

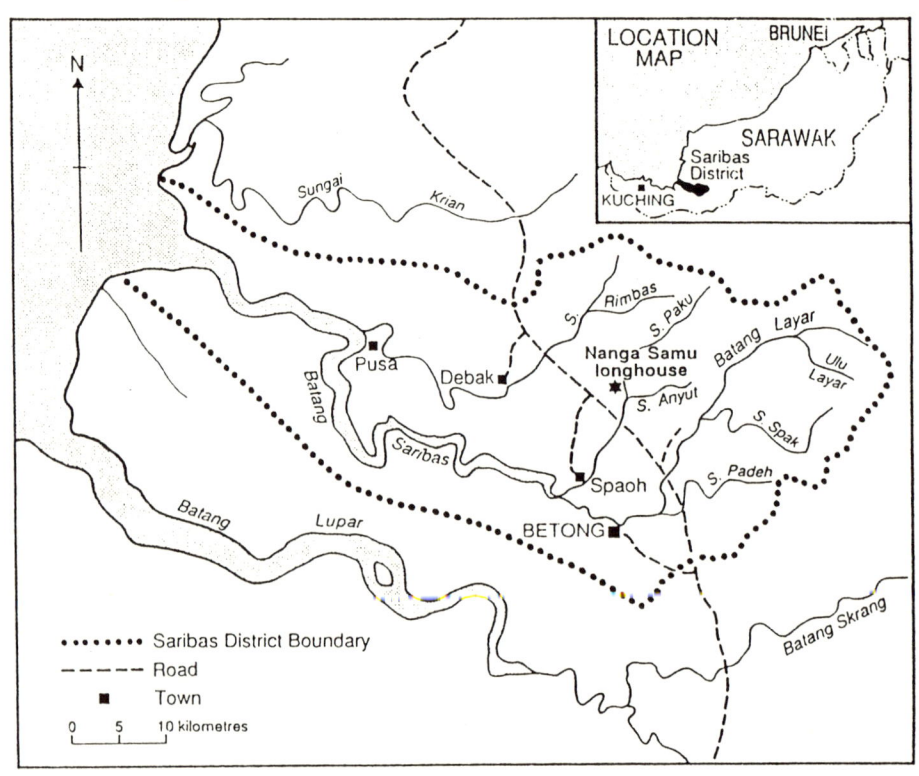

MAP 1

Saribas District

Handelman (1979:185-6) goes on to argue that the transformational properties of both play and ritual frames are embodied in the appearance of what he calls "symbolic types." The examples he cites include the Fool, Madman, Clown, and Prophet. Symbolic types are essentially consistent forms, constituted above the level of social roles, which unify the contexts in which they occur by transforming them in terms of their own consistency (cf. Kapferer 1979a:11). According to Handelman (1979:185) symbolic types are likely to appear when the logical unity of a context is threatened, or cannot be maintained; they arise, in other words, "in situations of social inconsistency, where routine typifications of reality become discrete, contradictory, anomalous [or] paradoxical." By its intrusion into a social field, a symbolic type thereby restructures the meaning of its context, eradicating discontinuity by rearranging "reality" in keeping with its own image (1979:186; Kapferer 1979a:11-13).

Ritual and play in the communicative terms outlined here are not necessarily mutually exclusive domains. Thus Handelman (1979) shows, for example, how the medium of play restructures meaning within the *naven* ritual described by Bateson, while Kapferer (1979b, 1983), arguing along similar lines, shows how the insertion of comic drama into Sinhalese exorcism ritual makes possible its therapeutic efficacy. In this latter case, ritual initially constructs a cultural order in which human beings are portrayed as dominated and controlled by demons. Comedy, as a form of play, renders this otherwise consistent representation of "reality" inconsistent by introducing discordant and mutually incompatible understandings, thereby making possible a reconstituting of the ritual context in a way that denies demons their position of dominance, instead making them appear laughable, and so allows patients to see themselves as outside and apart from their own subjective experience, no longer subject to demonic control (1979b:145-8). Comedy thus introduces, Kapferer argues, an "anti-rite" into ritual which, in this instance, "destroys the demonic and unmasks its illusion" (1983:205; see also Barrett in this collection).

In the essay that follows I consider two "symbolic types:"--the Fool and Shaman--examining, in particular, their conflation in a genre of Iban comic narratives. These narratives, called the *ensera Paloi*, are basically morality fables. For the Iban, they represent a form of narrative play. Here play is constituted within the boundaries of the narratives themselves, in the character and actions of their actors, particularly their central protagonist, the comic Fool (*tambap*), "Paloi" or "Father-of-Aloi." The "reality" of what occurs within the narrative world represented in these tales is acknowledged to be "untrue" (*enda' bendar*), "not real" (*enda' amat*), that is to say, a product of the story-teller's imagination. Thus a disjunction is asserted between the narrative "reality" of the fables and the "real world" that exists beyond their boundaries. As the primary hero of the fables, Father-of-Aloi is a figure of contradiction, a trickster as well as a fool, whose actions, free from the constraints of the "real world," characteristically violate both common sense and everyday social conventions. His appearance signals a suspension of belief, an entry into a world explicitly set apart from everyday experience in which the normal guidelines of behavior are suspended, everyday social life is satirized and in its place paradox and comic fantasy prevail. The tales thus open a discursive space within which the very nature of "reality" itself is open to question.

In a small number of tales the Fool assumes the role of Shaman (*manang*), and, in this role, his appearance within the narratives is marked by ritual. The result is a paradoxical conjunction of framed domains, i.e., of ritual located within an act of play. But here, in contrast to the situations explored by Handelman and Kapferer, "make-believe" is the overriding message communicated and the effect of this conjunction is to subvert, and bring into question, the validity of those very transformations of cognition on which ritual itself is predicated and made to seem "true." Iban morality fables thus reflect on the multivocality of Iban religious experience-- its interplay of belief and skepticism-- and so project, as we shall see presently, a strikingly ambiguous image of the shaman and his ritual practice.[1]

IBAN SHAMANISM

Here I look at three morality fables. All are part of a familiar story-telling tradition, well-known to Iban throughout Sarawak, and were recorded, together with a number of others, in August 1984, at Nanga Samu longhouse, in the upper Paku river region of the Saribas District (Map 1). My source is a single Paku story-teller, Henry Gerijih anak Jabo,[2] a man well-known in the river as a master of the *ensera* tradition.

The Paku river on which the Nanga Samu longouse is located is a major tributary of the main Saribas, lying between the Rimbas and upper Layar rivers, in the lower Second Division of Sarawak. The river drains an area long-settled by the Iban (Sandin 1967:16-23). Today some 4000 live in 33 longhouses along its banks and those of its principal tributaries, the Anyut, Bangkit, and Serudit streams, above the sub-District center at Spaoh bazaar (cf. Sather 1980, 1985). Most earn their living by cultivating hill rice and growing cash crops, principally rubber and pepper. In addition, many younger people engage in migratory labor, or hold permanent jobs outside the region, mainly in Kuching, Sibu, Miri, and Brunei, returning chiefly on holidays, in times of family illness, or for major ceremonies.

In the Paku, as elsewhere, shamans are called *manang*. The rituals they enact are known as *pelian* and are performed primarily to maintain the health and psychic wellbeing of individual clients. In the Paku shamans continue to be consulted with some frequency. At present there are, however, no *manang* actively practicing in the upper Paku, with the result that families requiring the services of a shaman must generally summon one from the lower Paku, or from the Rimbas where they remain numerous. In the lower Rimbas in particular, the profession tends to be practiced as a family vocation within closely related *bilek*-families.[3] In addition, *manang* from the lower Rimbas annually visit the upper Paku following the main hill-rice harvest, beginning usually in late April or May. News of their arrival typically sets off a flurry of invitations and, for a short time nightly *pelian* rites become a common occurence. In 1984 Nanga Samu longhouse was visited, according to Gerijih, by nine *manang* from the Rimbas and one from Serudit in the Paku.

The Iban *manang* is a shaman in the classical sense, of one capable of passing at will "from one cosmic region to another" (Eliade 1964:259; cf. Freeman 1967, Graham 1987). The Iban cosmos is divided primarily into "this world" (*dunya tu'*), the realm of living human beings, plants, animals, and spirits (*antu*); --the otherworld of the dead (*menoa sebayan*), which is invisible to "this world" and identified with the unseen Mandai river;[4] --and the sky (*langit*), the principal domain of the gods (*petara*) and celestial shamans, which is said "to cover" (*bap*), or overlay, "this world" like the lid of a rice bin. Beneath the central zenith of the sky is Mount Rabong associated with the Shamanic Goddess Ini Inda.[5] Here, at its summit, the *manang* regularly call down and return their spirit assistants at the beginning and end of each of their healing missions through the cosmos.

Further differentiating the Iban cosmos is a dichotomous distinction between "the seen" and "the unseen," the delineation of which is both fundamental, yet pervious and alterable. Corresponding to this distinction, all "living things" (*utai idup*) are believed to possess both a visible body (*tuboh*) and an animating, but unseen spirit or soul (*semengat*). The individual, as a living totality, is comprised of both. The body itself, although outwardly visible, envelops invisible interior spaces, the location of organs which are, for the Iban, the seats of emotion, intelligence, intentionality and moral agency, and so the most frequent site of symptoms diagnostic of health or of illness-causing disorder. In addition, human beings (*mensia*) also possess, as attributes of both body and soul, "appearance" (*gamal*), name (*nama*)[6] and "vitality." The latter is symbolized by an unseen plant-counterpart (*ayu* or *bunga*) representing the mortal aspect of personality. Thus the *ayu* flourishes in health, but in sickness is said "to wither" (*layu'*); and in death, "to die" (*parai*). Similarly, illness, dreaming, and death are also related to the disassociation of the soul and its separation, temporarily or permanently, from the body. Continued life and wellbeing are thus believed to depend upon the proper conjunction of these differing aspects, or attributes, of the person, both seen and unseen, and upon their preservation from both physical and spiritual injury. This task of maintaining their proper conjunction, and preserving them from harm, falls largely to the shaman, who, as a ritual agent, is thought to work chiefly through his soul within the unseen plane of the spirits, souls, gods, ghosts of the dead, and plant counterparts.

In his *pelian*, the *manang* assumes the properties of what I have called, following Handelman, a "symbolic type." This he does by uniting in his person, and so resolving, opposed elements of human experience conceptually represented by the dichotomies I have outlined here. For the Iban, the *manang* is a being set apart, whose nature transcends these oppositions. Thus, in the course of his *pelian*, the *manang* is thought to be capable of altering his ontological status at will. Suspended from a swing, or wrapped in a pua',[7] he temporarily transcends the limitations of ordinary human experience by dispatching his soul into the unseen plane of the *semengat* and spirits. There, aided by a personal spirit-helper (*yang*), his soul contends against molesting spirits, retrieves the wandering or ensnared *semengat* of his patients, and protects endangered individuals by effecting their invisible separation (through the erection of unseen "barriers") from other human and spiritual inhabitants of "this world." As distinct from ordinary human beings, the *manang* alone is believed to be able to see and identify individual *semengat*, and through his control over his own soul, and with the aid of his *yang*, to be capable of sending his *semengat* out into the unseen world to recover the souls of his patients; restore their invisibility; defeat malevolent *antu*; erect invisible fences; and to travel to where the *ayu* grow and there to "clear around" (*mensiang*), "transplant" (*nusop*) and otherwise "nurture" (*nupi'*) these plant images of mortality and healthful vigor. In each case, the shaman is thought to restore particular elements of the cosmos, repairing their disruption or damage and maintaining, within the individual and his surroundings, their life-sustaining boundaries and inter-connections.

The ritual action of the *pelian* moves between the family apartment (*bilek*) and the longhouse gallery (*ruai*). Nearly all *pelian* are enacted around a complexly symbolic apparatus, set up on the gallery floor, called the "fence (or barrier) of fire" (*pagar api*).[8] This consists chiefly of a spear set, blade upward, inside a *kebok* jar, bound with a banana stalk, and attached to a frame draped with a *pua' kumbu'*. The *pagar api* represents, at once, a spiritual barrier--a "fence of fire" that intimidates spirits and so prevents them from invading the human world--and a means of access to the unseen realm--a "ladder" or "dangerous crossing" by means of which the shaman is able to enter the unseen plane and there contend against its potentially adversarial forces and return again to the visible world, often accompanied by the lost or captured souls of his patients (cf. Graham 1987:148; Barrett this volume). Thus the shrine is simultaneously the starting and ending point of the *manang's* journeys. As Graham (1987:148-50) observes, encapsulated in the complex symbolism of the *pagar api* is a sense of the dual role of the shaman, as one who both transcends the human condition and at the same time enforces a degree of separation between antithetical aspects of the cosmos. Underlying this dual role is a cultural logic that posits a degree of separation between "human" and "spiritual" dimensions of the universe, the seen and unseen, while at the same time credits the shaman with the ability to move across this ontological divide at will, thereby enabling him to articulate these dichotomies in ways that restructure, and so render coherent, the experienced reality of his clients.

In the confines of the ritual role he plays, the shaman is thus seen as an empowered, effectual agent. He creates in his *pelian* a mediating reality in which he is able, mutually, to effect both "the seen" and "the unseen." Thus the deeds he performs in his *pelian* are thought to have instrumental consequences in the visible world through the effects they produce on unseen forces, while the words of his invocation (*leka pelian*) are said to be *bisa*, strong or visably efficacious. In this regard, the *manang* is often likened to a man or woman of action in the mundane world.[9] Historically the Iban were the most successful and expansionist of all inland swidden cultivators of Borneo and reflecting this history, Iban society was, and remains, intensely competitive. Hereditary ranking is lacking, and those who were most esteemed in the past were the *raja berani*, literally the "rich and brave" (Freeman 1981). Today, as formerly, competitive success is predicated in the Iban view on self-assertion, resourcefulness, personal adequacy, initiative, and daring. Significantly, within his *pelian*, the *manang* is expected to demonstrate these same qualities. Thus his rituals of healing are marked by symbolic analogies to warfare, farming and travel, all avenues through which social honor was traditionally acheived (Sather 1978), and in his incursions into "the unseen," the shaman is expected to project these same qualities into the realm of *semengat* and spirits.

Yet there exists in these symbolic analogies a series of profound incongruities. The prowess that the shaman asserts in his *pelian* does not, as a rule, carry over into other spheres of Iban life. Instead the shaman's role is to some degree marginalized and his ritual achievements are removed from the main arenas in which Iban men and women compete for power and worldly reputation. This does not mean that individual shamans are not respected, or even, in some cases, held in awe. But success for the Iban is measured primarily in tangible, this-worldly terms, as exemplified, in particular, by the *raja berani*. In contrast the shamans deal chiefly with "unseen" powers, repairing disturbed relations between mankind and the spirits, gods, and the dead. Moreover, the *manang's pelian* comprise a separate category of ritual, distinct from those sponsored by successful men and women of action to valorize status and gain recognition for personal achievement. These latter rituals--focusing, for example, on farming success, the acquisition of prestige wealth, memorialization of the dead and their accomplishments, male honors, or the demonstration of personal competence in warfare or weaving--are conducted, not by the *manang*, but by the bards (*lemambang*), and are the occasion of major regional gatherings, calling together whole longhouse communities allied to one another by extended "co-feaster" relations (*sapemakai*). In contrast, shamanic rituals focus primarily on individual clients and their immediate families.

Something of this social incongruity can also be seen in the behavior of individual shamans. Thus, in a somewhat extreme example, Freeman (1967:320) describes the character of the redoubtable "demon-slayer," Manang Bungai, a Saribas-born shaman practicing in the Baleh:

> Haughty and boastful in manner, he strove to create the impression that he somehow stood apart from other *manang*. On the crowded gallery of the long-house he would pour scorn on the rites of other shamans and on the farfetched tales they told upon emerging from their 'trances'..."What liars these shamans are!" he would exclaim with a great show of feeling, "Such lying is not pleasant. I alone am honest, so people say." (*Manang bula! Enda nyamai bula. Aku aja betul, ko orang*). Or,..he would comment laconically:... "I am no shaman" (..*Ukai manang aku*). Then this would be followed, often soon afterwards, by the assertion that nowhere was there a shaman to be remotely compared to himself, and that there were many Iban who believed him to be a spirit possessing supernatural powers. As a measure of his importance he had, he insisted, to be summoned (i.e. to another long-house) by a party consisting of three, five, or seven persons.

Although obviously self-assertive, and clearly projecting confidence in his own spiritual powers, Manang Bungai is, nevertheless, intent upon disassociating himself from other *manang*. The latter he describes, signficantly, as liars and fakes.

For many Iban, the practice of shamanism is regarded, in fact, as antithetical to mundane success. Reflecting this view, Spencer St.John (1863:I:73), an early observer of the Iban, noted that among their numbers Iban *manang* "often" include persons who are "blind and maimed [and] who, by following this profession, are enabled to earn a livelihood." In fact, actual blindness, or severe physical disability, is unusual in *manang*. Considerable physical stamina is required in travelling to visit patients and in conducting all-night healing sessions. The view, however, is widely held that those who practice as shamans, whether physically disabled or not, suffer harm as a consequence of their calling and are less likely than others to achieve material success. Thus *manang* tend to be viewed with a mixture of wonder and pity. In this respect, Sutlive (1976) has described the shaman's role as an "alternative route to normality," interpreting it as a means by which Iban men who deviate from ideal norms of masculinity may achieve social acceptance. Here, I would argue, instead, that this incongruity is not a matter of individual normality or deviance,--for *manang*, as individuals, are rarely either abnormal or lacking in manliness--but is, rather, a matter of conflicting cultural constructions of the *manang's* status and of the relegation of the ritual role he plays, despite its analogies to worldly success, to areas removed from those in which power and reputation are, in fact, contended for and valorized.

A further expression of this incongruity is a widespread skepticism regarding the shaman's claims to ritual prowess. Not only do the *manang's* achievements tend to be marginalized, but they are also widely believed to be based on deception. "All fully initiated *manang*," as Freeman (1967:317) observes,

> are believed to have the power...to confront and overcome malevolent demons, but this power...resides in the shaman's *semengat*, or soul, and his deeds of valour are performed without surveillance in the shadowy world of the spirits. Thus, even quite devout Iban will sometimes express doubts about the extraordinary feats of daring that *manang* claim to have performed.

The *pelian* rituals which the *manang* enact are rich in dramatic theatricality, incorporating trance (or fainting), invocational journeys into unseen realms, spirit encounters, and the use of charms and complex ritual apparatus (cf. Freeman 1967). As Sutlive (1976:69) notes, dramatic effects are greatly appreciated:

> The lengthy chants which the *manang* recite, the sleight of hand acts which they perform, and the *materia medica* which they manipulate, elicit from spectators cries of "good, *manang*, well done.."

But what is valued, above all, is a "deception" well-performed, that is to say, a performance which is both convincing, yet produces an effect which seems to contradict ordinary, here-and-now experience. Iban shamans operate within a cultural milieu of skepticism. Yet, to be perceived as effective requires trust. Thus, if a shaman is to succeed, he must be able to convince his audience of the underlying reality of his "deceptions." Since this reality involves the actuation of unseen forces, he must be able to represent this actuation tangibly, in a visible form within the mediating reality of his *pelian*, as, for example, by extracting bits of stone from his patient's head, or by producing the latter's "soul" in the form of a small seed. *Pelian* thus tend to be characterized by virtuosity, and through their performance, each *manang* seeks to establish the authenticity of his actions and so overcome the skepticism of his clients and gain their assent to the assertion of belief and cognitive consistency on which the communicative efficacy of his *pelian* can be said to depend.[10]

Finally, in addition to skepticism, it is generally recognized that the material and social rewards of shamanism are small, and that, in travelling among his clients, the *manang* must often leave farmwork unattended and absent himself for varying lengths of time from the practical, this-worldly affairs of his longhouse and family. In addition, although *manang*, as individuals, are only rarely blind or disabled, it is nevertheless commonly believed that they gain the assistance of spirit-helpers to heal others at some expense in terms of their own physical health. As the Rimbas shaman Manang Jabing explained, the *yang* often threaten a new initiant with madness or death if he refuses to take up the "calling" *(kumbai)*, and, once he does take it up, the "work" *(penguwa)* he performs is itself potentially "hot" *(panas)*. In curing others, a *manang*, through his contact with unseen forces, exposes himself to spiritual heat. For this reason, male *manang* were exempt in the past from active participation in warfare, otherwise, significantly, the *sine qua non* of masculine achievement.[11]

Some *manang* use this lack of material gain, and the calling's dangers, as proof that those who pursue it cannot be considered "deceivers" or "cheats." Thus Manang Jabing insists,[12]

> But this thing [being a shaman] does not make me rich,...nothing, I make no profit from it, but do it to save myself, to protect myself from harm. No one tells me to do it. (*Tang ukai ngasoh aku bisi', ..nadai, nadai ngasoh bisi', tang ga sayau kai seput diri empu utai ulih nadai. Nadai orang madah.*) This calling might be 'hot'; perhaps this work is 'hot'...but we must save the lives of people. We do not cheat them. (*Ka kumbai enda' panas, panas ga pengawa' nya'...ga ngidup kai mensia, ukai nya' musin orang.*)

Indeed, in the Paku, Manang Jabing's views were widely accepted by his patients, who generally looked upon him with affection, as a skilled and compassionate healer.

The morality tales play upon these incongruities. Doubt, as we shall see, is made an occasion for humor and skeptical commentary. But, more than this, the comic hero, by burlesquing ritual and conflating the identities of Fool and Shaman, emerges as a subversive dissembler, a comic trickster who, like the "dissembling" figure of the shaman himself, performs miracles in defiance of reality. Through a comic parodying of ritual, the Fool at once transcends the limitations of everyday experience, performing deeds that seemingly contradict ordinary expectations, and at the same time he turns the social order on its head, reasserting the primacy, as we shall see presently, of its egalitarian social values.

FATHER-OF-ALOI AND THE ENSERA TRADITION

Within a rich and varied oral narrative tradition, the Iban distinguish between the *ensera,* composed, fictional narratives, and the *cherita* (or *jerita*), a complex category that includes myths, historical narratives, prose anecdotes and eye-witness reportage. The *ensera* comprise primarily the hero sagas (*ensera Orang Panggau*), many of them complex, poetically structured epics that relate the adventures and romances of the Iban spirit-heroes and heroines (*Orang Panggau*), and the morality fables, much shorter narratives told in prose, and including both animal tales (*ensera jelu*)[13] and comic fables (ensera Paloi, or *ensera Apai Aloi*).[14]

Within the comic fable tradition, many story elements are "traditional," being part of the repertory of most Paku story-tellers. Others represent new and continually changing innovations, some of them dealing, as elements of narrative, with novel situations or institutions, such as schools or agricultural subsidy schemes. When told by skillful story-tellers, the *ensera Paloi* are embellished by qualities of voice and spoken dialogue.[15] Most often, the stories are told at night, before sleep.

Father-of-Aloi (*Apai Aloi*), or *Paloi,*[16] the central hero of the comic fable tradition, is both a fool and a trickster. Most often he is depicted as greedy, lecherous, cowardly, and lazy, an impulsive figure of absurdity who lives in a reality of his own making. At other times, including the small number of fables in which he appears as Shaman, Paloi emerges as a figure of wit and cunning. Very often these contradictory elements of his character are merged in the same narrative.

As culturally constituted, the shaman and fool have much in common. Both are interstitial figures. While the shaman can be described as a mediator between "the seen" and "the unseen," humankind and the spirits, the living and the dead, the fool, as represented in the comic fables, mediates between ordinary, taken-for-granted experience and a make-believe world of contradiction and paradox. The fool's actions, although a reflection on everyday life, defy its rules and expectations, thereby revealing, through the imaginary medium of play, the arbitrariness and inconsistencies of taken-for-granted categories, rules, and cultural paradigms. Underlying his actions is a denial of necessity to any one "reality." Similarly, the shaman, in his *pelian*, creates and acts within a ritually-created reality distinct from, yet joined to both "the seen" and "the unseen."

Although the Fool is not identified with actual social actors in the same sense as the Shaman--in everyday social life an individual who behaves foolishly--contrary to common sense or his own best interests--who appears, in short, to inhabit a separate reality--may be called *aloi* or *aloh*. Significantly, these terms are used, not to convey disapproval, or condemnation, but with fondness and affection. The same is true of *tambap*, "fool" or "idiot."[17] Thus between close male friends, *aloi* (or *aloh*) may be used in mutual address, as a reciprocal friendship-name (*peremberian*), to connote a personal bond of special camaraderie. In addition, some persons are said to possess Paloi charms (*ubat Paloi*) which give them the power to deceive others or make them behave foolishly. Such charms, although their use is generally kept secret, are greatly coveted.[18]

In the Paku *ensera Paloi* tradition, Father-of-Aloi has a wife, Mother-of-Aloi (*Indai Aloi*) or Enchelegit; a son and namesake, Aloi; and a number of other children, usually seven in all. Most commonly Father-of-Aloi and his family live at Emperan Embawang, within the Panggau-Gelong world inhabited by the Iban spirit-heroes and heroines (Sather 1981, 1984).

In contrast to the latter, whose epic sagas of war, wanderings, and love-affairs exemplify Iban ideals of manliness and femininity, Father-of-Aloi's adventures satirize the most basic relationships of everyday life: those between husband and wife, parents and children, and friends. Here the ideals celebrated in the sagas are regularly violated or turned on their head. In the fables, Father-of-Aloi repeatedly tries to deceive his wife and children and occasionally his neighbors and friends as well. For example, he tries to keep the fish and game he has caught in his traps, so that he can secretly eat them himself without sharing with his family. But such schemes invariably fail, and in the end Paloi's greed and selfishness bring about his own undoing. Again and again he is outwitted by Enchelegit and his children, and when he attempts to get revenge, the results are even more disastrous. In one story, for example, Mother-of-Aloi frightens Paloi into sharing with his family a turtle he was about to cook for himself in the forest by impersonating an "Eye-gouger Demon" (*antu ngingit*). In revenge, Father-of-Aloi decides to pretend to be a "Buttock-biter" (*barukap*).[19] He steals up under the longhouse at night while Enchelegit is frying sago cakes for their children. Assuming the voice of the Buttock-biter, he demands that she drops the cakes to him through the floor slates. Instead, she heats stones in her cooking fire until they are red-hot and then, using fire-tongs, drops them into his outstretched hands. He is severely burned, of course, and in the end Mother-of-Aloi nurses his wounds, while lecturing him on the foolishness of stealing from his own family (Sather 1984:23-24).

As a fool, Paloi lives in a world of fantasy, and a number of stories play upon his literal-mindedness or refusal to come to terms with "reality" as others understand it. In another story, for example, Paloi finds a sleeping barking deer. Not wishing to share it with others, he dresses the animal in his own clothes to make it appear as a human being. But only Paloi himself is taken in by this deception. Having blurred the categories of animal and human, he is dismayed to find, when the deer wakes up, that it refuses to listen to "reason," but, instead, escapes into the forest wearing his clothes, leaving Paloi to return home naked (Sather 1984:11-13). In other fables, Paloi encounters powerful outsiders, whom he overcomes, not by bravery or physical prowess, but by cunning and trickery. Most of the fables are cautionary tales. Although told overtly for amusement, nearly all carry a "moral," but one which is set, consistent with their comic nature, in a transposed world where belief is suspended, ordinary expectations are confounded, and nothing is quite as it seems.

Those who tell the *ensera Paloi*, and form their principal audience, are, as a rule, like the *manang*, socially marginal, persons removed from the main centers of power and reputation. They consist, as story-tellers, chiefly of elderly "grandparents" and, as audience, mainly of "grandchildren." As a general rule, person-to-person relations in an Iban longhouse are structured along generational lines, and in everyday social transactions, courtesy requires the use of teknonyms between neighbors and longhouse members. Thus every individual is characteristically addressed as "mother" (*indai*), "father" (*apai*), "grandmother" (*ini'*), or "grandfather" (*aki'*), plus the name of a child or grandchild, or by a more specific kin term in the case of a particularly close relationship. Only those of the most junior generation, without children or grandchildren, are addressed by personal name. Respect is most marked in relations between members of adjacent generations, while a close identity exists between those who are generationally related as "grandparents" and "grandchildren." To parents falls most of the work of rice-farming. As a consequence, in families with small children to look after, much of their care is entrusted to "grandparents," particularly during periods of heavy farm work, and it is chiefly in this context--in the privileged relationship between "grandparents" and "grandchildren"--that the morality fables are told, characteristically forming, as it were, in contrast to the hero-epics, a body of non-hegemonic narratives giving voice to those living, like the *manang* himself, at the margins of society.

PALOI TRAVELS TO FOREIGN LANDS (*PALOI BELELANG KA MENOA BUKAI*)

The first story that follows begins with Father-of-Aloi's childhood and youth and is in part an etiological tale that "explains" the origin of the hero's name *Paloi*, or "Fool."[20] This origin emphasizes, significantly, the hero's contradictory nature.

The action of the fable centers around a journey. This is described as *belelang*, or "wandering." When applied to shamans, the term refers to the traditional practice of travelling from longhouse to longhouse, especially between farming seasons,[21] to treat patients and perform, in particular, the *pelian beserara' bunga* ("severing the flowers").[22] But here the action of *belelang* is universalized. Paloi journeys to the very limits of the known world. He travels downriver, and then across the sea, to a maritime kingdom ruled by a Malay sovereign. As a riverine people, the Iban have long engaged in external trade through coastal Malay enclaves, the latter linked in Borneo to a number of maritime and river-mouth trading states. As reflected here, the Malay world was looked upon in the past as a source of riches. From here traditionally came the durable prestige wealth so greatly valued by the Iban down through the early decades of the present century: gongs, brassware, Chinese jars and porcelain. But the Malay world also represented the pinnacle of autocratic power and hierarchy. As such, it constituted a political order familiar to the Iban, as a people living at its peripheries, but alien to their own essentially independent, chiefless society.

Here the shaman's *belelang* is transformed into a classic story of *bejalai* or journeying abroad in quest of reputation, adventure, and wealth. Such journeying is for the Iban, in contrast to the *manang's* wandering, a major institution of male achievement (Freeman 1970:222; Kedit 1987). But, here, as a prior condition to success, the hero must first, paradoxically, acquire a knowledge of curing and so prove himself an effective "healer." This Paloi does by performing the seemingly impossible feat of bringing a dead princess back to life. In doing so, he assumes his trickster character. Realizing that the young woman is not dead, he performs the "miracle" of restoring her to life through a sham ritual. Here, at one level, our suspicions are confirmed. Paloi's ritual is a deception. Yet, at another level, it "works." Thus, as a "curer," Paloi outwits the

Rajah. Later, as a guest in the Rajah's palace, Paloi makes love to the king's daughter. His success and triumphant return home may be read, in part at least, as a testimony to the superiority of the Iban way of life and of wit and deception over worldly wealth and autocratic power.

What follows is a translation of the first fable. I have shortened the text somewhat, indicating omitted materials with brackets [...].

[...] Paloi has brothers and sisters[..] He is the eldest.[23] His siblings (*menyadi*) include Gila Gundi ['Mad Gundi'], the father of Keling.

He was not always known as Paloi[..] As a youngster he is mischievous. Everything he does is amiss (*pengawa' ke salah enggau ke ngena sama bisi dikerja iya*). When he speaks, his speech is often wrong way around (*tunsang sebut*). At other times he speaks wisely, like an elder (*orang ke besai tuai*). So it is that people call him "Paloi" [Fool], and Paloi becomes his name.

As a youth [..] he is overcome by a desire to visit distant lands. Leaving home, he travels far. [...] He comes at last to a land where he meets a healer (*beliau*).[24] "Where do you come from?" (*Ari ni penatai nuan*) asks the healer.

"I come from Panggau Libau" (*Aku datai ari Panggau Libau*), Paloi answers, "and Keling is my brother's son" (*Keling nya anak menyadi aku*).

Unknown to Paloi, the healer is the brother of Beliau Pulau, a powerful enemy whom Keling killed in battle. [...] Out of fear, the healer befriends Paloi and for three years teaches him the curing arts[..].

Having acquired a deep knowledge of curing, Paloi resumes his travels. He journeys by sailing vessel. On the voyage he and the ship's captain (*jeragan*) become friends. When they reach their destination, [..] the captain offers to lodge Paloi in his house and Paloi accepts the captain's invitiation. [...] At this point Paloi reverts to his contrary character. When he is indoors, he dresses in finery; in public, outside the captain's house, he wears only rags, like a beggar.

[...] The Rajah of the kingdom in which the captain lives has only one child, [..] a daughter. The princess falls ill and the Rajah invites all the healers in his kingdom to treat her. Every day Paloi goes to the palace but each time he is turned away because of his appearance. The princess's condition grows steadily worse and on the seventh day she dies.

As news of her death spreads, the people flock to the palace to pay their last respects, Paloi among them. Standing before the crowd, the Rajah announces: "If anyone is able to bring my daughter back to life, I will reward him handsomely." Paloi alone perceives that the princess is not really dead. She is only in a deep coma (*luput*). So he offers to try to restore her to life. "If you have the knowledge," says the Rajah, "please help me" (*Enti' nuan bisi penemu, tulong meh aku*).

"I have studied much," Paloi replies, "but whether I can or not, I cannot say, as I have never tried before to apply what I have learned." [...]

Paloi recites seven spells over the princess (*puchau disebut tujoh kali*), [..] blowing each time over her body, starting from her head and ending with her feet. As he completes the last spell, she awakes [..] and is soon well again. The Rajah and his subjects rejoice.

The Rajah asks Paloi to marry the princess and become his heir. Paloi asks for a month to consider the Rajah's proposal. [...] During this time he lives in the palace and he and the princess become lovers[..]. In the end, however, Paloi decides that he does not want to make his home among strangers, even as their Rajah. He also remembers that his father has arranged his future marriage with Enchelegit, his cousin. Therefore, at the end of the month, Paloi informs the Rajah that he wishes to return home. [...] Disappointed, the Rajah rewards him with precious jars, cannons, gongs, and drums, and equips him for the return journey with seven attendants and a large, well-made longboat. The princess gives him a gold ring. [...] Finally, the Rajah presents Paloi with all the goods necessary to set up a new household.

[...] Paloi then returns home. The people of Panggau come down to the riverside to meet him and help carry his things into the longhouse. There the Rajah's gifts are laid out on the gallery floor [..] for everyone to admire. Sempurai comments [..] on the large number of things that Paloi has brought home and Paloi replies that such is only fitting for those who return from travels abroad (*endang baka orang pulai pegi*). [...]

That night the entire longhouse gathers to listen eagerly to the newly returned traveller tell of his adventures in distant lands and of how the Rajah only reluctantly allowed him to return home. Among them is his shy [..] but proud bride-to-be, Enchelegit.[25]

At the conclusion of the tale, the close identification of the story-teller and the hero is emphasized by Paloi becoming, within the story itself, the teller of his own adventures. This narrative device adds a further layer of "play" to the fable. It links the unfolding of the story to the "real world" of the story-teller and his audience, thus highlighting the Fool's mediating role between "reality" and play--both mirroring "reality," yet freed by the exercise of his trickster nature, from its constraints.

FATHER-OF-ALOI AND THE RAJAH (*APAI ALOI ENGGAU RAJA SIKO*)

The action of the second *ensera* also centers around a journey, but one which is undertaken by the hero, now in his more familiar form--as an old man with a wife and family--not voluntarily, but against his will. It takes Father-of-Aloi once again to the Malay world.

> There once lived a Rajah [...] who owns a ring of immeasurable value, which gives him great pleasure for it is the inherited treasure of many generations of his royal ancestors. One day the ring disappears. The Rajah suspects theft.
> [...] He orders his shamans to look into their crystals. None, however, can name the thief, or tell the Rajah where the ring is hidden.
> [...] One day news comes that there lives in the kingdom of Rajah Merom a man with a miraculous gift for finding lost property. His name is Father-of-Aloi. The Rajah at once sends his two ship captains to bring Father-of-Aloi to him. He orders them to bring him without fail, by force if necessary, on pain of death.
> The two captains sail to the kingdom of Rajah Merom. [...] There they are told that Father-of-Aloi lives in a longhouse at the far edge of the kingdom, near a crossroads, on the main Panggau river [..]. "But," people say, "he is a well-known curer and is often away answering the calls of his many patients." The two journey, following the directions they are given, until they meet an old man. "Where is Father-of-Aloi's house?," they ask. "If you are looking for Father-of-Aloi, then I am the one you seek" (*Enti' saduai deka' ngagai Apai Aloi, aku tu' meh iya*).

Father-of-Aloi leads the two captains to his longhouse. There they tell him that he has been summoned by their Rajah and must come with them at once in order to find the Rajah's lost ring. Father-of-Aloi answers that he is unable to do as they ask[..]. Hearing this, they threaten to beat him and make ready iron chains with which to bind him.

"Wife, they want to kill me," says Father-of-Aloi. "I won't go with them, so they threaten to bind me with chains and throw me in the river. Yet if I do as they ask, and fail to find the Rajah's ring, I will also be killed. Either way, I loose my life."

Mother-of-Aloi weeps[..]. "My poor husband. I never thought you would have such a short life[..]. And now who will look after us when you have gone to the Otherworld?" (*Sapa ke ngidup ka kami menyanal ditinggal ka nuan parai?*)

Father-of-Aloi then tells the captains that he cannot go with them just at that moment. "I must first build a new house. This one of mine, as you see, is old. The walls lean and the roof leaks. Besides, I don't know how to find lost things."

The two captains answer that his reputation for finding lost property is well known[..]. As for the house, they will have their followers begin to build a new one in the morning. "When it is finished, we will set off." And so, early the following day, work begins on Father-of-Aloi's new house. Even the captains join in and in five days the house is finished and Father-of-Aloi and his family move in.

Next morning, the party sets off with Father-of-Aloi for the Rajah's kingdom. After reaching the sea, they sail for two days and three nights.[...] Father-of-Aloi carries with him all of his charms, including a small black bottle without a bottom (*puchong chelum siti ke udah rumpung burit*). Whenever Father-of-Aloi practices as a shaman, he uses this bottle--so he tells his patients--to spy upon the souls in the Otherworld (*kena nilik samengat di menoa sebayan din*). [...] As they sail across the sea, Father-of-Aloi looks through his bottle like a telescope, searching out distant lands beyond the horizon and looking at things on the bottom of the sea. As he gazes through his spy-glass bottle, he speaks to himself [..].

"There is a demon on the horizon (*Nyin antu ba tisau langit*),
Fish at the bottom of the sea (*Nyin ikan ba buntut tasik*),
A dragon in the east (*Nyin naga ba mata-hari tumboh*)"

It happens one day that Father-of-Aloi is standing beside the two captains. High in the sky, well out of sight, two eagles are diving at each other. One eagle is black, the other is white. Father-of-Aloi studies them through his bottomless bottle. "If black wins, white loses," he says to himself. "But if white wins, black loses."

The two captains hear his words and begin to whisper to one another. One captain wears a black uniform, the other white. "He knows we have stolen the Rajah's ring. Whichever one of us he names, when the Rajah asks him to identify the thief, will be executed." But, unknown to the captains, Father-of-Aloi is only watching eagles.

Father-of-Aloi continues to gaze through the bottle. "If not black, then white loses. If not white, then it must be black."

"Did you hear what he said?" one captain again asks the other. "He knows we have stolen the Rajah's ring. What shall we do? If Father-of-Aloi comes before the Rajah and searches for the thief with his spy-glass, one of us will surely be executed." [...] After a long debate[..], the two captains decide that their only hope is to take Father-of-Aloi into their confidence. And so they call to him[..] and invite him to sit beside them.

"As you know, it was the two of us who stole the Rajah's ring. We ask that you agree not to reveal our guilt when the Rajah calls on you to make known the whereabouts of his ring. Otherwise, we will surely be executed." [...]

"All that you say, I of course know well," answers Father-of-Aloi. "That is why I refused to come with you at first. I knew that you had stolen the Rajah's ring. But now you ask for my help. I am very reluctant to give it. If the Rajah knew, he would be even angrier. But I feel sorry for you, for if I don't agree, you will surely be executed."

Father-of-Aloi then tells the captains that they must give up the ring and bury it beneath the largest durian tree they can find near the Rajah's palace. First, he tells them, they must put the ring in a small jar. Then, after they bury it, they must mark the tree by tying a red string around its buttress roots. [...] The captains gratefully agree.

After voyaging a further two days and nights, they reach the Rajah's kingdom. It is mid-morning when they tie up at the royal wharf. Seeing the vessel arrive, the Rajah sends messengers to find out whether the captains have brought Father-of-Aloi with them. Finding that they have, he hurries to the wharf to receive him. [...] The Rajah greets Father-of-Aloi and they walk arm-and-arm back to the palace. Father-of-Aloi wears his finest attire; a yellow loincloth and a woven turban.

After supper, the Rajah relates the entire history of the missing ring. "I have called on all my wisemen," says the Rajah, "but none could tell me who has stolen it [..]. This greatly distressed me, for the ring is a royal treasure, a possession of my family for many generations."

"Truly you had reason to feel distressed," Father-of-Aloi agrees. "But have no worry. For tonight I will find out where the thief has hidden your ring." Hearing this, the Rajah is grateful and promises a handsome reward [..]. He then asks what preparations should be made. "Wait a moment," answers Father-of-Aloi. "It is not yet time."

Later that evening [..] Father-of-Aloi unwraps his charms (*pengaroh*). These include stones, horns and tusks, large and small bottles, and the black spy-glass bottle without a bottom. The Rajah asks Father-of-Aloi where he obtained such charms. Father-of-Aloi tells him that they were all given to him by the spirits (*samoa ubat tu' diberi' antu magang*).[...] He then asks for a live chicken [..].

As soon as the chicken is produced, Father-of-Aloi recites a prayer over his charms, waving them with the fowl.

> One, two, three, four, five,
> > *Sa, dua, tiga, empat, lima,*
> six, seven.
> > *enam, tu--joh*
> Thus I wave you my charms,
> > *Aku tu' miau kita ubat,*
> Be effective, do as I command.
> > *Minta' kita sidi', minta' ngasi.*

The prayer [..] concludes:

> Let it no longer be hidden.
> > *Kita anang ngasoh iya sekong, iya lindong,*
> Make it shine, make it flash.
> > *Tang asoh marak, tang asoh tampak.*
> Cause it to be seen, reveal it to us.
> > *Asoh ayan, asoh nyeratan.*

He then lustrates his charms with blood drawn from the chicken's comb and begins his ritual scanning. First he looks into his crystal (*batu ilau*) and announces that the ring was indeed stolen. [...] He then scans with his spy-glass [..]. After gazing through it for a long time he announces to the Rajah: "This ring is difficult to find, for it has been hidden by the thieves in a very secure place."

Concerned, the Rajah asks Father-of-Aloi to spare no effort.

Father-of-Aloi pretends to fall asleep, wrapped in a *pua'* (*Udah nya Apai Aloi lalu ngelulu ka diri tindok bebungkor pua'*). Moments later, he awakes. "What is it, Uncle?" (*Kati baka, aya*) asks the Rajah.

"Everything is fine. I have seen the ring, and early tomorrow morning you and I will go to where it is hidden and take it back."

Early next morning Father-of-Aloi again studies his crystal. He then scans the horizon with his bottomless bottle. First he scans to the right, then shakes his head. Next, he scans in the direction of the river. Then, again, he shakes his head. He next turns his telescope toward the rising sun. Again, he shakes his head. With this, the color drains from the Rajah's face. [...] "Can't you see it?" he asks.

"Ess! Be still. It is, as I told you, very hard to find."

Father-of-Aloi then turns his spy-glass in the direction in which the sun sets and holds it there for a long time. "Your ring," Father-of-Aloi says at last, "has been buried by thieves under the roots of a durian tree. First the thieves hid it in their house. Now they have put it inside a jar and buried it near your palace under a large durian tree. Come, [..] follow me." [...]

[...] Reaching the foot of a durian tree, Father-of-Aloi orders the Rajah's attendants to dig carefully beneath its roots. They soon uncover a small black jar wrapped in cloth. Father-of-Aloi hands the jar to the Rajah. He quickly removes the cloth and inside he sees his ring.

The Rajah shouts with joy. "Never have I ever met anyone as wise as Father-of-Aloi" (*Nadai aku kala' nemu orang besai penemu baka Apai Aloi tu'*).

[...] Next morning Father-of-Aloi lets it be known that he wishes to return home. And so the Rajah orders that preparations be made for his departure. But first he asks Father-of-Aloi to name his reward (*upah*). Father-of-Aloi replies that in his dreams the spirits who gave him his charms said that he must not ask for payment [..]. "It is up to those you help," said the spirits, "whether they wish to reward you or not" (*Nya barang pengasih orang, pia' ko ajar antu, nya alai nya meh kabuah aku enda' minta' upah*).

Hearing this, the Rajah calls for his two captains and orders them to return with Father-of-Aloi to the kingdom of Rajah Merom. But first, he gives Paloi an enormous reward, consisting of rare jars, cannons, brass gongs, porcelain plates, bowls and cups, and countless other things too numerous to name. Father-of-Aloi and the two captains then depart and sail for two days and two nights.

Arriving home [..], the crew carries Father-of-Aloi's possessions into his longhouse [..]. There Mother-of-Aloi weeps with joy to see her husband safely home again with such riches (*pulai gerai nyamai lalu buih perengka reta*).

Here the fable proceeds through a series of deceptions. A Malay Rajah finds that a precious ring has been stolen. After his own wisemen fail to discover its whereabouts, he learns of Father-of-Aloi's gift and orders his ship captains to bring the shaman to his kingdom so that he might recover the stolen ring. The story, as it opens, emphasizes the life-and-death power that the Rajah and his captains hold over the hero.

The captains, when they arrive at his longhouse, threaten Father-of-Aloi's life and prepare to carry him off in chains. Undaunted, the hero soon gains the upper hand. He first tricks the captains into building a new house for his family. Then, aboard their ship, he convinces them that he knows their secret, having learned it by chance: that it was they who stole the Rajah's ring. Because of their belief in Paloi's powers, the captains are easily taken in. Their lives now depend upon the hero's silence. From being their prisioner, Father-of-Aloi has now, in effect, made prisioners of the captains, and under his instructions, they agree to a plan he devises for returning the Rajah's ring. This return, forming the dramatic climax of the narrative, takes place once again as a miraculous act of "ritual."

Arriving at the Rajah's kingdom, Father-of-Aloi immediately asserts his power over the king as well. Welcomed at the wharf, Paloi, attired in a royal yellow loincloth and turban, is led arm-and-arm by the Rajah to his palace. There Father-of-Aloi stages an elaborate scanning "ritual." This, of course, is a hoax. After another elaborate search the following morning--using once again his "magical" crystal and spyglass--Father-of-Aloi leads the Rajah and his attendants to where the captains, by pre-arrangement, have buried the ring, and there, pretending to be guided by the results of his scanning, he directs its "discovery." The awed and grateful Rajah presents Father-of-Aloi with a lavish reward. This the captains help Paloi transport to his longhouse. There they are met by Mother-of-Aloi, who weeps with joy at her husband's return.

Here, as in the first fable, the tale sets up a contrast between the Fool as Shaman and a Malay Rajah. Again, the latter epitomizes, in opposition to the former, worldly wealth and power. But the Fool subverts the relationship, and from an initial position of advantage, the Rajah is soon outwitted, and by deception, subordinated to the Fool's designs.

PALOI BECOMES A SHAMAN (*PALOI NYADI MANANG*)

This final story involves, again, a case of stolen property. But here the theft is an act of revenge--of paying back a wrong. The thief is Father-of-Aloi himself and the victims are his nephews, the principal spirit-hero companions of the epic sagas: Keling, Laja, and Sempurai.

When this story opens, Paloi lives with his wife and two children, Aloi and Laminda, in a longhouse above Nanga Gelong and below Nanga Panggau Libau.[26] One day he decides to make a boat. He plans to make it from a *nyatu pelaga* tree,[27] growing above the mouth of the Gelong river, which his father claimed years before when it was still a small sapling.

A day after this, [..] Laja, Sempurai, and Keling also decide to make a boat. [...] Several days later they fell the very same *nyatu pelaga* tree. Next morning they cut its trunk to the proper length [..] and begin to fashion it into a boat.

Having made ready his tools, [..] Father-of-Aloi learns that someone else has felled his tree. "Ha! What is this?" (*Hah, deh*) he cries "Have I looked after this tree all these years so others can steal it?" (*Nya ga' kayu ke udah di-inak, nya ga' tebang orang. Lebu endar meh ke udah nginak nya, udah ga' dichuri orang?*)

At noon, Laja, Sempurai, and Keling stop work to eat their lunch beside the river. While they are eating, Father-of-Aloi arrives. He has come to see who has cut down his *nyatu pelaga* tree. As he approaches, he hears the sound of Keling and his friends eating their lunch beside the river. While they eat, he hides their tools under one end of the boat they are making. He then conceals himself nearby.

After eating, Keling, Laja, and Sempurai [..] bathe. They amuse themselves by swimming in a river pool. When they return, they discover that their tools are missing. They search everywhere. [...] "Who would dare steal our things?," asks Sempurai. "If I set eyes on him, I'll cut off his head" (*Ti' aku meda' tentu pala orang nya dipumpong aku*). [...]

[...] Keling and his friends wait two days before they resume work. On the third day they set out again with a new set of boat-building tools. They work with a fury to make up for the two days they lost. As they work, Father-of-Aloi again arrives and conceals himself nearby. At noon, the three go bathing again. Father-of-Aloi creeps from his hiding place and takes their lunch and tools and hides them at the foot of a large tree some distance away, covering them with dead branches. He again hides.

After bathing, the three friends return to where they left their things and discover that their lunch and tools are gone. "Bah!" shouts Sempurai. [...] The three search everywhere [..]. In his fury Sempurai uproots the surrounding trees, tossing them to the left and right. [...] Seeing that they are not going to find their tools, Keling advises his friends to return home so that they might call a meeting of their followers.

At lunchtime they arrive at the longhouse. The youngsters call out, "Have you finished your boat already, uncles?" Sempurai is too angry to answer. [...] Later Keling calls a meeting to seek the help of the longhouse in searching for their lost property. Everyone takes part in the search, but they find nothing, not even the thief's footprints. "The undergrowth ought to be trampled. But there is no sign of such a thing. Perhaps," some suggest, "your tools were not taken by a man at all." [...] Finally, Keling calls a halt to the search and they return home [..].

In the evening, [..] Keling calls the people of the house to his gallery [..]. He reviews the events of the previous days. "First, someone steals our tools. We search for them to no avail. Then, this morning, we are robbed a second time. That is why we called for your help. But, again, we find nothing. Now, in calling you together, I ask for your advice. What should be done?" Keling's followers suggest that the views of the elders be sought. So Uncle Bujang Tuai speaks:

"It is my opinion that we should call for a shaman. He can search for the tools in his crystal. Whether they were taken by a demon or by a human thief--the shaman will be able to discover the culprit" (*Enti' iya di-ambi antu, manang ga' ulih meda'; ti' iya di-ambi mensia, manang ga' nemu meda'; ti' iya dilalai ka orang iya ga' nemu alai orang engkah*). Everyone agrees with the wisdom of Bujang Tuai's advice.

"Who will fetch the shaman?" asks Keling. "And who will this shaman be?" "It is best," advises Laja, "that we engage our local shaman." "And who is that?" asks Widow Jantau. "There is no other shaman living among us than our Uncle, Father-of-Aloi. He is well-known for his wisdom (*udah di-dinga rita bisi penemu*). Once he brought a princess back to life and another time he recovered a precious ring stolen by thieves." [...] Laja and Sempurai [..] offer to summon Father-of-Aloi the following morning.

Early next day Sempurai and Laja set out. At Father-of-Aloi's landing place, they meet Mother-of-Aloi [..]. As they bathe, she goes ahead to tell her husband of their arrival [..]. When Father-of-Aloi hears that Sempurai and Laja have come, he pretends to be sick. He begins to shiver and pretends to have pains in his knees. He lies on the gallery floor and wraps himself in a blanket. [...] When the two enter the house, his son Aloi is rubbing his back. "Welcome cousins, come in and sit down."

After bringing out areca-nut, Mother-of-Aloi asks Sempurai and Laja the purpose of their visit [..]. "We have come to call for your husband, our uncle [..]," they tell her.[...]

"Let me call him for you, then," says Aloi. "There, Father! Wake up."

Father-of-Aloi gets up slowly and comes to where the two visitors are sitting. Laja asks him why he has wrapped himself in a blanket and Paloi tells them that he is sick [..]. Laja and Sempurai then explain the reason for their visit. [...] They tell Paloi how they have twice lost their tools. And they are not just ordinary tools but tools fashioned by their ancestors. They have come to ask his help in finding them. Also they wish to know whether a demon or a human being has robbed them. Father-of-Aloi replies that he is too sick to leave home [..].

"If you are sick, we two," Sempurai says, "will take turns carrying you on our backs." [...] Father-of-Aloi gives in [..] and enters his family room to collect his medicines.

He gathers all his stone, tusk, and antler charms. But Father-of-Aloi is not, in fact, a real shaman, nor is he a curer (*Paloi tu' ukai manang, lalu ukai mega dukun*). He only collects odd stones, antlers, and tusks in order to trick people by pretending to be a *manang*.

When he has finished, he comes out onto the gallery carrying his medicine box. It is very heavy. Pretending to be unable to walk, he falls down. [...] Three times he tries to stand up, but he is unable to get to his feet.

"Oh! How can I perform my rites? I can neither stand nor sit" (*Kati ko aku beliau, din ila, enda' tau bediri, enda' tau dudok*).

"That's no problem," says Sempurai. "I will carry you. And when I get tired, I will let Laja have a turn." So Sempurai puts Father-of-Aloi on his back. Laja takes up his medicine box and together the three set out for Panggau longhouse. Midway, Sempurai asks Laja to take his turn. And so Laja carries Paloi right into the Panggau longhouse.

Inside, he puts Father-of-Aloi down on the gallery. Paloi pretends to be unable to sit upright. [...] At noon Keling's mother cooks chicken livers for Father-of-Aloi to eat. She also prepares smoked *semah* and roasted fish (*ikan lempis*) for his lunch. After lunch, Keling's father goes out to catch more fish for Father-of-Aloi. Luckily he makes a large catch. Selecting only the choicest fish, Keling's mother cooks them in bamboo tubes.

That evening Kumang and her mother-in-law prepare an enormous feast for Father-of-Aloi's supper. When all is ready, Kumang goes to the gallery [..] and invites him to enter the family room. Keling must help him [..]. Father-of-Aloi is soon gorging himself. After this, when he has eaten his full, he forgets to act sick. [...]

After supper, Father-of-Keling asks what preparations are needed. Father-of-Aloi tells him that he must first look into his crystal in order to decide what type of rite to perform. Father-of-Aloi then asks that his medicine box and three large plates be brought to him. Opening his box, he fills one plate with stone charms, the second with tusk charms, and the third with antlers. [...] He then prays over his charms and waves them with a chicken. [...] Taking up the crystal, he stares into it for a long time. Everyone falls silent and watches. He continues to gaze into the crystal. At last, Sempurai asks, "What do you see, Uncle?" (*Kati baka peda' nuan, aya?*)

"Ah! This is very difficult (*mar tu'*), Sempurai, my son. Your things have been stolen by the Demon-Huntsmen (*Antu Gerasi*)."[28] On hearing this, everyone is speechless. Father-of-Aloi takes an areca quid and begins to chew.

At last, Sempurai asks, "How will we get our things back?"

"There is but one way. We must visit the Demon's house [..] and ask him to return them."

"And what about our headcloths, Uncle? They were taken when our lunches were stolen."

"I just now saw the Demon wearing one. He had it wrapped around his head. If you insist on having it back, you can come with me and take it from him yourself."

"Ess! I'm not brave enough," confesses Sempurai.

"If you lack the courage, then I will have to go by myself," says Father-of-Aloi.

"Do you plan to kill the Demon?" asked Sempurai.

"No. It shouldn't be necessary, unless he refuses to return your property. In fact, the Demon had no intention of stealing. He was simply out for a walk in the forest when he noticed your tools scattered all over the ground. He thought they had been thrown away by someone who didn't want them any longer. Therefore, let this be a lesson to you. When you are working in the forest, keep your tools together when you stop work. Or else put a stick fence around them, or cover them with leaves. Then others will know that they belong to someone."

Father-of-Aloi continues: "The rite I will perform tonight is called "The Rite to Visit the House of a Demon-Huntsman on Top of the Hill" (*Pelian namuai ngagai rumah antu gerasi di tuchong bukit*). The people then bring out a *dekoh* jar and erect a "Fence of Fire" (*pagar api*) on the gallery. When all is ready, Father-of-Aloi [..] sits beside the "Fence of Fire" and starts to recite his chants. He then falls into a trance (*iya pan lalu luput*). [...]

He remains unconscious for a long time. Sempurai and the others begin to worry [..]. Sempurai gets to his feet. At that moment, Father-of-Aloi awakens. "Why were you in trance so long, Uncle?" Sempurai asks.

"I had to quarrel for a long time with the Demon-Huntsman. He denied stealing your property. 'If Sempurai suspects me of being a thief, let him come here and accuse me himself.' So the Demon-Huntsman told me. 'I'll teach him a thing or two. As for Keling and Laja. If they think I stole their things, let them come here, and I'll settle with them, too.'"

"After telling me he didn't steal your things, I climbed to the Demon's loft (*sadau*) and there I saw your adzes and other tools. I also pointed to the headcloth the Demon was wearing.

'That's Sempurai's,' I told him. 'All this property must be returned. I don't want to see a quarrel between you and my nephews, so do as I say.'"

"'So be it', the Demon replied. I'll give them back if you insist. I didn't really mean to take them anyway.'"

"'That's as it should be', said I, 'for you and Sempurai are related. You are Merisi, "Whose Sword Never Looses Its Edge Biting Through Bone" (*Nyemilu tisi enda' beramuya makai tulang*). Your brother Nising, "Whose Ears are the Size of Winnowing Trays" (*Lambing pending mesai daun chapan senggang*), is Sempurai's father.'" [...] Thus Father-of-Aloi describes his visit to the mountain-top home of the Demon-Huntsman.

"This is a great feat that Father-of-Aloi has performed," everyone agrees. "He is truly a powerful shaman."

"But where will the Demon put our things?" asks Laja.

"For now, you must not ask. But tomorrow morning, everything will be returned."

[...] After that all who have witnessed the *pelian* eat the ritual *makai salau* meal.[29] No one sleeps the whole night [..], for everyone wishes to talk to Father-of-Aloi.[30] [...]

Next morning, at the first light of day, Father-of-Aloi calls for Keling, Laja, and Sempurai. "Why do you call us, Uncle?"

"It is about your property. The Demon-Huntsman came this morning to return it. He arrived a short time ago while it was still dark. If you would like to meet him, we might be able to, if we hurry." Sempurai and Laja admit that they are not brave enough. "I will try." says Keling, "if all three of us go." "Not I," says Sempurai, "even if we were five."

The three friends ask Father-of-Aloi where the Demon left their things. He tells them that he put the first set of tools under the end of their boat. The second set can be found at the foot of a large tree some distance away covered with dead branches. Later that day, after Father-of-Aloi tells them that the Demon has returned home, the three set off. They find their tools, even their three headcloths, just where Father-of-Aloi told them to look. "This certainly shows what a powerful shaman he is," says Sempurai.

When they return home, the three friends lay out their tools on Keling's gallery. "Did the Demon leave them where he said he would?" asks Father-of-Aloi. "He did, indeed! Everything was just as you told us. By this deed, you have proven yourself to be a truly great shaman, Uncle."

"Yes, I realize I am effective (*aku amat sidi ti' belian*), not an ordinary kind of shaman (*ukai manang ngapa*)." [...] Keling, Laja, and Sempurai then pay Father-of-Aloi his fee of two pieces of cloth, a chicken, a knife, and an *irun* jar. In addition, Keling gives him an adze and a headcloth, Sempurai a loincloth, and Laja a piece of *kebat* cloth. [...] The three friends then paddle him home, as he is still too sick to walk [..]. From that day onward, news of Father-of-Aloi's reputation spreads far and wide (*udah nya berita Apai Aloi mansang ditemu orang maioh*).

Here the hero displays more fully his comic trickster character. He is clearly a charlatan masquerading as a shaman. Thus he collects curious looking tusks, stones, and antlers in order to impress his clients, and is lazy and greedy, feigning illness so that the heroes will carry him on their backs and their wives will gorge him with special delicacies.

The story itself centers around Father-of-Aloi's revenge upon his nephews for felling a tree which he himself was preparing to use. In carrying out his revenge, Paloi invents an elaborate hoax in which the heroes' lunches, headcloths, and boat-building tools are made to appear as if they were "stolen" by a cannibalistic Demon Huntsman. But it is Paloi himself, of course, who is the "thief," and, as the story-teller's audience, we are made a party to the deception he perpetrates. Clearly, Paloi already knows where the heroes' tools are located, since he hid them himself, yet he goes through the charade of a *pelian*, as if it were by this means that he "discovers" their whereabouts. The comic travesty concludes with a make-believe dialogue between the "demon" and the hero in which the Fool trades places with the heroes, outwits them, and exposes their claim to "bravery" to be as much a deception as his own.

The result of this insertion of a "ritual" into what can be described as an "anti-rite"--a comic narrative constituted as play--is to juxtapose two opposed readings of the "reality" that this "ritual" represents. On the one hand, for the story-teller's audience, perceiving events through Paloi's eyes, what takes place within the ritual frame is clearly "make-believe." It constitutes a clever deception that deliberatedly misrepresents, or blurs conventional categories of experience, notably those between the "spiritual" and "human." For the heroes, on the other hand, belief persuades them of the genuineness of Father-of-Aloi's incursion into "the unseen" and of his heroic encounter there with the Demon culprit responsible for the theft of their tools. As a consequence, both attribute totally different meanings to the "recovery" of these tools that follows. Yet both readings of reality "work," although the fable, paradoxically, suggests that the greater truth is to be found in "make-believe."

Both Malay sovereigns and spirit-heroes exist outside the world of immediate experience, yet both constitute for the Iban important images of power, wealth, and, in the latter case, of physical prowess and daring. Here the Fool's principal antagonists are the *Orang Panggau*. For the Iban, the spirit-heroes and heroines are associated with this-worldly success in all of its traditional forms. In contrast to the *manang's yang*--who aid him in performing deeds of bravery in the unseen world--the *Orang Panggau* are thought to act as spirit-patrons to successful men and women in the world of visible deeds. Thus, as spirit-patrons, they enable those whom they aid to distinguish themselves, for example, as orators, warriors, blacksmiths, or weavers. In addition, as hosts and hostesses during major status-valorizing rituals, successful men and women enact the parts of the *Orang Panggau* when they receive the gods and goddesses whom the bards have invoked so that they may bear witness to human achievements and feats of daring. Yet, the Fool triumphs over both the sovereigns and the spirit-heroes. At one level, his triumph can be read as a denial of hierarchy itself. Thus the Fool is everyman's equal. In this sense, by humbling the powerful and exposing as cowards those whom society extols as heroes, the comic fables can be said to reaffirm the central place of egalitarian values in a competitive society in which the outcome of competition is far from equal. But at another level, the Father-of-Aloi fables can be read as a celebration of deception itself.

SHAMANISM AND DECEPTION

Early European writers portrayed the *manang*, almost without exception, as a charlatan and confidence-trickster (Graham 1987:16-17). Brooke Low (Roth 1896: I:265), for example, argued that,

> The entire system of the *manang* is based upon...imposture...His reputation depends upon...the trickeries his superior cunning enabled him to practice upon the credulity of the people...To ensure success in his profession his cunning must be of a high order.

What such commentators failed to realize is that the Iban themselves share much the same view. Thus the shaman's audience frequently expresses doubts, as we have noted, about the genuineness of his performance. While such doubts may reflect upon a shaman's claim to this-worldly status, they in no way, it is critical to note, rule out a belief in his ritual efficacy. On the contrary, rather than being condemned, cunning and deception are viewed by most Iban as essential to a *manang's* success. In dealing with spirit adversaries, the shaman, like the comic hero, is ideally a trickster. The spirits and other malevolent forces he contends against are believed to work through deception and trickery. Thus they change form at will or employ other subterfuges to capture souls or to injure human victims. To match such adversaries, the *manang* must, by necessity, be a master of deception himself, and, in defeating or thwarting his enemies, he regularly engages them in what are, in effect, unseen duels of cunning, bluff, and deception. But more than this, those visible actions which the *manang* performs in the course of his *pelian* that appear to be "trickery," or sleight of hand, such as producing bits of stone from a patient's head, or wrapping his shoulders in cloth to serve as "wings," may nevertheless have potent effects in the unseen plane in ways which are not immediately perceptible. Just as the shaman's performance during his *pelian* appears to produce visible "miracles" that defy ordinary comprehension, so the unseen effects of his actions, may, in the same way, bring about visible consequences through means that are not directly perceptible to the senses, but which are no less "real" all the same. Here the comic fables clearly reflect upon this complex conjunction of skepticism and belief, playing in particular on distinctions between "the seen" and "the unseen," efficacy and deception, reality and make-believe.

But, more than this, the Fool in the guise of Shaman, openly champions deception itself. In doing so, he gives licenced expression to a view that is much more widely represented, though less overtly, in other cultural contexts as well, for example, in the hero sagas, where the *Orang Panggau*, too, regularly triumph through magical transformations, cunning and deception, and in historical narratives (*cherita lama'*) where men of action, pioneers and warleaders, are honored as often for their cunning as for their bravery and physical prowess.

CONCLUSION

One way of reaching an understanding of Iban shamanism is through a close reading of the shaman's ritual actions. These actions are believed, by most Iban, to be instrumentally efficacious, i.e., to have effects in the "real world." Their efficacy rests, as I have argued here, on a belief in the *manang's* ability to both transcend and enforce opposing aspects of the cosmos, and on the operation of symbolic analogues between this ability and the qualities displayed by successful men and women of action in the visible world. Not only are the shaman's ritual actions modelled on worldly achievement, but they act as well to validate a belief in the *manang's* own efficacy. Thus, through his *pelian*, the shaman repeatedly demonstrates the authenticity of his behavior and so generates confidence in his claims to expertise and daring. Shamanism exists "at the point where direct experience on the part of individual Iban...gives way to trust in the actions of an intermediary considered capable of skilled intervention" (Graham 1987: 134), and, as in the case of this-worldly renown, such trust does not come automatically, but must be won.

The shaman's success, as a ritual intermediary, thus depends upon his ability to unite within his person what the Iban conceive to be "seen" and "unseen" planes of experience and to render consistent within himself the potentially fragmenting principles inherent in this dichotomization. Yet, when the shaman's role is more broadly situated, beyond the framed domain of ritual, profound incongruities are apparent in the way in which this role is socially constituted. Within the wider social system, the *manang* himself is a figure of contradiction. The shaman's ritual prowess, as we have seen, is not only structurally isolated from, but is seen, to a large degree, as antithetical to this-worldly power and status. What is paradoxical here is that these incongruities-- while they find little resonance in the shaman's ritual actions--are richly explored in the realm of narrative play.

Within the *ensera Paloi*, Father-of-Aloi, as Shaman, both highlights, and at the same time transcends these incongruities. The miraculous acts he performs are a sham, produced by deception and stage-props, and sustained by the credulity of those he deceives. He is thus a master dissembler. Yet the hero does, in fact, perform miracles. His nature, as a comic trickster, reconciles all contradictions. He thus overcomes the incongruities of his role by subverting both nature and the social order. Through a parody of ritual, he achieves the seemingly impossible--seeing the invisible and bringing the dead back to life-- and at the same time he inverts the taken-for-granted social order, proving himself, by deception and the quickness of his wit, to be more powerful than worldly sovereigns and more courageous than the spirit-heroes. In the process he dissolves the taken-for-granted credibility of these very images of hierarchy, this-worldly power and achievement.

The more general irony revealed by these fables is that "play," while outwardly disengaged from "reality," may hew more closely to the objective realities of society than does ritual, notwithstanding the latter's claims to this-worldly efficacy. Thus through the medium of play, the Father-of-Aloi stories offer what is, in effect, a penetrating commentary on the nature of Iban shamanism itself. While ritual, as Turner (1982:29) observes, is bound by the sanctity of its frame to censor the commentaries on...society that it generates...Play [in contrast] in the guise of drollery and folly and in the ephemerality of its presence is licensed to comment on a great range of issues.

Thus play allows its participants "to escape from the 'should' and 'ought' character of ritual...and to see themselves as free to fabricate a range of alternative possibilities of behaving, thinking, and feeling," thereby exposing the assumptions and ambiguities of both ritual and society generally to critical scrutiny. Thus, "Seemingly amoral, [play's] moralism may cleave more...closely to the facts of contemporary life than the moralism of ritual" (1982:28-29). It is in this capacity, Turner suggests, that inheres play's special virtue.

Finally, writing in another context, Turner (1974:256) applies the notion of play to institutions of initiation, arguing that such institutions must act, not only to produce adherence to rules and patterns, but through the introduction of play--of paradoxical features that challenge accepted conventions, cognitive categories and boundaries--must equally generate a level of skeptism and initiative so as to allow those who pass through them to be able to cope with novelty and to imagine new cultural paradigms and schemata. Play, Davis (1977:16-17) argues, has what he calls both "positive" and "negative" aspects, that is to say, elements of both *ludus* and *paidia*. On the one hand, play contributes to the development of cognitive skills, self-awareness, and a mastery of the rules that govern social interaction and role behavior, and, on the other, it entails a "playing with" these rules and skills, of exploring and crossing the limits of cognitive boundaries, and of juxtaposing images or combining them in ways which contradict ordinary experience. The Iban comic fables clearly constitute play in both these aspects. At one level, the tales appear to be absorbed in rules and categorical distinctions and to dwell on the disasters that flow from their confusion or intentional violation. At another, they represent a kind of "initiatory play." Transmitted across the generational order--from "grandparents" to "grandchildren"--they confront their audience with contradictions, juxtapositions, and paradoxes, and so generate an awareness of the fissures and ambiguities in taken-for-granted understandings; skepticism, and an openness to the possibilities of new paradigms and cultural givens.

ACKNOWLEDGEMENTS

A number of persons read and commented on earlier drafts of this paper. In particular I wish to thank George Appell, Robert Barrett, Penelope Graham, Christine Helliwell, Margaret Jolly, and Rozanna Lilley. In writing this paper I enjoyed the support of a research fellowship in the Department of Anthropology, Research School of Pacific Studies, Australian National University, under the auspices of the Comparative Austronesian Project.

NOTES

1. Barrett in this volume reveals the reverse side of this ambiguity by pointing out that the term most commonly used to refer to ritual performance, *main* has much the same range of semantic meaning as the English term "play."

2. These fables are taken from a much larger body of *ensera Paloi* collected over a number of years in the upper Paku (cf. Sather 1981, 1984). Here I wish to thank Henry Gerijih, my main *ensera* source, and the many others who aided me, both on this occasion and during earlier fieldwork (1976-79 and 1981-84). Henry Gerijih was born at Nanga Samu in 1917. Both his father and paternal grandfather were well-known Paku traden'-travellers. Gerijih studied with *lemambang* Luat ak. Jabu and became, at the young age of 18, a member of Lemambang Luat's company of bards. He later attended teachers' training college and, beginning in 1949, taught at a number of Iban mission schools in the Second Division. Among his first pupils was the current Deputy Chief Minister, Datuk Alfred Jabu. He retired from St. Christopher's school, Debak, in 1972 and since then has lived with his wife and son Jatan at Nanga Samu longhouse, where he continues to farm and manage the affairs of his *bilek*. According to Gerijih, he first heard these particular *ensera Paloi* from his grandmother, Krandang ak. Sang (Sather 1984:vi).

3. These observations expressed by Paku informants are born out by Robert Barrett (personal communication; see also his contribution to this volume), who carried out a survey and collected family histories of *manang* in the Rimbas and Krian rivers as part of a study of Iban mental illness and traditional methods of therapy. Not only does the practice of shamanism tend to be concentrated, and pass down within specific families, but *manang* themselves are aware of this tendency, linking it to conditions of spirit-inspiration and apprenticeship. It is not, however, as Barrett makes clear, an inherited status. Those with whom Barrett discussed the question maintain that families that produce *manang* are also likely to produce *dukun* and *lemambang* (healers and bards) and today, very often, hospital dressers as well. Manang Jabing ak. Incham of Tarum, Rimbas, the principal shaman informant of the late Benedict Sandin and myself, was, during the last years that he practiced as a shaman, before his death, the father of a *lemambang* (bard) and the grandfather of an Anglican clergyman (Rev. Ubun ak. Renang).

4. Reflecting the basic "seen":"unseen" dichotomy of Iban thought, the Mandai river also exists simultaneously as a visible river in the human world (in West Kalimantan).

5. Mount Rabong is uniquely sacred to the *manang*. In the Paku, an evocation of the mountain ends every *pelian* invocation. In it the shaman calls upon the celestial shamans and spirits of past *manang*, who have come to aid him during his *pelian*, to return to its summit (*tuchong*) which represents their special abode (cf. Sandin 1978:80fn). In addition, this return symbolically parallels the recovery of the patient's soul and its reinsertion into the body through the fontanelle. Mount Rabong is an actual mountain located on the true left bank of the Ketungau river in West Kalimantan, and is visible from many parts of the Second Division. Mount Rabong is thus a natural landmark in the world of man. It is also the site of Manang Raja Menjaya's consecration as the first *manang bali'*, "transformed" or transvestite shaman, by his sister, the Goddess Ini Inda, and the abode of the souls of deceased *manang*, in short, their own special land of the dead (cf. Graham 1987:36; Sandin 1983:236-38).

6. As "seen" (*meda'*) by the gods, spirits and souls, and, in its visible bodily form, by other human beings. *Gamal* or "appearance" is thus identified with an individual's unique persona, both spiritual, as seen by the gods and spirits, and social, as seen in the everyday social world by human beings. To an individual's social persona is associated "name," or reputation, and individuating aspects of "character" (*pendiau*). To an

individual's spiritual *gamal* are associated conditions of ritual jeopardy or favor, as revealed, for example, by omens and dreams (cf. Sather 1985:3).

7. A ritual ikat textile.

8. There are exceptions. In the *pelian bejereki*, for example, described by Sandin (1978), this central ritual apparatus consists, instead, of the *sabang ayu*, literally the "cordyline of vitality." This is represented by a cordyline plant (*sabang*) set in an *irun* jar (1978:59), which, after the *pelian* is over, is planted by the *manang* in the earth below the longhouse entry ladder. In the *pelian bejereki* the plant symbolizes the "image," or plant counterpart, of the about-to-be-born child in the womb of the expectant mother whom the shaman spiritually "fences" (*bejereki*).

9. An Iban *manang* may be either a man or a woman; female shamans, however, are comparatively rare. None are currently consulted by patients in the upper Paku, although several women, all from the Rimbas, were active in the river in the recent past.

10. Approaching performance somewhat differently, Barrett (in his volume) shows, in a rich and powerfully vivid analysis, how this sense of efficiency is established through the interaction of shaman and audience, particularly through their mutual metacommentary on the nature of ritual itself.

11. This was a matter of expectation. The *manang* were not debarred from warfare. They were free to join war parties, if they chose to, and a few, such as the turn-of-the-century Paku-Julau rebel Manang Bakak "Asu Rangka" (Greedy Dog), distinguished themselves as both warriors and shamans. Unlike other men, such participation, however, was not expected. As a result of their healing practice, shamans are said by many to lack the physical strength and endurance of other men. For a discussion of the symbolic associations of shamanism and warfare, and the relation of both to notions of gender, see Sather 1978.

12. Field notes, Kerangan Pinggai, Ulu Paku, 1978.

13. Concerned chiefly with tortoise (*tekura'*) and Mousedeer (*pelandok*).

14. Similar comic tale traditions appear to be widespread in Borneo. Klokke-Coster, Klokke, and Saha (1976: 66-121) record an extensive collection of similar Ngadju Dayak tales. Here the principal comic hero is known as

Bapa Paloi. Christine Helliwell (personal communication) reports a similar comic tradition among the Malayic-speaking Gerai Dayaks of West Kalimantan. Here, significantly, the comic hero, Pa' Aluwi, also appears in a small number of tales, as a shaman. Sander Adelaar (personal communication) reports similar traditions among the Malayic-speaking Salako (or Selako) and the Tamanic-speaking Embaloh. Among the former, the hero is known as Pa' Aiai; among the latter as Ma' Alui. The Sarawak Malay have also a comic fable tradition, but, according to Anthony Richards (personal communication) its hero, Abu Nawas, is more purely a trickster figure. His actions are directed nearly always against the Raja or more well-to-do members of his *kampong*. Regretably, to my knowledge, Abu Nawas stories have not been recorded for Sarawak. Elsewhere, in Indonesia, collections of Abu Nawas stories have been published in Indonesian (Iskandar 1964) and Sudenese (Tanoewiredja 1928) and in Malaysia, in Bahasa Malaysia (Shamsudin 1966). There is also a Sama-Bajau tradition of Abu Nawas stories in eastern Sabah and the southern Philippines.

15. Father-of-Aloi, for example, speaks with a peculiar nasal voice (*idol*), which is instantly recognizable and adds greatly, for Iban audiences, to the hilarity of the dialogue (Sather 1981:74). Thus in analyzing written versions of the *ensera Paloi* an important element of irony is lost. Even at his most brilliant, the moment Father-of-Aloi speaks, the story-teller's audience at once realizes that behind the brilliance lurks the Fool.

16. Also known as *Saloi, Sali, Sali-ali, Pak Sali*, or simply *Tambap* (Fool) (Sather 1984:vi).

17. Thus, for example, between friends, *tambap lap!*, You idiot!, is an expression of affection (see Richards 1981:363).

18. Two brothers in the Paku, the eldest of whom is now dead, inherited from their grandfather a charm in the form of a hair from Paloi's head (*bok Paloi*). The hair is kept rolled in a ball inside a small bamboo-node container (*bungkan buloh*). According to the surviving brother, the hair is grey and when unrolled is about three to four inches long. The elder brother was a man of some prominence in Sarawak and according to his younger brother, used the charm when dealing with other government officials and during court cases. The younger brother, on the other hand, used it as a youth to make girls "foolish" and so easily seduced. Except for a few close friends, the two brothers have kept their ownership of the charm secret. Although I have not been able to verify this, others in the

river are said to possess charms in the form of small pieces of Paloi's loincloth.

19. Both, significantly, are make-believe "demons." The first is the sound of cicada, the second of a frog, which are used by parents to frighten and so quiet unruly youngsters, especially at night (cf. Sather 1984:viii). This use of make-believe "demons" by parents against one another, rather than children, is another example of comic inversion in the fables. Also, considering that these stories are told to children, it gives an interesting commentary on the practice of make-believe itself.

20. For a different version of this origin see Sather 1981.

21. The month following harvest was traditionally known as *bulan pelelang*, literally "the month of travelling."

22. This *pelian*, held sometime after burial and following the conclusion of initial mourning (*pana*), is considered by the older generation as an essential part of Iban death rites. In it the *manang* removes, or "separates" (*serara'*), the dead *ayu* of the deceased from the clump made up of the *ayu* of the other members of his or her *bilek*-family. Following death, this plant-counterpart must be separated from the family clump; otherwise its presence threatens the health of the deceased's surviving family members. *Beserara' bunga* is thus essentially a rite of separation.

23. Victor Turner (1982) has stressed the role of the Fool, as a "leveler," a figure who, by his paradoxical character, subverts established hierarchy. In this connection, the Fool is almost always the eldest among a set of siblings; thus, by his very existence, he subverts the normal birth-order status between brothers and sisters.

24. *Beliau*, which I translate here as "healer," is a Malay, not an Iban term. When used by the Iban it refers to a healer who employs Malay methods of healing. Among the Saribas Malays of the lower Paku, *beliau* is also used as an honorific, in address, and refers to anyone who commands a specialized body of skill or knowledge (*ilmu*), including medical doctors and visiting anthropologists. Beliau Pulau appears in the Paku hero sagas as an extraordinarily powerful magician.

25. Historically, for a young unmarried man, the accomplishment of a successful journey (*bejalai* or *pegi*) represented the first rung on the

achievement ladder (Freeman 1970:223). As here, it was also thought to enhance a young man's attraction as a prospective husband.

26. Gelong and Panggau Libau are the rivers inhabited by the spirit-heroes and heroines. Keling is the chief of the Panggau Libau heroes; Laja is the second in command and the smoker of trophy skulls; while Sempurai, whose ancestry is semi-demonic, is the strongest and most daring of their warriors. The Gelong heroes are led by Tutong, whose sister Kumang is the wife of Keling. Tutong is the spiritual patron of blacksmiths (*tukang kamboh*) and, among the heroes, the principal forger of weapons. While Keling leads the other heroes by cunning, strategy, and the power of his personal magic, Sempurai, by contrast, is a figure of mercural temper, unreflective directness, and brute physical strength.

27. *Ternstroemia spp.* Forest trees may be claimed by clearing around their base and by bringing the claim to community notice. Such claims, once recognized, are inherited by the descendants of the first-finder (cf. Sather 1990: 31-32).

28. Forest-dwelling ogres that feed on human souls. The *antu gerasi* may also act as *yang*.

29. Or *asi salau*, a mid-night meal eaten generally half-way through the series of *pelian* rituals performed by the *manang* in one nightly session. No one who has come from another longhouse to attend the *pelian* may leave the house until he or she has partaken of this meal.

30. After the shaman completes his entire series of *pelian*, others who have gathered on the gallery to witness the rite are free to seek his advice concerning their own health, or to ask questions regarding inauspicious dreams, or other signs of spiritual danger. The shaman ministers to minor complaints, using masage, blowing and other techniques. News is also exchanged at this time, particularly during the season in which the *manang* are travelling from longhouse to longhouse. On such occasions the shamans not only affirm kinship with their clients but acquire information useful to their practice.

REFERENCES

Davis, Richard
    1977   Myth, Play, and Alchemy. Canberra Anthropology 1:15-23.

Eliade, Mircea
    1964   Shamanism: Archaic Techniques of Ecstasy. London: Routledge and Kegan Paul.

Freeman, Derek
    1967   Shaman and Incubus. Psychoanalytic Study of Society 4:315-344.

    1970   Report on the Iban. London: The Athlone Press.

    1981   Some Reflections on the Nature of Iban Society. An Occasional Paper, Department of Anthropology, Research School of Pacific Studies. Canberra: The Australian National University.

Graham, Penelope
    1987   Iban Shamanism: An Analysis of the Ethnographic Literature. An Occasional Paper, Department of Anthropology, Research School of Pacific Studies. Canberra: The Australian National University.

Handelman, Don
    1977   Play and Ritual: Complementary Frames of Metacommunication *In* It's a Funny Thing, Humor. A.J. Chapman and H. Foot, eds. London: Pergamon, pp. 185-192.

    1979   Is Naven Ludic? Paradox and the Communication of Identity. Social Analysis 1:177-192.

    1981   The Ritual Clown: Attributes and Affinities. Anthropos 76:321-370.

Iskandar, N. St.
    1964   Abu Nawas. Djakarta: P.N. Balai Pustaka.

Kapferer, Bruce
    1979a   Introduction: Ritual Process and the Transformation of Context. Social Analysis 1:3-19.

Kapferer, Bruce
  1979b Entertaining Demons: Comedy, Interaction and Meaning in a Sinhalese Healing Ritual. Social Analysis 1:108-176.

  1983   A Celebration of Demons: Exorcism and the Aesthetics of Healing in Sri Lanka. Bloomington: Indiana University Press.

Kedit, Peter Mulok
  1987   Iban Bejalai. Ph.D. Dissertation. University of Sydney.

Klokke-Coster, A.; A. H. Klokke and M. Saha
  1976   De Slimme en de Domme: Ngadju-Dajakse Volksverhalen. Verhandelingen van het Koninklijk Instituut voor Taal-, Land-en Volkenkunde, 79. 's-Gravenhage: Martinus Nijhoff.

Roth, Henry Ling
  1896   The Natives of Sarawak and British North Borneo. London: Truslove and Hanson, 2 Vols.

Sandin, Benedict
  1978   The *Pelian Bejereki*: Iban Rite of Spiritually Fencing an Expectant Mother. Sarawak Museum Journal 26:57-80.

  1983   Mythological Origins of Iban Shamanism. Sarawak Museum Journal 32:235-250.

Sather, Clifford
  1978   The Malevolent *Koklir*. Bijdragen Tot de Taal-, Land- en Volkenkunde 134:310-355.

  1980   Symbolic Elements in Saribas Iban Rites of Padi Storage. Journal of the Malaysian Branch of the Royal Asiatic Society 53(2):67-95.

  1981   Origin of the Iban Comic Hero Apai Aloi: A Saribas Saga Version. Sarawak Museum Journal 29:73-96.

  1984   Apai Aloi Goes Hunting and Other Stories. Kuching: Persatuan Kesusasteraan Sarawak.

  1985   Iban Agricultural Augury. Sarawak Museum Journal 34:1-35.

Sather, Clifford
    1990   Trees and Tree Tenure in Paku Iban Society: The Management of Secondary Forest Resources in a Long-Established Iban Community. Borneo Review 1:16-40.

Shamsuddin, Wan
    1966   *Hikayat Abu Nawas*. Kuala Lumpur: Penerbitan Pustaka Antara.

St. John, Spencer
    1863   Life in the Forests of the Far East. London: Smith, Elder and Co., 2 Vols.

Sutlive, Vinson
    1976   The Iban *Manang*: An Alternate Route to Normality. *In* Studies in Borneo Societies. G. N. Appell, ed. Center for Southeast Asian Studies. DeKalb: Northern Illinois University, pp. 64-71.

Tanoewirendja, M.A.S.
    1928   Tjarita Aboenawas. Weltevreden: Bale Poestaka.

Turner, Victor
    1974   Passages, Margins, and Poverty: Religious Symbols of Communitas. *In* Dramas, Fields, and Metaphors. Ithaca: Cornell University Press, pp. 231-72.

    1982   Introduction. *In* Celebration: Studies in Festivity and Ritual. Victor Turner, ed. Washington: Smithsonian Institution Press, pp. 11-30.

NOTES ON CONTRIBUTORS

G. N. APPELL, Ph.D. (Australian National University), is Senior Research Associate, Department of Anthropology, Brandeis University; Director of the Sabah Oral Literature Project; and a consultant in organizational development and social change.

L. W. R. APPELL, B.Sc. (McGill University) is Assistant Director, Sabah Oral Literature Project, and co-author with G. N. Appell of a Cultural Dictionary of the Rungus Language (in preparation). She has conducted research in the Northwest Territories of Canada, and on female roles and religion in East Kalimantan, Indonesia, and Sabah, Malaysia.

ROBERT J. BARRETT, Ph.D. (University of Adelaide) is Senior Lecturer in Psychiatry, at the University of Adelaide and has done post-doctoral study at Harvard in medical anthropology. His major research interest, and the topic of a forthcoming book, is the cross-cultural study of schizophrenia. He has conducted fieldwork among the Saribas Iban on illness beliefs and healing rituals.

JAY BERNSTEIN, Ph.D. (University of California, Berkeley) is a Research Officer, at the University of Kent at Canterbury. He has done field research among the Taman in West Kalimantan on medical anthropology and is currently engaged in research in Brunei. He is the author of a forthcoming study of shamanism among the Taman of West Kalimantan.

RICHARD C. FIDLER, Ph.D. (University of Pennsylvania) is Assistant Professor of Anthropology at Rhode Island College. His research interests are in the overseas Chinese, and in ethnicity, religion, and economic life of small towns in Borneo, on which he has presented and published various papers.

SIAN E. JAY, D.Phil. (Oxford University) is currently a commissioning editor for a publisher in London. She has carried out fieldwork in Borneo among the Ngaju on mythology and religion and has written numerous ethnographic articles on these topics and on Southeast Asian art.

H. S. MORRIS, Ph.D. (London University) taught for many years at the London School of Economics. He conducted one of the pioneering social anthropological studies in post-war Borneo, on the Melanau sago industry. He is the author of *The Oya Melanau*, recently published by the Malaysian Historical Society.

JÉRÔME ROUSSEAU, Ph.D. (Cambridge University) is Professor of Anthropology, McGill University. He is the author of *Central Borneo: Ethnic Identity and Social Life in a Stratified Society* (Oxford University Press) and other publications based on research in the Baluy area on the Kayan and in the middle and upper Mahakam.

CLIFFORD SATHER, Ph.D. (Harvard University) is currently Courtesy Professor, Southeast Asian Studies, The University of Oregon. He has done fieldwork in both Sabah and Sarawak, the latter among the Saribas Iban and is the author of numerous publications on folklore and social organization, and of forthcoming studies of Iban architectural symbolism and Southeast Asian ecological adaptations in historical perspective.

VINSON H. SUTLIVE, JR., Ph.D. (University of Pittsburgh) is Professor of Anthropology, The College of William and Mary, and Director of the Borneo Research Council. He has done extensive research among the Iban of the middle and upper Rajang on history, ecology and social change and is the author of *Tun Jugah of Sarawak: Colonialism and Iban Response*, recently published by the Sarawak Literary Society.

ROBERT L. WINZELER, Ph.D. (University of Chicago, Anthropology) is Professor of Anthropology, the University of Nevada, Reno. He has done fieldwork in Kelantan, in peninsular Malaysia, as well as in Sarawak, on various topics and is the author of a forthcoming book on latah in Malaya, Borneo and Java.